HITLER
ON THE
DOORSTEP

HITLER ON THE DOORSTEP

Operation 'Sea Lion':
The German Plan to Invade
Britain, 1940

EGBERT KIESER

TRANSLATED BY HELMUT BÖGLER

Naval Institute Press
Annapolis, Maryland

This book is dedicated
to those Germans and British who lost their lives
in the summer of 1940

Original German-language edition published 1987
by Bechtle Verlag, Esslingen, Munich.
This English-language edition published 1997.

This edition © Arms & Armour Press, 1997

First published in Great Britain in 1997
by Arms and Armour Press
An Imprint of the Cassell Group
Wellington House, 125 Strand, London WC2R 0BB

Published and distributed
in the United States of America and Canada
by the Naval Institute Press, 118 Maryland Avenue,
Annapolis, Maryland 21402-5035.

Library of Congress Catalog Card No. 97-68137.

ISBN 1-55750-390-7

This edition is authoprized for sale only in the United States
of America, its territories and possessions, and Canada.

Designed and edited by DAG Publications Ltd.
Designed by David Gibbons; edited by Gerald Napier;
indexed by Maureen Charters. Manufactured in Great Britain.

Translator's Note
Several military, political and other typically Nazi
German terms, as well as some other foreign-language terms,
have been left in the original and set in italic. Where these require
translation or explanation, this is given in square brackets where
the term first occurs. All other parentheses are either original
to the text or enclose a comment or note by the author.

Contents

CONTENTS

Preface

For a long time I had not had the slightest inkling that there had been an 'Operation Sea Lion' during the summer of 1940, nor that German troops had been intended to land in England. In the British Isles however, this episode has not been forgotten, as I was bound to discover during my frequent visits to Kent. For the British, the threat is still as vividly alive today as it was then. A friend showed me the spot near Dover where the British had intended to pump oil into the Channel and set it alight. By chance, we were standing on a block of concrete which had served as an anchor for a barrage balloon. The numerous barbed-wire barricades that festooned the coast in those days have disappeared, but the concrete humps that were intended to stop the panzers are still there: they now protect entryways and car lots from unauthorised parkers. German planes that were shot down are still being dug out of the marshes, and today the third generation of children is busy collecting mementoes, pieces of metal and insignia. There are still bombs and chunks of shrapnel about, pill boxes adorning the fields, and Martello Towers jutting up along the coast facing defiantly towards France.

On British television, a comedy series about the Home Guard that is a great favourite with all the viewers has kept the memory alive. Even little children know that German paratroopers fell down from the sky disguised as nuns and that they themselves would not be alive today if the German U-boats had had their way.

The summer of 1940 was a nightmare for the British. Why has the German side forgotten all about it? To discover the answer to this question was naturally a fascinating challenge. The result of my investigations was astounding: 'Operation Sea Lion' was one of the greatest German endeavours of the war and was intended to bring Great Britain to its knees. It did not succeed. Hitler really lost the Second World War in the summer of 1940. After 'Sea Lion', there were only setbacks for the German war leaders. Why then did Hitler not occupy Britain? All of Britain was convinced that the Germans would come – the British had nothing left with which to oppose the German panzers.

At the beginning of the campaign in the West, on 10 May 1940, Hitler had admonished his troops: the British and the French wanted to prevent Germany ever becoming great. They wanted to deprive it of its basis of existence and split it up into numerous minor states. 'The hour has now come for you. The battle which begins today will decide the fate of the German Nation for the next thousand years. Do your duty.'

And the soldiers had done their duty. In only five weeks they had beaten down France for Hitler and they now stood on the Channel and were waiting for him to send them to England. In a procurement effort without precedent, the *Kriegsmarine* [German Navy] had already converted all available ship space for the transportation of troops and brought it to the Channel coast. By day and by night German bomber and fighter formations flew into England in order to break British resistance. The *Luftwaffe* [German Air Force] was to create the primary condition for 'Operation Sea Lion': gaining command of the air, without which a landing on the English coast was impossible. The fight developed into the 'Battle of Britain', in which the very existence of Great Britain was at stake. If the German squadrons could not only gain the upper hand in the air battles, but also destroy the major ports and paralyse the British aircraft industry, nothing more would stand in the way of the invasion.

The struggle for air supremacy has been give more space in this portrayal than was originally intended. The *Luftwaffe* was the only branch of the German armed forces which actually fought heavily in connection with 'Operation Sea Lion'. The individual phases of this battle – 'the Channel Battle', 'Eagle Day' and the 'Blitz' on London – allow us to evaluate the chances for success of 'Operation Sea Lion' and show us the lack of coordination between the branches of the *Wehrmacht* [German Armed Forces] and the flexibility and determination of British resistance. Far more than the preparations undertaken by the *Kriegsmarine* and the *Heer* [German Army] the result of the air battle would determine the start of the invasion. By early September, the Royal Air Force had its back to the wall and Hitler could have issued the order to send over the troops at any time.

However, there is not a single clue that Hitler ever really did intend to occupy the British Islands. There is much evidence that in a complete misapprehension of the actual situation, he intended from the outset to force Britain into concluding a peace agreement by means of a massive threat, in order thereby to clear the way for his attack upon Russia. Did the many German pilots and British civilians therefore die only for the sake of a bluff? In the face of all existing evidence, this must be assumed to have been the case. But there is a further question in connection with 'Operation Sea Lion' that requires an answer. Were the German generals and admirals so naive, not to have seen through Hitler's directives? Why, despite all their misgivings, did they stand fully behind Hitler in the end?

The documents that have become available since the end of the war, particularly in more recent times, provide the answer. In the summer of 1940 there was actually no reason for the generals and admirals to doubt the earnestness of Hitler's intentions. They did not recognise Hitler's directives for a bluff, even though they had a multitude of reasons to question the success of such an operation. As late as June, the chiefs of the three services were convinced that it was hopeless. But when Hitler confronted them with his directive No. 16, the staffs suddenly began to feel that anything was possible. All one had to do was to prepare a plan. This was then done with such precision, speed and thoroughness, that the *Wehrmacht* needed only two months to prepare for the crossing of the Channel, something that took the Allies the same landing in the opposite direction more than two years to accomplish.

With his directive, Hitler had relieved his generals and admirals from all responsibility. In this sense, 'Operation Sea Lion' becomes a paradigm for the whole of the Second World War. Based on a mere word from the *Führer*, a gigantic military bureaucracy was set in motion which, without regard for men and *matériel*, requisitioned, acquired, ordered and administered foreign territories as if they were their own. Raeder, von Brauchitsch, Halder, Jeschonnek, did not need to ask why Britain was to be destroyed and occupied. They did not need to ask why hundreds of thousands were to be driven from home and hearth, thousands killed, cities and whole districts laid waste. Hitler's directive was alibi enough, the 'struggle for the Fatherland' served as the motivator, hubris as the driving force, to set masses of men in motion who did not hate the British, as little as they had hated the French or were to hate the Russians.

The war machine had become independent, an end in itself. Here yawns a chasm that even today has lost none of its dangers: the interaction between political power and military potential. In the pursuit of his dreams of a *Großdeutsches Reich* [Greater German Reich] and the enslavement of his neighbours, Hitler could rely without reservation on the outstanding professionalism of his generals. Sworn to unequivocal obedience, the generals did everything within their power to fulfil this political hubris by military means, without regard to morality and civil responsibility.

Bismarck said that it is always minorities, not nations, who start a war. By this he meant politicians and the military – and he did not mean only the Germans. History, as well as today's world, offers many examples showing how an inflated ideology imposes its political claim to power by means of a military machine and how the military is able to help politicians gain more power. The equation is always made without regard for the majority, the people, who willingly pay with their blood, because they have had it drummed into them that they are suffering for a noble cause.

For his dreams of *Großdeutschland*, Hitler could rely on his military machine. After he had brutally broken all resistance within its ranks during the 'generals' crisis' in November 1939, it did everything within its power to fulfil his hubris, only following the laws of military logic, which made an occupation of the British Islands inevitable.

Hitler himself had declared the invasion to be politically senseless. But would he have stopped it, had the *Luftwaffe* won and the British still not thrown in the towel? 'Operation Sea Lion' is a classic example of how an omnipotent military machine develops its own rules of behaviour and can function without any sort of intellectual corrective. Had the operation succeeded, and there is very little evidence that it would not have, had Hitler but given the order to attack, then the world today would probably look very different. One may assume however, that in the end the operation would have failed because of the higher morale of the British, even though the fears it engendered are still very much alive today along the coast in Kent and Sussex. Why this is so, this book attempts to help explain, and also to serve as an admonition not to forget man for the sake of the machine. A war machine is also a machine, which is only good if it serves man and does not become an end in itself, obsessed solely with the destruction of others.

I
The Phoney War
Peace still has a chance

After the German invasion of Poland and the partitioning of the country between the *Großdeutsche Reich* and the Soviet Union in September 1939, a deceptive calm reigned throughout Europe. On 3 September, Great Britain and France had reluctantly declared war on Germany and left it at that. The stereotyped German *Wehrmacht* bulletins spoke only of patrol activities and light artillery fire in the West, and of the reconnaissance activities by the *Luftwaffe*. In the *Reich* people were preoccupied with the regulations on food rationing following upon the introduction of the *Reichskleiderkarte* [rationing of textiles and clothing]. In the *Generalgouvernement* Poland [the part of Poland not annexed by Germany, but left as an 'independent State' under German control], the first mass executions of Jews were taking place. From time to time British aircraft flew in over the Bay of Heligoland and dropped bombs on Borkum and Sylt without causing much damage.

In Paris, Simone de Beauvoir noted in her diary in December 1939: 'And so this strange war drags on. At the front, as in the rearward areas, the main problem is to kill time, to patiently sit out this period for which it is hard to find a name – is it fear or is it hope?'

Hope, that was the wish that this war would go away again all by itself, that the Germans would be satisfied with their conquests to date. This also reflected the basic attitude of the German people themselves, who had not displayed any great enthusiasm at the end of the Polish campaign. Nobody had displayed flags on their house. Coal and potatoes were becoming scarce and everybody expected peace. Now that Danzig and the Corridor had been regained, there was no further reason to continue waging war.

The resistance group around Carl Goerdeler used the hiatus to contact the British Government. They wanted to explore the possibilities of a peace agreement with a democratic German Government. Chamberlain, however, was not prepared to make any commitments, because some members of the group insisted on retaining the frontiers that had meanwhile been reached. An initiative by the Americans also failed. Roosevelt sent Sumner Welles to Berlin and Rome as his personal representative, in order to persuade the Axis Powers to end the military conflict. His proposals did not find any favour. The French and British also declined, since Hitler gave no sign of withdrawing from Poland.

Far more pronounced than the feeble glimmer of hope, were the fears within the Allied camp. In particular the French, who had been the major victims in the First World War, already saw the Germans again standing where they had stood 25 years ago: on the Somme, on the Marne and in the Vosges Mountains. Memories of the blood sacrifice were still far too fresh. And the war of 1870/71 had not been forgotten either. Many French were convinced that it was a trait of the German character always to follow the ideology of force, regardless of whether their leaders were called Friedrich, Wilhelm or Adolf. In their eyes, the Germans were not only dangerous, they were incorrigible. 'Il faut en finir' ['we must make an end'], they said, and they did not mean the war, they meant Germany itself, which was again threatening to devastate their country.

On the other hand, the British had expressly stated that they did not intend to wage this war against the German people, but only against Hitler and Nazism. Goerdeler's emissaries had made some impression after all, particularly that one had to differentiate between the Germans and the Nazis. The conservative British in the Foreign Office for example, were not sold on the French idea, reported by the British Ambassador in Paris, that the Germans were an aggressive race. John Colville, who later became Churchill's private secretary, gave much thought to what was to become of Germany after the war. He considered the 'il faut en finir', in other words extermination, to be neither Christian nor civilised. One should treat the Germans with extreme magnanimity and draw a line under the past after the war. Germany should be put back on its feet economically and disarmed, as by the way, should the Allies as well. The Germans should not be made to feel to be pariahs. None of the territories legally belonging to them should be taken away, nor should the country be partitioned.

Even after the initial reports from the concentration camps and the first pictures of shipments of Polish Jews went around the world, and the British White Paper on German concentration camps was ready for publishing, men like Colville still did not condemn the Germans indiscriminately. On the other hand, Lord Halifax is said to have urged the publication of the White Paper, whose *spiritus rector* is alleged to have been the 'fanatically anti-German' Sir Ivone Kirkpatrick who had been First Secretary in the British Embassy in Berlin from 1933 to 1938 and was later to become British High Commissioner in Germany from 1950 to 1953.

In Paris the horror stories were also received with scepticism. Simone de Beauvoir noted in her diary in April 1940: 'Hitler announced at the beginning of April that he would enter Paris on 15 June. Nobody took... that seriously. Horrible stories were circulating about the occupation in Poland. The

Germans were rounding up all the patriots, putting them into concentration camps and deliberately letting them starve to death. Some stories mentioned closed waggons that were being stuffed with prisoners and then having poison gas led into them. One hesitates to believe such rumours when one remembers the fairy tales that were spread during the First World War. But one also does not believe the optimistic talk circulating.'

Fear of the Germans prevailed. While the British were transferring their Expeditionary Force and some air force squadrons to France, the French were reinforcing the Maginot Line and concentrating the core of their forces along the Belgian border. They were not in any doubt: if the Germans were to come, they would again follow the Schlieffen Plan and come from the north.

The fears were more than justified. Hitler wanted to begin the campaign in the West already on 12 November 1939, but postponed it because of the objections of his generals. Goebbels had instructed his propagandists to rein-terpret the term 'neutrality' in the sense of the Nazis, after two British agents had been enticed to the Dutch border and kidnapped. Out of this, Goebbels construed a breach of neutrality by the Dutch. To outward appearances, everything remained quiet. The theme of the *Wehrmacht* reports was still: nothing new in the West.

It was the Russians who started the ball rolling. On 30 November 1939 the Soviets attacked Finland. World public opinion was outraged by this breach of international law. No government officially offered to help the little country, because nobody wanted to risk an open conflict with Russia. The alarming warning by Sir W. Seeds, the British Ambassador in Moscow, that Soviet Russia would probably overrun all of Scandinavia and that a declaration of war by Great Britain against Russia would possibly soon become necessary, was quietly shelved in the Foreign Office in London. Berlin also remained quiet. Unofficially however, a wave of sympathy swept through Europe. In the Finnish consulates throughout Scandinavia, many Norwegians, Swedes and Danes volunteered for service against the Soviets. Secret arms shipments arrived from Italy, Hungary, Sweden and Great Britain. The Finns defended themselves so courageously, that within a short time four Russian divisions had either been destroyed or stopped in their tracks.

The general public in England took little notice of the drama being enacted on the Arctic Circle. However, for the First Lord of the Admiralty in London, Winston Spencer Churchill, the attack on Finland by the Soviet Union came as a godsend. For him, the supply of Swedish iron ore to the German armaments industry via Norwegian ports had long been a thorn in the side. Tenaciously he had worked towards getting his colleagues in the Cabinet to agree to mining the Norwegian ports and seizing the ore freighters. Now the Soviets had provided him with an excuse to seize the Swedish ore fields of Gällivare and the Norwegian ore port of Narvik connected to them.

The plan was simple: the Finns were to ask the Norwegians and the Swedes officially for permission to have *matériel* and troops from other nations moved through their territory. Following the time-honoured method of 'non-intervention', Great Britain was then to land 'volunteers' for Finland in Narvik and Trondheim, but then station most of them in Norway and Sweden for the defence of these countries.

On 7 February 1940 this plan was approved by His Majesty's Cabinet. The French had been informed about the plan long before and had declared their willingness to participate. Preparations were begun and carried forward even after the Soviets and Finns had concluded the Moscow peace agreement. On 20 March the troops were ready for embarkation in French and Scottish ports: three British divisions, a contingent of French *Chasseurs Alpins* and several battalions of Polish volunteers. Under British command, they were to seize the ore mines in Gällivare, or at least to destroy their equipment, and to interrupt the railway line Gällivare–Narvik. The planned operation suffered from only one minor defect: rumours about the forthcoming Franco-British expedition had been circulating in Stockholm since February. The leak was assumed to have been in Paris. The results of this indiscretion were to be fatal for the whole operation. On 5 April the *Daily Telegraph*'s correspondent in Stockholm reported that the Nazis intended to occupy Norway if the British blockade were to affect the shipment of Swedish iron ore.

On Sunday 7 April, when the British troops were already partly embarked, British naval reconnaissance reported strong units of the German fleet at the entrance to the Skagerrak, steering north. In the ports of the British Home Fleet the alarms went off. At 20.30, the first task force consisting of three battleships, two cruisers and ten destroyers left Scapa Flow in order to confront the Germans and bar their way north. At 22.00, a second squadron followed, composed of two cruisers and fifteen destroyers. With this, almost all of the available units of the Home Fleet had been committed in order to anticipate a major operation by the enemy and to protect the deployment of their own forces.

At this time, there were already four British destroyers off Narvik engaged in laying mines in the coastal waters. The battlecruiser *Renown*, cruiser *Birmingham* and a further eight destroyers had been ordered to protect them. On Monday morning the minelayers had completed their job in the West Fjord and were steaming south with their consorts in order to lay minefield 'Wilfred'.

Only the destroyer *Glowworm* had had to turn back in order to search for a sailor who had gone overboard during the night.

The sea was choppy, grey rain-clouds chased across the sky and visibility was poor. Captain Gerard Roope was just in the act of breaking off the search and turning back, when two German destroyers appeared before him and immediately opened fire. *Glowworm* returned fire with all guns, but the choppy sea made aiming almost impossible. In the middle of the engagement the German cruiser *Hipper* appeared and straddled *Glowworm* with salvos from her heavy guns. The British made smoke. *Hipper* followed into the smoke and seconds later the side of the cruiser burst inwards under a terrific blow. Captain Roope, having seen that he could not escape, had rammed *Hipper* under full steam. *Glowworm* lay burning in *Hipper*'s wake and shortly thereafter exploded. The German cruiser was able to rescue 40 survivors, Captain Roope was not among them.

On the evening of the same day, the badly damaged *Hipper* ran into Trondheim and lay there in dry-dock for many months while the huge hole in her side was being repaired. In the British Admiralty *Glowworm* was written off, without the reason for her loss being known. Far too late, the British were to learn that *Hipper* had been escorting German troop transports to Norway.

On the morning of 9 April German troops had not only occupied Trondheim, Bergen and Narvik but Oslo and its hinterland were also soon in German hands. The British had come too late. While they still landed the Franco-British expeditionary force, they had to withdraw it again after only a few weeks of heavy fighting.

The British fleet was also unable to destroy its opponent. In the course of the two-months-long battle for Norway, the British lost an aircraft carrier, two cruisers, nine destroyers and six submarines, losses they could cope with, given the size of their fleet. Not so the *Kriegsmarine*: it lost four cruisers, ten destroyers, three U-boats and one torpedo boat. That came to almost half of the available units. After this adventure, they were left with four destroyers compared with 184 British.

During the debate on Norway which raged in Parliament on 7 and 8 May, the opposition poured the most severe criticism on Prime Minister Chamberlain declaring him responsible for the defeat. The old animosities against the 'appeasement politician' broke out anew. Lloyd George, the grand old man of the Liberal Party, blamed him for the fact that the declarations of mutual support to Czechoslovakia, Poland, Finland and Norway were now worthless.

The First Lord of the Admiralty, Churchill, who had helped drop his Prime Minister into this soup, delivered an emotional speech in defence, but had to admit: 'We were taken completely by surprise and out-manoeuvred by the Germans.' Churchill himself had no easy time of it. It was not the first time that, as First Lord of the Admiralty, he had had to admit to a self-inflicted disaster. On 25 April 1915, acting against the advice of the First Sea Lord, Admiral Fisher, he had sent ill-prepared, mainly Australian and New Zealand troops to land on the steep coast of the Gallipoli peninsula from old warships destined for the scrap-yard, in an attempt to seize the Dardanelles. The forces, which were virtually unable to protect themselves on the narrow beaches, were destroyed bit by bit by Turkish troops under the command of the German General Liman von Sanders. When the sorry remnants were finally evacuated after many months, the casualties amounted to 213,000 Australians and New Zealanders, but also including a number of British. At the time, Churchill had had to resign and volunteer for service at the front in France, where for one year he served as a lieutenant-colonel in the 6th Royal Scots Fusiliers, before he dared to return to Parliament as a humble Member. There were many who had not forgiven him this senseless sacrifice, which only came about because of his unbridled impetuosity. However, Churchill was able to compensate for this defect in character by an extraordinary willpower, a tenacious, sometimes even ruthless sense of purpose, the ability to handle an incredible workload, assertiveness and an irresistible personal charm. His reputation was so good that Lloyd George was able to shout at the Prime Minister, that he should not try to hide behind Churchill's skirts.

Confidence in the Chamberlain Government had been seriously shaken, all the more so since the press was maintaining the same line as the opposition. Speculation about a new cabinet and rumours of resignations filled the air in the corridors of Parliament and government offices. Chamberlain spent the whole of 9 May in conference. He not only consulted the members of his cabinet but also included the leaders of the opposition. The word 'coalition', which to British ears sounds almost like the end of democracy itself, was to be heard more and more frequently. It became increasingly more clear that in the serious straits in which England found herself, Parliament and government could only master the situation by a united will. 9 May passed without any solution having become apparent.

10 May was a Friday and bright sunshine promised a lovely weekend. In their minds, Londoners were already occupied with their Whitsun excursions. In the suburbs the electric milk-vans purred from house to house, the first commuters thronged into the trains of the Underground, only to fill the streets of the City with their busy bustle soon thereafter. The topic of conversation everywhere, as far as people were interested in politics at all, was the recent political developments at home.

In its morning newscast at 07.00, the BBC's reporter announced in dry terms that this morning German troops had crossed their western frontiers and engaged the defenders in heavy fighting. One hour later, the first extras of the papers were being touted in the streets and torn from the hands of the paper boys. They repeated what the Supreme Command of the *Wehrmacht* had announced on German radio: 'At 5:30 this morning, German troops crossed the Dutch, Luxembourg and Belgian frontiers. Enemy resistance along the borders was broken everywhere by sharp attacks, often in close cooperation with the *Luftwaffe*.' Hitler's threadbare excuse was only made known to the English later on: 'By means of a gigantic diversion in the southeast, England and France are attempting to advance to the Ruhr via Holland and Belgium.' In actual fact, neither the French nor the British had had any intention of advancing to the Ruhr. The 'gigantic diversion' had been a British commando operation, during which several agents had vainly attempted to block the Danube, and thereby the oil shipments from Rumania, by sinking barges and laying mines. Nobody put any credence in Hitler's statement. All that counted was that within one month, from 9 April to 10 May, he had attacked five neutral countries.

The excitement about the beginning of the campaign in the West soon abated. With the weekend before them, the majority of the British were optimistic: this time Hitler would not find it as easy as in Poland. The Allied armies were prepared for the attack, and the powerful British Expeditionary Force stood in support of the French and Belgians. Hardly had the extras been sold out than the streets of London returned to normal. The British remained calm. First and foremost Prime Minister Chamberlain, who took his wife for a walk in St James's Park before returning to 10 Downing Street towards 10.00. Foreign Secretary Lord Halifax was also out for a walk with his wife and dog.

In the offices of the Admiralty, the War Office, the Foreign Office and the Office of the Prime Minister however, there was hectic activity that morning. Since 06.00 a flood of reports and alarms had begun to sweep over the desks. Those responsible passed the messages on as quickly as possible. Nobody wanted to have his Whitsun weekend spoiled.

In the offices of the First Lord of the Admiralty several Ministers from Holland were waiting, having flown to London from Amsterdam to ask the British for aid. The First Lord had been called to an important meeting at 10 Downing Street. There, together with Foreign Secretary Lord Halifax, he was sitting opposite 71-year-old Chamberlain in the Prime Minister's office. The subject of the discussion was the terrible state of the Chamberlain Government. The Prime Minister coolly reported on the new situation. The German attack made a closing of the ranks by all parties the order of the day, even if they all deeply detested the idea. Only an all-party government would be able to impose the necessary war effort.

Chamberlain saw himself forced to transfer power to a man who, unlike himself, also enjoyed the confidence of the other parties. Lord Halifax, aged 59, and Winston Churchill, aged 65, were the only Conservative politicians who could be considered for the job of Prime Minister.

It was obvious that Chamberlain preferred Lord Halifax, the *grand seigneur* who had already gained so much experience with the Germans and their *Führer*, to the unpredictable, impulsive Churchill. He asked the two colleagues facing him, whom he should recommend to the King as the new Prime Minister. The endless silence, as Churchill remembers it, which greeted this weighty question was broken by Lord Halifax. In a long-winded declaration he explained that as a member of the Lords, he did not have the support or confidence of the Commons which was necessary to lead the nation in such a war. With this, the die had been cast: Chamberlain would recommend to King George VI the First Lord of the Admiralty as his successor.

Churchill returned to the Admiralty towards 11.00, where he immediately devoted himself to the Dutchmen. His visitors described the desperate situation of their country and reported that the Germans had already advanced to the Rhine and were threatening the dikes of the Zuider Zee. Churchill tried to calm them down as far as he was able and immediately ordered a flotilla cruising off the Dutch coast to enter the Zuider Zee and take the dikes under fire. Simultaneously, he had messages sent to the Dutch naval units at sea in order to initiate joint action. That was all he could do at the time.

That same afternoon, King George VI asked Churchill to form a government. By 22.00 the new Prime Minister had not only reached agreement with the leaders of Labour and the Liberal Party and assured himself of their support, he had also presented the list of his cabinet to the King. Towards 03.00 Churchill went to bed in his apartment in the Admiralty: 'I slept well and did not require any encouraging dreams. Facts are better than dreams.' And it was a fact that the descendant of the Duke of Marlborough was now the most powerful man in the British Empire and would lead his people against the Germans.

As serious as the situation appeared to be, Churchill did not worry unduly. The idea of a possible invasion of the British Isles from Norway had seemed very real and had disturbed both political and military circles. With the attack in the West, this danger no longer loomed so threateningly, because Hitler would need all of his forces for this campaign. On the other hand, the chances of beating Hitler on the Continent were not bad. About 135 German divisions were opposed by 156 Allied divisions. The 2,800 German panzers could be met with 4,000, mainly French, tanks, to say nothing of the advantages of having fortified defensive positions. However, Churchill was soon to be in for a nasty surprise: on 14 May the Dutch surrendered, a fortnight later King Leopold of Belgium capitulated, whereupon the French front also collapsed. The Germans stood on the Channel.

II
German Panzers on the Channel
A nightmare for the island

'Much to our regret, Germany is organised as a war machine whereas England has just begun to think about the means of waging a modern war.' This appreciation by General Thorne, commander of the British forces in Kent, was factually true. The initial confrontation with the German 'war machine' was to give the British such a shock that nobody was able to imagine the perfected *Wehrmacht* ever failing and not overrunning England. Only this explains the almost hysterical fear of invasion that the British developed later on. Hitler's glorious campaign in the West was proof enough that militarily, nothing was impossible for the Germans.

The shock was all the greater, because until the early days of May 1940, the *Wehrmacht* had been criminally underestimated. British military leaders, together with the French, had naively prepared themselves for a set-piece war following the pattern of the First World War and placed their trust in the French fighting fiercely for every square metre of ground, as they had done in 1914-1918. The bunker system of the Maginot Line had been built up into an imposing line of fortifications stretching from the Swiss border to the Belgian frontier at Charleroi. There were whole armies of French soldiers quartered in subterranean passages many kilometres long and casemates reaching down to 100 metres under the surface. Thousands of bunkers, whose armoured towers with their wide gun embrasures stuck up from the ground everywhere like oversized tree trunks, housed the artillery whose gunners like the infantry in their countless machine-gun positions, had been waiting for months for the German attack to unfold. A furious hail of fire would greet the attacking enemy. Churchill was so impressed by a visit to the fortifications that he exclaimed: 'The Germans will never get through here!'

In an extension of the Maginot Line, the French northern armies were ready to oppose any advance over the battlefields of the First World War. With them were the divisions of the British Expeditionary Force [BEF] whose soldiers had practised trench warfare during the winter and the spring in the old, partially caved-in trenches of the Great War. The marching speed of the infantry was still considered to be the standard for all movements. The French and British tanks, only the former of which were in any way equal to the Germans except in speed, were split up among the infantry divisions in small units. There were only four armoured divisions in the whole French army. One of these divisions was under the command of General de Gaulle, who had vainly argued in favour of a more mobile form of warfare and larger armoured units.

The Allied staffs had taken their strategic planning far too lightly and, without any contingency planning at all, had counted on the Germans following the Schlieffen Plan as in 1914: an advance through Belgium and then southwards towards Paris. Up until the final moment General Gamelin, the French Supreme Commander, had let himself be deceived by the Germans massing troops along the Belgian and Dutch borders. Hitler's memoranda to the Belgian and Dutch Governments, notifying them that German troops would enter their territories to protect their neutrality, may have contributed to the deception.

The Spanish Civil War, the campaign against Poland and the occupation of Norway should have taught the Allies a lesson. The *Wehrmacht* had at its disposal battle-proven panzer forces who were capable of conquering huge areas at speeds never experienced before and cutting off and surrounding entire enemy army groups, and also motorised infantry that was able to keep pace with these forces. Already during the early 'twenties, the *Reichswehr* [German Army during the Weimar Republic] had turned a liability into an asset by practising mobile warfare, because the Versailles Treaty's restriction to an army of 100,000 had made it too weak for trench warfare. The role of the *Luftwaffe* had also become apparent to everybody since the Spanish Civil War. Its bombers and fighters had demonstrated how enemy forces can be destroyed in advance of the panzer spearheads and the enemy air force eliminated by bombing its bases. And Germany also had at its disposal the most mobile infantry, the most modern service of the times: paratroops and airborne troops, who had made their debut in Norway.

These factors were already enough to shift the alleged balance of power in favour of the *Wehrmacht*. However, the *Wehrmacht* gained the decisive advantage by means of a brilliant strategic move that had been devised by the Chief of Staff of Army Group A, General von Manstein. The old Schlieffen Plan had been modified into a daring pincer movement which was designed to encircle and annihilate the mass of the French northern armies.

On the first day of the campaign in the West, the panzers of Army Group B had already penetrated about 120 kilometres into Holland and were advancing on Rotterdam. Several thousand paratroops had been dropped on important bridges and were holding them until the arrival of the motorised infantry, thereby preventing their demolition, and also tying down enemy forces. On 14 May, the centre of Rotterdam was laid waste by German bombs. Following Warsaw, this was the second blow against an open city. 78,000 people became homeless, 1,000 civilians were killed. On 15 May, Dutch armed resistance was broken and the Commander-in-Chief sued for a cease-fire.

On the southern flank of Army Group B the fortress of Eben Emael near Liège, considered to be impregnable, was taken within a matter of hours with the help of airborne troops. With this, the road to Lille was open. In the royal palace of Laeken, the Queen Mother Elisabeth barely escaped being captured by German paratroopers who had landed in the park and were overpowered by the palace guards. Queen Elisabeth, a descendent of the Wittelsbacher, watched the struggle from a window on the first floor of the palace. She pooh-poohed it as an 'incident' and went back to business as usual, until German troops suddenly occupied the residence. However, the resistance by the Allied forces in Belgium had not yet been broken, even though they were retreating under heavy losses.

For three days it had looked to the Allies as if the Germans actually were following the old Schlieffen Plan and General Gamelin had fallen into the trap: French and British troops had marched north to unite with the Belgians. In the meantime, however, in the south, German panzer forces of Army Group A had crossed Luxembourg and penetrated into Lorraine. They took Sedan on 12 May and next day crossed the Meuse after the *Luftwaffe* bombers and *Stukas* [Sturzkampfbomber, i.e., dive bomber] had softened up the extension of the Maginot Line for attack. Only near Monthermé were the French, otherwise completely demoralised by the screaming of the *Stukas'* sirens, still resisting fiercely. Despite the *Stukas* and the panic breaking out among the defenders to their right and left, two machine-gun brigades with colonial troops from Mada-gascar and Indochina held out for two whole days against parts of Panzer Corps Reinhardt. It was not until the morning of 15 May that they were smoked out with flame-throwers and their bunkers overrun. Out of the 5,000 men from the two brigades, only 1,000 survived, of their 150 officers only 20.

On 16 May, the first bastion of the extended Maginot Line was also breached. On a wide front, 1,500 German panzers closely followed by the motorised infantry were rolling westwards towards the Channel coast behind the French front. On 17 May, General Rommel and his 218 panzers of the 7th Panzer Division reached Le Cateau. About 30 kilometres to the South, Panzer Corps Guderian had reached the same line. Between both was Panzer Corps Reinhardt.

Rommel's panzers had jumped off at 04.00 in total darkness, an act of daring that gained him a large lead over his immediate neighbouring units. 'The roads were crowded with French troops and refugees', he noted in his diary. 'Our shouts of "a droit!" [keep right] had little effect and we made slow progress.' At the sight of a panzer, the French soldiers surrendered, threw away their weapons without any show of resistance and followed their officers on the march to the east into captivity. Completely surprised, nowhere were the French able to improvise any sort of line of resistance. And wherever French tanks appeared, they were shot to pieces by the Germans.

On the evening of 20 May, Guderian's panzer divisions reached the Channel coast at the mouth of the Somme. The French northern armies and the BEF had been cut off from the south and their bases of supply. In the face of the approaching catastrophe, Marshal Pétain had relieved the Commander-in-Chief Gamelin the day before and replaced him with General Weygand. Gamelin had issued a final desperate appeal to the troops, which demonstrated his complete helplessness: 'Victory or death!' and 'Stop the panzer tide!'

But it was not only the panzers which were spreading paralysing horror among the defenders and driving hundreds of thousands of civilians into flight southwards with their possessions. The blows delivered by the *Luftwaffe* were having just as devastating an effect. 1,400 aircraft, Do 17, Ju 88 and He 111 bombers, Ju 87 *Stukas* and Bf 109 and 110 fighters, were attacking enemy airbases and positions day and night. The *Stukas* especially, hurling themselves down on troop columns and artillery positions in screaming dives, contributed much to the demoralisation of the enemy. The Dutch and Belgian air forces had been almost completely annihilated within a matter of hours. Many of the 275 day fighters and 70 bombers of the French air force had been destroyed on the ground on the first day. What was left, were 400 bombers, 69 Hurricanes and about a dozen of the outdated Gladiator fighters of the British, which were stationed in France as an advanced striking force. Against the superior numbers and the combat experience of the German pilots they did not stand a chance. After five days they had already lost 105 aircraft and with each further day the losses mounted.

In London, everybody was awe-struck by the disaster. Churchill angrily maintained that in the whole history of war he had never heard of such mismanagement as that displayed by the French. 'The French are not fighting properly!', said Lord Ismay, Churchill's Chief of Staff, and was thereby only expressing what everybody was thinking. The British felt themselves shamefully betrayed by the French, as if the unprecedented German victory had only been made possible by the alleged cowardice of the French. However, the elite of the British army was also on the Continent and faring no better than the despised ally.

It was difficult for the British to comprehend the magnitude of the military catastrophe, the shock was too great to be able to recognise the underlying actual reasons, or the inevitability of the events. Churchill and his War Cabinet clung to the hope that the BEF would be able to hold out and that the French would finally pull themselves together for an effective defence.

On 22 May, Churchill flew to Paris accompanied by Field Marshal Sir John Dill and General Lord Ismay. He intended to convince Reynaud (the French Prime Minister) and General Weygand, that there was little sense in trying to operate against the German armoured columns. The French should finally decide to attack the mass of the German armies following behind. After a short discussion in Paris, Churchill and his companions, together with Reynaud, flew to French Headquarters in Vincennes where they met with General Weygand. In contrast to his predecessor Gamelin, the 73-year-old Weygand made a 'youthful and forceful impression' on the British. He was thinking along the same lines as they were and had already developed a plan of attack for the French forces and the BEF. A concentrated attack against the German flank was to cut off the panzer columns, bring the German advance to a standstill and reopen the lines of communication to the south. Twenty French divisions had been concentrated on the Somme to come to the aid of the northern armies.

Now everything depended on French initiative and on how quickly they would convert their plan into actions. However, virtually nothing happened. Communications to the encircled northern armies were almost completely cut off. General Billotte, who was supposed to execute the Weygand Plan, was killed in a motor accident on the evening of 21 May. His successor, General Blanchard, needed days to understand the situation. London urged Paris in vain to finally order the attack.

The British Expeditionary Force would have fallen victim to the confusion and the apathy of the French leadership, had not its commander kept a cool head and trusted only in his own judgement. 54-year-old Lord Gort was one of the most highly decorated officers of the First World War. He was not particularly popular due to his rather brusque manner and pedantic ways. A protégé of War Secretary Hore-Belisha, he had been Chief of the Combined Staff until 1930, a position that had not suited his highly developed sense for detail and the practical side of matters. His initial headquarters in France had been Chateau Harbacq, about which he had written home: 'a castle without water, light or a loo.' He had then pitched his tents in Arras, only to subsequently move to De Panne, 16 kilometres up the coast from Dunkirk, where the undersea cable, his 'umbilical cord', led through the Channel to London.

Just like his generals, Lord Gort had also believed himself to be more than prepared for the Germans and was therefore all the more surprised when his troops had constantly been forced to retreat under the assault of the *Wehrmacht*. When Guderian's panzers reached the Channel, not only were Lord Gort's divisions cut off from the rest of the BEF in the Pas de Calais and in Normandy, but also he had lost all contact with the French on his southern flank. Gort's operative superior had been General Billotte, whose troops had disintegrated under the blows of Army Group A. From the beginning, Billotte had shown very little inclination to cooperate with the British staff and had mostly kept them in the dark about his operations. This only changed with the appointment of Blanchard.

Since the remaining French and Belgians were drawing back on both flanks of the British, there were only two possibilities left to Lord Gort to save his soldiers: either an advance south to reunite with the French on the other side of the German penetration, or a retreat to the coast. Gort attempted the former and attacked near Arras on 21 May. His troops caused the SS Death Head Division to falter, but Rommel's 7th Panzer Division, together with two further panzer divisions from Reinhardt's corps, contained the attack. Gort had to give up Arras and pull back.

Things looked bad for the British contingent. Guderian's Panzer Corps had meanwhile turned north and, having passed Boulogne and Calais, was on the direct road to Dunkirk. If the Germans were to succeed in entering Dunkirk, the British would be caught in a trap and close to 200,000 soldiers and officers would become German prisoners. Lord Gort had little hope left. On 23 May he was forced to put his troops on half rations, because his lines of supply had depended on the ports in Normandy. Fighting power was still good, but he believed that there was no further prospect of saving his troops and their equipment.

On 24 May, something completely unexpected happened: after a meeting with Hitler, the Commander-in-Chief of Army Group A, Colonel General von Rundstedt, ordered the panzers to halt their advance and to stop on the Aa Canal on a line Gravelines–Béthune. In several telephone calls from his headquarters in Bruly, Hitler assured himself that the order had actually been carried out.

The commanders were stunned: now, with the final objective so close at hand, the pocket almost closed, they were supposed to take a break? Quite rightly, they felt themselves cheated of a major victory. 'We were speechless', Guderian said later, 'but since we did not know the reason for the order, it was difficult to object to it.' However, Colonel Warlimont at the OKW [Oberkommando der Wehrmacht = Armed Forces Supreme Command], whose plan of operations had just been thrown out, certainly did. His protests, like those by the army commanders, were ignored. This time, Keitel and Jodl stood behind Hitler. They had successfully sabotaged another idiotic order when, during the occupation of Norway a panicking Hitler had demanded that General Dietl let himself and his troops be interned in Sweden. At that time, they had simply suppressed the telex. This time it was not so easy, because von Rundstedt was Hitler's favourite and the order had originated with von Rundstedt.

General Jodl took it upon himself to interpret Hitler's intentions: the valuable panzer troops were not to be worn out in the lowlands of Flanders with their canals and swamps. In actual fact, the sluices had been opened and the hinterland was partially flooded. This would not seriously have impeded a further advance by the panzers, but the intention was to give them a sorely needed rest before 'Study Red', the final blow against the French in the south. For Guderian, the order had already gone out to form a new panzer corps in the Ardennes out of parts of his own and Panzer Corps Reinhardt, and to paralyse the Maginot Line by an advance to the Swiss frontier.

The order to halt came in for much discussion later on, because it allowed the British to escape from the eye of the needle that was Dunkirk. Many saw it as a mistake by Hitler that was decisive for the outcome of the war. It was suggested that he had not intended to spare the panzers, but rather the British, in order not to endanger an agreement with the British Government. This is contradicted by the fact that he voluntarily forewent a weighty bargaining-counter: he could have wished for no better means to put pressure on Churchill than the capture of the elite of the British Army. Whether he would have been successful in this is another matter entirely.

Beyond any doubt, the desire to halt the panzers originated with Colonel General von Rundstedt and Guderian's superior, General von Kleist. Von Kleist had already ordered the panzers to take a break near Ribemont on 17 May, whereupon Guderian wanted to resign his command and only remained at his post on the express order of von Rundstedt. A few days later, von Kleist, always after consulting with the Chief of the Army Group, again interfered and placed one of Guderian's three panzer divisions in reserve, in other words, withdrew it from the line. One should not forget that waging war with fast panzer forces was something quite new at the time and that the speed of the advance caused many a senior general to have qualms: the panzers charged across the battlefields of the First World War, the scenes of years of murderous trench fighting, as if war were child's play. It was believed it could not work, particularly since the extended southern flank was dangerously exposed. Against this military and psychological background, Hitler's alleged political motives are of little account.

Hermann Göring was not prepared to forego the victory over the British which the Heer had thrown away. The Commander-in-Chief of the Luftwaffe requested Hitler that he leave Dunkirk to his bombers and fighters. They would inundate the port in a sea of flames and thereby prevent the British from escaping. Hitler agreed.

The order to halt was rescinded on 26 May, but Dunkirk remained reserved for the Luftwaffe. Through the regrouping of the panzer corps for 'Study Red', the elan of the attack had been lost. The tenacious resistance in the pocket had increased. Particularly the French 16th Corps, deployed to the south of Dunkirk, was fighting ferociously, so that gains on this sector of the front were hardly achieved any longer.

The halting of the German advance on the line Gravelines–Béthune–Lens had no direct influence on the decisions of the encircled forces. Lord Gort and General Blanchard had reached an agreement to follow the Weygand Plan and break out to the southwest with an attack by eight divisions on 26 May, in order to link up with the French divisions advancing from the Somme. This attack, which would have been the only means of saving the situation for the Allies, was prevented by the increased pressure of Army Group B against the Belgian forces in the North. On 24 May, the Belgian front was broken near Menin and a wide gap then opened on the British left flank. Communications to Dunkirk were now also threatened from the north. Gort and Blanchard were forced to withdraw to the west in order to save what they could. The last chance for a break-out to the south had been missed. On 26 May, Lord Gort received a telegram from the War Office in London: 'According to our information, French offensive on the Somme cannot be launched with sufficient forces.' For Lord Gort all that now remained, was to keep the roads to Dunkirk open and to withdraw his troops to the coast.

III
Broomsticks Against Paratroops
A Home Defence Force is set up

Invasion – for the British the word has always signified something far worse than plague, fire, flood, or war: it has simply meant the beginning of the end of their lives as islanders. In the light of the history of the British Isles, this can be taken as a dramatisation hard to justify. After all, the Phoenicians had landed, as had the Celts; the Romans had overcome the Channel with their armies, the Vikings, the Jutes, the ancient Saxons and the Normans had come over and won through – only the Spaniards, the Dutch, and the French had tried and failed – and each time life on the islands had gone on and the inhabitants had profited from the invaders.

If one looks at it in the proper light, one must come to the conclusion that the British had more luck with their enemies than did the people on the Continent. The Spanish Armada of 1588 turned into nothing more than a spectre, just as did Napoleon's gigantic Montgolfières which were never built, although in the imagination of the British they still seem forever to float threateningly in the pale blue skies over Sussex and Kent. At the time, 3,000 men were supposed to be transferred across the Channel in order to take London. Every schoolboy knows the date 1797, when during the Anglo-French war, the French General Hoche gathered together 1,200 mercenaries, mostly criminals from French prisons, put them under the command of William Tate, a 70-year-old American adventurer and sent them to the south coast of Wales. The French did not know what they were supposed to do there and after landing began to plunder the countryside indiscriminately. All over England and Wales, able-bodied men took to the roads in carts, carriages, on horseback and on foot. The French were soon surrounded and had to surrender.

Many of the so-called Martello Towers have survived the ravages of time. In 1805 they were built along the southern coast of Kent and Sussex at intervals as a defence against Napoleon. The prototype for these round brick towers had been a circular fortress in Corsica that had successfully withstood a British attack some years previously. With great effort – one tower required a quarter of a million bricks – 74 such bastions were erected, from which British soldiers kept watch along the coast. After Waterloo they were no longer used and began to decay. In 1914, 26 of the remaining towers were again occupied and armed with light cannon and machine-guns. This time, it was invasion by the Germans that had to be reckoned with. As late as 1915, the British military leadership was expecting an assault on the south coast by anything from 70,000 to 160,000 German soldiers. The fears were totally unfounded, because the German Imperial General Staff never even considered crossing the Channel. However, the fear remains. It is a part of the island mentality, the price Neptune demands for the protection he grants his Britons.

Since the fear is always latent, even the slightest cause is enough to reawaken it and let it grow into a monstrosity. Already weeks before the German surprise victory in France, which brought the German divisions to the Channel coast, the first voices in England had been raised warning of an invasion. The occupation of Norway had shown that the German forces were not only capable of victory on land and over short distances. The *Luftwaffe* and the *Kriegsmarine* had supported the huge landing operation so successfully, that the British had not been able to bring their superiority in the North Sea to bear.

On 7 May, Clement Wedgwood, MP, declared in the Commons: 'While the British Navy is capable of holding open the sea lanes to the West and thereby protecting Great Britain from starvation, it does not appear to be capable of cutting off the German occupation forces in Norway. It is therefore conceivable that in the event, it will not be able to oppose a landing by the Germans in Lincolnshire or on the Wash.'

Only a few days later, on Friday, 10 May 1940, the spectre of invasion arose fully. The British Air Ministry sent the following 'urgent' message to the Admiralty, the War Office and the Ministry for Home Defence: 'According to information received from Norway, German paratroopers hold both arms above their heads during descent, just as if they were surrendering. However, in each hand they conceal a grenade which they throw at anybody who tries to oppose them when landing. In order to counter this trick, paratroopers numbering more than six (the largest British bomber had a crew of six) should be regarded as hostile and shot while still in the air if at all possible.'

Even the British Air Ministry should have known that paratroopers hold the lines with both hands above their heads in order to steer the parachute. The issue here was more likely only an attempt to justify the order to shoot. The officials probably counted on the fact that many people have scruples about shooting at someone floating in the air unable to defend himself. Later on, such scruples were in fact to save the lives of many German pilots who had been shot down.

Paratroops also played a part in the next far more important news bulletins. On 10 May 1940, German troops had crossed the Dutch and Belgian frontiers at 05.30. Half an hour before, paratroops had landed in the rear of the defenders and had taken the fortress of Eben Emael, previously considered to be impregnable, as well as several important bridges. The British reaction to this, after they had recovered from the shock, could be read on 12 May in the *News of the World*, which headlined a letter to the editor on its front page:

'Just let them come! The Germans are dropping troops by parachute. It is possible that they will attempt to do this here as well! I speak for thousands, if not millions, of former soldiers who all know how to shoot. We are too old for active service, but we can handle a gun! Just let them come!'

In pubs and clubs, in offices and factories, in every household, the possibility of an invasion was the topic of the day. The main question was: how does one deal with enemy paratroopers? The many former soldiers and officers of all branches of the services, who had served in India, Arabia, Africa, during the Boer War, and the First World War, were now jolted out of their nostalgia and called upon to meet a completely new kind of danger: a war without a front. Paratroops can come down out of the sky anywhere. Every city, every town, every house, every individual, would then be 'the front'.

Thousands of letters were written to the papers, to MPs and to the War Office. Everybody wanted to take part. In Leeds, a number of elderly businessmen, all of them former officers, had met for lunch. 'We agreed', one of them, a former major, reported later on, 'that one can only meet such a threat to our country by arming every veteran soldier.' The group wrote a letter to their MP: 'Can you induce the War Cabinet to call former soldiers up as volunteers for a militia against paratroops? We here in Leeds are willing and able to organise such a unit in the shortest possible time. All we need are weapons and the proper authorisation. Up to now, nothing of the kind has been initiated here in Leeds. We therefore appeal to you.'

Already on Saturday and Sunday, while the alarming reports from Holland and Belgium began to pile up, representatives of the War Office and the Ministry for Home Defence were meeting with the Chiefs of Staff of the services and discussing setting up a Home Defence Force. They agreed that every Briton between 17 and 65 years of age who had ever handled a weapon and did not suffer from any physical disabilities, could serve as a Local Defence Volunteer (LDV) in a Home Defence Force organised on military principles. The weekly service time was set at ten hours, initially for the forthcoming six months, and either side could terminate the agreement with a notice period of two weeks, the so-called 'maid clause'. Each volunteer had to bring his own food. The basic equipment to be provided by the Army was twenty rounds of ammunition for guns that were yet to be supplied, tea, a straw mattress, a shelter half and three blankets. The assignment: finding and combating enemy paratroopers.

Then it was Monday, 13 May 1940. The British returned from an uneasy weekend only to begin an even more uneasy week. The new Prime Minister

Winston Churchill gave his famous speech containing the shortest govern-mental programme in history: 'Victory, victory at any price!' And the price he named became the byword of those dark days: 'I have nothing to offer but blood, toil, tears and sweat.'

Churchill also believed in an imminent landing by the Germans. In one of his almost regular letters to the American President, F. D. Roosevelt, he wrote: 'We expect to be attacked here ourselves, both from the air (i.e. with bombs), and by parachute and airborne troops in the near future, and are getting ready for them!' One of his first acts in office as prime minister had to do with the inva-sion: he asked the three chiefs of staff for an analysis of Great Britain's military situation should France lose the battle on the Continent. Based on the erro-neous assumption that the *Luftwaffe* was four times as strong as the Royal Air Force, the military came to the sad conclusion that they were almost powerless: 'Prima facie Germany has the better hand; in the final analysis it will depend on whether the morale of our troops and civilian population can compensate for the numerical and *matériel* superiority of the Germans. We believe that it can.'

They were to be proven right. Long before Goebbels hysterically called for a 'total war', the British had prepared themselves for one as a matter of course. It began on the evening of 14 May, which was also the date the Dutch forces capitulated before superior German strength. The new War Secretary in Churchill's cabinet, Anthony Eden, went on the air with a speech in which he proclaimed the formation of a Home Defence Force and called for volunteers to register immediately with their local constabulary.

The response was overwhelming. While Eden was still speaking, the first volunteers set out. In Gillingham, Cranbrook, and Folkestone, as in many other communities throughout the islands, they left their pints standing in the pubs in order not to miss out. The police had not been informed – one normally forgets to inform the officials responsible in such cases – and there were no forms prepared for writing down the necessary information. However, the stunned police officers did not lose their composure and continued to take down names and addresses until long past midnight.

Next morning, a virtual storm broke over the constabularies. In Oxford, professors, students, businessmen and workers queued up together as early as 06.30, in Canterbury, the whole sixth form of King's School registered as a unit. Never before had so many false dates of birth been registered as on this occa-sion; old men made themselves ten or even twenty years younger, boys two to three years older. In Great Britain such a thing is not easy to check, because there is no system of police registration. Within the first twenty-four hours after Eden's speech, more than a quarter of a million men had registered in England, Wales, Scotland and Northern Ireland.

The Home Guard, as the LDV was later to be called, was put under the authority of the Commander Home Forces, originally Field Marshal Sir Edmund Ironside, and later General Sir Walter Kirke, and organised strictly along military lines: regiments (zones), battalions, companies and platoons. There were no weapons available for the newly created force and it was left up to each individual 'parashot', as they were soon to call themselves, to solve the problem as best he might.

Experienced former officers were appointed as leaders and it was not uncommon for a lieutenant general (retired) having to serve as a major, a former colonel as a captain or lieutenant. In great haste, hundreds of thousands of registration forms were printed and sent by lorry as quickly as possible to even the most remote police post. All the formalities were handled locally, so that units were often set up within a matter of hours. The bureaucrats were given no chance at all, because the danger was far too great that thousands of heavily armed enemies might suddenly fall down from the sky.

In London alone, 60 battalions of the Home Guard were formed in these few days. In the City, in apartment houses and places of business, in factories, and on the docks, there could now be seen groups of patrolling civilians armed with sticks, old rifles and sabres, who asked to see identification documents or spent hours staring into the heavens. In Fleet Street, the typesetters and printers had joined together to form a battalion. The Westminster Battalion, in which generals and members of the peerage dominated, also included a platoon from Buckingham Palace comprising officials of the Court. The City had its own battalion, as did both Houses of Parliament, the gas works, the BBC, the refuse collection service and the taxi drivers. A stretch of 125 miles was patrolled by a River Battalion made up of the owners of the private motor and house boats lying in the Thames.

Even the Americans living in London had formed a unit of the Home Guard. They called themselves the 'American Squadron', numbered between 60 and 70 men, and were commanded by General Wade H. Hayes. Their formation caused the Foreign Office to take notice: if members of one neutral nation were permitted to form an armed unit in Great Britain, this right could then not be denied to other neutrals, and in England there were, among others, a considerable number of Japanese. However, these misgivings turned out to be unfounded. Not so those held by the American Ambassador Joseph Kennedy, who did not like the idea one bit: 'If London were to be occupied, this could lead to all US citizens living there being shot as *franc tireurs*!'

Several of the lord lieutenants in the Counties had expressed similar doubts about the Home Guard. According to the Hague Convention, irregulars had to display insignia, carry their weapons openly and be under the command of responsible leadership. Whitehall reacted immediately, prescribed armbands for the 'parashots' with the letters L.D.V. and simultaneously began to put them in uniforms; fatigues, overalls and khaki caps.

This did not prevent German propaganda from seizing this heaven-sent opportunity. An information brochure put out by the Nazis pompously declared: 'Under no circumstances can a nation be permitted to set armed civilians against an enemy under any sort of excuse or disguise. Whoever incites the population of his country, as the Churchill–Eden Government is doing, to such militarily senseless methods of combat, which are prohibited by international law and dangerous for the individual concerned, is committing a crime against his people and therefore his nation. Such an irresponsible action is a sign of hysteria on the part of the government, which is seeking refuge in any method of murder out of a sense of military weakness.'

The department in Goebbels' Propaganda Ministry charged with observing the foreign press, had attentively followed the development of the 'art of cowardly murder' in the British dailies. These spoke of hand grenade depots in the villages, of stone piles in the fields against airborne landings, of dynamite, with which German soldiers should be treacherously blown up. Every farmer a soldier, every horsewoman an Amazon, was the motto of the British Home Defence. The German comments on this speak for themselves, viz. the following: 'Out of a misapprehension of true soldiery arises the pernicious ideology under which War Minister Eden incites to guerrilla warfare. It is the spawn of the unrestrained will to annihilate the enemy, for whose destruction any means will serve and any weapon be of value... and so he knows no bounds in his breaches of the law, his brutality and his murderous actions, and still expects "Our Lord" to bless even guerrilla warfare... here the mantle of Christian civilisation has fallen.'

It had not escaped the notice of the German propagandists that former Spanish freedom fighters were playing an important role in the Home Guard; they spoke of machinations by the Red Guard, of murderous scum – it was but a short step to 'Bolshevist sub-humans'. The man they were mainly aiming at was Tom Wintringham, military expert of the *Daily Mirror* and former freedom fighter in Spain, who was teaching his countrymen the techniques of guerrilla war.

This propaganda made no impression on the British target group, nor on the Germans. In its broadcasts to England by the Propaganda Ministry, 'Lord Haw-Haw', an American of Irish descent, poked fun at the Home Guard. He quoted from letters to the papers in which the strangest suggestions on how to deal with German paratroops were being made. Someone had advised in the *Daily Mirror*, for example, to put miniature sewing machines under the seats of bicycles deliberately left standing about, so that when German soldiers tried to ride off with them, they would automatically sew their trousers to the seat. Someone else suggested equipping the Home Guard with lassoes, because that was the best method by which to catch a paratrooper. Boomerangs were also being discussed as weapons.

The British laughed about it. The ranks of the Home Guard continued to swell. The islanders were well aware of their idiosyncrasies. For a foreigner it was virtually impossible to tell where the fun left off and things became serious, for example, in the matter of the golf club.

Whereas in the cities, the units of the Home Guard had almost automatically developed out of existing connections from people's places of work, factories, offices, shops, in the country there was normally only the village society in which the local squire, the landowner, gathered his tenants, hired hands and small business owners about him, just as in the days of Napoleon. Besides this, there were a number of church choirs, amateur theatrical groups and various clubs, whose members joined together in the paramilitary organisation for the defence of their homeland. So too did the Cobble Hall golf club in Leeds, which improvised home defence in so typically an English manner, that it could just as well have taken place in India, Burma or Africa. The club did not lack for retired officers. Many of the stiff, white-haired gentlemen, with their moustaches and faces reddened by whisky, had already fought in the Boer War or in China, but certainly all during the First World War. There was no question but that the club would unanimously form the 2nd Platoon of the Leeds Company. After three days of recruiting – the club bar served as the recruiting office – the club, augmented by some useful non-members, reported for its first tour of duty. Dress: golfing togs; weapons: heavy walking sticks. The duty room was the club hall and people slept in the leather armchairs around the place.

The military assignment was clearly defined: high ground was to be occupied providing observation points, road blocks were to be manned and patrols were to cover the countryside in search of enemies that had landed, spies, and members of the fifth column. The term 'fifth column' stemmed from the men who had fought in Spain. It described an enemy inside the country about whom there was no clear conception whatsoever. All that was known was that he was omnipresent and very dangerous. He could be a traitor or a saboteur in the guise of a churchwarden, or a retired colonel, an interned 'enemy alien', as easily as a man out of work. People were therefore living in enemy territory, so to speak, and anybody could be a potential enemy. This was a feeling they were already familiar with from having lived in the colonies and the golfers from Leeds knew exactly how to conduct themselves. And who was to gainsay them if, after having completed a patrol, they were to play a round of golf?

Two members brought along their guns, because one cannot shoot a spy with a walking stick. Unfortunately, one of them had to be reprimanded because when on observation duty, he whiled away the time by shooting rabbits instead of keeping a lookout for paratroops. Discipline and combat morale took a turn for the better, however, when everybody was issued a rifle and could regularly drill with weapons. The duty room was moved to the tea room, where there were now beds installed. A textile manufacturer, who was also a member of the club, donated mattresses and blankets. The drying room became the arsenal. Otherwise, club life continued as usual. A symbiosis of guerrilla warfare and golf. One day the duty officer of the Leeds company was making his rounds and arrived at the 2nd Platoon towards 22.30, precisely at the moment that a smartly dressed waitress with a white lace cap and starched apron came into the duty room with a tray of tea and sandwiches. That caused talk. The other platoons scoffed at the life of luxury being led by the 2nd Platoon, which had a gardener and helpers who tended the hand-grenade throwing range and kept the dummies for bayonet practice in order. 'Golfers are actually the ideal home defenders', said the platoon leader, 'only sometimes they forget this when playing golf. It may then occur that they report "tracers over the 13th green" or "searchlight 105° from the 7th hole!' The golf club platoon became so popular that the older members could soon be sent home. Many of them subsequently reappeared time and again under the most threadbare excuses, pointing out their indispensability, and it was not only the bar, or the bridge games, or the billiards that kept bringing them back.

Being a member of the Home Guard also meant that one had a certain authority over one's fellow citizens. Whether from an inflated need for recognition or an exaggerated sense of duty, the men of the Home Guard did not show themselves to be over-scrupulous when it came to controlling 'suspects'. According to the motto: 'a spy can also be found wearing the uniform of a Bobby', they stopped police patrols and demanded to see their identification. This led to a heated controversy between the Home Office and the Ministry of Defence, which resulted in the police henceforward demanding to see the identity cards of the Home Guard.

When King George VI was visiting a munitions factory in southern England, a member of the Home Guard of the plant even went so far as to stop the King's car and demand to see papers. Only after an adjutant let him have a peek inside the car did the over-zealous man salute and let it pass.

Things really got out of hand, however, when patrols at roadblocks or in open country began to shoot because something aroused their suspicion. It happened far too often that harmless citizens who were 'acting suspiciously' in the country – in one case in the person's own garden – or who did not stop their cars because they had not seen the roadblock, or simply drove on because they were afraid to stop, were shot out of hand. During a single night there were four such incidents.

A doctor in Kent said of the Home Guard what many people were thinking: it was more of a liability than an asset. He had been called out at 01.00 to treat a patient in Benenden School, which lay only three miles from his home. When halfway there, his car was stopped by a wild-looking youth brandishing a musket. The doctor became frightened and shouted at the youth: 'For God's sake, put that damn thing down. Your are liable to shoot one of us!' Cowed, the young man obeyed and carefully put the murder instrument on the ground in front of him. He then asked to see papers. Carelessly, he stepped in front of the car's bonnet and studied the doctor's identification card in the weak shine of the dimmed headlights. The motor was still running. A mere nudge with the foot would have sent the 'guard' into the hereafter. 'If I were a German, you would be dead by now!' said the doctor when he was handed back his papers. He then did not wait for any further explanations, as the barrel of the musket was again dangerously approaching his head, but drove off as fast as he could.

The Home Guard was not very popular with the average citizen. Sometimes its members were mocked openly because for want of rifles, they had to drill with broomsticks, or because they themselves were infected by the paratrooper hysteria. Far too often false alarms were sounded and huge search actions initiated, because some observer's imagination had run away with him. A patrol out in the mists of an early summer morning had mistaken the stamping of cattle for the thuds made by landing paratroopers; on a bright moonlit night, a vicar had taken a landing swan for a parachute; a Home Guard had been deceived by a shred of cloth from a barrage balloon floating in the air. Nonetheless, what this did prove was that, over the British Isles not even a needle could fall from the sky without being detected.

It was hardly fair to make the Home Guard responsible for all of the fantasies. They were but an expression of the 'island syndrome' against which not even men in the highest offices were immune. Sir Edmund Ironside, commander of the Home Defence Forces, went so far as to claim at a meeting of the commanders of the Home Guard: 'We have definite proof that there are people in this country who are preparing landing areas for the enemy.' The Admiral commanding Dover, Sir Bertram Ramsay, discovered 'numerous signs of acts of sabotage and fifth column activities', including the fact that 'used cars are being bought up at fantastic prices and parked on various car lots'.

Apart from the fact that the German paratroops and airborne forces were still in the process of being built up, and were far too weak for an invasion, there is not a shred of proof that anything excepting pollen had fallen from the sky onto the British Isles. The haul gathered in by the 'parashots' usually consisted of harmless bird watchers who had been observing birds with their field glasses, holiday-makers who were sketching country scenes, aeroplane enthusiasts who were hanging around near airbases, or lovers who were detected in lush grass.

For the British, devoted to the theatre as no other nation on earth, the initial phase of the invasion threat took on the character of a patriotic melodrama. Everybody attempted to draw his own moving picture of the invasion. Nothing was safe from the dark fantasies of the British: from the alleged disguises the paratroopers were going to use, to the French woman who fled across the Channel with her two small children and, on reaching the coast, was holding a child in one hand and with the other supposedly clutching the dead hand of the other child; German bombs had torn the child from her side and severed the arm in the process.

In such a mood, the British even gave up hallowed privileges, sacrifices that they made on the altar of the mother country: they willingly let themselves be registered in lists (something they normally never did), obeyed orders from above without complaining and even carried a personal identity card, a thing that every Briton hates, with them all the time. They dug trenches and dugouts right through the centres of their beloved flowerbeds and carefully tended lawns. They donated their aluminium cooking pots for aircraft production, took down the iron railings protecting their front gardens and painted over the bumpers of their cars with white paint.

It was soon to become apparent, however, that the British were not only play-acting. When the curtain actually rose on this sinister drama, they were at least morally prepared. Even the German Intelligence Service reported with indignation on 1 June: 'The English are not even considering defeat.'

IV

Jews and Nazis in the Same Bag
The British intern everybody

The presence of thousands of 'enemy aliens', mostly Jews and other refugees from the Nazi regime, proved itself to be an interference with British defence efforts. That at least is what a great many conservative politicians believed, who were also inciting fear of espionage and the fifth column. Long before the declaration of war, the internment of 'untrustworthy elements' had already been planned and was put into practice from September 1939. Under this policy, both Germans and Austrians, supporters of the Nazi regime, as well as its victims, were to be put into the same bag.

The fate of the refugees, particularly the Jews, had not touched public opinion, even though much had become known about the atrocities of the *Kristallnacht* ['Crystal Night', term commonly applied in Germany for the days in November 1938 when Jewish homes and places of business were wrecked by Nazi hordes and much glass and crockery broken], or those committed during the *Anschluss* ['attachment', i.e. Hitler's seizure] of Austria and the campaign in Poland. The stories just sounded too barbaric to be believable.

This was clearly expressed in a letter that the well-known diplomat and writer Harold Nicolson wrote to his wife from London in June 1938: 'Yesterday I chanced upon an Austrian who had just escaped from Vienna. What he told me made me sick. There is a devilish sense of humour in their cruelties. Last Sunday they arrested all the people out for a walk in the Prater [park and fairgrounds] and separated the Jews from the rest. The Jewish men were made to take off all their clothes and crawl around in the grass on all fours. They made old Jewesses climb into the trees on ladders and perch there. Then they told them to chirp like birds. The Russians never committed atrocities such as these. One may kill a person, but to take his dignity away from him is barbaric. This man told me that he had seen with his own eyes, the Duchess of Starhemberg scrubbing the urinals in the Vienna railway station. The suicide rate is horrifying. Maybe I should have said to myself that the man was exaggerating, because I had my doubts that even the Germans could act in such a manner. However, I had dinner with Count Bernstoff (author's note: diplomat, retired in 1933, active in the Resistance, murdered by the SS in 1945) who said, when I repeated the stories to him: Yes, they are true. A Nazi friend of mine who was transferred to headquarters in Vienna told me that he was unable to stand it. He said "I saw grownup men acting like nasty little boys who tear the wings off flies".'

Only the British Foreign Office had initially differentiated and carefully classed the enemy aliens into three categories. Category A comprised Germans and Austrians who could be expected to support their own country (sic!) or impede the defence efforts on the island. This category was to be interned.

Category C included all refugees who had had to leave Germany for racial, religious or political reasons. It also included those who had been living in Great Britain for a longer period of time and had identified themselves with the country, provided they had a good reputation and could credibly prove their loyalty. They were to retain their freedom and go on living as before.

Whoever did not fall into category A or C was automatically put in category B and had to accept serious restrictions on his personal freedom. These foreigners, for example, were not allowed to travel further than five miles from their place of residence, were not permitted to own cameras or maps, and had to report to the police at regular intervals.

In England, Scotland and Wales, 120 tribunals were set up to hear each individual case and decide into which category a person was to be put, very similar to the tribunals that carried out the denazification in postwar Germany. The chairmen were either judges, lawyers or justices of the peace, the jurors were normally recruited from the local town councils. A total of 73,800 cases were heard by these tribunals. About 64,200 people were put into category C, so that in the beginning, only a few thousand were interned, in other words imprisoned, in hastily improvised camps.

It could have remained at that. However, with the start of the German campaign in the west, the situation changed over night. The surprise actions by the German paratroops and airborne troops in Holland, the rapid advance of the German panzer divisions and the collapse of all resistance on the Continent fired fears in England of an invasion and a fifth column. From conversations he had with Dutch refugees, including members of the Dutch Government, the Director of Propaganda in Enemy Countries, Sir Campbell Stuart, painted a grotesque and horrifying picture of the occupation of Holland, which was expressed in a widely circulated memorandum. This said that German paratroopers alone had killed between 35,000 and 40,000 Dutch soldiers. They had come down from the skies in manifold disguises: in Dutch, Belgian, French and British uniforms, as normal civilians, as priests, as schoolboys, 'some of whom were dressed as girls'. All of them carried automatic weapons and hand grenades and distributed poisoned cigarettes and chocolates to passing troops and civilians.

Sir Neville Bland, the British Ambassador in the Hague, who, together with other refugees from Holland, reached the English coast in a British destroyer on 14 May, reported his experiences to Lord Halifax and also painted a horror picture of the overpowering of Holland by the Germans, in which fighting forces and fifth column were impressively amalgamated: 'The paratroopers are boys of 16 to 18 who are so thoroughly indoctrinated with Hitler's ideology, that all they can think of is to spread as much death and destruction as they can before they are themselves killed. They land on rooftops, in the open countryside, even in private gardens.' According to Sir Neville Bland, they were thoroughly familiar with Holland and knew exactly where each unit of the Dutch Army lay and where the air bases were located. From whom? From the Dutch themselves, who had not been wary of their German and Austrian servants or employees. 'The most lowly kitchen maid', he claimed, ' may not only be a threat to the safety of our country, she normally is.' He also meant the many poor Jewish refugee women and girls, who had found employment as servants in English homes. From this Bland concluded that the moment Hitler gave the signal, the 'vassals of the monster' would set off a wave of sabotage against military and civilian installations all over the country, and he demanded: 'All Germans and Austrians should at least be interned immediately.'

One may take into account that Bland, like the Dutch refugees, was still under shock. He had seen German paratroopers in the flesh, heard their shots, and the destroyer that had brought him back had been repeatedly attacked by *Luftwaffe* aircraft. But his exaggerated portrayals fell on fertile ground. From right and left, the 'enemy aliens' were suddenly being regarded as dangerous agents.

The extreme right had been inciting against the foreigners for quite some time, had been calling them henchmen of the Communist International, who were aiding and abetting the Bolshivisation of England. In Lord Rothermere's paper, the *Sunday Dispatch*, it had been possible to read in February: 'Here (in Glasgow) there are more than 2,000 subversive agents under orders from Moscow. They disguise themselves as peace societies or legitimate organisations of the working class. It is time they be exposed for what they really are.' In April, the paper became even more outspoken: 'The Great Foreigner Scandal' the headline proclaimed. Czech Communists had received two million pounds and used them to form Red Cells and print Communist brochures.

After the conquest of Holland by the Germans in May, however, the issue was no longer only Communists, but all Germans without exception. Consequently, the Intelligence Staff of the Armed Forces under Sir William Cavendish-Bentinck came to the conclusion, based on an analysis of the events in Holland, that all enemy aliens, male and female, between sixteen and 70 years of age should be interned.

Home Secretary Sir John Anderson, who had propounded a liberal stance towards the refugees, because he had had legal reservations, was unable to assert himself in the face of the hysteria against foreigners which now broke out. Internment fell under the Royal Prerogative, the right of the King in times of war, which permits the government of the moment to undertake any measures outside the law which it considers to be necessary. Already in May, the Home Office had reluctantly requested the General Staff to intern all foreigners between sixteen and 60 years of age living in the counties bordering on the coast, including those in category B. With this, 5,000 Germans and Austrians were rounded up in two police actions.

Among those arrested were men like 43-year-old journalist Richard Broh. Having fought in the First World War, he had later been an employee of the *Reich* War Ministry and a member of the Citizens' and Soldiers' Council of Berlin. From 1926 on, he had worked as a journalist associated with the trade unions, until Goebbels discovered in 1935 that there were still twelve Jewish journalists registered with the *Reichspressekammer* [Reich Press Association]. Broh was one of them. Goebbels ordered their expulsion, which was tantamount to a prohibition to work. The twelve thereupon took the matter to court. The proceedings were delayed due to the Olympic Games, because Goebbels did not want a scandal at that juncture. In 1937, however, the court upheld the expulsion order. Broh recognised in time the danger he was now in and escaped to England. The other eleven were arrested and put into a concentration camp. From England, Broh had continued to work for his paper until the advent of the war put an end to that as well. The tribunal had classed him as category B. That he was now being put into a different camp, albeit a more humane one, where he was to meet his arch-enemies can hardly have given him much satisfaction.

Italy's entry into the war on 10 June inflamed the anti-foreigner mood even more and there were anti-Italian excesses in London. By 14 June, 1,687 Italians had already been arrested, without their having been put before a tribunal. By no means all of them were dedicated Fascists or had flown to Britain for political, racial, or religious reasons. They were mostly teachers, businessmen or cooks who had come to Britain, and the majority had been assimilated long ago.

Anderson's categories had by now been discarded for good. In June, the first Germans and Austrians in category C were arrested and put into camps. One of the better known ones was Olympia, a former exhibition hall in London, which was initially occupied by 40 men, of whom seventeen were declared anti-Nazis and a high percentage Jews, who now had to share sleeping facilities with active members of the Nazi party.

In the Onchan camp on the Isle of Man alone, there were – in addition to zealous Nazis – 121 artists and writers who had fled, 113 scientists and university professors, 67 engineers, 38 physicists, 22 chemists, nineteen men of the cloth, and twelve dentists, out of a total number of 1,491 inmates of whom 82% were Jews.

In the camps, vehement altercations broke out between Hitler's followers and those that had fled before the terror of the Nazi regime. The former attempted to assume the roles of camp leaders and 'kapos' and to take over command. They wanted to show the British what German discipline and order was all about and to demonstrate brown power as 'Germans abroad'. If they had had their way, they would even have held party rallies in the camps.

Conditions in the camps and the lack of interest on the part of the British contributed to such excesses, because the issues always included such matters as better quarters, a greater share of the meagre provisions and the control of the flourishing black market. Food often consisted of nothing more than biscuits and tea, watery vegetables and potatoes.

The accommodation was atrocious. Those who were unlucky enough not to be put into a camp equipped with the Nissen huts that were standard for the British Army could, for example, find themselves in the changing rooms under the tiers of a race track such as Lingfield or in the bathing cabins of a seaside resort such as Seaton. The bathing cabins had the advantage that one could catch eels through a hole in the floor and open a brisk trade with them.

The arrests continued until July. In the end, there were 27,200 Germans, Austrians, and Italians in the camps. Many men of rank and stature, whose loyalty to their host country could not be questioned, had fallen victim to this mistreatment. Max Braun, former chairman of the SPD [German Social Democratic Party] in the Saar, Dr Martin Freud, the son of Sigmund Freud, the conductor Hans Oppenheim, the pianist Frank Osborne, the famous jurist Professor Fritz Pringsheim, the painter Kurt Schwitters who had fled from the Nazis in Norway in May, journalists Robert Neumann and Sebastian Haffner, the novelist and editor of Knaur's Encyclopedia, Richard Friedenthal. Even Ernst 'Putzi' Hanfstaengl, Hitler's former intimate and protector, was among those interned. The *Führer's* erstwhile 'court jester', who had fled from Germany to escape Goebbels' jealousy, was not taken seriously by anybody in England, except by the officials in the Home Office, who put him on their list as one of the first to be arrested and then hastily deported him to Canada.

Hitler stood on the Channel like a threatening, oversized spectre and in almost panicky fear, people were to grasp the shadows he seemed to be casting on the English countryside. After the Germans, Austrians, and Italians, the press next turned public attention to those groups that many newspapers openly referred to as 'Quislings' and 'Hitler's future *Gauleiter* [district party bosses] in Great Britain', the British Union of Fascists of Sir Oswald Mosley.

These imitators of Hitler, with about 5,000 registered members, had long descended into political obscurity. After street fighting in Cable Street in London in 1936, they had been forbidden to wear uniforms and they had lost virtually any support in the population due to their anti-Semitic gangs of bullies. In recent years, they had never gained a seat in general or by-elections.

Sir John Anderson opposed the internment of Mosley's followers even more strongly than that of the foreigners, and this time brought political arguments to bear, after referral to the Bill of Rights and habeas corpus had not borne fruit: 'Even though the political objectives of the BFU include resistance to the war effort and attacks on the Government, there is no proof that they are supporting the enemy. Their propaganda even contains patriotic overtones. In my view, a blow against this organisation, such as the detention of its leaders, would be a mistake at this time.' The government however, bowed to public opinion. On 29 June, Anderson presented Prime Minister Winston Churchill with a list of the names of 150 people he had had arrested the day before. Churchill was annoyed, because among the top three on the list were two of his relatives, his cousin Lady Mosley, better known as Diana Mitford, daughter of Lord Redesdale and sister of Unity Mitford, and another cousin, Geo Pitt-Rivers, Mosley's deputy.

The camps were beginning to fill up and the enemy could land on the coasts of the island any day. What better then, than to send this gigantic factor of insecurity, this massed fifth column, as far away as possible? After secret agreements with Canada and Australia, the first shipments of internees into the safekeeping of the Canadian and Australian governments already started in June.

In Liverpool lay the *Duchess of York*, a 20,000 BRT passenger liner that had regularly plied the North Atlantic route for the Canadian-Pacific Line until the outbreak of war. And now again, on 20 June 1940, a long line of passengers was boarding for a trip to Canada. Men in badly fitting, rumpled suits and uniforms without insignia were dragging cases and cardboard boxes past British soldiers lining the route with their arms ordered. The passengers consisted of 500 German prisoners of war and 1,600 internees of category A and B. About 1,100 of them were members of the German merchant marine, whose ships had been seized, or German sailors who had been taken from aboard neutral ships against all maritime conventions. While the other civilians went towards their unsure fate with heads bowed and full of bitterness or resignation, the German sailors openly showed their disdain for the British. Some of them attempted to provoke the soldiers wherever they could. They had no inkling that the *Kriegsmarine* had done exactly the same thing and that only thereafter, had Churchill directed the Admiralty to arrest three Germans for every Briton taken into captivity.

With this, Churchill seriously endangered the British reputation abroad and lost much of the sympathy with which the neutral world regarded Britain's struggle, for the Royal Navy had no scruples at all and paid no heed to the numerical relationship decreed. On 2 December 1939, a British warship had taken 22 German passengers off the Brazilian liner *Itape* and, ignoring Brazilian protests, brought them to England. The British had even disregarded warnings by the US State Department.

On 21 January 1940 a major incident took place. A British cruiser stopped the Japanese *Asama Maru* only 35 nautical miles off the Japanese coast and took 21 Germans, including several sailors, into custody. The State Department joined in the enraged protests by the Japanese, after the American Embassy in Tokyo pointed out that the incident had also seriously endangered Japanese–American relations.

The British finally saw their way clear to returning nine of the captured Germans to the Japanese. The German Foreign Ministry had not let this oppor- tunity slip by and, via the American Government, had offered permission to leave Germany to any British citizen who applied, provided the measure was reciprocal. But Churchill had not been prepared to give in. While pressure by the USA had led to about 100 people being exchanged and the Germans had freed about 400 Lascars, the number of German sailors interned in Great Britain had continued to grow. Now the attempt was being made to get rid of them by sending them to the Dominions.

The internees knew nothing about this squabble. For them, the grey painted *Duchess of York* was just another prison on the way to another camp. For this, the guards were given many a look of hatred. On board, a crisis began to develop. Only with great ill-will did the German sailors obey the orders of the British, who in their turn were becoming increasingly more nervous.

The *Duchess of York* had left Liverpool and passed the New Brighton light when the first incident aboard occurred. A lieutenant of the guards ordered German sailors lounging on deck to clear the deck and go to their sleeping quarters below. Nobody moved. A sergeant repeated the order in a loud voice. Someone then shouted: 'Speak German'. Thereupon the lieutenant lost his nerve and ordered the sergeant to shoot. The sergeant lifted his weapon, intending to shoot over the heads of the internees, when the lieutenant pushed the weapon downwards. The shot killed one man and wounded two others. Under protest, the Germans cleared the deck, taking their dead and wounded comrades with them. The captain immediately sent a cable to his owners reporting the incident and closed his report by saying he expected a mutiny by the internees. The guards on board were put on constant alert. As it soon turned out this was an exaggerated assessment because the prisoners bowed to their fate and were delivered to Canada in good shape. Later on, the lieutenant was court-martialled and convicted.

Another shipment of internees was far more dramatic and was to cost hundreds of them their lives. On 1 July 1940 the 15,000 BRT former luxury liner *Arandora Star* left Liverpool. On board were 712 Italian and 478 German internees, 200 British soldiers as guards, and a crew of 174 British sailors. The Germans included 242 seamen: officers and sailors of the *Adolph Woermann* under the ship's captain, Burfeind. Their ship had been seized by the British several months before. Now they too were to be shipped to Canada.

The *Arandora Star* had been built in 1927 for the Blue Star Line. Like many other ships, her employment reflects contemporary history. Originally a passenger and freight carrier on the South America route, in 1928 she achieved greater honours. The world economic crisis was casting its shadows and the freight business was stagnating, so the owners decided to convert the ship into the 'most pleasurable excursion cruiser in the world', exclusively reserved for first class passengers who were to be offered every conceivable amenity. From then on she served the deceptive optimism of the rich, who steamed heedlessly past all of the crisis of the 'thirties.

The ship undertook spring cruises in the Mediterranean and along the Atlantic coast of Africa, in summer to Stockholm and Oslo, during the winter to the Pacific and the Caribbean. The passenger list included such illustrious names as King Carol of Rumania, Lord Nuffield and George Bernard Shaw.

From 1927 onwards, the ship's captain was 50-year-old Edgar W. Moulton, a tall, polite gentleman who was esteemed and respected by both passengers and owners. Moulton was a master of his trade. He had sailed in large sailing ships for many years and his father had been captain of the famous four-master *Pegasus*. He knew every ocean like the back of his hand.

For 1939 there had been twelve cruises in the *Arandora Star*'s programme. The summer cruise included the Faroes, Iceland, the Norwegian Fjords, Denmark and Sweden. She was supposed to return to Southampton on 31 August 1939 via Danzig and the Baltic–North Sea Canal. However, having been warned by his owners, Moulton broke off the cruise in Sweden, and without stopping in Danzig, steamed through the Skagerrak to Southampton, where the ship arrived on 26 August. On 1 September she was already under way to New York with 441 Americans for whom Europe was becoming too hot. When war was declared, the ship was still at sea and the crew spent the rest of the voyage painting stacks and upper works grey and blacking out windows and portholes by simply covering them with dark blue paint.

After her return, engineers of the Royal Navy came on board. They were disappointed to discover that the conversion into a pleasure cruiser had made the *Arandora Star* top-heavy, so that she could not be employed as an auxiliary cruiser. Nonetheless, she could still be used as a target ship for practising defensive techniques in the war against submarines. By then, the German U-boats had already sunk more than 100 British merchant ships, without the Royal Navy being able to find an effective response. The only thing that had proved any value were torpedo nets hung in front of harbour entrances. It therefore seemed a good idea to attach such nets to ships and the *Arandora Star* became one of these trial ships: her massive hull draped in heavy nets, she had to let herself be torpedoed by British submarines in the Channel. The trials were successful: all the torpedoes fired became entangled in the nets. Despite this, later on nets were only used on rare occasions, even though they only reduced the speed of a large ship by about one knot. *Arandora Star* had to give back her nets too.

The next order Captain Moulton received promised a far less exciting assignment: *Arandora Star* became the censor boat in the Straits of Gibraltar. During late winter and early spring of 1940, the crew spent their time examining mail carried by Italian ships. But most of the time Moulton and his men were just waiting around; it was the Phoney War at sea.

When the war really started in May, the ship was ordered back north in order to bring 10,000 men of the British Expeditionary Force back to Glasgow from Norway. On this trip, she almost ran under the guns of a German flotilla with *Scharnhorst* at its head. Some miles away, the British destroyer *Acasta*, defending the aircraft carrier *Glorious*, carried out a courageous diversionary manoeuvre. Steaming full speed ahead, her captain ran his ship towards the German battle cruiser and as soon as he was in range, opened fire with everything he had. The *Scharnhorst* with her superior armament, had no trouble at all in shooting the little warship to bits within minutes. But even in sinking, *Acasta* succeeded in damaging *Scharnhorst*, and this sacrifice saved the *Arandora Star*, which escaped without the Germans intervening. She delivered the troops from Norway to Glasgow unscathed.

Only days later she made fast in several French ports in Brittany, where she saved British and Polish troops encircled by the Germans. By now, her decks were adorned with a 4.7-inch cannon and a 12-pounder anti-aircraft gun. Armed in this manner, she lay at anchor in Liverpool during the final days of June to take the internees aboard.

There was nothing left to be seen of the former splendour of the luxury liner. The valuable furniture had disappeared. The large dining room had been converted into a primitive canteen with screwed-down benches and rough wooden tables. There was no longer a captain's table. For Captain Moulton, as for all the other British, the fight for sheer survival had now begun.

In another sense, this was also true for the internees, who now came on board in long lines. In particular the crew of the *Adolph Woermann* was well aware of this, with a sound appreciation of the danger from U-boats. The first thing Captain Burfeind and his officers did after coming aboard, was to closely inspect the lifeboats, and to note down those that were in good condition. In secret, he divided his 241 men among these six boats.

The rest of the almost 1,000 internees had hardly any conception of the danger they would be in during the voyage across the Atlantic. Among the Italians were the chefs of the Ritz and the Savoy in London, the Café des Anglais in Paris, and of many another famous restaurant. In their ranks was also Anzanis, the Secretary General of the Italian League for Human Rights. The Germans included the Socialist Karl Olbrich, the labour leader Louis Weber and many respected Jewish businessmen. Among the Austrians were eleven anti-Nazi politicians, who had had to flee their country after the *Anschluss*. Most of them had never been to sea and lifeboats were something they took no interest in. Nor apparently did Captain Moulton who, curiously enough, did not conduct the customary boat drills.

On the morning of 2 July, the *Arandora Star* was 200 nautical miles off the west coast of Scotland and 125 nautical miles northwest of the Irish coast. She was not alone in the watery wastes of the Atlantic. A German U-boat crossed the track of the passenger ship. U-47 under *Kapitänleutnant* Günther Prien was on the way home from a three-week combat patrol. Prien and his crew had already sunk eight ships, including the 5,000 BRT freighter *Balmoral Wood* and several tankers. There was one torpedo left, waiting to be fired.

The situation was favourable for an attack. A light wind from the southwest, a calm sea with a slight swell, overcast sky but excellent visibility. Prien went to attack depth when he had approached to within 2,500 metres of the big ship. At 06.58 the torpedo surged out of the torpedo tube. As if she were motionless, *Arandora Star* lay in the cross-hairs of the periscope. 60, 70, seconds went by. Maybe the distance had been to great after all. Prien was just about to turn away when a huge fountain of water arose midships on the *Arandora Star*. Exactly 97 seconds had passed.

When the torpedo's explosion shattered the calm on *Arandora Star*'s bridge, the officers only looked at each other in silence. Automatically, Captain Moulton rang the engine room for full stop, but the sound of the engines had already died away. He then called the engine room but did not receive any answer. In a calm voice he brusquely ordered all water-tight doors in the bulkheads amidships closed and the clearing of the fourteen lifeboats. A few minutes later he realised that there was no further hope for his ship: *Arandora Star* took on a distinct list. Moulton ordered all hands on deck. It was the captain's last order, a final gesture of authority, before chaos swamped them all.

The explosion in the engine room had caused a panic among the internees below decks. Screaming, they had overpowered the guards in the gangways and seized their weapons. Half dressed, they viciously battled their way upwards. There the guards attempted to control the demented mass. They advanced towards the mob surging around the lifeboats with fixed bayonets and tried to force them into orderly lines. Shots were fired and several Italians were killed. At one spot, a sergeant knocked obstreperous internees down with the but of his rifle and had their unconscious bodies heaved into the boats.

The officers and men of the *Adolph Woermann* had seized the six previously selected lifeboats, which were quickly lowered to the water completely over-loaded. Even though the guards gained the upper hand, the fight for the remaining lifeboats, liferafts, and lines hanging down to the water from over the sides, continued to rage. Most of the elderly men hit out, pulled at each other and climbed all over each other in naked fear of death. In a lifeboat designed for 70 people, over a hundred internees and five members of the crew crowded together. Others just clung desperately to the railing and waited for the end.

On the bridge, Captain Moulton continued to try to bring order out of chaos. He was supported by the German captain Burfeind. However, their orders and shouted commands went under in the general panic. Moulton threw a life-jacket to one of the Italians. Major Bethel, commander of the guards, gave his to a member of the crew. After twenty minutes it was all over. Moulton had sailed 85,000 nautical miles in his *Arandora Star* and he stayed on her bridge when she went down gurgling. Next to him stood Captain Burfeind and Major Bethel as the water closed over their heads. The wireless operator also died. He had sent SOS until the water rushed into his office and he was no longer able to escape. The gunner, who up to the end had kept his weapon aimed and ready to fire on the spot in the water where he suspected the U-boat to be, also died.

The sea was covered with pieces of wreckage, planks, boats, rafts, people swimming. And the battle among the castaways was still raging. James Hunt, a sailor who survived, reported: 'I was in the pantry. The explosion had buried me under a heap of cutlery. The door was stuck; I had to kick it down in order to get out. We then cleared the rafts on the railing and jumped in after them. I was hardly on the raft when I was surrounded by screaming Germans and Italians, who caused it to capsize. One Italian pushed me under water and hit me in the face. When hitting back, I broke my knuckles. There were eight of us on our raft.'

One of the Germans kept his head in the chaos. When an over-loaded lifeboat capsized he took over command and ordered helpers to his side. Despite the fact that others constantly threw themselves in between in their panic, the boat was turned back right side up. Thereupon he began to collect people swimming about and on the verge of drowning. Half an hour later the last screams and shouts had died down at the place of the sinking. Mute and grimly keeping their heads above water, or crammed into the boats, the survivors waited for a rescue ship.

Four hours later a Royal Air Force Sunderland flying boat flew over the scene of the disaster and dropped tins with biscuits and bully beef. However, the survivors still had to wait until 13.30 before the Canadian destroyer St Laurent arrived. Her captain, Commander de Wolf reported later that only ten of the fourteen lifeboats had been found on the water. Therefore the others had either not been cleared or had gone down in the suction of the sinking ship.

Rescue work lasted until 16.00 St Laurent then set course for Scotland and arrived in Glasgow at 06.30 next morning. Besides 79 British members of the crew, 689 of the interned Germans and Italians had died.

The news of the sinking of the ship full of internees caused an outcry throughout the western world, because the attack had taken place in daylight and without warning. But the outrage was also directed against the British, who had sent defenceless prisoners on such a voyage. In London, the news fell victim to the censor. However, the incident and the reaction to it by the rest of the world had shown the British Government, how senseless the mass internment and deportation of victims of the Nazis and long assimilated 'enemy' aliens together with Hitler's supporters was. The shipments were discontinued, the regulations governing internment loosened and with time, most of the internees were set free.

V
Where to Hide on an Island?
The trauma of evacuation

Since 1938, protection against air raids and the service to provide it (the ARP) had dominated the lives of the British. Even more than in Germany, people were attempting to protect themselves against attacks from the air, especially in eastern and southeastern England and London. The bombs dropped by the *Zeppelin* monsters during the First World War were still remembered by many. The bombing attacks by *Legion Condor* against Madrid and Guernica had again demonstrated how dangerous the *Luftwaffe* was.

Included in the measures for air raid protection was the registration of children, mothers, the handicapped, and the blind, who were marked for evacuation out of the threatened cities. This was done neither systematically, nor was it obligatory. It was left up to the parents, for example, whether they preferred to register their children for evacuation, send them to the country themselves or keep them at home.

In Greater London, 136,502 children and adults had been listed. Three days before the outbreak of war, the authorities began with the evacuation of more than 39,000 people from the Medway towns such as Rochester and Chatham, the presumed approach path of enemy bombers bound for London, to districts further east between Sittingbourne and Herne Bay. From 5 September 1939 on, it was the turn of 97,320 Londoners, of whom 12,999 alone were to be brought to Folkestone on the coast and between 5,000 and 7,000 each to Ashford, Tunbridge Wells, Maidstone and other smaller towns in Kent. Special trains and whole armadas of buses were sent off for this purpose, and within three days the operation had been completed.

The speed with which the evacuation was carried out, was not due to an especially efficient organisation, but rather to the simple fact that most people had stayed at home. In the end it became apparent, that only about 47,000 had made use of the offer of evacuation. Most parents had not been able to give their children away. And during the course of the Phoney War, when nothing was happening and the measure appeared more and more to have been pointless, the majority of those evacuated returned to London and the Medway.

The government, which was concerned for the fate of the children and convinced that sooner or later the air attacks would begin, again began making preparations for an evacuation in February 1940. New lists were drawn up, but only 2.6 per cent of the parents concerned registered their children for evacuation. The plans again disappeared in the drawers of the Home Office desks.

With the invasion of Holland by German troops, this situation changed completely within only a few weeks. This time, no lists were needed. Appeals in the press and on the radio brought thousands of children, mothers, the sick, and the elderly to the train and bus stations in London, on the Medway, and in the most endangered communities in Kent, such as Ramsgate, Dover, Folkestone and Canterbury.

For the first time, and before the bombs began to fall, war was showing its true countenance. During the days that followed the evacuation of the BEF from Dunkirk, the evacuation of the children and segments of the civilian population in Kent was also in full swing. The station at Ramsgate had four platforms; two of these were being used for the troops returning from France, who were being brought from the ships to the station by bus; on the third stood trains with wounded and evacuees, while only the fourth served normal rail traffic.

The sight of the defeated army, the dirty, torn uniforms, the completely exhausted soldiers, many of whom were lightly wounded, many barefoot and only dressed in shirt and trousers, the long rows of stretchers, the moaning of the wounded, came as a shock to the patiently waiting evacuees, which made them forget their own pain at being separated from home. They waved gaily to the soldiers and looked forward to the long journey that was to take some of them to Wales and others to the Midlands.

The children were loaded with full kit just like soldiers. Over their school uniforms they wore a white tin box containing a gas mask, Band-Aid, ointment for burns and a bottle of iodine. From their belts, like hand grenades, hung brown paper packages with sandwiches, socks, a raincoat. In their pockets they had notes with name, school, home address and, probably already smeared with chocolate, a postcard pre-addressed by mother, for posting after arrival at their destination. In their left hand most of them carried a small case or carton with clothing, their right hand clutched a package with comics, a doll or another, particularly beloved toy, which was turned into a wildly brandished weapon in the pushing and shoving to grab a window seat.

The waggons dated from the time of Queen Victoria and had gold lettering on the first, second and third class compartments; the benches were hard, the windows covered by a yellow patina, and above the seats hung pictures in wooden frames, showing seaside promenades on which girls with straw hats were strolling about with boys in light flannel suits.

Stephen from Dover, who was eight at the time, recalled 40 years later how he arrived at the home of a miner's family in Blackwood, Monmouthshire, on the borders of Wales. Even though the hosts did everything they could to make him feel at home, treated him as if he were their own child, and gave him many a penny for sweets that they begrudged themselves, the appeal of the new surroundings soon wore off and home-sickness gained the upper hand.

This was not only due to the different style of life and the strange dialect, but also to the food. Children from the poorer sections of East London, for example, were seldom able to adjust to the middle-class eating habits in the country. They were used to a diet consisting exclusively of bread and margarine, fish and chips, and sweets. Meat, vegetables, and puddings were as strange to them as stews and soups. Some of them had never eaten a warm meal at home; they were content with a few slices of bread and margarine munched on the door-step. In the best cases, their mothers had given them a few pennies with which to buy their own 'meal'. Now they were served 'Sunday dinner' every day and it was just too much for them. One five-year-old demanded 'beer and cheese' for supper from her foster parents, others tried to eat soup with a knife and fork. The children from the city knew milk only in bottles, which to their knowledge were filled in factories. Cows, which they had never seen before, scared them, and in disgust they refused to drink milk fresh from the cow.

The children shed many tears. Some could not stand being with strangers and like stray cats, simply set off for home. Stephen also ran away. He arrived back home on the very day that Dover was being shelled from the other side of the Channel for the first time. That was much more exciting, especially since all the schools were closed and had troops quartered in them.

In London, and in all the other cities, classes continued, as they did for the two daughters of King George VI and Queen Elizabeth, fourteen-year-old Princess Elizabeth and her nine-year-old sister Margaret. In May the two royal children had been sent to Windsor Castle with their teachers and ladies and had their rooms in Lancaster Tower.

Windsor is only 22 miles west of the centre of London and was therefore just as much threatened by bombs as the capital. As a precaution, all treasures such as paintings, crystal chandeliers and porcelain had been removed, the tall glass display cabinets and cupboards had been turned with their doors to the wall and most of the other furniture covered over. The royal children were mainly occupied with classes and riding lessons; only Princess Elizabeth already had extensive correspondence to attend to. As the air raids increased, they obediently packed their bits and pieces and moved into the lower vaults of the castle. They saw their parents only at weekends, which King George and Queen Elizabeth still habitually spent at Windsor Castle.

In October, Princess Elizabeth surprised everybody with a message broadcast over the radio in which she spoke for all of the children in the British Isles. She had already written the first draft weeks before, after one of her cousins had been killed in action. Derek McCulloch, the 'uncle Mac' of the BBC Children's Hour, helped her with the correct pronunciation and breathing technique, which she practised untiringly for days on end. The BBC recorded the broadcast in the King's office. Elizabeth and Margaret sat before two microphones with serious expressions, and the older of the two read out in a firm voice:

'I can honestly say that we children at home are full of confidence and in good spirits. We want to do everything in our power to help our brave soldiers by land, by sea and in the air and we want to carry our share of the dangers and sorrows of the war. Each of us knows that all will be well in the end.'

At the end she said: 'Come Margaret, say hello to the children', just as if it was only Children's Hour after all.

Without really intending to, by this action Princess Elizabeth captured a place in the hearts of the British people. Abroad, the fighting spirit of the young British princess and the naturalness of her gesture were greatly admired. 'If the coming generation in this world will still have queens', said a well-known writer, who had heard the address in South Africa, 'then this child will be a good queen.'

Given such patriotic support, the evacuation made good progress. By the end of the year, far more than one million children had been evacuated. In the coastal communities of Kent, many adults who were not needed for defence or other indispensable functions had also followed the appeals by the government and had moved to the west and the north.

All of the seaside resorts had become depopulated within only a few months. The promenades were closed, the beaches were mined and covered with tank traps and barbed wire. Many houses were boarded up. In Margate, the population dropped from 40,000 to 10,000. 7,208 private homes and places of business had been abandoned, and in the streets life had come to a stop. The town was bankrupt, because the holiday-makers no longer came and business was at a standstill. The government in London had to step in so that on-going costs could be paid. And it was the same in Dover, where only 16,000 out of an original 36,000 still lived, or in Folkestone, where only 6,000 out of 40,000 remained.

The famous writer, J. B. Priestley, who visited Margate in June 1940, described the almost empty town as 'unreal and ghostly'. The impression was reinforced by the absence of the household pets which normally enlivened the streets: far and wide, there was neither a dog nor a cat to be seen. Andy Thompson, a veterinary surgeon in Dover, had already been swamped with work the day after war was declared. People queued up before his practice with their animals, in order to have their pets put to sleep. And the more people that left the town in the days to come, the busier Thompson became. For a time, he had to use a lorry provided by the town to cart off the bodies and plead with the health inspector when there was a hitch in disposal. 'It was both sad and disgusting', Thompson said later.

His wife, who had a pet shop on High Street and stayed on in Dover despite the bombs and shells, was able to take quite a few animals in and thereby save them until the end of the war. She succeeded, despite the food rationing, in finding sufficient food for the few remaining animals in the town. Once a sailor brought her 28 pounds of white millet from Spain and thereby saved all of the town's budgerigars.

Another rescue action was more important and at least of more nutritional value to the population. When the German panzers appeared on the other side of the Channel, fear of invasion also clutched Romney Marsh, an extensive marshy area with fat pastures between Hastings and Folkestone. The region is famous for a breed of sheep that produce both excellent wool and outstandingly good meat. The sheep-owners feared for their flocks and organised a move to the safer counties of Bedfordshire, Hertfordshire, Middlesex and Wiltshire. The sheep were shorn and sorted out, and every day 2,000 animals left Romney Marsh for the north and west in lorries. After nineteen days, 125,000 sheep had been brought to safety. The breeders, with their families and their helpers, left with the last loads. Perhaps this evacuation was possibly based on special intuition, for Romney Marsh was designated as an operational area in the German invasion plans.

The appeals by the Home Office to the population to evacuate the possible landing areas and London were not made only for humanitarian reasons. They were also a result of the events in Belgium and Northern France, where the civilian population, caught by the fighting, had blocked all the roads in its panicky flight south and made movements by French and British forces almost impossible. This was not to repeat itself in England.

Despite this however, in certain circles probably aroused by Churchill's pugnacious speeches, the evacuees were regarded with much contempt. They had shirked the front, abandoned their towns and cities. This contempt was even vented on children. A twelve-year-old London girl who had been evacuated to Brighton in September 1939 returned to her parents in July 1940. When she reapplied to her former school, the Headmistress refused to take her back: 'We have no use for cowards in this school', she said, and that was that. The child had to change to a school where she was not known.

Elderly, well-off people who took up residence in hotels in the country were also looked at askance. The advertisements of most of the hotel refuges in Scotland and Wales were therefore couched in euphoric hyperbole: 'Today more than ever before', said an advert for the Aviemore Hotel in Inverness, 'Aviemore is a bulwark of peace and tranquillity. Here, in the fresh air of the pine forests, you will find refuge from the stress and nervous pressure of the world outside.'

Through court officials, the government had suggested to Queen Elizabeth that she and her husband should leave endangered London at least for a time, and retire to one of the more remote royal residences. The Queen had laconically replied: 'My place is at the side of His Majesty and the King will not leave London. He will share the fate of his subjects.' That was the end of that as far as the Royal Family was concerned.

However, King Haakon of Norway and Queen Wilhelmina of the Netherlands were now also living at Buckingham Palace, where, by the way, there were no air raid shelters. For the British Government, which had to take into consideration a coup by enemy paratroops similar to the one in the Hague, this meant a threefold responsibility from which it could not be so readily absolved, even by the words of the Queen. With the consent of the King therefore, Lieutenant Colonel J. S. Coats was stationed in Buckingham Palace with a company of the Coldstream Guards and four armoured personnel carriers of the 12th Lancers and Northamptonshire Yeomanry. In the event, they had the assignment to take the King and Queen as well as the two foreign monarchs to safety. Four remote country residences had been selected as alternative refuges. Only after the danger of invasion had passed, was the military contingent withdrawn.

A further crowned head almost came to join those in Buckingham Palace. On 21 May the cabinet discussed the possibility of offering asylum to the German *Kaiser* Wilhelm II, who had been living in exile in Holland since 1918 and whose residence in Doorn had been overrun by German troops. After some hesitation, it was agreed to make the *Kaiser* such an offer if he were to request it. Wilhelm II, however, preferred to remain where he was. He died in Holland the following year.

The odium of flight in the face of the enemy clung heaviest to those prominent artists and writers who could afford to remove themselves across the Atlantic on ships that also took many children to the United States and the Dominions.

The reports from the Dutch, Belgian and northern French theatres of war, had created a wave of sympathy throughout the world for the children who had become entangled in the machinery of war. In early June, Australian women's clubs had provided places for Dutch, Belgian and British war orphans and asked the Australian Government to initiate and finance the transports, and not without success. On 2 July, the Australian Ministry of the Interior announced that the first group of British children were expected in two months. By then, 17,000 offers of adoption of the children from overseas had been received.

There were similar efforts being made in Canada and the United States. Australian Prime Minister R. G. Menzies informed Parliament on 4 June, that the government had made enquiries in London about taking in children. At the same time the Americans were stretching out semi-official feelers to the Germans as to whether US ships would be given safe conduct for the transport of children. The British Government now felt compelled to initiate action of its own. On 19 June, Lord Privy Seal Clement Attlee told the Commons that the financial means for shipping children to the USA and the Dominions would be provided and that the matter was considered to have utmost priority.

The programme was then set in motion. Before long, 200,000 applications had been received, far more than could ever be taken into consideration, so the government's action was discontinued after only a few days. Churchill was far from pleased by this development, the 'stampede' smacked far too much of defeatism for his taste.

However, the German U-boats very quickly put a sad end to the shipping of children. The German naval command had objected strongly to 'any special treatment of any sort of transports, because otherwise the advantages for our forces of the new political-military situation would quickly evaporate'. In late August, the Foreign Ministry had transmitted this message to Washington in answer to the American enquiry.

On 21 September 1940 a German U-boat sank the British steamer *City of Simla*, 10,138 BRT, to the northwest of the North Channel, which separates Ireland from Scotland. There were 320 children on board. They were saved by the steamer *Guinan*, which rushed to the rescue, and brought back to Greenock in Scotland on the morning of 22 September.

Three days previously, on 18 September, a catastrophe, which provoked great outrage in the western and neutral press, had taken place in mid-Atlantic. U-48 had attacked a convoy and torpedoed the steamers *City of Benares*, *Marina* and *Magdalena*. Only eleven of the 90 children on board the sinking 11,100 BRT *City of Benares* were rescued.

The official programme was immediately cancelled. 2,666 children had already left England by this means. More than double that number had privately been sent overseas by their parents, including little Elizabeth Taylor. In all, Canada and Australia took 5,000 and the United States 2,000 children. The shipments had no effect on the situation in Great Britain.

VI
Dunkirk, the Defeat that Was Not
The British come up with a miracle

On the European continent meanwhile, the drama of Dunkirk was being enacted, which was to bring fear of invasion in Great Britain to its peak. For the *Wehrmacht*, it provided several insights that were to be important for 'Operation Sea Lion': the British field army could be beaten, shipping large numbers of troops across the Channel in a short time was possible, and the *Luftwaffe* proved by its assaults against troops and evacuation vessels, that an orderly military operation required the interdiction of enemy air attacks. What many Englishmen seriously dreaded in those days was not even being considered on the German side: during the last days in May and the early days in June an attack against the British coast right in the middle of the evacuation effort would have put the most important port of Dover and the neighbouring airbases into the hands of the Germans with only minor losses. At no point in time later on were the British so helpless and vulnerable. Far sooner than the staffs in London, Lord Gort, commander of the British troops in Belgium and France, had recognised the desperate situation there. While Churchill was still encouraging him at least to relieve encircled Calais, which fell on 26 May, he had already worked out a plan, together with his military superior General Blanchard, for a retreat to the Dunkirk area. His troops only had rations for two days left, were worn out and, against the superior German forces, had not the slightest chance of changing the situation in their favour.

Tall and somewhat corpulent, Lord Gort was known for his personal bravery, but beyond that not very much was expected of him. Field Marshal Montgomery, at the time one of his subordinates as a newly appointed corps commander, still pokes fun at him in his memoirs: 'His first remark... after my appointment... was: "Make sure tonight that your front is well safe-guarded by patrol activities".' But even Montgomery is forced to admit that Lord Gort, 'even if only at close range, saw quite clearly that he must at least bring the men of the BEF and their handguns back to England'. And in this, the so greatly underestimated Gort was to succeed brilliantly. His withdrawal movement planned down to the last detail, succeeded without major loss and under strict discipline, and preserved for England the core of her Army. It was a major factor in the 'miracle of Dunkirk'.

On 27 May, Lord Gort gave the order to withdraw into an approximately 35-kilometre-wide bridgehead around Dunkirk, which was to be defended on a line Gravelines–Bergues–Nieuport. Gort moved his headquarters to de Panne on the coast, sixteen kilometres northeast of Dunkirk. Already during the night of 28 May, the British pulled back to the line Poperinghe–Cassel about 40 kilometres east of Dunkirk, which they were to reach the following day.

Poperinghe, a small Belgian town on the border, had already been heavily damaged during the First World War. With the advent of British troops in northern France in the autumn of 1939, life had returned to the sleepy little town; Poperinghe became an excursion site for the Tommies. Actually, they were not supposed to put foot on the soil of neutral Belgium, but nobody took that at all seriously. However, after 10 May this changed, because French and British soldiers were deployed in Belgium in order to bring the German steam-roller to a halt.

There was always highlife in the little café near St Bertinus' church. Until long past midnight, the two waitresses, seventeen-year-old Elaine Madden and nineteen-year-old Simone Duponselle, carried beer and coffee to the small tables around which boisterous young British soldiers crowded. It was fun, particularly for Elaine, who spoke fluent English. Her father was an Australian who had taken part in the First World War and then married her mother. He had stayed in Europe until 1932 as a member of a war graves commission until he had felt the urge to go back to Australia.

On 24 May the first bombs fell on Poperinghe. Soon the first artillery shells were exploding in the streets and *Stukas* screamed over the rooftops. Fires broke out in the narrow rows of houses. The water supply was out and the soldiers no longer put in an appearance in the café. Elaine and Simone decided to retreat westwards as well. They did not want to fall into the hands of the Germans.

In the early morning hours of 30 May, the two girls marched through the burning streets of Poperinghe towards Dunkirk. Each carried a blanket slung across her back as the soldiers had advised them to do. They had stowed their meagre belongings in a few carrier-bags. They made good progress. High in the sky above their heads, a wide black cloud of smoke drifted from west to east: the burning oil storage tanks in Dunkirk were showing the two refugees the way. Without knowing it, they had chosen a way through no-man's-land. For hours they constantly heard artillery fire on their left. In the afternoon they stumbled into a fire-fight. German panzers with their black crosses had suddenly appeared from behind a copse and were shooting northwards over their heads, from where French or British artillery was returning the fire. The girls ran for their lives until they found a barn in which they hid and out of fear of the panzers spent the night.

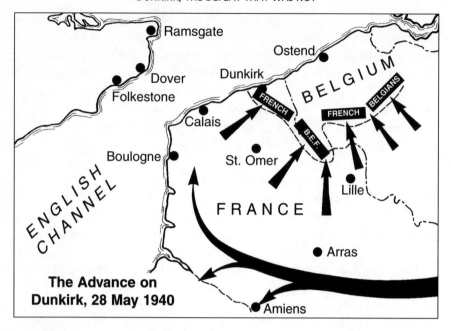

The Advance on Dunkirk, 28 May 1940

Next day they reached the main road leading to Dunkirk, on which columns and columns of French and British soldiers were marching westwards. There were only very few civilians to be seen. A British lorry gave them a lift. After only a few kilometres, however, their escape was again interrupted. The bridges over the Yser had been destroyed. Soldiers helped them cross an emergency bridge to the other side and gave them khaki jackets and English helmets with which to continue their journey, because as civilians they would not have got much further.

With every kilometre the confusion grew: soldiers, wherever one turned; the roads lined with abandoned equipment. Time and again shells came in to explode and in between the rattle of machine-gun fire. And when the sky cleared, the German planes came flying in low. Far ahead, *Stukas* were screaming above the Channel. British fighters were weaving in and out and the smoke from machines that had been shot down stood against the sky like black-brown strokes with a paint brush.

The *Luftwaffe* was trying to prevent embarkation with all of its might. But Göring had once again bitten off more than he could chew. The German bomber squadrons had to be brought forward from far behind the lines and their numbers were far too small to compensate for the interruptions caused by bad flying weather. During the whole of 'Operation Dynamo' there were only three and a half days during which the *Luftwaffe* could be deployed.

31 May was one of these days. Several hundred aircraft of all types had taken off for the Channel coast from the bases of *Luftflotte* 3 [air fleet, a self-

contained unit of about 1,000 aircraft, bombers, dive bombers, fighters and reconnaissance units under one unified command]. As opposed to attacks on French targets during the advance against a completely surprised enemy, here they faced unremitting barrages by light and heavy flak. Besides the destroyers, the British Admiralty had deployed an anti-aircraft cruiser off Dunkirk. On top of that there were the Spitfires and Hurricanes of Fighter Command who flew against the Germans from bases in Essex and involved them in dogfights behind the lines. These came from 11 Group under Keith Park. 'Every time our squadron flew over,' Lieutenant Bartley recalls, 'we met up with from 50 to 60 German machines which our 12 Spitfires had to cope with. We attacked them and shot until our ammunition ran out. And while we were tangling with them at 3,000 metres, down below us the *Stukas* were causing horrifying damage.'

Between 10 May and 4 June the pilots of 11 Group flew 213 sorties with 7,154 hours in the air. They shot down 402 German aircraft and damaged 201 others, against losses incurred of 141. Some of the British pilots shot down were able to save themselves, like Al Deere, the New Zealand ace.

Deere was hit on 29 May by the tail gunner of a Do 17 and had to crash-land on the beach 25 kilometres north of Dunkirk. Part of the way back he hitched a ride, for the rest he used a bicycle he had managed to get hold of. With great difficulty he made his way through the columns flooding towards the beach, finally reached a destroyer on foot and was in for a curious experience: 'What are you doing here', an Army major snarled at him. 'I'm an officer of the Royal Air Force and want to get back to my squadron!' 'I don't give a shit who you are,' the enraged major said. 'For all the good you chaps are doing here, you can just as well stay on the ground!'

The major was only articulating what almost all of the BEF was thinking: to its mind the Royal Air Force had failed because they had had to suffer far too much under the attacks of the *Luftwaffe*. In actual fact, the intervention by the Royal Air Force had prevented a much greater bloodbath on the beaches of Dunkirk. They had handed the *Luftwaffe* its first setback and in many cases prevented precision bombing. In their thousands, the soldiers stood on the dunes four abreast in snakelike lines many kilometres long for hours on end and were completely unprotected. Systematic strafing and bombing would have cost thousands of lives. But only occasionally did the Bf 109s or 110s dare to attack the beaches at low levels.

Night was just falling as the two girls from Poperinghe arrived at the port in Dunkirk. There were no further planes in the air. Three soldiers had taken charge of the girls and shielded their telltale skirts from curious eyes. This was not a place for women. In the port basin, progress was measured in steps. The east pier was still standing, even though the German bombers had been trying for days to destroy it.

It was past midnight before Elaine and Simone finally came in sight of the iron ladders at whose feet the boats lay. In complete apathy, the Tommies were inching along foot by foot to the end of the line of people. Many of the exhausted and dirty soldiers who were supporting each other had hardly slept for days, received little food and nothing to drink. The thirst was particularly torturing for the many wounded in the lines. But discipline was maintained. In the roar of battle which did not abate even at night everybody had only one thought: get out of here as quickly as possible!

Simone was the first to climb down the ladder, immediately causing cries of protest from below. The two girls had been discovered. But in the press, there was no way back. With many shouted insinuating remarks, the over-crowded boat brought them to a destroyer where they were immediately taken to the captain. 'He was very nice', Elaine recounted later, 'he gave us his cabin and we landed safely in England.'

They had been lucky. Shortly before, the steamer *Mona Lisa* carrying 1,420 members of the BEF had sailed. The German batteries between Gravelines and Les Hemmes had taken her under fire over a considerable distance, then *Stukas* and Bf 110s took up the pursuit. After running this gauntlet, the ship put in at Dover. The German attack had cost 23 dead and 60 wounded.

The two girls had no inkling that they owed their escape to 'Operation Dynamo'. On 20 May, when the German panzers reached the Channel coast, the idea of evacuating the back area troops and wounded from the Continent in order to free the fighting forces from 'useless mouths to feed' had been proposed in Churchill's War Cabinet. As a precautionary measure, it was decided to collect a large number of ships ready for sailing to French ports and points of embarkation.

The very same afternoon, when Guderian was entering Abbeville, members of the Admiralty, the Marine Ministry and the Port Authority held a meeting in Dover Castle in order to prepare emergency evacuation of large numbers of people across the Channel. It was all still theory, but the assumption was that every 24 hours 10,000 men of the BEF would be evacuated from Boulogne, Calais and Dunkirk.

Vice Admiral Bertram Ramsay was appointed admiral in command of the operation. His headquarters were in Dover Castle, the fortress high on the chalk cliffs that tower above the town and the port. At the outbreak of the war, Ramsay had been called back from retirement and given the important position of Naval Commander Dover. Ramsay was well known in Dover. As a young officer during the First World War he had been in command of a destroyer belonging to the 'Dover Patrol' and knew the port and the waters of the Channel like the inside of his pocket. Ramsay also knew the castle and knew about the labyrinth that had been dug deep into the chalk cliff under the castle by French prisoners of war during Napoleon's day, a defensive measure the sense of which is still not quite clear to the present day.

In view of the increasing danger of air attacks, the Admiral moved his offices into these catacombs. Next to Ramsay's room, the only one enjoying daylight from a hole in the wall of the cliff 160m above the beach, there lay a gallery. This was where, during the First World War, the emergency generators of the castle had been kept, and it was still called the dynamo room. Now, boasting a huge table covered with green felt, this dungeon served as a conference room. The code name for the operation planned in the dynamo room was therefore, logically, 'Operation Dynamo'.

The energy which was now set free under the cold lighting of the cavern was without precedent. The naval officers sitting in their small plywood cubicles telephoning day and night in order to pull an evacuation fleet together, hardly had time for sleep. The whole southeastern coast from London through Rams-gate and Folkestone to Plymouth was mobilised. Port after port, shipyard after shipyard was contacted. Whereas in the beginning, only 40 destroyers and 35 transport ships, including the Channel ferries, were available, within only a few days the fleet grew to 848 ships. The units of the Royal Navy had been joined by 230 fishing boats, 203 motor boats, 27 yachts, all of the life-boats along the coast, port launches, tugboats and barges. The many small motor and sailing boats, whose owners simply set off on their own to bring the boys home, remained uncounted. The youngest crew member on such a boat was eight, the oldest 78.

From 27 May on, 'Operation Dynamo' had become an heroic race across the Channel, just as if neither the German artillery and Luftwaffe existed, nor the greatly feared German E-boats. In the beginning Churchill had believed that the Royal Navy would not be able to save more than 20,000 to 30,000 men, but in only four days the number reached 126,000.

The Supreme Command of the Wehrmacht reported on 30 May: 'By swimming and in small boats, the enemy is trying to reach the English ships lying in the roads, which our Luftwaffe is assaulting with devastating effect as already reported in a special bulletin. More than 60 ships have been hit, of which three warships and sixteen transports have been sunk, and ten warships and 21 merchant ships of all sizes heavily damaged or set on fire.'

Motor vessel Triton under Navy Lieutenant R. H. Irving, with a crew of two Naval Reserve who had never been on a ship before, reached the beach at De Panne shortly after dawn on 30 May. This most easterly of the evacuation beaches was under constant fire from German artillery in the region of Nieu-port. All morning, *Triton* towed barges crammed with troops through the shallow waters to the destroyers and other ships waiting further out. Towards noon, *Triton* had just delivered another load of soldiers to a destroyer and was laying off, when an officer called down from the railing: 'Well done, motorboat! Wait for me!' He came down a jack-ladder. He was wearing a sheep-skin coat and was completely soaked through. 'If you carry on as you have been doing', he told Lieutenant Irving, 'then I have one or two further jobs for you.' Again the motorboat sailed back and forth between the beach and the ships. The number of soldiers waiting did not appear to be getting any smaller. Late in the afternoon the strange officer ordered the captain to put him ashore at a certain spot on the coast. He wanted to look for Lord Gort on land and bring him back directly to England. Irving was to wait for him with his boat. The enemy artillery fire lay very close to the little boat and Irving was asking himself, how long he would be able to wait. At the end of an hour the officer reappeared on the beach, alone! Wading through the light waves up to his neck in water, he came back on board. He did not mention Lord Gort. Instead, he told Irving to carry on and stayed aboard while *Triton* tirelessly continued to tow barges full of soldiers out.

Night fell and the efforts continued mechanically. At 01.00 on 31 May the log entry read: 'Seven soldiers rescued from drowning'. An hour later the boat ran aground at low tide and was only able to float off on the rising tide towards 04.00. Slowly but surely the physical effort and exhaustion began to tell on the four men. But they carried on. The strange officer was still on board. By now Irving had learned that he was a commodore and that his name was Stevens. 'I must say', Irving recalled later, 'the commodore sometimes called me a fine chap and sometimes a stupid ass. It is not my place to judge superior officers, but this officer, without a cap, soaked to the skin, with nothing in his stomach, was a great inspiration to me. He helped me to steer, to throw lines, to pull soldiers from the water. Sometimes he commended the men, at other times he cursed them for their stupidity.'

On the afternoon of 31 May, Irving put Commodore Stevens aboard a minesweeper. 'I was the last naval officer to leave this sector of the beach', said Irving. *Triton* continued her rescue work further south and collected stragglers: 'A full load of soldiers aboard, six of them wounded, a full barge in tow, and a bunch of soldiers clinging outboard to the stern.' Lieutenant Irving and his crew of two stuck to their task until their fuel ran out and they had to return to Ramsgate.

On 31 May fog descended. This at least protected the escapees from the *Luftwaffe*. On this day, 68,014 soldiers were evacuated. The total so far was close to 200,000 men who had been able to escape from the Germans. However, hundreds still lost their lives on the way to the safety of the English coast. The *Luftwaffe* alone sank seven destroyers and damaged another nineteen.

As late as 22 May, German air reconnaissance of the 9th Air Division under Colonel Czech had reported the sea area under the Channel coast between Ostende and Boulogne to be completely empty of the enemy and that only off South Foreland had eight large steamers running north been sighted and attacked. However, the deceptive calm did not make the observers jump to the conclusion that the enemy had already given up the Channel ports and discontinued embarkation, because other aircraft had detected transports and smaller vessels.

The *Luftwaffe* reconnaissance flights during the ensuing days confirmed the assumption that embarkation and disembarkation activities were still going on in the ports on the French and Belgian Channel coast. The observers reported heavy traffic by steamers and other vessels, probably connected with shipments to and from the Belgian and French ports, in the Downs, the sea area off Ramsgate, and in the Thames estuary. 9th Air Division recommended mining these sea areas.

On 29 May, 30 transports and about eight destroyers were observed taking people on off Nieuport and Dunkirk. 'The situation at the front', the report said, 'leads to the conclusion that tonight the English will use the final opportunity to take off troops in increased numbers.' The *Kriegsmarine* therefore felt it would be desirable to deploy E-boats against the enemy that night, but had to admit that it was not possible to deploy more than four boats, because the fuelling and loading of torpedoes required time-consuming passing of ships in and out between their berths and the open sea. Then the weather deteriorated, which caused great problems for the E-boats so susceptible to high waves. In the seas around Den Helder, the wind was at force 6. In the ears of the German Naval Staff, the reconnaissance report by 26th Bomber Squadron must have sounded like mockery, when it reported on 3 June: 'In and off the port of Dover about 50 ships, including many warships. Between Dover and Dunkirk heavy steamer traffic.'

For days now the German E-boats had been operating out of the Dutch port of Den Helder. Before the start of the evacuation, they had already sunk the French destroyer *Jaguar* off Dunkirk. During the night of 28 to 29 May, the German E-boat S-30 under Lieutenant Commander Zimmermann had run into a group of the evacuation flotilla and had sunk destroyers *Wakeful* and *Grafton*, both laden with troops. Of the 600 men aboard *Wakeful*, which broke in half, only 150 were rescued. In *Grafton*, 35 officers of the BEF died when a torpedo exploded in the mess.

North of De Panne, 2nd Army Corps under General Montgomery had held the line in front of Nieuport. During the night of 31 May to 1 June, it had to retire in the face of the huge German superiority in strength. De Panne came under increasingly heavy German artillery fire. Montgomery's units were ordered to withdraw along the beaches towards Dunkirk and to embark wherever the opportunity offered itself.

The improvised piers along the beaches – lorries and other vehicles connected by planks – were only partially still serviceable, because the tide was slowly washing them away. Most of the soldiers were only able to reach the boats to take them to the waiting transports at Bray-Dunes and Malo-les-Bains.

General Montgomery and Brigadier Ritchie, together with their adjutants and batmen, were among the last to leave De Panne in the early morning hours. They walked to Dunkirk along the firm sand above the groynes, where they then reported in by radio. Like Lord Gort before them, they were taken across the Channel in a speedboat.

In Dunkirk itself, thousands of British and French still pushed and shoved their way over the southern pier in order to reach one of the ships waiting there. Bombs had torn huge holes in the planks and it became more and more difficult to carry the wounded across the improvised wooden gangplanks. However, there is not a single instance on record of a wounded man having fallen into the black gurgling water far below the narrow boards.

The British embarkation officers had great difficulties in communicating with the Frenchmen crowding forward. Hardly any of them spoke more than a few words of French and all too often sidearms were brandished and even warning shots fired. These however, mostly went unheard in the screaming of incoming German shells, which began to cause heavy damage.

On the evening of 2 June, the last British troops left French soil. The men of the Coldstream Guards even brought their small arms on board the destroyer *Sabre*. The remaining elements of the Green Howards, whose job was now over, were the last to join the waiting line.

Admiral Wake-Walker, who despite the danger, had been patrolling up and down the coast all day in his MASB 10, took Generals Alexander and Percival and their staffs aboard towards 21.00 and brought them to the destroyer *Venomous*, which was already overloaded with soldiers.

The destroyer *Winchelsea* began loading at 22.30. By now there were only Frenchmen left waiting on the pier. Captain Tennant, the British embarkation officer, radioed to Dover at 22.50: 'Operation concluded. Am returning to Dover.' Shortly thereafter, torpedo boat MTB 102 cast off with the captain on board.

But 'Operation Dynamo' was still going on. In the port lay the destroyers *Express*, *Codrington* and *Malcolm*, the car ferry *Autocarrier* and a host of other ships. Under German artillery fire they waited for over an hour for the mass of the remaining French troops to appear in the harbour. They steamed back across the Channel empty, because the *poilus* [French common soldiers] were ferociously contesting every metre of ground in the assumption, that the evacuation was still going on.

German troops had already penetrated into the outskirts of Dunkirk when General Fagalde finally gave the order to retire. With this, the crews of the English boats again had their hands full. During 3 June and in the morning hours of 4 June, another 53,000 men, mostly French and Belgians, were loaded from the pier at Dunkirk.

The human flood which descended on the ports on the coast in eastern Kent, Folkestone, Dover, Ramsgate, and Margate, was barely manageable during these days. The piers and reception halls had only been designed for tourist traffic, which was still modest in prewar days, so that the masses had to be kept constantly in motion in order to make it at all possible to unload them. In the comparatively small railway stations of the ports, chaos reigned supreme.

Admiral Ramsay and his men, local officials, the officers of the railway and port authorities, and many volunteer helpers succeeded in passing this stream of returning soldiers on into the interior without mishap or check. The population on the coast was seized by a wave of solidarity when the dead and dying, the wounded and sick, were carried off the ships. There was always someone there to help. Doctors and nurses worked round the clock until utterly exhausted, just like those that had brought the soldiers across. Without pause, community and private buses, as well as hospital trains, took those wounded and sick able to travel to hospitals further inland.

Healthy soldiers able to walk, had to drag themselves on to the stations immediately after having disembarked, regardless of how exhausted they might have been. There was hardly time for a mug of tea, which volunteers brewed in large tubs on the docks and in the stations and hastily distributed.

During the nine days of the evacuation S. W. Smith, station master at Ramsgate, checked out 82 troop trains in addition to the regular traffic, the trains with evacuated civilians and children, and the hospital trains. 'The platform looked like a huge laundry, so high did the clothes pile up which our women kept bringing, because many soldiers only had a blanket wrapped around their naked bodies, while others were completely covered with oil.' In these few days 42,783 soldiers went through Ramsgate, from Folkestone 35,000 travelled on in 64 trains. 'Everybody worked like mad', Smith recalls, 'and even if an engine driver had already clocked fourteen hours, he kept on and rode off.'

It was only in the stations further inland from the coast that the soldiers were able to fortify themselves. Ashford, Paddock Wood, Headcorn, were only three of the many stations at which the trains could take turns and stop for a slightly longer period. In the small village station at Headcorn, 50 kilometres from Dover, things were particularly hectic: Here, 145,000 British, French and Belgians received the first meal they had had in days. In a large barn next to the station food was cooked and sandwiches prepared, which were then hastily brought to the trains; a total of 207, which were only allowed to stop for eight or, at the most twenty, minutes. The food was provided by the Army, which had also commandeered 40 men for distribution. The same number of women and girls worked side by side with them in eight-hour shifts. Tea and coffee was prepared on nineteen stoves, 2,500 loaves of bread were sliced every day and made into sandwiches, 1,000 tins of sardines and corned beef were consumed. On one evening alone, 5,000 meat pies, 5,000 eggs and the same number of buns and sausages were delivered. The farmers in the area donated eggs, chickens, vegetables, meat, the bakers baked bread in shifts, grocers contributed from their stores. In Canterbury the Mayor had had a loud-speaker installed in the Guildhall over which he called upon the citizens for donations and for means of transport to Ramsgate and Dover of the food and clothing collected.

As suddenly as the human flood had broken over the coast, so did it ebb away again. Within only a few days, the units of the British Expeditionary Force were being reformed in their home barracks. There were 60,000 men and officers missing who had fallen, been wounded or captured by the Germans. Missing also were the weapons they had had to leave behind: 2,472 guns, about 400 tanks, 63,879 vehicles of all kinds, as well as mountains of ammunition and other equipment. This counted for little against the fact that close to half a million British troops had safely been brought back from France. 'This has dramatically changed our position in home defence', Churchill told his Chiefs of Staff. Nobody spoke about the military defeat. Out of the total of 846 ships, 235, including 40 belonging to the Royal Navy, had been lost due to the *Luftwaffe*, German artillery, mines, E-boats and accidents.

The 'Miracle of Dunkirk' was a psychological victory. The fighting morale of the British now grew almost to fanaticism. At Victoria station in London a young interpreter was engaged in helping Belgian refugees who in many cases had only managed to save their naked lives. A police officer who was assisting her became more and more taciturn. Then he looked sideways at the young woman and said: 'You know, Miss, this is a serious business. This could happen to us too.' He was not so much referring to flight, but to the feeling of fighting backs to the wall. As a London taxi driver assured one of his passengers: 'We are all alone now, and now we will show them!'

The realisation that now the German hordes could so quickly and easily cross the water and that virtually nothing had been prepared for the defence of the coast, that the core of the Army was beaten and without weapons, made even the most peaceful citizen begin searching his house for a weapon with which he could confront the enemy at the front gate. Everybody was convinced that the Germans had to come and everybody was ready to fight to the last. After all, there was no place they could run to.

VII

A Powerful Guerrilla Force
Snipers that scared Goebbels

The débâcle at Dunkirk was a body-blow for the British. It was as if the seas had parted and all the Germans needed to do was to march across. However, with the expectation of invasion from the sea any day now, determination grew to fight for every house, for every stone. In a Cabinet meeting on 28 May Churchill declared: 'During the past few days I have given serious thought as to whether it is not my duty to consider opening negotiations with this person (Hitler). It would be pointless to believe that we could achieve more favourable terms if we sued for peace now than if we continue to fight. I am also convinced that you would rise up and chase me from office if I were to favour negotiations or a surrender. If the long history of our islands is to come to an end, then it shall only end when every last one of us is beaten to the ground and lies choking in his blood.'

Churchill's rather bloodthirsty appeal to the individual will to resist grew out of his realisation that Britain's military situation was desperate and that she must now turn to the most basic means of defence. The Army would need a long time to recover from the defeat in Northern France. Its best troops had been decimated and were without weapons or transport. Approximately 29 divisions were ready for combat. Given the length of the coastline to be defended, twice that number would have been insufficient to meet the massed assault by the enemy at a given point.

The Royal Navy had had to realise in Norway and at Dunkirk that its heavy units were doomed to inactivity as long as the enemy was able to operate with a strong air force. The Navy's aircraft carriers, battleships and heavy cruisers were lying in Scapa Flow, at Liverpool, in Iceland, in the Mediterranean, or they were protecting convoys in the Atlantic. As a striking force, there were only 40 destroyers and three cruisers available between the Tyne and Portsmouth. Approximately 400 fishing vessels and 700 patrol boats of all kinds were deployed to guard the British coast from Duncansby Head on the most northeasterly point in Scotland, down south round the coasts of Kent, Sussex and Cornwall and then back north again to the Solway Firth, to await the invasion. The Royal Navy was unable to bring its tenfold superiority over the *Kriegsmarine* to bear.

The Royal Air Force was still in the process of being built up, due to inexcusable delays during the prewar years, and in particular was suffering from a lack of pilots. It believed itself to be facing a *Luftwaffe* that was four times stronger and in addition had already gained much more combat experience. In actual fact, the relative strengths were about equal. However, this overestimation of the enemy's strength had its positive side as well: it convinced the British, that they now had to mobilise their final reserves in order to be able to survive the inevitable battle.

There was also a question of the lack of weapons. With teeth clenched, the men of the Home Guard shouldered their broomsticks, while some resignedly gave up and invoked the 'maid clause'. There were only 70,000 rifles available throughout the whole kingdom. The commander of Zone Kent had been issued 1,500 with which to defend an area one and a half times larger than the Saarland. It is understandable that when the opportunity arose, the commanders on the coast turned to improvisation.

At Margate on the northern coast of Kent, the 900 men of the Home Guard under Major (retired) Witts, at the time a manager with Lloyd's Bank, had only 100 rifles with five rounds of ammunition apiece. When London issued the warning 'enemy landing imminent', the men armed themselves with shotguns, garden hoes, golf clubs and clubs. Desperately Major Witts tried to find guns, as did his comrades in Dover and Folkestone, and he made a find on the harbour wharf: there were piles of rifles and handguns lying about, which had been left behind by the soldiers returning from Dunkirk. Ammunition was also found. Witts obtained a lorry and some men, drove under the pier and hauled the rich prize away.

Understandably, the arms caused great jubilation among the men of the Home Guard, and Witts could finally begin target practice with his men. When the Army demanded to have the weapons back, he delayed their return under all sorts of excuses until all the ammunition had been used up on the practice range and even the greenest of his recruits had at least some idea of how to shoot.

The realisation, however, that the enemy could appear on the coast at any time with tanks and artillery dampened such feelings of success considerably. Even if it had been known at which point on the coast the Germans would land, there was virtually nothing with which to oppose them. How then could the advance of the German troops into the country be delayed, how could the fight be continued in their rear, their supply lines paralysed and their fighting morale destroyed?

The British are a nation of improvisers and the time had now come when it appeared that only the spirit of inventiveness would be able to save the island kingdom. One of the most spectacular ideas, which has always been kept a secret, was to set the ocean on fire at the points of landing. Several military departments were involved in this grandiose project. Pipes were laid into the sea from the oil tanks that served to supply fuel to ships and oil pumped into the water. The resulting oil slick was to be set alight and so turn any landing craft into a burning pyre. However, waves and currents tore the oil slick apart and turned it into a non-flammable emulsion. There was no single successful attempt to set it alight. After weeks of very expensive experiments, the idea was dropped.

Never before had so many pencils been chewed in England as during these days and weeks. In the offices of the planning staffs the lights stayed on all night. One of the planners, Captain Stringer, told a friend, the well-known novelist Dennis Wheatley, of his woes. Like all the British, 43-year-old Wheatley had been thinking hard. He had gained combat experience during the First World War and had also closely followed the Spanish Civil War, something which had found expression in a number of war games he had invented. Consequently, Wheatley sat down and on thirteen typewritten pages put down his ideas on how one could, by the simplest means, make a landing on the British Isles more difficult and prevent troops penetrating further after having landed. Wheatley believed that if even one out of a number of wild ideas were to prove of value, then the whole effort would have been worthwhile. Besides many strategic and tactical leads for the Army, he also came up with dozens of practical tips. How to dig tank traps, for example, or how to erect road blocks, employ dynamite, protect the coast and river deltas with fishnets and logs weighted with mines, bury boards studded with nails in the sand, and produce concrete slabs full of glass splinters.

Wheatley's paper was passed on to the War Office. It was circulated and copied. Not only did the military planners find it useful, the novelist's ideas also became the basis for many information brochures for the civilian population, which were sold that summer at all the news stands and which carried titles such as: 'What to do when the invaders come', or 'How to stop them'.

The first official measure was intended for the disorientation of the enemy. On 31 May, the Home Office ordered that all road signs were to be removed and place names on railway stations, post offices, police posts and other buildings taken down or painted over. In those days, it was not advisable to drive through the countryside without local knowledge. Southern England is criss-crossed by a network of small, hedged lanes. Without road signs, even local residents are helpless in this labyrinth. H. R. Pratt Boorman, owner and publisher of the *Kent Messenger*, a weekly published in Maidstone, was on the way to one of his branch offices which he seldom visited. In the idyllic village of Smarden he came to a three-way crossing. It was only days after the order had been published, but already there was not a road sign to be seen far and wide. Boorman asked an elderly man standing on a corner. 'I know the way', the man replied, 'but I'll be damned if I'll tell you.'

The next step was the erection of road blocks. Every town, every village, every collection of houses put up barricades. Anything that could serve as an obstruction was dragged onto the road at the town entrances. At Chillingham, for example, it was the thickest logs from a nearby saw mill; at Newing Green a heavy plough, an iron steam boiler, a water tank, a refuse truck and the wreck of a car. In other places the locals had dragged out steam engines and heavy farm equipment, cobblestones, tar vats and sandbags. In their enthusiasm, the men often forgot to leave gaps wide enough for their own lorries. At Margate on the Thames estuary, where old bathing carts and beach chairs had been filled with sand and used as obstructions, an important bridge had been so thoroughly stopped up overnight, that it took almost all of the following day to make it passable for local traffic again.

Traffic had almost come to a complete standstill, because at petrol stations more and more signs were appearing saying: 'No petrol'. Some of the stations near the coast were mined. At others, tanks containing water had been prepared with which to render the remaining petrol useless. For private cars still in service, the strictly obeyed rule was: when parking, remove the distributor cap, so that no German falling down from the sky, nor any member of the fifth column, would be able to steal the car!

For the delaying tactics of the Army, the most immediate measure was the securing of the advanced positions scattered throughout the coastal area. Whoever had two good hands was enlisted to help. During this summer there were over one million unemployed, most of whom were just burning with desire to get going. 150,000 men were put to work constructing pillboxes for machine-gun nests and digging tank traps. One of Wheatley's suggestions had been to put cans of petrol equipped with remote control detonators into the traps in order to set stalled tanks afire. Another had been to build 'tiger traps', holes into which sharpened stakes were rammed pointing upwards, just as they were employed by the Viet Cong in Vietnam twenty years later.

Basically, it was left up to each community, to each individual, how he intended to protect and defend himself. When a lady in Buckinghamshire was asked what she would do in case of a landing, she said: 'I would ask all the German officers in for a glass of champagne.' After a dramatic pause she added dryly: 'Poisoned, of course.' One housewife intended to smash all of her jars of jam preserves with a hammer, so that they would not fall into the hands of the jam-hungry Germans. The increased demand for dynamite proved that people were building their own booby traps: many a person put a charge of dynamite under loose floor boards, in the garden shed, in wall cupboards, beneath staircases, in garages, and under unused vehicles. There is little the British did not think of: from boats loaded with explosives all the way to charges attached to trees along the roads which, when blown up, were intended to fall on enemy tanks.

The closer a landing from the sea seemed to threaten, the more panzers now took the place of paratroops as enemy No. 1. But how does one fight tanks, if one does not have an anti-tank gun? The freedom fighters had brought the answer back with them from the Spanish Civil War: Molotov Cocktails. The Home Guard had enthusiastically seized upon this means of defence because it was cheap and easy to prepare. Soon the preparations to produce this most simple weapon were under way in all the zones.

One fine Sunday morning in Bexley, a London suburb, Captain R. G. K. Barker was driving from house to house, from pub to pub, collecting bottles. He was accompanied by the sergeant of his Home Guard company, a smith, and his adjutant, a bank manager. Whisky bottles, lemonade bottles, vinegar bottles were soon piled up by the hundreds on their lorry. Beer bottles were eliminated because they were too thick and hard to shatter. They drove their spoils to a copse in a park nearby. There a local pharmacist, together with a local builder and his men, had already lit a wood fire under a tar vat. When the tar was melted, they extinguished the fire and filled the mass, generously mixed with petrol, into the bottles which had been collected. In the end, the company had several hundred Molotov Cocktails at its disposal, which were stored at various strategic points in case of need. As late as 1986, in connection with the purchase of a house in Kent, such a large store of Molotov Cocktails, ammunition and explosives was discovered in the attic, that the Army bomb-disposal experts had to be called in.

Even the most beautiful Molotov Cocktail will fizzle out harmlessly if not accurately thrown at the target. To practise throwing with the precious bottles was out of the question. Therefore wooden 'bottles' were produced. With chalk, Captain Barker drew the silhouette of a panzer on the wall of an empty house and marked the tank's vulnerable spots exactly according to the book. The men never tired of bombarding the objective for hours on end. Later on, at least in Bexley, the method of practice was even refined. A broken down car was given the upper works of a panzer made out of tin, and pulled through the streets by a tractor. The men of the Home Guard lay in the ditches on the right and left and hurled their missiles against the vehicle. They had named it the 'Hitler bus' and covered it with slogans such as 'The road to Berlin' or 'Don't miss me!' When, later on, the exercises were often interrupted by air raid warnings, this only made it all the more realistic and fired the men to greater efforts.

Besides the Molotov Cocktail, the fighters from Spain had brought something else back with them: experience in guerrilla warfare. In Osterley, a western suburb of London, the Earl of Jersey had donated a part of his property as a training ground for the Home Guard. There, the publisher of the *Picture Post*, Edward Hulton, together with Tom Wintringham and several British instructors, who had also taken part in the Spanish Civil War, as well as three Spanish miners, who had made a reputation for themselves as tank busters, started up a guerrilla school for the Home Guard. The curriculum consisted of: conduct of a lone fighter in open country; camouflage; taking out enemy sentries; patrols; house-to-house fighting; single combat. The members of the Home Guard learned the use of anti-personnel mines, the various types of hand guns, hand grenades, fog grenades, wire nooses, and how to decapitate enemy motorcyclists by stretching a steel wire across the road. The school was so successful that the regular Army, including regiments of the Guards, sent officers and men there for training and later took the school over completely.

This recalls the time in 1805 when a sort of Home Guard, comprising as many as 350,000 men, had also been formed. At that time, a far-sighted colonel had demanded that the men were not to be trained by drill sergeants from the barracks, but rather by poachers and gamekeepers. Similar ideas also surfaced in 1940.

Many of the preparations for invasion were carried out under the strictest secrecy. Only a very few among the civilian population, and even in the armed forces, knew about the formation of a partisan force. Its members were to let themselves be overrun by the Germans and then conduct a guerrilla war in their rear. The volunteers consisted of civilians, as a rule specially selected members of the Home Guard. Later on, several Home Guard battalions were formed, secret units that did not appear on any official listings. They did not receive any pay and wore the same uniforms as the rest of the Home Guard.

The whole thing started with a captain of the Grenadier Guards, Peter Fleming, the brother of Ian Fleming, creator of James Bond. He established his headquarters in The Garth at Bilting, a country house on the road from Ashford to Canterbury. With him was another captain, two sergeants and several soldiers, who acted as drivers, batmen and clerks. The core of the unit was formed by a platoon of the crack commando force, the Lovat Scouts, who were later to become one of the most famous units in the British Army.

Within a short time, Fleming and his helpers recruited men from all of the tactically important areas in Kent. There were no written records on any of the recruits and they were all sworn to strictest secrecy, even towards members of their own families. One poor wife believed for four years that her husband was having an affair out of town, because he never trained with the Home Guard and disappeared every weekend.

The Garth became a guerrilla school similar to Osterley. Every weekend from 50 to 80 men were gathered there to practise guerrilla warfare in the neighbouring woods. Since the activities of the resistance would mostly take place at night, by day the trainees wore welders' goggles in order to accustom themselves to fighting in the dark. Each man was equipped with a pistol, a truncheon, a knife, and combat boots with thick rubber soles, which permitted silently creeping up on German sentries. Each of the five to eight man teams had a light machine gun, hand grenades and a supply of plastic explosive, which was still quite new at the time.

Slowly The Garth turned into a richly equipped munitions and weapons depot. The latter also included six longbows. Fleming was an excellent shot with a bow, and could kill a deer with an arrow at 90 metres. This silent weapon was ideal for use against enemy sentries. It could also be used to send an incendiary charge into his ammunition or fuel dumps. The bowmen were able to practise in public, because they disguised themselves as a sports club.

The duties of the men of the future resistance were not over with their arduous training in single combat. They also had to help dig their hideouts, even though the major part of the job was carried out by pioneer units sworn to secrecy. During the early weeks of summer, at least 25 hideouts were built in Kent, in which six to seven men could stay hidden for a minimum of two weeks. As a rule, such a dugout was about seven metres long, three to four metres wide and deep enough so that the men could stand upright. It contained bunks, a stove, a paraffin lamp, and the necessary supply of food. When occupied, there was enough room for ammunition, weapons and explosives. The dugouts were normally dug in woods, covered with planks and carefully camouflaged. The entrance was usually covered by a wooden box containing soil from the surrounding area.

Old tunnels and caves on the steep Kentish coast, which the smugglers had used in the seventeenth century, were rediscovered during the search for adequate hideouts and prepared for their new purpose. One of these tunnels led directly under the landing strip of the RAF station at Manston, from which one could easily reach the hangars and administrative buildings in case the Germans were to take over the base. The partisans also made themselves comfortable in the cellars of the ruins of a country house and even in enlarged badger tunnels.

The largest hideout was located near Bilting in Godmersham Park. This installation was designed as a place of refuge for partisan troops who, for whatever reason, were unable to return to their own hideout. It offered shelter, food and water for 120 men and was called the 'Air Ship'. In the course of his investigations, Fleming had stumbled upon a twenty-metre long, ten-metre wide and ten-metre deep overgrown excavation in the middle of the park. It was soon discovered that it stemmed from the First World War and had been intended for an airship. The Germans would never look for a hole underneath a hole, Fleming reasoned. He therefore had the pioneers deepen the depression by more than three metres, cover it with beams and put the surface back into its original condition. A long shaft was dug as an access, whose entrance lay about fifteen metres from the edge of the depression. The trap door consisted of a tree stump, which was balanced out with counter-weights in such a manner, that it could easily be pushed aside with one hand after first having withdrawn a bolt.

The earth dug out when building the hideouts posed a major problem, because it lay about in the countryside far too conspicuously, particularly since the lower strata often consisted of chalk and showed up so brightly, that they could be detected from an aircraft even at great altitude. Army lorries carried the earth to 'official' construction sites or tipped it into the sea. Fleming's successor had an idea straight from Hollywood: using explosive charges, he had the mounds of earth converted into 'bomb craters'.

The more time passed without the Germans appearing, the more perfectly the nests of resistance were extended. As well as in Kent, guerrilla fighters were also trained in Sussex and East Anglia, but also in the Midlands and in Scotland, and hideouts were built for them. By the close of 1940 they numbered 300, later on this rose to 500. In the end, the strength of the 'Auxiliary Units', as the partisan forces called themselves, reached approximately 3,000 men.

On the German side nobody knew of the existence of this dangerous force, which Churchill called 'a useful extension of the Army'. The German OKH [Oberkommando des Heeres = Supreme Army Command] underestimated the will to resist of the British, who, unlike the Poles and the French, could no longer be surprised and were preparing themselves for the day with all their might. In Berlin they only had a vague idea about the much-discussed Home Guard, which was obviously based on a random selection of English newspaper articles. On 9 August the OKH published the following appreciation of the Home Guard under the title 'Troop observations': ' 'For local security services, particularly against paratroops and airborne forces, the 'Home Guards', formerly 'Local Defence Volunteers', have been formed in addition to the terri-torial defence forces. They consist of an auxiliary volunteer force without any military training. Instead of a uniform, sweaters and civilian trousers are being worn, apparently as standard dress. Equipment with steel helmets is probable. The units of the Home Guard are part of the traditional infantry regiments and wear their badges. Arming them with guns, including sports guns, and hand grenades is intended, but has apparently only been partially carried out. Their assignment, in addition to combat, consists of controlling traffic, particularly with a view to movements by refugees; it is obviously the intention to prevent the flight of the population from combat areas by all possible means.'

The numerical strength of the Home Guard was also underestimated by the German observers, probably partly due to the fact that they were unaware of the mass of one million unemployed, from whose ranks the Home Guard received a surprisingly large turnout. The British press had made no bones about the fact that during the first 24 hours after Eden made his appeal on 14 May, about 250,000 applications for the Home Guard had been received and that by mid-July its strength had grown to over one million. 'The total strength of the forces deployable at home at this time, including coastal defence forces but excluding anti-aircraft units,' the OKH continued in its 'Troop observation', 'is assumed to be 230,000 men. Adding the five active divisions which escaped from France, this number is increased to around 320,000 men.'

The Germans completely ignored the contribution women were making to the defence of the country. There were thousands of Boadiceas ready and waiting, not all of them with red hair like the legendary queen of the ancient British tribe of the Iceni, who revolted against the Roman conquerors in Norfolk. But in them too, 'the originality of the oppressed British character engaged in desperate resistance', as Leopold von Ranke once wrote about Boadicea, was manifest.

'We demand the right to stand shoulder to shoulder with the Home Guard', Nora Robbins, founder of the Amazon Defence Corps proclaimed. 'The fighting spirit of our soldiers also lives in their mothers and wives and it should be integrated into our joint war effort.' The Corps 'became very much in demand' when she called her sisters to the battle. The Army provided instructors to train the Amazons in the use of a rifle and in combat. 'I personally carry a truncheon', said Nora Robbins, 'and with it I can easily kill a man if there is no rifle to hand.'

The seriousness of the situation led to nervous tensions, which both male and female dispositions were not always up to dealing with. The wildest rumours were in circulation and false alarms occurred daily. Horsewomen who had joined the mounted Home Guard spent many days searching the fields for 'arrows' that members of the fifth column had allegedly mowed in the already tall grain to show landing troops the way.

One of the many rumours took a long time to die out: on the southern coast, the naked bodies of 40 German soldiers had been washed ashore. In one version, the whole Channel coast was 'white with dead bodies'. There was much speculation where they could have come from. The source of the rumour was never identified, but it corresponded to the wishful thinking of most Britons.

This probably also explains the many false alarms: imagination ran ahead of events, because the expectant tension had become too great. A typical example is the alarm that was sounded one day in Burton. This little village is not far from the River Dee, a bay in North Wales, in an area in which a landing by the enemy could never seriously have been expected.

In the early hours of a Sunday morning, the commander of the Home Guard battalion was awakened by shouts outside his bedroom window: 'Invasion, Sir, Invasion!' Hastily the elderly gentleman, a lieutenant colonel, scrambled out of bed and put on some clothes. He rushed outside buckling on his revolver as he went. In the street he found some wild-looking men armed with shotguns, sabres, iron bars and sticks. They were waiting for him to lead them against the Germans. The local constable stepped forward, saluted, and in a low voice asked to see the Commander's identity card. Nobody found this funny or impertinent, after all, there was a blazer and a pair of pyjamas pants to be seen under the Commander's military greatcoat.

The situation was clear enough: a farmhand had just reached his observation post in the dunes, when he detected the Germans on the beach. Many Germans. He had immediately rushed back to report. The men only spoke in whispers. A patrol had to be sent out.

Led by the commander, a handful of volunteers set off, including the vicar and the local pub owner. They first wanted to go by the post office to make a telephone call to Denhall, a group of houses not far from the beach, because there anyone would be in the best position to know more. The postmaster was also up and about. He was carrying a heavy axe on his shoulder: before the Germans came, he wanted to demolish the telephone cabinet. When he rang Denhall, nobody answered. The farmhand said that it was small wonder, there had been hundreds of Germans on the beach.

It was now time to make haste. The Commander and his intrepid men set out on the road to the farmhand's observation post. It was not easy to climb across the dunes in a straight line in the light of dawn that was just breaking. They took almost an hour to reach their objective about three kilometres away. Carefully they crept up the final dune and looked over.

'Down there', whispered the farmhand, 'there are...'. He fell silent. 'Idiot!' shouted the Commander in the uncanny stillness. 'Don't you know what those are? Those are stakes! Stakes that have been rammed into the sand to prevent German planes from landing at low tide!' How was the farmhand to know? He worked inland on a farm and hardly ever came down to the beach.

As curious as some of these marginal details may appear to be, they are also an expression of the general stance of the British: any day, any hour, they expected the Germans to appear and they were prepared to fight for their bare existence. But what was keeping the Germans?

VIII

Then Let Us Make a Plan

How *Großadmiral* Raeder set off an avalanche

Since the declaration of war on 3 September 1939, the island kingdom had been a red rag to Hitler. The British were interfering with his grandiose plans on the Continent instead of only minding their Empire. He had no intention of subjugating the British, but if they insisted on forcing their concept of European politics down his throat, they would have to be made to see reason and brought to their knees.

On 23 September Hitler had a meeting with the Chief of the *Seekriegsleitung* [literally: Sea War Leadership, i.e. Supreme Naval Command] in the seaside resort of Zoppot near Danzig, at which Colonel General Keitel was also present. *Großadmiral* Raeder reported on the war situation at sea in the Baltic, North Sea and Atlantic. He tried to play down the substantial successes of the German U-boats. 232,000 tonnes of enemy shipping had been sunk so far but so that nobody would harbour any idea that things could go on in this way, he explained that at the outbreak of war a large number of French and British steamers had been on their way back to home ports and become a relatively easy prey to the U-boats, because they were not yet armed. On the other hand, the boats were operating under restrictions for political reasons – no attacks on passenger liners and closed season on the French navy and merchant marine – so that British and French troopships from Africa and the British Isles could still run to French ports unmolested.

Raeder asked Hitler what measures were to be taken in case the war against England and France had to be 'fought through'. This was far from clear at the time, because Hitler had also said that he hoped to split France off from the western Alliance. Hitler consoled his naval chief by telling him, that within a fortnight he intended to give a presentation on the political situation to his Supreme Commanders and would then announce the siege of England, which was to be carried out by the *Kriegsmarine* in cooperation with the *Luftwaffe*.

In his notes on this discussion Raeder wrote: 'If war continues, siege of England must be carried out immediately and with strongest measures. Foreign Ministry, Economics and Food Ministry to be informed beforehand about the consequences. All objections must be rejected. Even threat by America to enter war, which appears unavoidable if war continues, must not lead to restrictions. The sooner the start and the more brutal, the quicker the effect and the shorter the war. All restrictions prolong the war. Chief OKW and *Führer* are in complete agreement.'

No mention was made of a landing on the British Isles. Neither at this time nor later on did Hitler mention this possibility by so much as a single word. This 'crazy idea' first occurred several weeks later to the Commander-in-Chief of the *Kriegsmarine* himself. During a visit by Raeder to the Chief of Naval Command West on 6 November 1939, talk turned to the continuation of the war after a possible victory over France. Would the *Führer* decide to starve Great Britain out by means of a blockade or intend to land on the islands with masses of troops? Hitler had just designated 12 November 1939 as the date for the attack in the west.

The General Staff of the *Heer* had informed the *Kriegsmarine* in late autumn that they could count on hard fighting with heavy losses and a lengthy duration of the campaign in the west. The *Heer* planners assumed that the German troops would 'reach about the same line as in 1914/18 and that the Belgian and Dutch ports on the eastern approaches to the Channel will thereby possibly also fall into our hands.'

Raeder recalled: 'As our mental as well as *matériel* preparations before the war had not been aimed at an armed conflict with England, I was anxious that we should at least give some initial thought to the matter.' Before the leader-ship of the *Wehrmacht* or Hitler came up with the idea to invade England and caught him unawares with a demand for sea transport, Raeder at least wanted to be prepared.

On 15 November *Großadmiral* Raeder created a small team under Naval Chief of Staff Vice Admiral Schniewind, which was to study the military, naval, and transportation aspects of a possible invasion of England. The members of the team were sworn to strictest secrecy. Nobody outside the Operations Staff was to learn anything about these considerations.

Schniewind's subordinates, Rear Admiral Fricke and Captain Reinicke, immediately went to work at the Tirpitzufer in Berlin. It was a formal exercise that did not fill them with any great enthusiasm, because everybody knew that in the Royal Navy, they were facing an opponent who was ten times stronger than they were and had much more experience in war at sea. Furthermore, the matter was a completely new topic for them. While there had been troop ship-ments on a large scale before, a German naval staff had never before planned an invasion nor had the other two branches of the armed services ever had to be included in a naval operation.

After five days, the two staff officers presented *Großadmiral* Raeder with a document of twelve and a half typewritten pages, the so-called 'Study Red'. They had chosen an approximately 100 kilometres wide sector of the English south coast between Portland and Yarmouth on the Isle of Wight as the landing area and found the ports particularly suitable because of their accessibility and freight handling capacities. They had devoted little attention to the actual transportation problem; more however, to the dangers a landing fleet would face from the Royal Air Force and the Royal Navy. Fricke and Reinicke therefore made the success of a landing operation dependent on four conditions being met:

1. The enemy naval forces had to be kept away from the landing area or else destroyed there.
2. The enemy air force had to be eliminated.
3. The enemy coastal defences had to be destroyed.
4. Attacks by enemy submarines during the crossing had to be prevented.

The landing fleet was to embark from German home ports. As assembly points for the invasion forces, the Belgian and French Channel ports, provided they had even been taken, appeared far too vulnerable to the navy planners. Despite all the risks, they came to the cautious conclusion: 'If a victory in the West or a stabilisation of the front permits forces to become available, a landing operation across the North Sea on a large scale and under the aforementioned conditions would appear to us to be a possible means of forcing the enemy to sue for peace.'

It was not only the superiority of the enemy's naval forces and the danger the German troop transports would be exposed to from the air which made the naval officers so hesitant. They were still thinking in the categories of the First World War: engagements at sea and war against the merchant marine were their job. Landing operations were more properly the responsibility of the *Heer*. In this they were also confirmed by *Führer* Order No. 9 which exhaustively defined the job of the *Kriegsmarine*: merchant war was its only assignment. 'Study Red' therefore, was basically only intended as an alibi. In the *Reichsmarineamt* [Reich Naval Office] it wandered into a desk drawer and was forgotten for the time being. However, copies were sent to the OKW and the OKH.

At the OKW, Major General Alfred Jodl, Chief of the Armed Forces Operations Staff noted reception of the study and passed it on to the Chief of Department L [Landesverteidigung = Home Defence], Colonel Walter Warlimont, who also filed it for the time being. Not so at the OKH, which apparently developed military ambitions: after receipt of 'Study Red', Colonel General Walther von Brauchitsch initiated a counter-study by the *Heer* on 13 December 1939 under the code name 'Study Northwest'. Major (i.G.) Stieff was made responsible for drawing it up.

The leadership of the *Heer* was not weighed down by the heavy scruples that had troubled the *Kriegsmarine*. The problem was approached without any undue misgivings, as in a sand-table exercise. The main objective was to be the occupation of London. The given assumptions for the operation were: possession of the Belgian and Dutch North Sea and Channel ports, and that the core of the British Army would be on the Continent committed, together with the French, to countering a German attack on the battlefields of the First World War.

Taking the difficulties into consideration that the *Kriegsmarine* had been confronted with in 'Study Red' in assuming a landing on the English southern coast, Major Stieff and his team moved the landing north between the Thames estuary and the Wash. Air Division 7, reinforced by the 16th Infantry Regiment, were to take the ports of Great Yarmouth and Lowestoft in an airborne operation, while one infantry division and a brigade of cyclists landed in the ports from the sea. South of the ports, a further infantry division was to land on the open coast near Dunwich and on Hollesley Bay in front of Ipswich, in order to prevent enemy counter-operations from there. A second landing wave consisting of two panzer divisions, a motorised infantry division and a reinforced infantry division, was to follow. The empty transports returning to the Belgian and Dutch ports were then to embark a third wave of six panzer and infantry divisions and take them over. As a deception, a diversionary landing was to take place north of the mouth of the Humber. The actual objective was the area north of London. Thus being cut off from its lines of communication to the North, the metropolis could be seized ('taken away') and occupied.

In order to allow this text-book operation to unfold without interference. The *Heer* assigned the following tasks to the *Kriegsmarine*:

1. Closing of the Strait of Dover against enemy naval forces approaching from the south.
2. Prevention of actions against the landing operation and its supply by enemy surface and undersea forces in the North Sea.
3. Clearing the routes and landing areas of enemy and own forces mines.
4. Carrying out the transport by sea.
5. Providing the necessary landing equipment.
6. Fire support from the sea for the invasion forces.
7. Carrying out the diversion north of the Humber.
8. Impeding the return of the BEF from the Continent.

From the *Luftwaffe*, the OKH expected:

1. Command of the air in the approaches and landing areas.
2. Support of the *Kriegsmarine* against enemy naval forces.
3. Airborne landings in Great Yarmouth and Lowestoft and near Cambridge.
4. Support of the final operations in England.
5. Impeding the return of the BEF from the Continent.

Chief of Staff, General Franz Halder, and Colonel General von Brauchitsch approved the study and sent it to the *Seekriegsleitung* and the Commander-in-Chief of the *Luftwaffe* for comment. The echo was characteristic for the lack of cooperation and understanding between the three branches of the *Wehrmacht*. In their reply on 30 December, the Staff of the *Luftwaffe* simply announced that they were incapable of meeting the requirements of the *Heer*: 'The planned deployment is therefore only possible under a condition of total air superiority and even then, only if complete surprise is guaranteed', said one of the key sentences of the reply. The *Luftwaffe* drew the attention of the *Heer* to the fact that the planned airborne landings would strike at the strongest point of the enemy's air defence and that even weak enemy air forces would already suffice to make transport virtually impossible. There was not a word on how the *Luftwaffe* intended to alleviate this. Instead, the study was rejected in total: '(A landing in England)... could only be the final act in an already victorious war against England, otherwise the conditions for the success of such a combined operation would not exist.'

In its comment, the *Seekriegsleitung* was at least prepared to discuss the matter. The *Kriegsmarine* people however, were hard put to disguise the degree to which they were astonished by the naivety of the *Heer* planners. They drew Halder's attention to the fact that in the attempt to capture the ports, one would not only have to count on a defence by light naval forces and lines of interdiction in the approaches, but that beyond any doubt the whole British Home Fleet with its heavy ships, cruisers and submarines would be fully deployed. And 'the English Home Fleet will always be able to appear in greater strength than our own, if the will to do so is there.' This also precluded the deployment of German U-boats, which were not capable of facing such an opponent.

The *Kriegsmarine*, which in its study had not preferred the southern ports without good reasons, declared that the restrictive port conditions in Great Yarmouth and Lowestoft were no less problematical for unloading operations than the open coast. In other words: The *Heer* leadership did not have a clue how difficult unloading in narrow ports really was and how fatal a loss of time would occur because of the need to manoeuvre the ships. Major Stieff had obviously not given any thought at all to how to disembark as few as only one company of soldiers on a steep pebble beach. Even using small boats or lighters, this was almost impossible for men without any experience.

On several points, the *Kriegsmarine* simply turned the tables and, for example, demanded that the *Heer* eliminate coastal defences beforehand. Simultaneously, it categorically rejected any possibility of systematically clearing enemy and friendly mines in the sea areas indicated. It also did not wish to entertain any ideas about a diversionary operation north of the Humber, because that would have meant splitting up its already weak forces.

It was apparent, that at the Tirpitzufer no one was able to warm to any of the suggestions from the *Heer*. The two points of view were furthest apart on the key question. The *Kriegsmarine* was aghast at the dimensions of the transport requirements. In their own investigations, Fricke and Reinicke had assumed fifteen ships and 7,500 men. Now 100,000 men and heavy equipment were to be hauled across the Channel. 'The number of troops mentioned', Admiral Schniewind wrote, 'requires a transport fleet of 400 medium-sized ocean-going ships, furthermore a large collection of sea-going tugboats, barges etc. for disembarkation on the open coast.' The ships themselves, of which only a fraction was available in any case, would have to be modified for the transportation of troops and heavy weapons (tanks, artillery), for which shipyard capacity would have to be provided. This would take all of one year. Landing equipment was not available to any mentionable degree and would first have to be obtained.

The *Kriegsmarine* used the opportunity to fire a broadside at the *Luftwaffe*: 'Support of the *Kriegsmarine* by the *Luftwaffe* cannot be counted on with any degree of assurance. The weather, the time of day, and other circumstances could totally preclude the participation of air forces over the sea.'

Two of the three branches of the *Wehrmacht* therefore did not believe an invasion of the British Isles to be feasible, at least not in this manner. On one point only did *Heer*, *Kriegsmarine*, and *Luftwaffe* agree completely: without command of the air above the approaches and the landing areas, a landing was not to be thought of. There was nothing for General Halder to do but to have 'Study Northwest' disappear in a desk drawer.

But this did not mean that the idea of a landing on the other side of the Channel was dead. It was only sleeping. It was slumbering so deeply that Hitler's next act, while awakening British fear of invasion, did not even make the German General Staff put two and two together. On 10 April 1940, the landing operations in Norway began. The landing followed the same pattern on which *Kaiser* Wilhelm had transported his troops to China 40 years before. Soldiers and their weapons were brought to Norwegian ports in large ocean-going ships and simply unloaded there. After four months of planning, nobody had thought of using the opportunity to practise having troops land on a defended coast or disembarking them on beaches.

It was only after his breathtakingly victorious dash through France had brought Guderian's panzers to the Channel coast at Abbeville on the mouth of the Somme on 20 May 1940, that there was again talk of beaches and of England. As they turned north in order to reach Calais and Dunkirk, where they were supposed to meet Army Group B descending from the North, the panzer crews could clearly see the white chalk cliffs of Dover. Guderian wrote about this in his memoirs: 'During the night (from 20 to 21 May) the Spitta battalion of 2nd Panzer Division passed Noyettes and thereby became the first German force to reach the Atlantic (sic!) coast.'

Guderian's geographical mistake is characteristic of German general officers' appreciation of all things maritime. In the course of the coming weeks, this was to become a major factor: on the one hand, the Channel was regarded as an insurmountable part of an ocean, an endless waste of wild water that could not be understood or mastered; on the other hand the Channel was not much more than a puddle of water that many people had already swum across. But for the time being, the operations against France were still occupying all the attentions of the military. Nobody thought about crossing the Channel, while only a Sunday's excursion away, millions of men and women were trembling in fear of a German invasion.

Only one man among the leadership of the German *Wehrmacht* had been electrified by the break-through to the Channel coast: *Großadmiral* Erich Raeder. He was tormented by the thought that Adolf Hitler would now demand of him to have the two victorious Army Groups still filled with the spirit of attack, transported across to England. 'The time had come, when I had to raise the question of an invasion with Hitler. I was afraid that otherwise some irresponsible person would make the obvious suggestion to invade, Hitler would take up the idea, and the *Kriegsmarine* would then suddenly find itself faced with an insurmountable problem.'

On 21 May 1940, after the *Führer* conference in the *Felsennest* [cliff nest] headquarters, Raeder asked the *Führer* for a private meeting. He began his presentation with the successful occupation of Norway, which had come off far better than anyone had expected. This could therefore easily lead to the idea, that one could now proceed against England in the same manner as in Norway. At first glance, the jump across the Channel might even appear to be less dangerous than the long distance to the Norwegian ports, whereas in actual fact, the opposite was true: a landing on the British islands was extremely difficult and entailed great risks. Raeder explained to Hitler that the Channel was one of the most dangerous and treacherous stretches of water in the world and that its coasts were protected against attack by reefs, shallows, currents and steep cliffs. The British fleet, which was superior to the German, was at home in these waters, besides which a massed, and consequently slow, landing fleet was virtually helpless against the powerful Royal Air Force.

The *Großadmiral* went on to state that the most important condition for a landing operation against England was absolute command of the air over the Channel. German air superiority would have to be so overwhelming that besides control of the air, it would prevent the British fleet from intervening, or at least make its intervention very costly. Otherwise the risks would be far too great and could not be justified.

Hitler listened attentively and did not express an opinion. However, he insisted that no preparations should be undertaken for the time being. Together with Raeder, Hitler left the conference room. He was in high spirits and even recounted that during the night he had heard a nightingale for the first time in twenty years.

However, the thought of an invasion of the British Isles would not leave the Commander-in-Chief of the *Kriegsmarine* in peace. He still feared being faced with such an order. The experts at Naval Command were also under no illusions. 'The degree to which our fleet can become effective', wrote Rear Admiral Fricke, 'will remain modest. Only the further course of the war will be able to show whether the small German fleet will be able to play any role at all in such a gigantic operation. Its inferiority compared to the English fleet will hardly permit fleet operations. Nonetheless, possibilities will also arise here, as in Norway, for the remaining light forces, and over short distances also the auxiliary forces (steamers, fishing vessels), at least quickly to throw personnel on to the English coast.'

Fricke dug out the old *Kriegsmarine* 'Study Red' of November 1939 and based on it, prepared a new 'Study England', which he presented to his Chief on 27 May. As opposed to the old plan, the opinion expressed by the OKH in its 'Study Northwest' had been taken into consideration, and Fricke now saw landing possibilities both in the Portland–Yarmouth area as well as between the Thames estuary and Newcastle far up in northern England. For the former, the points of departure were to be the ports between Cherbourg and Texel, for the latter, the ports between the Schelde tributary and Hanstholm in Denmark. For reasons of tactics and navigation however, the *Kriegsmarine* still preferred a landing west of the Strait of Dover, which was easier to mine and to protect from the air.

The new appreciation was due to the fact that in the meantime, the *Kriegsmarine* had taken over the ports that had been captured in Holland, Belgium and France and had begun to repair and extend them for its purposes. On 31 May, the preparations for a landing fleet were also set in motion, even though the *Kriegsmarine* had not received any orders and nobody in the *Heer* was yet thinking of an invasion.

Raeder ordered Admiral Schuster, Admiral in Chief in France, and Captain Degenhardt, Chief of Sea Transport z.b.V. [zur besonderen Verwendung = on special assignment], to prepare a list of the available shipping capacity in case this would be needed. He ordered the Naval Staff to study the possible means of closing the Strait of Dover and to prepare mine-sweeping. A job of no less importance had been assigned to Department 3 of the Naval Staff. On 7 June, it handed its chief a twenty-page study on the conditions of navigation in British coastal waters and the landing possibilities between the Isle of Wight in the south and the Wash in the north. Every single port had been scrutinised for its overall condition, freight handling facilities, total water surface, depth, and traffic connections. The distances to the closest base of the Royal Navy had not been forgotten. With the help of maritime manuals, the open coast had also been checked out for landing possibilities.

The listing of shipping capacity for transport was to take weeks. Mine-sweeping off the enemy coast and closing off the Strait of Dover depended on so many conditions, that this was left in the balance for the time being. Only the investigations of the coast and its ports produced any results. The Wash, for example, was found to be difficult and unfavourable for a landing attempt: dangerous sands, strong tidal currents (up to 5 knots), heavy tides (6m to 6.5m), which would cause a landing fleet great problems on an otherwise low coast. Further south, the coast was more suitable for a landing; only when reaching the region of the Thames estuary did navigation become difficult again, due to the many sunken wrecks and strong currents. Marshy areas made a landing hardly advisable. On the southern coast of the Thames estuary, near the Isle of Sheppey, there were several favourable anchorages. The adjoining coast from the North Foreland through Dover to Dungeness was described as difficult: this was where the Channel was most dangerous as a seaway, because of the many sandbanks and strong tidal currents. The *Kriegsmarine* considered a landing between Folkestone and Dungeness to be theoretically possible. Otherwise, this coast only offered steep sides and cliffs 18m to 36m in height. The nautical experts of the *Kriegsmarine* had procured charts of several of the coastal sectors on which a landing could be considered. These showed the geological make-up of the seabed off the coast: fine sand, clay, rock, pebbles, where the bottom was uneven, the steepness of the beaches. Even the petrified forest off the coast of Dungeness was marked down.

None of this information produced any enthusiasm among the *Kriegsmarine* leadership, as little as did the fact that the British destroyer packs at anchor in distant Scapa Flow would only need 24 hours for the run to Dover, not to mention the other units of the Royal Navy. Why then play about with this dangerous idea at all? The impression was gained that Raeder, in his battle against the idea of a landing operation, was tilting at windmills. Who was compelling him to prepare a quiver full of counter-arguments? Whoever it was, it was certainly not Hitler, because at this point in time, nothing was further from his mind than an invasion of England.

In his order of the day on 5 June, Hitler had lauded his soldiers for having fought the tough battle at Dunkirk and in only a few weeks, forced two nations to capitulate, destroyed France's best divisions, and beaten the British Expeditionary Force, taken it prisoner or chased it from the Continent. As far as England was concerned, this appeared to satisfy him for the time being. 'As of today's date, the western front will again stride forward .... .' The objective was not London, but Paris, which fell into German hands without a battle on 14 June. On 17 June Marshal Pétain sent the first peace negotiator to German headquarters at Bruly on the Franco-Belgian border.

The victory over France stirred the emotions. Hitler's secretary reports that, to the speechless astonishment of his entourage, Hitler performed a 'St Vitus' dance' for sheer joy. The only one who was not amazed by this was Keitel. He gave a little speech in which he celebrated the military success and called Hitler the greatest commander of all time (which later led to the nickname 'Gröfaz').*

Peace was in the air. When Hitler flew to Munich next day, 18 June, to meet Mussolini, he first met Göring at Rhein-Main airport. The pair fell into each other's arms in a gesture full of pathos. 'We will reach an understanding with England,' an emotional Hitler declared. 'That means we will finally have peace again,' a beaming Göring replied.

The conference with Mussolini was also dominated by Hitler's generous stance towards his only remaining adversary. The two dictators agreed in their discussion that all that would be needed was to increase the pressure on England. Mussolini offered his air force for the purpose. Only as an aside was a landing in England mentioned as an additional means of putting on pressure, but not discussed any further. Count Ciano, the Italian Foreign Minister, asked Ribbentrop, his German counterpart, straight out: 'Does one now want continuing war or peace?' Ribbentrop did not hesitate for an instant before answering: 'Peace, of course!' and added that England's willingness to make peace was already being sounded out via Sweden.

Despite this, Raeder was not far wrong in already attempting to prepare himself to meet a possible demand for transport space for invasion troops. The OKW had also become uneasy about this question. It had not escaped the attention of General Jodl and his staff, who were responsible for coordinating the plans and operations of the three services and bringing them in line with Hitler's directives, that Heer, Luftwaffe, and Kriegsmarine were toying with plans to invade England and had already begun with preparations, even though no directives had been issued and Hitler was only talking about peace.

* Translator's note: Keitel called Hitler the 'Größte Feldherr aller Zeiten'; later on, when Germany began to lose the war, this was abbreviated to 'Gröfaz', which, while not a term existing in the German language, contains the syllable 'faz', sounding like the first syllable in 'Fatzke', which in English means 'twit' and in American English 'jerk'. Combined with the 'grö', people in Germany, by now thoroughly disenchanted with Hitler and his conduct of the war, understood the meaning to be 'greatest twit (of all time)'.

This may have been the reason for a visit that Colonel Warlimont, Chief of Department L at the OKW, paid Rear Admiral Fricke of the naval Operations Staff on 17 June. Warlimont broached the subject of what was to be done with England. Fricke cleverly evaded: 'Throughout the world, England for all intents and purposes, epitomises the reputation of the white man, therefore the destruction of England would have a negative effect on the whole white race.' Warlimont confirmed to him that this also reflected the *Führer's* opinion, who was attempting to come to a peace agreement with the British at the expense of France, based on the conditions that the British would return the colonies and refrain from any interference on the Continent. The *Führer* had not made any statement about a landing on the British Isles, nor were there any preparations or studies for this being carried out at OKW. He was astonished therefore, that indications of such preparations had become apparent, not only with the *Kriegsmarine*, but also with the other two branches. The Commander-in-Chief of the *Luftwaffe*, for example, had ordered the formation of a paratroop division and General Schell was working on plans for large transport pontoons. Fricke had no difficulty in explaining the *Kriegsmarine* point of view to Warlimont's satisfaction.

Even though it is quite reasonable to suspect that the OKW had been less concerned about the subject itself, but rather in preventing its being outplayed by the three services, Warlimont's visit was still a new signal of alarm for the *Kriegsmarine*: the others were working towards an invasion and the *Kriegsmarine* would have to carry the risks of transportation. At the next *Führer* conference on 20 June, *Großadmiral* Raeder therefore again broached the subject of the difficulties facing a landing in England: selection of an appropriate coastal sector, the still open question of mines, and the lack of suitable transport space were just as much of a worry as was the fact, that the *Heer* engineers were developing special vessels for transport at sea without reference to the *Kriegsmarine*.

Hitler did not address a single word to the preparations for a landing. Instead, he ordered Keitel to ensure that the construction of the special vessels would be put under the control of the *Kriegsmarine*. With that, the topic was closed. Nevertheless, Raeder was again able to make his point: the only appropriate way for his *Kriegsmarine* to fight the British was a blockade by U-boats. One could only seriously begin to consider a landing, after command of the air over the British Isles had been achieved. With this, the matter had again come full circle and not a single step forward taken.

Maybe the British defence efforts would have been less hectic if those responsible in London had been aware of the fog eddying about the German planning tables in heavy drifts. There, nobody seemed to know how the war was to continue, if it was to continue at all. After the occupation of Paris on 14 June, the OKH actually began to send 40 divisions home, because it did not know what to do with the many soldiers in France. It was considering having them help with the harvest at home, work in the armaments industry or even total demobilisation.

This question was troubling General Halder, Chief of Staff of the Heer. When he arrived in Berlin on 30 June to attend a family reunion, he immediately went to see his friend Ernst von Weizsäcker, State Secretary in the Foreign Ministry, in order to sound out the political situation. Weizsäcker offered the opinion, that there could be no question of peace or demobilisation. In the East, one had to be even more watchful than before, and in the West England would prob- ably need a further demonstration of force before she would be prepared to give in. This information was of no use to Halder. Like most of the generals, he was unable to imagine that the Führer did not have any clearly defined objec- tives. Weizsäcker assured him that he had not held anything back, but had only expressed himself in cautious terms.

At this time, no mention was made of Russia. All eyes were turned on the West. In the Reich, and particularly in Berlin, rumours were rife about an impending invasion of England. It was even claimed that the battle had already begun and had only not been made public due to a ban on information. On this day of 30 June, German troops had occupied the Channel Islands and therefore stood on British soil. Others were expecting the Republic of Ireland to ask the German Reich for military protection. From there, German troops would then strike the great blow against the British home country.

Halder was unable to free his mind from all this. Moreover, as Chief of Staff of the Heer, he felt himself very poorly informed. It never entered his head that everybody else was in the same boat. In the hope of at least learning something from the Kriegsmarine, he went to see Admiral Schniewind at the Tirpitzufer. In the preceding months, he had already corresponded with the Kriegsmarine Chief of Staff about the various invasion studies, albeit without results. In the mean- time, however, the situation had undergone a fundamental change: the Channel coast was in German hands. An army that had proven its immense power of attack was looking west: only 30 kilometres of water separated it from the English coast, 30 kilometres which, if overcome, would bring final victory. The troops themselves were not thinking along such lines; after their long string of victories, many officers and men would have preferred to march for home. But Halder suddenly had a vision: now was the time to hit the British over the head. His calculation was simple: the Heer had more soldiers than it knew what to do with, the Kriegsmarine more harbours and ships than it could count. What then argued against an invasion of the British Isles? It was no more than a simple problem of arithmetic: ships plus soldiers equals invasion.

Schniewind made the mistake of voluntarily giving Halder all the information he asked for and thereby set the ball in motion. All the former jealousies between *Heer* and *Kriegsmarine* seemed to have been forgotten when Halder began to warm to the new plan, and Schniewind kept throwing him new pieces like a child playing with building blocks. Ports of departure for the landing would be those between Le Havre and Ostend. The two of them discussed their condition, then the open coast and its variation between high cliffs and flat beaches, the marshy areas between Hythe and Hastings, where the Normans had landed in 1066. Tides, water levels, the beaches, some of which fell off surprisingly steeply, navigation at night. Schniewind impressed Halder with his expertise and he appeared, at least to Halder, to be far less opposed to an invasion than his chief: he considered it to be politically necessary and now, also militarily feasible.

Halder took copious notes. All they needed was a smooth sea and clear visibility; half moon would be best. This meant that within any moon cycle only one week would be favourable, provided the weather played along. The next possible date was mid-August, then one week in September, from mid-October on fogs and rough seas normally settled in the Channel, which would make a crossing impossible. Halder and Schniewind could not know that in the same way, the British had already calculated 8 July to be the attack date of the German troops.

Halder wrote: 'A large number of small steamers (about 1,000) can be gathered together... 100,000 men in the first wave.' Schniewind did not correct him, although he knew that there were not more than 300 suitable steamers available in the whole of Europe. 'Artillery protection on the second leg of the journey and on the beaches must come from the *Luftwaffe*', Halder continued to note. 'Threat from enemy submarines can be dealt with by net barriers; mines, and German U-boats can hold off the Royal Navy.' There was nothing to which a positive answer could not be found. In his overly optimistic evaluation of the situation, Halder now saw the military objective clearly before him and already knew how mine barriers and tank traps on the beaches could be cleared by army engineers, how the British coastal batteries could be silenced. He already saw the German panzers running ashore and setting off straight for London.

On returning to the OKH, he ordered Lieutenant Colonel Pistorius to begin developing a new invasion plan immediately: the first wave of six divisions with strong panzer support was to storm ashore on 15 August. Halder also believed that he had reached an agreement with Schniewind about the appropriate stretch of the English coast. The landing should take place between 1°30' East (Margate) and 1°30' West (Isle of Wight), in other words along the whole length of England's southern coast.

There were many technical problems to be solved: deployment of schnorkel tanks, which could run towards the beaches under water; rocket launchers and rocket mortars had to be installed in boats. How to load and unload heavy equipment from a Rhine barge? How to transport storm boats close to the coast? At this point, von Brauchitsch stuck his oar in. He knew of the opposing course Raeder was steering and simply ordered General Alfred Jakob to solve the transportation problem without the *Kriegsmarine* and to concentrate on pontoons.

And, as if it were the most natural thing in the world and they were afraid of missing the boat, the *Luftwaffe* now also joined in. *Luftwaffe* Chief of Staff General Jeschonnek had it announced that there were 25,000 airborne troops available, of whom 6,000 to 7,000 were paratroops. There were still only very few gliders which, besides the pilot, could carry eight men and their equipment. Parachutes were also scarce and supply teams combed the whole of Belgium and France to requisition parachute silk. On 11 July the *Luftwaffe* was already able to report to OKH that there were 400 Ju 52 transport planes, which could each carry twenty men, and 110 gliders available. Only five days later the number of aircraft had grown to 750, the number of gliders to 150.

In the meantime, the OKH had collected thirteen divisions on the Channel coast. The divisions were split into two waves: the first consisted of 90,100 men with guns, rocket mortars, panzers, an additional supply of machine-guns, mortars and anti-tank guns, as well as 4,600 vehicles, and 4,433 horses. They would launch the first attack on the enemy coast. The second wave for the follow-up attack comprised 170,300 men with the heavy weapons, 34,200 vehicles, and 57,550 horses. In addition, 26,000 bicycles had been provided.

A gigantic striking force appeared slowly to be forming up. Completely contrary to his original intention, Raeder had set off an avalanche. Within the staffs, all the talk now was about the invasion. Only one person remained silent: Adolf Hitler, the 'greatest commander of all time' left his generals stewing in their own juice.

On 29 June, Hitler had left to spend a few days at his headquarters on the Kniebis in the Black Forest near Freudenstadt and then continued on to the Obersalzberg. He had let the OKW know: a landing in England only as the ultima ratio, at least that is what General Jodl had noted down.

On 11 July, a *Führer* conference took place in Hitler's Alpine refuge. Keitel took part, as did *Großadmiral* Raeder. Hitler held forth a long monologue about a beautiful German city that was to be built next to Trondheim, also a large autobahn through Norway and Sweden, the gigantic works would take ten to fifteen years to complete. Then without warning he declared that he would shortly give a speech in the *Reichstag* with which he would change Great Britain's mind. This was water on Raeder's mill: as the commander of the *Kriegsmarine* he could not recommend an invasion of England as he had earlier in Norway. Again, he listed all the difficulties and risks of such an operation: the Royal Navy, the Royal Air Force, the mines, the lack of transport space. In no case should preparations be undertaken before the *Luftwaffe* had forced a decision. The English people should be made to feel the effects of the war on their own bodies. Raeder demanded a total blockade of supply by sea and more concentrated air attacks than before on Liverpool and other centres, for example. Hitler agreed and repeated that a landing was the last resort. Raeder left the Obersalzberg in the belief that he had sunk the invasion operation for good.

He had not reckoned with the *Heer*. Two days later von Brauchitsch and Halder arrived at the Berghof. Their adjutants were carrying heavy briefcases. These contained the latest invasion plans. Hitler, however, did not let the two officers get a word in. For two hours he gave them a military presentation from which many conclusions about the coming fateful developments could already have been drawn. For example: now, only the men from twenty, and no longer from 35 or 40 divisions, should be sent on leave. That did not exactly sound like peaceful intentions.

The *Führer* spoke about the Balkans, about Africa, about Russia and Spain, but always came back to Great Britain and the question as to why the British were not prepared to take the road to peace. Halder noted in his diary: 'The *Führer* sees, just as we do, that the reason is the hopes England places on Russia. He therefore believes that England must be forced into making peace. The reason: if we destroy England militarily, the British Empire will fall. Germany will gain nothing by this. German blood would have been spilt for Japan, America and others.'

This finally gave the two generals the chance to familiarise Hitler with the *Heer* plan of invasion. To their great surprise, Hitler accepted the plan developed by Halder together with Schniewind, in its entirety. Completely at odds with his normal practice, he asked no questions on specific operations, was not interested in details, and recommended no improvements. He declared the plan to be a practicable basis for preparations and ordered that these were to begin immediately.

On 16 July Hitler signed the famous *Führer* Order No. 16 which brought 'Operation Sea Lion' into being: 'Since England has still not given any sign of being prepared to reach an agreement, despite her militarily hopeless situation, I have decided to prepare an operation to invade England, and if this becomes necessary, to carry it through. The objective of this operation is to eliminate the

English home country as a base for the continuation of the war against Germany and, if this should become unavoidable, to occupy it fully.'

Preparations were to be completed by mid-August, the operation to have the code name 'Operation Sea Lion'. The war machine began to roll. Everybody believed it would crush England within a few weeks.

IX

The French Fleet Plays Coy
With or without Pétain? For or against Hitler?

The deadly danger of the situation in which the British believed themselves to be during these weeks, how heavily the thought of invasion weighed upon the men responsible in London, is demonstrated by Churchill's conduct during the political tragedy that had meanwhile unfolded in France. It had added a French component to the threat posed by the Germans: with possession of the Channel ports and the French fleet, with a pro-German French government in support, Hitler could cut the British lifeline in the Mediterranean and take the British Isles in a coup-de-main. Churchill had fought desperately to keep his French ally in line, above all his fleet, and thereby reduce Hitler's freedom of action.

In March, 61-year-old Paul Reynaud had taken over the office of Prime Minister from the Radical Socialist appeasement politician Edouard Daladier. Against the express will of Reynaud and the majority of his cabinet, Deputy Prime Minister Marshal Pétain and the Commander-in-Chief of the Armed Forces General Weygand, supported by the military and such people as two-time Prime Minister Laval and future Foreign Minister Baudouin, were working towards an armistice and the downfall of the government. Pétain and Weygand wanted to negotiate with the Germans 'without the civilians' and take over the leadership of the nation.

This over-hasty willingness to end the fighting did not only stem from military defeat. It reflected a deeply rooted feeling among a sector of the population. Within the anti-Communist camp, Hitler had always enjoyed much sympathy as an exponent of law and order. For example, perfume manufacturer Coty published an article in L'*Ami du Peuple*, a newspaper he had founded, under the headline: *France d'abord? Avec Hitler contre le bolchevisme* ['France first? With Hitler against Bolshevism']. In it he spoke out against the Franco–Russian alliance, against a Socialist International, and claimed neither Mussolini nor Hitler wanted to wage war against France. Many Frenchmen felt that Nazism was an antidote to Communism: 'Better Hitler than Stalin', they said. The right-wing paper L'*Action Française* attacked anybody who was unwilling to submit to a National Socialist Europe, and Beraud, who like Hitler wanted to see the link between France and Britain severed, wrote for the paper *Gringoire*.

In 1937 Alphonse de Chateaubriant, an influential writer, published *La Gerbe de Force* ['Concentrated Power']. In it he glorified Nazi upbringing and saw the salvation of Europe in 'a Teutonic renaissance, because the culture that grew from the womb of the Roman Empire is now dead'. Faced with a choice between Hitler and Stalin, France should choose Hitler, who 'exuded human kindness'. The basic feeling, admiration of German order and economic power, the deceptive display of the Olympic Games, was not only a political trend of the times, it even survived the war. General Weygand, who was also infected by it, was touting Chateaubriant's book in New York as late as 1950.

Public opinion was divided. The schism also ran through the established political parties. Only the Communists were universally pro-Soviet and wanted to introduce the Soviet system into France without any restriction. They only discontinued their anti-German tirades after the conclusion of the Hitler–Stalin Pact on 23 August 1939, until the German invasion of Russia, which turned the Communists into a pillar of the *Résistance* movement.

Whether Hitler or Stalin, before the war there was yearning in France for a strong hand which would change the terrible economic and political conditions for the better. Reynaud called this mood a 'conditional patriotism'. One side said: 'I am a patriot, provided neither Blum nor the Communists rule, otherwise I prefer Hitler'. The other side said: 'I am a patriot, provided France follows Soviet policy, otherwise I prefer Stalin.'

For many long war-weary, 'better-slavery-than-war' Frenchmen, negotiating with the Germans was therefore not necessarily a dishonour. Weygand and Pétain succeeded behind the backs of Reynaud and Interior Minister Mandel, in bringing a large majority of the cabinet over to their side. Their reasoning: it was necessary to prevent further fruitless bloodshed and to sound out the Germans on the terms of an armistice before officially asking for a cease-fire.

Reynaud first became aware of these events towards the end of May when the seat of the French Government became the issue. During a meeting of the War Council General Weygand declared: 'The government must stay in Paris and let itself be captured.' In this he was citing Livy, according to whom the Roman Senate had simply remained seated in their chairs and let themselves be massacred when the Gauls stormed Rome. This was true greatness. A flight by the government would demoralise the army and cause a revolution. However, Reynaud was able to prevail for the last time: from 14 June the seat of the French Government was to be moved to Bordeaux.

The French Prime Minister was determined to continue the war even after a capitulation by the armed forces in the mother country. France, after England, still disposed of the second largest fleet in Europe, of North Africa, and its extensive possessions overseas. If necessary Reynaud intended to escape from Bordeaux to North Africa with the government. This matched the contingency planning of the British government: in the event of a German occupation of the

British Isles, Churchill intended to evacuate his cabinet to Canada and to continue the fight from there.

On 11 and 12 June a meeting between the British and French took place at Chateau-Muguet near Briare (to the southeast of Orléans). The English were represented by Winston Churchill, Anthony Eden and Generals Dill, Ismay, Spears, and Howard-Vyse. On the French side there were present: Paul Reynaud, Marshal Pétain and Generals Georges and de Gaulle. At a second meeting Air Marshal Barrat and Admirals Darlan and Vuillemin took part.

Churchill had himself briefed on the situation by General Georges, Commander of the northeastern front. He listened with a grim face as Georges presented his figures: the armies on the northeastern front had lost at least 35 divisions out of 103, as well as three divisions of motorised cavalry and a large part of their few armoured units. Of the divisions still engaged, 20 to 25 had dissolved completely. Since 5 June the will to resist of the soldiers had grown, but the front had become a thin line of defence. Reims was already being threatened from the east. Georges ended his report with the statement: 'We are literally at the end of our tether.'

With forceful eloquence Churchill tried to convince his listeners that Great Britain would share the fate of its ally: it would not surrender until it had been crushed. If the French Army were to break off the battle, the British would continue to fight on in the hope that Hitler would destroy himself by his own victories. With their Air Force, their Navy and their Empire behind them, the British could continue to fight for many years to come and put Europe under a stringent blockade.

However, Churchill made no bones about his greatest worry of the moment. What would become of the French fleet if the land forces were forced to give up the fight? 'That is a nightmare we have to face', he said. If the French fleet were to fall into German hands, it would become an acute danger for the western access to the Mediterranean as well as to the British Isles themselves.

After the conference had ended he went up to Admiral Darlan once again: 'Darlan, I trust you will never surrender the fleet!' 'That is out of the question', the Commander-in-Chief of the French Navy assured him. 'That would not be reconcilable with the honour and tradition of our naval forces!' Churchill gained the impression that Darlan was serious in that he would rather sail his fleet to Canada, than to leave it to an enemy, even if he had to reckon with the opposition of certain political circles.

Meanwhile Reynaud was making desperate attempts to keep the 'defeatists' in line. To Pétain and Weygand he suggested that if the battle in the mother country had now become hopeless, to send the Army to Switzerland and have it interned there, or simply to put it into civilian clothes. Both the Marshal and the General rejected this idea. Reynaud tried to hold Pétain by his honour: France had given Britain its solemn word of honour on 28 March not to conclude a separate cease-fire or peace. In his soft, somewhat brittle voice the Marshal answered: 'You are looking at matters from an international point of view, I see them from a national point of view.'

Reynaud was convinced that his two opponents, who were being supported by such ambitious politicians as Laval and Baudouin, were less concerned with the fate and honour of France than with their own power. Even the consideration that after having betrayed Great Britain, France would stand all alone, at Hitler's mercy now and forever, did not make any impression on them. Weygand even threatened the Prime Minister: 'Our country will not forgive you, if you reject the possibility of concluding peace just for the sake of remaining faithful to the British.'

Despite this, Reynaud was still not prepared to throw in the towel. He was on the telephone almost constantly and sending telegrams and letters to Roosevelt and Churchill. At his instigation, Churchill asked the American President for a declaration by the United States that it would join the war in order to save France. A desperate and futile request.

On 13 June Churchill again flew to France, this time to Tours to a meeting of the French Council of Ministers. With tears in his eyes, he assured Reynaud and the presidents of the two chambers that come what might, Great Britain would make the French cause its own and, if it were to come out of this conflict victorious, would reinstate the dignity and sovereignty of France. He did not mention the French fleet. Instead, he spoke of another matter with Reynaud: during the course of the battles, 400 German pilots who had been shot down had become French prisoners of war. With the rapid German advance, it was probable that they would be freed and immediately employed against England. Churchill therefore suggested to Reynaud that the prisoners be taken to England for safekeeping.

Reynaud promised to initiate the handover immediately. That very same day he issued the necessary orders. In the evening, General de Gaulle took ship for London in the destroyer *Milan* in order to conduct the necessary negotiations. In addition the general had the assignment to arrange with the British the tonnage required to move the French government to North Africa. That this mission had been entrusted to de Gaulle is one of those small incidents that determine the march of history. De Gaulle was only to return from London four years later; then as the liberator and unifier of France.

In Bordeaux, the new seat of the government, the situation was coming to a head. The defeatists were beginning to gain the upper hand. Reynaud was still struggling. He did not want to submit to the Germans. It appeared as if many a

Briton was prepared to do more for France than many a Frenchman. In Tours, Churchill had not only promised new troops. On 16 June, Reynaud received an historically unique document that had been prepared in the London Foreign Office by Sir Robert Vansittart, together with de Gaulle, Pleven, and Monnet, and subsequently approved by the British government: a Declaration of Union. The key passage of this surprising offer said:

> At this most fateful moment in the history of the modern world the Governments of the United Kingdom and the French Republic make this declaration of indissoluble union and unyielding resolution in their common defence of justice and freedom against subjection to a system which reduces mankind to a life of robots and slaves. The two Governments declare that France and Great Britain shall no longer be two nations, but one Franco-British Union.
>
> The constitution of the Union will provide joint organs of defence, foreign, financial and economic policies. Every citizen of France will enjoy immediately citizenship of Great Britain; every British subject will become a citizen of France.

The fact that nobody in England seriously reckoned with its implementation does not detract from the weight of this proposal. The intention was clear: the solemn agreement of 28 March was to be cemented and a desertion by France prevented.

No one was more happy about this step than Paul Reynaud. In it he saw the only means of preventing the defeatists in his cabinet from making a proposal for an armistice. However, he was in for an humiliating defeat. Marshal Pétain roundly refused to even examine the document. The mood confronting Reynaud in the cabinet was explosive: 'England only wants to grab our colonies', 'the declaration will put us under the tutelage of the British', 'France will become an English dominion', were the major objections. Others were even more outspoken: 'In three weeks England will have her neck wrung like a chicken anyway', 'better a province of the Nazis, then we at least know what to expect.' In vain Reynaud admonished: 'I would rather collaborate with my ally than with my enemy!' Pétain had the last word: 'The union would only be a fusion with a corpse.'

The Prime Minister also suddenly saw himself confronted by a majority on the question of an armistice. He tendered his resignation to President Lebrun. Lebrun accepted and asked Pétain to form a new cabinet. It had also not been of any help that at the last moment the British ambassador had handed Reynaud a note in which the Government of the United Kingdom had agreed to the French Government's attempting to negotiate an armistice, provided the French fleet were to weigh anchor and sail to British waters. The new French Government ignored the proviso. Via the Spanish Ambassador de Lequeria, it asked the German *Reichsregierung* for a cease-fire at 00.30 on 17 June, and only hours later, Pétain sent the first negotiator to German headquarters at Bruly on the Franco–Belgian border.

The same day Churchill again made Pétain an offer to move the French fleet to British or American waters. On 19 June, First Lord of the Admiralty Alexander, First Sea Lord Sir Dudley Pound, and Lord Lloyd, personally set off for Bordeaux in a flying boat. Darlan, however, still refused to have the fleet set sail, because this would allegedly have caused the Germans to occupy all of France. Darlan gave the British his word of honour that his fleet would remain French or else sink itself. The British were embittered. Alexander is alleged to have said: 'Words of honour are of no help to us.'

Paul Reynaud, in the belief that he would soon be able to take over the government again, refused to give up. On 21 June he advised Pétain to let Darlan escape to the USA with the fleet. Pétain merely replied that one could then expect German reprisals against French cities. He was also not prepared to have Darlan's conduct explained to the Germans as an unauthorised action and insubordination.

Two days later Reynaud again went to see the Marshal. He had been alarmed by a terrible rumour: the armistice agreement contained a clause according to which the fleet, the last bastion of the *Grande Nation*, was to be handed over to the Germans. He demanded to see the document and his request was granted by Pétain. There, article 8 said:

> The French fleet will assemble in ports to be designated at a later date. There it will be demobilised and disarmed under German or Italian control. The German *Reichsregierung* solemnly avows to the French Government that it does not intend to use these naval units for combat operations, except for such ships as are necessary for the protection of the coast and for mine sweeping.

The question now was: what would the British do? Would they trust Hitler? Reynaud confronted Darlan with the fleet clause: 'Are you satisfied with it?' 'The armistice commission will have that changed', Darlan answered. 'Do you really believe that?' 'In any case, the fleet will receive the order to sink itself before it falls into enemy hands', the Admiral assured him.

All Reynaud could do was to accept this. However, he hastened to inform Churchill about this brief exchange, in order to set his mind at ease. For

Reynaud, a confrontation between the British and the French fleet would have been a political catastrophe that he would not have wanted to be made responsible for later on. This was an unnecessary worry, because a short while later Pétain had him arrested at Riom under the threadbare accusation that he had driven France into the war. He was tried by special court (together with Daladier, Léon Blum, and Mandel) and received a life sentence. Later on he was handed over to the Germans as a war criminal.

Admiral Darlan's order to all French naval units in all French and overseas ports was actually issued:

> The terms of the armistice agreement will be sent to you in clear under separate cover. I am taking the opportunity of one of the final coded signals to give you my opinion on them:
> 1. Demobilised French ships must remain French and under French flag, manned by skeleton crews and stationed in French home or overseas ports.
> 2. Secret preparations for self-destruction must be made, so that neither the enemy nor any foreigner may take a ship by force in order to employ it.
> 3. If the armistice commission reaches a different decision than the one expressed in paragraph 1., ships of war will sail for the United States or sink themselves without awaiting further orders, if this is the only way to escape the enemy.
> 4. Ships that seek safety abroad shall not be employed against Germany or Italy without an order by the Commander of the Naval Forces.
> Darlan (12.45, 24.6.40)

Churchill had not let himself be reassured by Reynaud. Darlan's order proved that he was right, because the foreigners referred to in paragraph 2 could only be the British. The British Prime Minister did not trust the new French Government one bit, even calling it a government of Quislings. For him it was clear that despite all of the solemn promises, the French fleet had fallen into German hands undamaged and fully armed. The consequences were unimaginable.

While these events were taking place, a marked francophobia was spreading throughout the British Isles, particularly as it now also became known that Pétain had returned the 400 captured German pilots to the *Reich*, well aware that they could be employed against England immediately. On 25 June, George Bernard Shaw wrote to Churchill: 'Why not declare war on France, seize its fleet (which will gladly strike its flag to us), before Hitler regains his breath? In the present situation, this is probably the most logical thing to do.'

At this time, the British Admiralty had already issued the order to its fleet in the Mediterranean to seize the new, modern French battleships *Richelieu* and

Jean Bart if they were to leave Dakar or Casablanca. One of Churchill's secretaries, John Colville, noted on 26 June: 'If things do not develop in a satisfactory manner, it will end with our seizing as much of the French fleet as we can lay our hands on.' Two days later there followed an entry from which can be seen how much the situation had escalated: 'Winston is toying with the idea of an act of force against French ships in African ports.'

'Operation Catapult' was beginning to take shape.

X
Churchill Strikes
All that matters is survival

'Operation Catapult' was the code name for the British attempt to seize all the units of the French fleet within reach and to immobilise them. Ships that would not let themselves be disarmed and taken into British custody were to be sunk. This rigorous action had been prepared in minute detail from the time the British had first begun to suspect the loyalty of the French.

Fortunately, a large number of French ships were already in British ports. Vice Admiral Muselier, who was responsible in London under de Gaulle for the armed forces of the French National Committee, had arranged that many units of the French Navy, as well as merchant ships lying in northern French ports, were taken to Portsmouth and Plymouth on the English south coast before the Germans moved in. Even ships under construction that could already float had been launched and hauled across the Channel, together with the dockyard workers who were to finish building them in England. Two battleships, four *contre-torpilleurs* [light cruisers], several submarines including the very large *Surcouf*, eight destroyers, and about 100 smaller units lay at anchor, mainly in Portsmouth, with some in Plymouth, and continued to proudly fly the French flag even after the armistice.

At 04.45 on 3 July, British marines with fixed bayonets stormed aboard the French ships anchored in the south British ports. In the great cabin of the battleship *Paris*, British Admiral Sir Dunbar Nasmith demanded of the French Admiral, who was only wearing his uniform jacket over his pyjamas, that he place himself under his command. Lieutenant Georges Blond delivered the short, classic reply: 'You cannot ask a French admiral to obey the orders of the King of England. I must obey the orders of my government.' The French were so surprised by the British action, that they offered no resistance and did not try to escape. Only on board the submarine *Surcouf* was there a brief fight in which three British and one Frenchman lost their lives.

The crews of the French ships were taken to the Royal Navy barracks at Devonport. In the officers' mess, the officers received a message from Admiral Sir Dunbar Nasmith: 'His Majesty's Government expresses its regret that it was forced to take the decision to seize your ships. It has done this in order to prevent your vessels from subsequently falling into Germany's hands, which would deploy them against Great Britain. Your government will never be able to accuse you of having tolerated this seizure, because you are here in my power. I hope that many, if not all of you, will be prepared to continue the war against Germany at the side of British Navy, be it on your own ships, or on the ships of the British Navy together with us. All such will receive British pay and be under British command.' The French were given one hour to make up their minds. The answer, however, was immediately forthcoming: the French Navy holds fast to its ranks and will only obey its own superiors.

In the afternoon, the French sailors were permitted to go back on board their ships to collect their belongings. In groups of ten, always under guard by armed British soldiers, they were taken to their quarters. When they arrived, some of them were in for a highly unpleasant surprise: cupboards had been broken open, drawers under the bunks and in desks pulled out and the contents thrown on the floor. Anything of value had disappeared. Protests proved to be useless.

After they had gathered their remaining belongings, mostly clothing, and come back on land, the French were loaded onto trains without further ado. Their destination was Aintree, the race track near Liverpool, where they arrived towards noon the following day. It was a cold, wet day and not at all summery. The race track lay in an industrial suburb and was surrounded by factories, gas tanks and long rows of ugly little brick buildings that were like peas in a pod and covered with a layer of grey dirt. The Grand National course was covered with the wrecks of old cars, obstructions against enemy paratroops, on the green there were hundreds of tents in which troops for the Norway expedition who only months before had been faithful brothers-in-arms, had lived.

One of the prisoners recounted later: 'The officers were permitted to move into the washrooms under the stadium. The rooms were absolutely bare. It was only in the evening, that the officers were told that there were sacks of straw at a certain place, which they could help themselves to. And so one could see the commanders of ships, who only days before had been received aboard British ships with full honours, lugging their own sacks of straw and trying to find sleep on the floor of the washrooms of an English hippodrome.'

About 10,000 members of the French Navy had been quartered in various camps which hardly differed one from the other in their primitive conditions. Only the admirals had received slightly better quarters in Oxford. The food was terrible, the treatment worse than that accorded prisoners of war.

The British were disappointed that the French had not joined the Royal Navy in its fight against Germany and let them feel this at every opportunity. In August, an announcement by the British camp commander, which threw a glaring light on the situation in the camps, was posted on the outer gateway of the camp at Arrowe Park on the Wirral peninsula in Liverpool. In it the prisoners were threatened with fines and incarceration for a long list of offences: attempt to escape, damage to camp property, not using the toilets, theft of camp supplies, refusal to obey orders, threatening or attacking a British soldier, theft of vegetables on the stalk, butchering of household pets, seduction of women or girls, fist-fighting with the civilian population.

When the imprisoned French admirals complained that their officers and men were not receiving any pay, they were told that according to the agreement between countries at war, only enemy officers that had been captured were entitled to pay. The French were merely being detained. Furthermore it was said that His Majesty's Government and the British Admiralty had taken into consideration, that they were under no obligation towards people who refused to continue the fight for Democracy at the side of Great Britain.

In a speech he gave on 20 August, Winston Churchill said: 'A puppet government has been installed in Vichy, which can at any time be coerced into becoming our enemy... The Czechs, the Poles, the Norwegians, the Dutch, and the Belgians are still fighting. Only France has humbled herself, and that is not the fault of this great and noble nation but of those whom are called "the men of Vichy".'

General Spears, formerly Churchill's liaison officer to Paul Reynaud and now to General de Gaulle, gave a talk to French naval officers in the camp at Aintree. 'The Vichy Government', he began and was immediately interrupted by several voices: 'The French Government!' 'Long live Marshal Pétain!' A tumult arose and several Frenchmen were arrested.

The *Daily Express* even went one step further: 'These Frenchmen are dangerous. They are part of a fifth column.' The author suggested treating them like the Irish political prisoners who were being held in the hulks of demobilised ships on the English south coast. This suggestion quickly made the rounds in the camps and contributed to increased opposition to all attempts at courtship and invitations to the French to betray their flag, which is at least how they chose to define the issue.

Pressure was not only being put on by the British. With the support of the British Government, General de Gaulle was organising the movement *France libre* ['A free France'] in London. His Admiral Muselier moved heaven and earth to have the interned Navy join de Gaulle's ranks. He sent recruiters, officers who had 'deserted' to de Gaulle, and visited the camps himself, but to very little avail. The Gaullists claimed: 'If you return to France, you will perish of hunger and have to learn humility'. The sailors answered: 'One cannot abandon one's country just because it is in a sorry state.' To them, the name of Marshal Pétain appeared to be a sufficient guarantee of national honour.

The opposing lines became so rigid that in November the British gave in to Admiral Darlan's urgings and let the sailors loyal to the government return to France. They were taken through the Strait of Gibraltar to Toulon on French ships and welcomed there as heroes.

The seizure of the French naval units in British ports on 3 July had, however, been only a partial operation. 'Operation Catapult', the more difficult and tragic part of the operation yet faced the British and the French, because the main force of the French Navy was in the Mediterranean and in North Africa. In Alexandria in Egypt lay Force X under Admiral René Godefroy: one battleship, four cruisers and a number of smaller units. Admiral Godefroy was a close friend of Admiral Cunningham, who commanded the British naval forces there. When Admiral Darlan ordered Force X to sail to Tunis, Admiral Godefroy ignored the order, put himself under Cunningham's command and fought with him against the Italians. Force X remained in Alexandria until the Allies captured North Africa.

Dangerous for the British was the *Force de Raid* [Attack Force] under Admiral Marcel Gensoul, which was stationed in the naval base of Mers-el-Kebir at Oran. It included the two modern battle cruisers *Strasbourg* and *Dunkerque* as well as the older battleships *Provence*, *Bretagne* and *Commandante Teste*. The two former ships were causing concern in the Admiralty: in German hands they would endanger the supply routes to the island kingdom even more than *Gneisenau* and *Scharnhorst*. And if they were to be deployed in an invasion of the British Isles, they could destroy British hopes for survival.

The new battleships *Jean Bart* and *Richelieu* appeared to be no less dangerous. *Jean Bart* had just been brought from Saint Nazaire to Casablanca where she was to receive her armament. *Richelieu* lay in Dakar and was almost completed: she could sail under her own power and her 15-inch guns were ready to fire. Not counting a few units in more remote ports, there then remained the French naval units in Toulon which were out of British reach because there an intervention by the large Italian Navy had to be reckoned with.

The decision to act had not been easy for the British War Cabinet. Their navy meant almost as much to the French as did the Royal Navy to the British and holding a knife to the throat of their ally went against the Navy's grain. Up to the end, it was hoped that the French would see reason and take their fleet out of reach of the Germans. 8 July however, the supposed date for the invasion, was coming ever closer without anything happening. The vision of French ships of war under German command appearing off the English coast had become intolerable.

The scene of the drama was to be the western Mediterranean. In Gibraltar lay the British Force H: the battle cruiser *Hood*, at 42,000 tonnes Britain's largest warship, the battleships *Resolution* and *Valiant*, the aircraft carrier *Ark Royal*, and eleven destroyers. Its commander was 58-year-old Vice Admiral Sir James Somerville.

At 02.25 on 1 July, Somerville received the order: 'be prepared for "Catapult" July 3.' The Admiral was anything but pleased about the assignment to sink naval units of an ally, and not only for humane and sailorly reasons. Somerville also had political reservations, which he did not conceal from the Admiralty in London. He signalled back that such an attack would 'turn every Frenchman against Great Britain and convert a beaten ally into an active enemy.' Laconically the Admiralty answered: 'Firm intention of His Majesty's Government that if the French will not accept any of your proposals they are to be destroyed.'

At 01.08 on 2 July a long signal was received aboard *Hood*. It contained the message with the alternatives proposed by His Majesty's Government, which Somerville was personally to convey to the French Admiral. The naval force stationed in Mers-el-Kebir was to:

a. join the British fleet and fight against Germany and Italy at Great Britain's side, or

b. sail to a British port with reduced crews under British control, after which the crews would be repatriated at the earliest possible time, or

c. (in case he, the admiral, believed he had to respect the armistice) sail to a French port in the West Indies, Martinique for example, where he could be demobilised or put under the protection of the United States.

Furthermore the French were to be told: 'If you refuse these fair offers, I must, with profound regret, require you to sink your ships within six hours. Finally, failing the above, I have the orders of His Majesty's Government to use whatever force may be necessary to prevent your ships from falling into German or Italian hands.'

With *Hood* in the lead, Force H left Gibraltar that very same 2 July and set course for Oran. Churchill had a signal sent to Somerville: 'You are charged with one of the most disagreeable and difficult tasks that a British Admiral has ever been faced with, but we have complete confidence in you and rely on you to carry it out relentlessly.'

On the morning of 3 July, Vice Admiral Somerville sent destroyer *Foxhound* ahead. On board was Captain Cedric Holland with the ultimatum to Admiral Gensoul. 50-year-old Holland had been Naval Attaché at the British Embassy in Paris before he had taken over command of *Ark Royal*. He spoke good French, knew his way about in the French Navy, and had already been introduced to Admiral Gensoul (he was later to call him a rigid old log). He felt the turn things had taken even more severely than Somerville. He was later to break down under the role he now had to play. And leaving aside all the other objections, it was clear to him from the beginning that his mission was not going to succeed.

While his motor launch was under way to the French ships, they were moored stern first to the mole at some distance from each other, *Foxhound* signalled his arrival to the French. The last sentence of the message read: 'There is a British fleet lying off Oran and will welcome you.' Whatever *Foxhound*'s Captain may have meant by that, the French took it for a provocation and were insulted.

Holland was made to feel this at once. Gensoul was of the opinion, and quite rightly, that Somerville should have come himself, instead of sending a subordinate. He sent his Flag Lieutenant Dufay, an old acquaintance of Holland's, off in a boat to meet the Briton. Holland, in accordance with his orders, insisted on delivering the message in person. Gensoul thereupon ordered *Foxhound* to stand off at once. Meanwhile Holland stayed in the harbour in his launch. After several fruitless attempts, at 16.00 he finally succeeded in coming aboard Gensoul's flagship *Dunkerque* and speaking with Gensoul. The meeting lasted for one and a half hours. In the beginning, Gensoul was a block of ice, but became more amenable when he saw the difficulties Holland was labouring under. Despite this, the negotiations did not lead to any result. Having been informed by Gensoul, Darlan had sent off a relieving force that was to take the English in the rear if they dared to use force. His signal, however, had been intercepted by the British and decoded in London, whereupon the Admiralty urged Somerville to act quickly.

17.15. While Holland was still with Gensoul, Somerville sent the French Admiral a signal: if one of the British alternatives was not accepted by the French within fifteen minutes, he would sink Gensoul's ships.

Holland was immediately disembarked from the French flagship with compliments. While he was still descending the jack-ladder, he could hear the French officers urging their men to battle stations. They were having problems, because the crews were not willing to understand what this was supposed to be all about. When Holland said goodbye to Dufay, both men had tears in their eyes.

17.45. Holland had approached to within a few miles of the waiting *Foxhound*, when Somerville gave the order to open fire. From a distance of ten miles the first salvo from the 15-inch guns rained down upon the French force lying as if on a plate. One of the first heavy shells hit *Dunkerque*, shattered a turret, destroyed one of the main generators, and knocked out the ship's hydraulic system. The crew of the shattered turret were literally squashed to death by the armour plating.

Bretagne took several hits and burst into flames immediately. Heavy smoke rose upwards. Suddenly she took on a list and sank with 1,000 men on board.

Her sister ship *Provence* was heavily damaged and had to be run aground by her captain. The destroyer *Mogador* had her bow blown off. But *Strasbourg*, one of the two main targets, remained undamaged.

The French shot back, but did not achieve any results, because the British ships were sailing westwards and had disappeared behind a promontory after only a few minutes. At 18.04 Somerville therefore ordered cease fire. There had only been two wounded on *Hood*.

In the harbour, *Strasbourg* cast off. Skilfully manoeuvring between the wrecks and under cover of the clouds of black smoke that were spreading over the surface of the water, the battle cruiser gained the open sea accompanied by five destroyers. Under full steam, she passed the mine barrier that *Ark Royal's* aircraft had laid and soon disappeared into the twilight. The British only noticed the break-out half an hour later. Swordfish torpedo planes, which were immediately launched from *Ark Royal*, soon returned without having detected *Strasbourg* in the gathering darkness. *Strasbourg* reached Toulon undamaged, where soon other units that had escaped from the British were to arrive from Oran and Algiers.

Somerville, who wanted to make sure that *Dunkerque* at least was given the coup de grâce, sent his torpedo planes against the heavily damaged and defenceless ship. This unnecessary attack only led to further loss of life, because the torpedoes hit a trawler loaded with depth charges which was in the process of rescuing the remainder of *Dunkerque's* crew. Dozens of sailors died in the gigantic explosion. In total, 1,200 officers and men were killed at Mers-el-Kebir, 210 on *Dunkerque* alone.

Full of bitterness, the survivors sent mementoes from many a former joint operation back to their 'comrades' in *Hood*. The French Government immediately broke off all relations with Great Britain. According to the war diary of German Naval Group West, the French Admiralty informed the British government on 4 July, that it would fire without warning on any British ship that approached closer than twenty nautical miles from the French coast or the coast of a French colony. All French naval forces had been ordered to treat the British as hostile. A closer tie to Nazi Germany lay in the air. Deputy Prime Minister Pierre Laval and Admiral Darlan spoke out in favour of a surprise attack on the British Mediterranean fleet. They were not able to have this accepted, much to the relief of the British, because that was exactly what the action at Oran had been designed to prevent. If Darlan had had his way, the risks of 'Operation Sea Lion' would have been reduced considerably. The British would have had to send part of their Home Fleet to Gibraltar.

At the time, it should have been easy for the *Kriegsmarine* to bring Darlan over to their side. Had not Churchill said of him, 'Darlan is one of those good

Frenchmen who hate England', after he had learned that Darlan's great-grand-father had fought against the British at Trafalgar? However, *Großadmiral* Raeder made no efforts in this direction. Nor did Hitler use the opportunity to gain political advantage from the affair. In Germany, they were content to follow events with undisguised glee. Goebbels joyfully made the most of 'Britain's criminal action': on many posters that were also distributed in France, Churchill was portrayed as a cigar-smoking monster looking down on the burning French fleet and the graves of French sailors. N'*oubliez pas* Oran ['Do not forget Oran'] one of the posters said, which showed a drowning French sailor holding up the *Tricolore*.

The effects did not linger long with the French. At least in Paris, the poster quickly disappeared from walls. And with the French who had arrived in England, hatred of the English also soon died away. However, in most Frenchmen, Mers-el-Kebir left a deep feeling of bitterness. Anglo-French relations were affected for a long time.

For the leading actors in the drama there were no medals or promotions, their careers were in ruins. Gensoul disappeared from the stage, neither Vichy nor postwar France wanted to have anything to do with him. Darlan perished from the bullets of a French royalist in December 1942, an assassination that did not appear to have any serious motive. Captain Holland had to give up command of *Ark Royal* soon after Mers-el-Kebir and died shortly after the war. And Vice Admiral Sir James Somerville was never again able to step out from under the cloud cast by this act of desperation that had been forced upon him.

The ships fared no better than their masters: *Hood* was sunk by *Bismarck* in 1941, and *Ark Royal* in the western Mediterranean by U-boat U.81 in November of the same year. *Strasbourg* was scuttled by her crew in Toulon harbour together with the other ships lying there, when German troops occupied southern France in November 1942.

The bitter irony of the Mers-el-Kebir affair lay in the fact that the coup-de-main was militarily completely unnecessary. Churchill should have been able to come to this conclusion at the time, if only British Intelligence had drawn the correct conclusions from the manpower strength of the *Kriegsmarine*. It would then have become quite apparent, that the German war leadership could not have made use of the French Navy at all. It lacked the trained personnel. On the other hand, Darlan would never have permitted any of his ships sailing under the German flag. This was proved two years later in Toulon by the carrying out of his earlier order to scuttle themselves.

Nevertheless, Churchill had no reasons to regret his brutal step: '(Mers-el-Kebir)... demonstrated that the British War Cabinet fears nought and will not baulk at anything.' This was meant for the British first of all. After Norway and

Dunkirk, they desperately need a victory to fortify their fighting morale. When Churchill reported in Parliament on 4 July that three French battleships had been put out of action, 'everybody jumped up from their benches, shouted, cheered, waved papers and handkerchiefs like mad'.

No less important for Churchill was the reaction in America. Up to then, the United States and its President had only half-heartedly reacted to his appeals for help, because many Americans, first and foremost among them Joseph P. Kennedy, Roosevelt's ambassador to the Court of St James, had not believed that the British could hope to survive this conflict successfully, nor that they really wanted to. Many months later Harry Hopkins, Roosevelt's intimate, disclosed that it was above all the sinking of the French ships that had decided the Americans to put their money on Churchill and not on Hitler.

The effusiveness with which the British greeted Churchill's speech also pointed to something else: Mers-el-Kebir was a very effective safety valve for the fear of invasion becoming more rampant in England. The spectre of an Armada now appeared to have been laid. With some Britons this led to premature optimism, as the American Military Attaché in London, Brigadier Robert Lee, observed: 'Now that the French fleet has been dealt with, the British are no longer talking about "beleaguered Great Britain", but are professing pity for Hitler on the "beleaguered Continent".' But even Lee had to admit on 15 July: 'I believe Hitler will attack this island with all he has at any moment now.'

XI

Ships, Ferries, Barges
The Armada of the *Kriegsmarine*

After Hitler had given the green light for the preparation of landing operations in his Directive No. 16, and the British Government had not reacted to his 'peace offer' of 19 July, the staffs at the OKH and the *Kriegsmarine* concentrated on what at the time was a gigantic undertaking: how to bring as big a force as possible over the Channel as securely as possible in the shortest possible time and land it on the open coast as well as in the ports.

The OKH had assigned the landing operations to Army Group A under Field Marshal von Rundstedt. 9th and 16th Army were to carry out the assault in three waves. In the first wave, six divisions were to be taken across the Channel in two groups, the remaining seven divisions were to follow in two further waves. This meant the *Kriegsmarine* had to find transport space for a total of 260,400 men, 61,983 horses, 34,200 vehicles including panzers, artillery, and 52 light flak batteries belonging to the *Luftwaffe*.

The officers in the Naval Transport Department were aghast. They had still been reckoning with the much smaller contingent from the *Kriegsmarine* 'Study Red'. The first wave of 90,100 men alone, would have embarrassed them, but the following waves of 170,000 men with all their equipment, only provoked peals of derisive laughter in many a naval office. Heavy exclamation marks, question marks and snide comments adorn the papers containing the requirements of the *Heer* and preserve the conflict between *Heer* and *Kriegsmarine* for posterity. For example: 'For 170,000 men we would need 400 ships of 5,000 tonnes each, that comes to 2,000,000 tonnes of shipping space!' In July, the whole German high seas fleet had only 1,200,000 BRT of cargo ships at its disposal. In addition there were passenger ships totalling 285,000 BRT. Even if one applied the broadest possible definition, hardly more than 100 steamers with about 700,000 BRT could be scraped together, and that included trawlers and train ferries. Most of the freighters were employed in transporting coal and could not be dispensed with.

The calculations were still based on the assumption that landings would only occur in ports. In the meantime however, the *Heer* had begun to consider landings on the open coast and this had been discussed in great detail between Halder and Schniewind. In a study dated 6 July, the *Kriegsmarine* leadership had already taken a different route and brought the transportation problem closer to solution. Besides the cargo capacity of the German high seas fleet, it was now also taking the inland fleet in Germany and the occupied countries into consideration. The results were promising: The ship capacity in Holland, Belgium and France of 1,500 BRT and below suitable for transport on the high seas, was sufficient for shipping 40,000 men and 1,300 vehicles.

Every ship, even the smallest boat, in the occupied territories was listed giving the customary data. The lists were sent to Naval Command. There the men behind the desks noticed that information was missing on the Dutch river gunboat *Barga*, whereupon they sent an urgent query to the Ship Department asking about the condition and state of readiness of the vessel.

A week passed and nothing happened. When pressed, the Ship Department had to admit that neither in Berlin nor at the naval staffs in Holland, were there specialists who could undertake such an investigation. Naval Command insisted on knowing everything there was to know about every ship, and moved heaven and earth to trace the gunboat. In early September a specialist was finally found for this important assignment, Naval *Oberingenieur* Bake at the Shipyard Office for Holland and Belgium. On 6 September Bake went to the *Barga*'s berth in Emmerich on the Rhine. His report should have satisfied Naval Command: 'Interior and bridge completely demolished, engine not running and needs a complete overhaul. An inspection of bottom did not take place. It must be assumed that screw and rudder are damaged, because ship lay on the beach. Repair of this ship not worthwhile with regard to extraordinarily poor condition and age (date of construction 1876). Still serviceable, 12cm gun on board manufactured by Krupp, Model 1899.'

From the German merchant marine, about 1,300 ships, fishing vessels, motor cutters, tugboats, motor sailing boats, ocean-going barges, and ferries could be gathered, increased by about 600 ships that were already in the employ of the *Kriegsmarine*. With this ship capacity, about 200,000 men and 3,000 vehicles could be transported. On the Rhine, Dutch and German passenger ships for 4,000 men, and 1,500 barges for the transport of a further 120,000 men and 4,500 vehicles, were to be requisitioned. In total this came to a capacity for 300,000 men and 8,500 vehicles.

As impressive as this total might sound it also meant, however, that only three divisions could take their vehicles with them. The reason for this discrepancy lay in the too weak loading gear and the too small hatches of most of the ships, which were completely unsuitable for tanks and artillery, for example, and which could not be suitably modified. As a solution to the problem, the authors of the study, probably Schniewind and Fricke, recommended using barges and lighters with shallow draught, of which there was a sufficient number available. On the open coast, they could be run close to shore and be easily unloaded without elaborate preparations, by means of on-board collapsible bridges.

With this, Naval Command had no further problems in bringing the requirements of the *Heer* and the potential of the *Kriegsmarine* under the same umbrella. Since the first wave of 90,000 men was to be landed mainly on the open coast, the *Kriegsmarine* could manage with 41 ships of 5,000 BRT each, the rest of this fleet being formed by 805 barges of between 130 and 200 tonnes, 241 tugboats and 482 motorboats. For the next wave of 170,000 men, a requirement for 100 ocean-going ships with a total of 440,000 BRT, 760 barges, 187 tugs, and 574 motorboats was estimated. The next job facing the *Kriegsmarine* was therefore to find 2,000 barges, 500 tugs, and 141 ocean-going ships, to have them modified, and then to bring them to the ports on the Channel and the North Sea occupied during the campaign in the West.

As was only to be expected, free cargo capacity was not readily to hand. The German inland fleet was fully occupied with the transportation of bulk cargo (ore, coal, grain and other bulk goods). The armaments industry, running at top capacity, also contributed to the lack of free capacity, and every last barge was fully employed. On the Oder River, there were already insufficient tugs available. An intervention of this magnitude would be bound to lead to bottle-necks in the supply of industry and the population. If barge capacity were reduced, the food supply to the large cities would also have to be reduced. Should the transport space be required beyond the last ten days of September, the supply of fertiliser would become doubtful and the 1941 harvest endangered. A cautious estimate by the *Kriegsmarine* showed that the withdrawal of only 700 to 800 barges for 'Operation Sea Lion' would reduce the performance of the inland fleet by 30 per cent, and in some sectors bring it to a complete halt.

The Dutch, Belgian and French inland fleets could not help out. Many of the Dutch and Belgian inland navigators had taken their vessels across to England or had lost them during the fighting. The rest were already earmarked for 'Sea Lion'. The French inland fleet was still stuck in the rivers and canals, because bridges and sluices had been blown up and the waterways were impassable. The barges and tugs in unoccupied France were out of reach for the Germans.

For the high seas fleet the picture was somewhat brighter. For traffic to Norway, Denmark and the fringe states, foreign shipping space and the railways could be used. There was however the danger that the important ore and coal imports from Sweden would pile up in Baltic ports, because they could not be moved further inland.

Großadmiral Raeder did not want to accept sole responsibility for these consequences and therefore stated several times at *Führer* Conferences, how heavy a burden 'Operation Sea Lion' would be for German industry. As always,

Hitler listened to him attentively and finally decreed, on 25 July, that all work and measures for the operation were to be given top priority, even ahead of armaments orders in priority category 1.

For Raeder this order was very important, because all of the ships and barges for the transportation of troops had first to be modified. This posed a huge problem and required that all sea and inland shipyards had to be put at the exclusive disposal of the Kriegsmarine for at least four weeks. All other work had to be postponed. This even applied to the urgent construction of U-boats. During 1940, there should actually have been a delivery of 46 new U-boats, but because of the work for 'Operation Sea Lion', the Deutsche Werft in Hamburg was only able to build two instead of three per month, the Howaldtswerke in Hamburg only delivered a boat every six weeks, instead of once a month. The same applied to the Danziger Werft and the Deschimag. At the Kriegsmarinewerft in Wilhelmshafen, completion of battleship Tirpitz had to be delayed by three weeks, not to mention destroyers and other types of ships.

The modifications required a substantial effort in time and material. Ships hulls and barge bottoms had to be strengthened for loading tanks and artillery, unloading ramps installed and new towing gear affixed. Some of the barges had aircraft engines mounted for propulsion and huge portal ramps for the loading of tanks and guns, in addition the bows were cut off and made swingable. 80 tugs had equipment for lowering stormboats installed, two each on each side. The holds of freighters were given tweendecks and traverses for housing troops and horses. In the train ferries, the rails mounted in the holds had to be covered by concrete or planks.

It was not only a matter of transportation but also about protecting the men from rifle and machine-gun fire during the crossing and while disembarking. Therefore the sides were strengthened with concrete and iron bars; bridges, helmsmen's positions and unloading ramps were fortified, as far as this was at all possible. On deck, protective shields of iron plates were installed, behind which the crews and soldiers could take cover. Finally, all of the ships and tugs were prepared for the installation of guns and machine-guns on deck.

So much iron on board was bound to have a drastic effect on the compass needles, but since there was no time left to compensate for this, the use of cement and wood was more and more resorted to as a means of protection. Wherever the ships had no equipment for protection against mines it had to be added. Iron barges had to be de-magnetised because of the danger from mines. This could only be done at very few specially equipped installations so that a large number of barges had to forego this form of protection.

In certain shipyards, fifteen smaller ships of 650 to 1,200 BRT were converted into hospital ships with 50 to 80 beds and equipped with mine protection. Nothing was forgotten, from bed pans to woollen blankets, life-saving equipment and additional cooking facilities.

The procurement of material was difficult, but went off without a hitch. 30,000 tonnes of iron girders and plates, 40,000m³ of wooden planks and boards, 75,000m³ of concrete were required. In order to bring such quantities to the shipyards, the *Organisation Todt* [German state labour organisation run by Mr Todt] had to be involved for their transportation. As many as 4,000 new towlines, clamps, stays, hooks, thousands of other bits and pieces and many square metres of sailcloth, had to be procured. For the barges, the *Reichsbahn* provided more than 1,000 covers normally used for open freight cars. Never again during the Second World War were such efforts made for a single operation.

The collection of transport space and the movement of the ships and barges made a slow start. That had been expected. From the beginning, the *Kriegsmarine* reckoned that a four-week period for modification would not be sufficient. There was much preparatory work to be done, the procurement of material, the provision of workers and housing, for example. The number of skilled workers required alone came to 6,500. Bringing the vessels to the shipyards and then moving them to their ports of departure would take much time. The *Kriegsmarine* had to calculate from eight to nine weeks from the day an order was placed to the day a completed vessel would reach Ostend or Calais.

Because of this, 15 August as D-Day for 'Operation Sea Lion' became an illusion. On 23 August, the *Kriegsmarine* reported 1,596 barges in the process of conversion in various dockyards, of which 802 were ready to be towed out. 100 barges were scheduled for completion each day. But it was to take until 19 September before the *Kriegsmarine* was to have completed its task. On that day, there were 168 troopships, 1,975 barges, 100 coastal motorboats, 420 tugs and 1,600 other motor vessels available.

But in what sort of condition were the embarkation ports on the Channel coast that had been heavily damaged during the battles? Could the landing fleet be assembled there at all, loaded and set in motion across the Channel? The naval authorities in the occupied territories had not been idle in the interim, as a telex from Naval Command West to Naval Command proves: '27.7. Top secret. Lieutenant Commander Fischer signalling: pass on immediately. Boulogne, Calais, Gravelines, Dunkirk investigated. Boulogne assumed to be fully operational on time. Calais no serious damage. Condition Dunkirk makes availability of two-fifths to three-fifths quays probable. Installation of gates, swing gates, on both sluices initiated.... Success doubtful however. Gravelines usable for smaller vessels. Minister Todt desires support of work teams, including electricians, tool-makers, carpenters. Immediate provision of two engineer companies and a construction battalion for Dunkirk, one engineer company and one construction battalion for Boulogne, total of two companies and one construction battalion deployed in Boulogne, two engineer companies and one construction battalion secured for Ostend, Nieuport and Zeebrugge. For supervision of works *Bauräte* [senior construction officials] from Port Construction Authority with staff required... '

Behind this brief report lie many weeks of effort, during which the ports of Dunkirk, Calais, Boulogne, Le Tréport, Dieppe, Saint-Valerie-en-Caux, Fécamp, Le Havre, Trouville and Cherbourg had been put back into service. Everywhere quays and sluices had been destroyed, sunken ships blocked the exits, quays, and entrances to the canals and rivers leading into the interior. Besides the military engineers, the army of workers of *Organisation Todt* were extensively made use of. There were no heavy cranes for lifting and disposing of wrecks in any of the ports. These had to be brought in from the *Reich*. On the way, these monsters had to be dismantled and later reassembled in record time, because they did not fit under the many railway bridges. Some locks which connected the ports to the inland river and canal system had to be completely rebuilt, several new sluice gates had to be installed and others needed extensive repairs.

The works advanced rapidly and in August the first ports were ready to take in parts of the landing fleet. Only the condition of the inland canals was still so bad, that the work of clearing was to go on there until September and even thereafter. Laboriously, the debris of many blown-up bridges had to be cleared from the canal beds, dozens of locks repaired and temporary bridges jacked up, so that ships could be brought to the coast via the Rhine, the Schelde, and the French and Belgian canals. The Marne–Rhine–Canal had to remain closed for the duration – estimated at one to two years – the canals Epernay–Paris–Le Havre, however, were soon navigable, as was the Belgian canal system, which connects the Schelde with Zeebrugge, Ostend and Calais.

In August however, the canals were not yet to play any important role. Barges and ships that had been made ready in German shipyards were taken by sea to the ports of embarkation in convoys under destroyer escort. This led to a problem that had been easy to anticipate and which had therefore already been addressed in July: lack of personnel.

When deployed as landing boats, the barges required crews and those of the tugs, ships and motorboats needed to be reinforced. In total the *Kriegsmarine* was calculating on a requirement of 20,000 petty officers and men. However, the manpower reserves of the *Reich* were still far from exhausted. The *Kriegsmarine* was to supply 4,000 men, *Heer* and *Luftwaffe* were to transfer 3,000 soldiers who had been seamen in civilian life to the *Kriegsmarine*. By means of a new draft on the Naval Reserves, another 9,500 men could be called up. Finding the missing 3,000 to 4,000 was left up to the draft boards. And everything worked like a charm.

During these weeks, the *Heer* was also in the process of making a gigantic nautical contribution to the preparations for the landing. It all started with the fact that the army commanders made their liaison officers with the *Kriegsmarine* enquire time and again, when which ship would be available for which unit. Time and again they were put off, because at this juncture (the end of July), the ships had not yet even been converted. When General Halder himself had not been able to obtain any commitment from the *Kriegsmarine*, Field Marshal von Brauchitsch lost his patience. He ordered General of Engineers Jacob and his troops to provide for means of sea transport independently of the *Kriegsmarine*.

It was probably the *Kriegsmarine* itself which had inspired him with the courage to take this step. On 9 July, Rear Admiral Fricke had written: '(The crossing of the Channel)... is similar to the crossing of a river, in which, because of the width and the peculiarities of the waters to be crossed, the *Kriegsmarine* as the branch of the services specifically trained for this sort of thing, is to be employed.' Halder enthusiastically seized upon this cue, even said thank you, which happened seldom enough, and answered: 'The opinion that the planned operation is only the crossing of a river on a grand scale and that the preparations are to be made accordingly, is in full agreement with the view held by the OKH!'

General Jacob did the obvious. He assigned Engineer Battalion 47 of VII Army Corps (its home garrison was Bavaria!) in Bray-sur-Somme as 'OKH experimental battalion for the construction of seaworthy ferries out of auxiliary equipment, local supply and bridging equipment'. The battalion was moved to new quarters in Cateret on the western side of the Cotentin Peninsula opposite Jersey.

The Engineers did not waste any time. They swarmed far inland in the search for buoyant material and 'auxiliary equipment'. What they found would have made any seaman break out in a cold sweat. In various French aircraft factories they found pontoons for seaplanes and fuel tanks that were designed for installation in aircraft. In a French Engineer supply dump they found canvas sacks filled with kapok, which the French used as 'assault foot bridges for riflemen' when crossing rivers, probable the most appropriate discovery they made. The German Engineers also requisitioned all petrol containers and wine barrels wherever they found any.

With these 'floats', which soon began to pile up in the little harbour in Cateret, they built rafts. Barrels, containers, pontoons or kapok bags were tied in rows underneath beams with ropes and covered with planking. On the first trial tow between Cateret and Saint Helier in Jersey, however, it became apparent that the whole thing was far too improvised. Some of the wine barrels tore loose and drifted away, the kapok bags proved to be not quite water-tight and became saturated, so that these rafts had trouble reaching the harbour before they were pushed under by their loads. Attempts to provide the rafts with their own power by means of outboard motors also failed, because the motors drowned in even the lightest swell.

When they then turned to putting the pontoons normally used for crossing rivers together to make rafts, the results were also not very encouraging. These were constructed with iron beams with simple bolt mechanisms, which then came apart in the waves and could only be secured by wire in a makeshift fashion. The open pontoons filled with water in even a light sea and sank, nor was covering them with canvas any help. Only after the pontoons were filled with empty containers did the coverings hold. One such 'ferry' tore itself loose in heavy seas and was hurled against the cliffs of the steep coast. The heavy iron beams broke like matchsticks, the pontoons were crushed like cardboard boxes. Fortunately, the crew had been able to save themselves by swimming.

At the end of August this playing around with 'auxiliary equipment' was discontinued, after the *Kriegsmarine* had repeatedly objected to such suicidal means of transporting troops, which would probably never have been resorted to if it had not itself used the fateful term 'river crossing' and had made a greater effort at keeping the OKH informed about its own efforts. Even so, at OKH someone suddenly recalled a 'floating bridging device' that the Austrian Colonel of Engineers, Hans Herbert, had invented during the First World War. Two ship pontoons, about 20m long and consisting of seven segments and closed at the top, carried a heavy 10m x 10m platform supported on beams on which guns or vehicles could be transported.

By 10 September, twelve of these ferries had been put into service and divided between the ports of Le Havre and Fécamp. However, during trans-shipment so much water had entered through the hatches, that several men with bilge pumps were needed to prevent the ferries from sinking. In one case this was not successful. It sank shortly after entry into Le Havre.

The Engineers, however, refused to give up. Besides the 'Herbert ferry' the 'Siebel ferry' had meanwhile been developed, which promised to be far more useful for the operation, not only because it was larger, but also because it had far more powerful engines.

The Engineers, without knowing it, had been the ones to set the ball rolling. While searching for floats and aircraft tanks, one of the Engineer officers had come across the aircraft designer Fritz Siebel in Albert near Amiens. Siebel, one of Göring's protégés, was in the process of putting the aircraft plant there back into commission. With some astonishment, he listened to the Engineers' project and then began to think about it. Apparently he had a far better understanding of the power of the sea and knew that one could not approach it with aluminium containers such as those for which the Engineers were searching. Siebel designed a pontoon ferry which was larger and stronger than the Herbert ferry. The pontoons were solidly connected by steel beams. In the two stern compartments he put two Ford V8 engines with 75h.p. each and on the stern section of the deck, three aircraft engines with propellers were mounted, each of which produced about 300h.p. The stern motors were for powering the crossing, the aircraft engines were to propel the ferries onto the landing beach with enormously increased power.

Siebel had no difficulty in selling his idea to the Arms Procurement Department at OKH. As early as September, the first Siebel ferries were made available to the Engineers. The power plant proved to be so good, that the Herbert ferries were now also being equipped with aircraft engines on deck and three Ford V8 engines below deck between the pontoons. The Siebel ferries, armed with 8.8 flak and 7.5cm guns as well as light flak, were earmarked for the transportation of heavy army equipment. Since they had a flat bow, as opposed to the Herbert ferries, they were difficult to manoeuvre and somewhat slower. However, they lay more firmly in the water and could even survive Force 6 waves.

In view of the short time-span available for the development and deployment of the means of transport, slightly more than two months, the preparation for 'Operation Sea Lion' is an astonishing piece of organisation. However, a revolutionary development in this context, the 'war crocodile' was left entangled in the thickets of bureaucracy.

Professor Gottfried Feder, one of the *Alte Kämpfer* of the NSDAP [literally 'old fighters', those party members who had been with Hitler before and during the 'beer-hall putsch' in Munich in 1923], an engineer and formerly State Secretary in the *Reich* Economics Ministry, had developed a 'completely new and unknown weapon' back in April for the, to his mind unavoidable, invasion of England: a 27m long, 6m wide and 3.5m high amphibious tank out of reinforced concrete. It was more properly a swimming bunker with two to four pairs of tracks on its underside. When in the water it was propelled by ship's screws, with the first touch on the ground offshore, the power of the engines was to be transferred to the tracks, which would then allow the monster to creep ashore. One 'war crocodile' could carry at least 200 men with their equipment, or take panzers and artillery across the Channel. When landing, the soldiers would be ideally protected by their concrete bunker.

Feder believed that this amphibious tank could be quickly produced in large numbers, because in the building of the *Westwall* about 10,000 reinforced concrete bunkers had been put up within a few months. Experience and material were therefore available and dirt cheap, when compared to wood or steel. The 'crocodiles' just had to enclose a large enough space and buoyancy would occur all by itself.

Feder initially sent his plans to the OKH, and on 21 May also to Naval Command, where many different departments occupied themselves intensively with the project. Opinions were divided, but it appeared that the proponents would gain the upper hand, because Admiral Schniewind also evaluated the invention favourably. The Ship Department even stated that the concrete tank could become 'of most valuable importance'. Only the Naval Department expressed doubts about the seaworthiness of such a monster. Would the concrete construction be able to withstand the vibrations of the motors? How would a 100m² concrete wall act as a ship's flank in heavy seas or a strong current? Time-consuming and elaborate trials would have been required in order to answer these technical questions. The 'crocodile' was therefore never built.

But even without the concrete tank, the *Kriegsmarine* and the *Heer* were in the process of collecting an imposing fleet, which should certainly be capable of bringing the troops and weapons necessary for a landing to the other side of the Channel.

XII
Kriegsmarine and Heer at Odds
Where do we land?

The gigantic effort that the *Heer* and the *Kriegsmarine* had been making since 16 July in order to prepare the crossing of the invasion force, could not disguise the fact that no agreement had been reached on the most decisive question of all: where to land.

The *Kriegsmarine* had had to give up its concept of a limited landing in the area west of the Isle of Wight, because the 260,000 men with their equipment and supplies, which the *Heer* had stipulated, would not have found enough room on this relatively narrow sector. The *Heer* too had had to take some things back: there was no longer any talk about a landing north of the Thames estuary. Halder had accepted Schniewind's proposal to land south of the Thames, between Ramsgate and Yarmouth on the Isle of Wight. From there on, however, opinions were sharply divided. Halder insisted on landings along the whole coast and in addition, even wanted Sixth Army put ashore in Lyme Bay to the west of the Isle of Wight. A river crossing was a river crossing in the eyes of the General Staff. In the final analysis, Halder was only concerned with establishing as many bridgeheads as possible, which he needed to develop a continuous front in Southern England. It was now up to the *Kriegsmarine* to prove that crossing the Channel was not just a river crossing, and that one had to take navigational factors into consideration and also reckon with the vagaries of the sea and a steep coast.

Time and again, Naval Command tried to bring the OKH to recognise these factors. On 20 July it presented a detailed 'evaluation of the landing possibilities on the English south coast from North Foreland to Start Point.' In it the difficulties, as well as the possibilities, of a landing were clearly spelled out, although actions by the enemy were, with one exception, left out completely.

From North Foreland and Ramsgate on the most northeasterly point of the Kent coast, to Pegwell Bay, the coast falls almost vertically into the sea from heights of up to 36 metres, but then turns into flat pebble and sand beaches until well past Deal. South of Deal, the high chalk cliffs which are typical for this coast, again rise up and dominate the scene until west of Folkestone, where they then recede until Dungeness is reached, giving way to a wide bay protected against winds from the west.

124

The *Kriegsmarine* considered approaching the steep coast between North Foreland and Ramsgate, two to five nautical miles north of the dreaded Goodwin Sands, to be a possibility, provided the troops were capable of overcoming the almost vertical cliffs. A landing on the adjoining flatter coastal sector was impossible, because of silt and mud flats and the sandbanks and shallows off the coast. An approach from the south through the Downs would have led through the ten-mile-long Ramsgate Channel directly under the coast. Considering that the landing troops would be in a slow train of barges, 'this line of march is impossible', because the awkward barges and their tugboats would have been under the artillery fire of the British coastal defences for at least two hours.

South of Deal, which has a very steep pebble beach hardly approachable by boat, the steep coast began again. This approach was dangerous, because of the many sand-banks off shore. Under certain circumstances the strong north-westerly tidal current could wash the landing barges on to the Goodwin Sands and drive them aground. For the whole sector from North Foreland to South Foreland north of Dover, the *Kriegsmarine* evaluation came to the conclusion that flat-bottomed, slow-moving vessels could not approach this coast.

From Dover to Folkestone, the situation was similar: a sheer, unapproachable steep coast made a landing impossible. This also applied to the shallow East Wear Bay east of Folkestone, where at low tide huge rocks stuck up out of the water like cliffs. Only west of Folkestone until well past Dungeness, does the coast become flat. When embarking from French ports, however, the shallows of Varne and The Ridge had to be circumvented, which every navigating manual warned about because of their low water of only 2.7m to 1.8m and their treacherous currents. The *Kriegsmarine* therefore refused to take trains of barges over these shallows and wanted instead to circumvent them to the north and south despite the grave loss of time this would entail. After this, no further dangers faced a landing between Hythe and Dungeness. The beaches there are flat, the water only shallows gradually and with tides of 5 metres, at low tide in the wide St Mary's Bay, the beach in the north runs dry to about 100m out, in the south even as far as 1,000m out. The *Kriegsmarine* nautical experts had discovered that the beaches consisted of firm sand and were suitable for a landing. Here about 200 barges about 125m apart could be put ashore simultaneously.

Adjacent to Dungeness are the West Road and Rye Bay. Here the water again only shallows very gradually, so that a landing could easily be managed and again 200 barges put ashore. West of this bay, from Cliff's End to Hastings and St Leonards, no landing possibilities exist because of the sheer coast. Eight kilometres west, at Bexhill, the coast again becomes flat. The *Kriegsmarine* description of Bexhill and the bathing beach to Beachy Head off Eastbourne

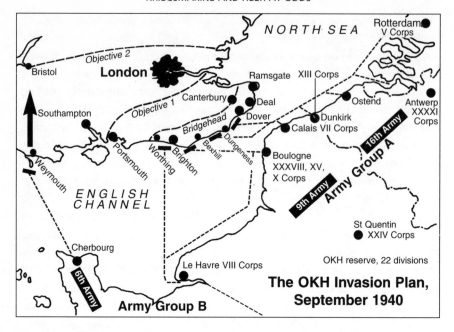

was almost affectionate: 'The town of 22,000 inhabitants lies on a rise of ground, has many red houses above whose roofs looms the red spire of St Peter's church.' The eight Martello Towers between Pevensey and Langley Point were also listed, as were the Wish Tower in Eastbourne and the 43m high lighthouse tower at Beachy Head, which is built of grey granite with wide horizontal black stripes, and stands on tidal cliffs under the steep coast which again begins here. There are several reefs off the long wide beaches between Bexhill and Eastbourne, which must be taken into consideration. But, according to the *Kriegsmarine*, 100 barges could land here simultaneously.

The *Kriegsmarine* did not consider a landing of any larger extent possible on the next sector of the coast between Beachy Head and the sea resort of Brighton, because of the steep shore, the rocky beaches, and some offshore cliffs. However, from Brighton to Selsey Bill, 21 nautical miles of easily approachable beaches again beckoned, on which ten reinforced regiments in about 500 barges could be landed.

After this, a description of that coastal sector should have followed, which in its 'Study Red' the *Kriegsmarine* had originally recommended as the best landing place of all: the stretch from the Isle of Wight to Portland. However, the authors of the 'Evaluation of the Coast' remained silent. Maybe they assumed that the *Heer* should still be familiar with this sector from the old study. In any case, in their evaluation of the coast, the naval experts continued with Portland and described a landing on the peninsula as being impossible. In the further stretch from Lyme Bay up to Exmouth, they only saw narrow valleys and two bays, in which units without heavy loads could be landed. Only between Portland and Bridport could 300 barges be put ashore by steamers on a very narrow front.

According to this evaluation, for the *Kriegsmarine* the only sector to be considered was the coast between Folkestone and Eastbourne, the 'narrow landing area'. According to this opinion, a landing north of Folkestone could not be justified for navigational reasons, operations west of Eastbourne would not be safe at sea. The time plan of Naval Command's Operations Department, however, extended the possible landings all the way to Brighton in the west and Dover in the north. These considerations had to remain pure theory, because they did not agree with the demand by the *Heer* to land the various contingents simultaneously. At least according to the *Kriegsmarine*, differences in tides and the long unloading times of the steamers made any extension of the landing areas unsupportable.

The *Heer*, on the other hand, had already committed itself on 15 July. Halder wanted to have as many bridgeheads as possible along the whole coast from Ramsgate to Lyme Bay. Accordingly, he had split the different waves equally between the Ramsgate area, Rye, Brighton, the Isle of Wight and Lyme Bay. With this, he intended to fragment enemy opposition. The necessary factor of surprise was to be provided by the width of the assault and the time of crossing.

On 26 July, Commander-in-Chief of the *Heer* von Brauchitsch confirmed his Chief of Staff's plans: 'The landing forces of Sixteenth and Ninth Army – first wave infantry divisions, second wave fast mobile forces – deployed in readiness between Dunkirk and Bayeux will, together with the specially equipped forward elements, gain as many bridgeheads as deeply as possible between Ramsgate and Portsmouth. Under rapid reinforcement by the second wave of infantry divisions and fast mobile forces, they will break out of these bridgeheads as quickly as possible, in order to gain the first operational objective: from the mouth of the Thames to Southampton.'

In particular, the attack from the Ramsgate–Dover area was to advance on London from the south. Simultaneously, the troops landed in the south between Brighton and Portsmouth, were to proceed towards Aldershot and, together with the forces landed further west in Lyme Bay, form a large bridgehead on a line Southampton–Thames estuary. Southwestern England was to be cut off by an advance on Bristol.

When the new Admiral Commanding France, Admiral Schuster, presented himself to the OKH in Fontainebleau on 27 July, the *Heer* Commander-in-Chief expressed his worry. The naval officers entrusted with embarkation and transport of the troops had still not established contact with the army units, so it had been necessary to forego conducting practice exercises on the coast. Von

Brauchitsch emphatically demanded now finally to be informed about how the various types of vessels were to be divided between the different ports, because on this depended the distribution of the troops for embarkation.

The talk then turned to the landing itself. Schuster was surprised how little account of nautical considerations was being taken by the army gentlemen at OKH, even how little they knew about such matters, so that he actually had to explain the difference between a windward and a leeward coast to them. In his turn however, the Admiral was unable to answer direct questions and had to refer to Commander of Naval Group West, Admiral Saalwächter and to Naval Command. That same day, Halder invited Admiral Schniewind to a meeting at Fontainebleau.

Schniewind took his time. On 29 July he noted down for his Chief that there were too many different conditions to be met for the success of the operation: moonlight, favourable tides, good weather with seas under Force 2, the ability to land simultaneously at widely separated locations, German air superiority, and absence of the British fleet. For Naval Command therefore, the operation appeared to be 'basically highly dubious'. Schniewind came down in favour of not attempting it that year. 'In case the air war, in combination with the other measures taken by the *Kriegsmarine* (he meant the blockade), do not lead to a willingness for peace, preparations can continue to an extent that is tolerable for the war economy. Execution itself could then again be considered from May 1941 onwards.'

Großadmiral Raeder took his Chief of Staff's notes along to a *Führer* Conference on 1 August, at which the Commanders-in-Chief of the other two branches and Keitel were also present. Raeder's reservations were accepted by Hitler, just as he had accepted the *Heer* plan from beginning to end two weeks previously. The preparations for 'Sea Lion' were to be carried out in such a manner, that the order to land could be given at any time from 15 September onwards. But Hitler made the final decision whether the operation was to take place that year dependent on the effects of the increased air attacks on the British Isles. In one important point however, Raeder only achieved a partial success: the crossings by the troops were now only to take place either side of the Strait of Dover–Calais, in a sea area that is marked by the lines Boulogne–Beachy Head and Ostend–Ramsgate. With this, the risky crossing near Deal and the trip through the Ramsgate Channel were back on the agenda.

How little the *Führer's* word really counted becomes evident from an order of the day from Keitel to the *Wehrmacht* that same day: the operational preparations are to continue for the time being on the previously planned wide front, despite the claim by the *Kriegsmarine* that it could only secure a narrow strip (westwards about to Eastbourne).

Above: The Germans test their submersible tank in preparation for the invasion. IWM HU7652

Below: A scene near Calais as a landing ship is worked on during the exercises for 'Sea Lion'. IWM HU2790

Abschrift. AOK 16

12 Ausfertigungen
3 .Ausfertigung.

Oberkommando des Heeres   F.Qu. OKH, den 17.7.40.
Gen St d H Op.Abt. (Ia)
Nr. 392/40 g.Kdos.   A.O.K.16, Ia Nr. 466/40 g. Kdos.

Der Führer hat die Vorbereitung des Angriffs gegen
England befohlen.

Die Vorbereitung erfolgt auf der Grundlage, daß

eine Angriffsgruppe Calais (A.O.K.16) aus dem Bereich
Ostende - Somme=Mündung gegen die feindl. Küste
zwischen Margate und Hastings

eine Angriffsgruppe Le Havre (A.O.K.9) aus dem Bereich
Dieppe - Caen gegen die feindl. Küste zwischen
Brighton und Portsmouth

eine Angriffsgruppe Cherbourg (A.O.K.6) aus dem Bereich
um Cherbourg gegen die feindl. Küste beiderseits
Weymouth

eingesetzt werden kann.

Näheres hierüber folgt.

Als Einleitung der Gliederung zum Angriff wird
folgendes befohlen:

1.) Befehlsgliederung:

a) 6.Armee (ohne Gen.Kdo.X mit 57.u.223.Inf.Div.) tritt
unter den Befehl der H.Gr.B.

Neue Trennungslinie zwischen H.Gr.A und H.Gr.B:
Port en Bessin (33 km nordwestl.Caen) - Bayeux -
Condé (Orte zu A) - Alencon (Ort zu B) - Nordost-
grenze des Departements Sarthe.

Left: The German High Command orders to mobilize for 'Sea Lion', issued on 17 July 1940, just four days after Hitler had given the go-ahead. IWM COL55

Right: German invasion barges concentrated at Boulogne in June 1940. IWM MR6657

Below: An invasion vessel is prepared. IWM HU72023

Above: An invasion vessel lies moored in a French harbour. IWM HU72002

Below: German troops at sea during exercises for 'Sea Lion'. IWM HU7969

Opposite page, top: More training for the landing, from an inflatable in a French harbour. IMM HU7970

Right: Göring and his officers view the white cliffs of Dover from the French coast. So near and yet so far! IWM HU1185

Above: A propaganda photo-montage showing Hitler amongst dead Allied soldiers. IWM HU4579

Left: A sombre rather than triumphant view of Hitler in front of the Eiffel Tower in Paris. Would such an image have been planned for Big Ben or Buckingham Palace? IWM HU3266

THE PREPARATIONS IN ENGLAND:

Top right: A coastal observation post. IWM H2337

Right: A coastal gun is test fired. IWM H2672

THE PREPARATIONS IN ENGLAND:

Top left: Flooded ditches were one defensive measure. IWM H2473

Centre left: A Beaverette armoured car and British infantrymen guard a coast road. IWM HU67472

Bottom left: Concrete barriers closed inland routes. IWM HU65874

Above: Many roads were also affected. IWM H2479

Right: Signposts were removed. IWM HU49250

HOME GUARD AND VOLUNTEER TRAINING INCREASED:

Above: A unit prepares 'Molotov cocktails', during a drill. IWM H8128

Left: A unit works with the Northover bomb projector anti-tank weapon. IWM H12239

Top right: A unit deals with an 'enemy' parachutist during an exercise. IWM H4755

Right: The men are taught some basic German phrases. IWM HU50154

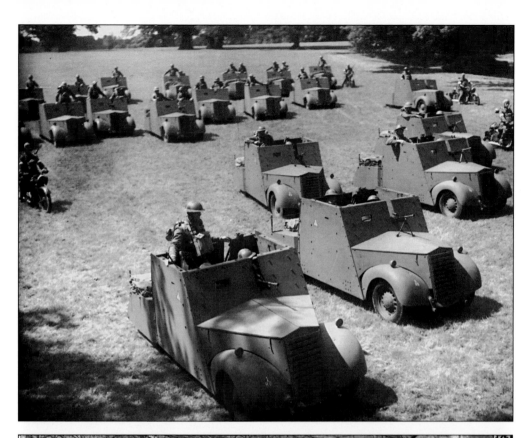

Top left: Troops training with the new 'Ironsides', armoured cars in an Essex field. IMM H2503

Left: Troops build a kapok bridge. IWM H7442

Above: The only time German troops marched on British soil – at Cheapside in Jersey. IWM HU5192

Right: The Forum Cinema in St Helier, Jersey, on Hitler's birthday on 20 April. The film being shown was *Sieg in Westen* (Victory in the West) IWM HU5188

Translation of a Communication addressed to the Governor of the Isle of Jersey.

1st July, 1940.

To the Chief of the Military and Civil Authorities

Jersey (St. Helier).

1. I intend to neutralize military establishments in Jersey by occupation.

2. As evidence that the Island will surrender the military and other establishments without resistance and without destroying them, a large White Cross is to be shown as follows, from 7 a.m. July 2nd, 1940.

   a. In the centre of the Airport in the East of the Island.
   b. On the highest point of the fortifications of the port.
   c. On the square to the North of the Inner Basin of the Harbour.

   Moreover all fortifications, buildings, establishments and houses are to show the White Flag.

3. If these signs of peaceful surrender are not observed by 7 a.m. July 2nd, heavy bombardment will take place.

   a. Against all military objects.
   b. Against all establishments and objects useful for defence.

4. The signs of surrender must remain up to the time of the occupation of the Island by German troops.

5. Representatives of the Authorities must stay at the Airport until the occupation.

6. All Radio traffic and other communications with Authorities outside the Island will be considered hostile actions and will be followed by bombardment.

7. Every hostile action against my representatives will be followed by bombardment.

8. In case of peaceful surrender, the lives, property, and liberty of peaceful inhabitants are solemnly guaranteed.

   The Commander of the German Air Forces in Normandie,

   _____ **General**

The States have ordered this Communication to be printed and posted forthwith, and charge the Inhabitants to keep calm, to comply with the requirements of the Communication and to offer no resistance whatsoever to the occupation of the Island.

Left: The proclamation of occupation of the Channel islands. No doubt a similar announcements would have accompanied 'Sea Lion'. IWM HU5183

Above: Though the beaches of Britain were riddled with defensive obstructions, the pleasures of sea bathing were not forsaken. IWM HU55536

Right: Once detected, the trains carrying ordnance to the French ports for use in operation 'Sea Lion' were attacked and destroyed by Allied aircraft. IWM HU72024

Winston Churchill inspects bomb damage in the East End of London. If Hitler could reach London by air, he believed Operation 'Sea Lion' would get him there by sea and land. IWM H3976

For the *Kriegsmarine*, this was tantamount to a massacre on the high seas. It would be easy for British naval units to descend upon the widely separated slow-moving landing fleet at night and to sink ship after ship with thousands of soldiers. Nobody could accept responsibility for this. And so Admiral Schniewind set off for Fontainebleau to explain the *Kriegsmarine* position clearly.

He arrived there with his immediate staff on 7 August. The welcome was very friendly, but the meeting, which lasted from 20.30 to 23.30 soon developed into a shouting match. Halder immediately launched into the question of the landing areas, on which the *Kriegsmarine* position was diametrically opposed to that of the *Heer*. Naval Command's proposal to land only in the narrow area between Folkestone and Beachy Head was completely unacceptable to the General Staff. The inland area behind this coast was marshy and unsuitable for the deployment of armour. Support from the air could only be counted upon in terms of hours and not continuously day after day. The three German divisions to be landed there were opposed by twelve British divisions. Halder insisted on further landings in Brighton Bay and in the area Ramsgate–Dover. Patiently Schniewind explained to him that the slow trains of barges would be exposed for hours to the British coastal batteries at Pegwell Bay and in the Ramsgate Channel and that, because of the differences in tides and the unapproachable coast, it was not possible to land simultaneously in the Brighton area.

Halder did not reply to this. He probably considered all this just to be pig-headedness on the part of the *Kriegsmarine* or an exaggerated need for safety. He knew the four conditions the *Kriegsmarine* kept piling up in front of itself like a mountain just as well as Schniewind did: 1. Weather, moon and tides had to be favourable. 2. In the Channel, German command of the sea had to have been established. 3. German command of the air over the sea and the coast must also have been achieved. 4. The English south coast was to have been 'ploughed over by bombs several times'.

One of the army officers present remarked, that all that really mattered was the moment of surprise. Even if the British were aware of the preparations, the advantage of tactical surprise could still be gained. Schniewind objected immediately: the transports would have to put to sea as much as eight hours before the crossing. That could be detected at any time from the English coast with simple field glasses, let alone from the air. The enemy would therefore have from twelve to fifteen hours to prepare himself for the landing. This in its turn surprised the *Heer* staff. They suggested distracting the attention of the British with deceptive manoeuvres. Again Schniewind objected, because there was not enough transport space available.

General Halder put an end to the to-ing and fro-ing and summarised: 'I categorically reject the *Kriegsmarine* proposal for carrying out the landing in the narrow area Folkestone–Beachy Head and, from the point of view of the *Heer*, describe this as suicide. I might just as well put the troops that have landed through the meat grinder straight away.'

Admiral Schniewind shot back just as sharply that Naval Command rejected a landing on a wide front on the same basis and not only considered this to be suicide, but a sacrifice of the troops to be landed there.

After this initial head-on clash the emotions calmed down again to some degree. The discussion turned to the effect of enemy actions at sea and technical details of the crossing by the troops. During this, the General Staff simply refused to believe that there were no more steamers to be found within the German sphere of influence, not even when Schniewind tried to explain why not every ship was suitable for the transportation of troops or for a landing operation.

And suddenly the partners in the discussion were again on a sharp collision course. The issue now was the time of day. The *Heer* wanted to land at dawn, the *Kriegsmarine* preferred daylight, because it feared meeting enemy surface vessels and because the waters, which in parts were very difficult, could not be navigated at night. Halder swept these reservations off the table with the remark that the *Führer* himself had decided in favour of dawn. And furthermore, the *Heer* would not undertake the landing on a narrow front in any case, militarily and operationally this was nonsense.

Schniewind might have pointed out that both the Romans and the Normans had landed on a very narrow front and had still conquered England. The most important confirmation of the point of view of the *Kriegsmarine*, however, would only be provided by history on 6 June 1944 with the landing of the Allies in Normandy: the landing area was only 70 kilometres wide, which just about equals the distance from Folkestone to Beachy Head. However, on this 7 August 1940 Schniewind had to content himself with opposing the army Command with repeated and loudly spoken 'no's!

Halder turned to his entourage. Colonel von Witzleben was to inform the Commander-in-Chief the following day, that General Staff and Naval Command had not been able to reach an agreement and that therefore a new presentation to the *Führer* had become necessary. Admiral Schniewind also made a note of the meeting 'for presentation by Chief Naval Command to *Führer*'. Apparently nobody was thinking about the Commander-in-Chief of the *Wehrmacht*, Field Marshal Keitel, even though it was his job to coordinate the operations of the armed forces.

It was not the first time that an army and a navy were at odds on the question of crossing the Channel. Back in 1804 Napoleon had had a row with his Admiral de Villeneuve. The Corsican had gathered 120,000 men on the Channel coast in order to conquer England and dictate a peace treaty to the British in London. He believed he could intimidate the English and weaken their will to resist by vociferous threats. The embarkation of his troops was to take place in the small ports in and around Boulogne. For this, he demanded 2,000 small ships from his navy, most of which had still to be built. His Admiral of the Fleet Pierre de Villeneuve was already indignant because the declaration of war had taken him by surprise in the middle of building up his fleet. He categorically announced to Napoleon, that the small vessels, flat-bottomed barges, stood no chance against the fast British sloops and frigates during the crossing. But Napoleon believed that fog and darkness would protect his landing fleet. Experiments however soon showed that a crossing by men, horses and cannon would not only take a few hours but days: the tides would play havoc and during manoeuvres over such a long period of time, bad weather and the loss of the whole fleet had to be reckoned with. Napoleon turned a deaf ear to all the objections, just as the German General Staff did 137 years later. He even had a coin minted with the inscription *Frappé à Londres en* 1804 ['Struck in London in 1804']. However, he had to give up his plan that very same year, because the nautical and technical problems could not be overcome.

Not so the German General Staff, which was slowly succeeding in softening up the *Kriegsmarine* position. Against all of the categorical objections of the *Kriegsmarine*, the OKW ordered the preparation of diversionary operations. From Norway and Denmark, a landing on the English east coast was to be simulated, from the Netherlands a second one north of the Thames Estuary, and from Brest and the Bay of Biscay, a diversionary manoeuvre against Ireland. With a suggestion of its own, the *Kriegsmarine* vainly tried to have the order reduced to reasonable proportions. Naval Command announced that it already intended a diversionary invasion of Scotland.

One can hardly claim that Keitel took sides for the *Heer*. He was only on the *Führer*'s side and just repeated what the 'greatest commander of all times' was prompting him to say. At some point in time Hitler must have noticed the length of the landing area, because on 16 August the OKW decreed that the preparations for a landing in Lyme Bay were to be cancelled due to lack of sufficient means to protect them. In the Brighton area as well, only a one-time landing without reinforcement by heavy equipment was to be kept open as a possibility. With this, at least the western flank of the *Kriegsmarine* had been substantially shortened.

The tug-of-war about the landing areas, however, was still far from over. Behind the scenes, the sniping continued. On 30 August the Commander-in-Chief of the *Heer* overrode the *Kriegsmarine* reservations and issued a temporarily final directive for the preparation of 'Operation Sea Lion' to the Army Groups on the Channel coast. In it, he takes the strategic pre-conditions as given: 'The *Luftwaffe* destroys the English air force and its production base and secures command of the air. The *Kriegsmarine* clears mine-free routes and seals off the flanks of the crossing strip.'

In his directive, von Brauchitsch avoided mentioning the awkward transportation question. That was the responsibility of the *Kriegsmarine*. As far as the *Heer* was concerned, he only ordered the utmost degree of mobility and independence in case of unforseen changes in the situation, as for example, 'if the peculiarities of transport at sea were to make a break-up of the forces unavoidable'.

Moreover, according to this directive, the landing plan was now as follows: Army Group A lands on the English south coast between Folkestone and Worthing with Sixteenth and Ninth Army. Sixteenth Army is assigned the sector Folkestone–Hastings. Advancing north, it takes the coast Ramsgate–Deal from the landward side and eliminates coastal defence, so that the *Kriegsmarine* can land reinforcements. Ninth Army lands between Bexhill and Worthing. Brighton, lying in between these two landing areas, is taken by airborne troops. Army Group B remains on alert and, if the situation develops favourably, is taken from Cherbourg to Lyme Bay by air and sea.

With this, after two months, there was at least a fairly workable plan, and one which was not unacceptable to the *Kriegsmarine*.

XIII

Spies and Secret Services
This is where they failed

Where then were the German spies, the saboteurs of the fifth column, the '*Gauleiter* in waiting'? They mainly existed only in the imagination of the British, who are just as much enthralled by spy stories as they are by crime and ghost stories. There was no German spy who, speaking perfect Oxford English, insinuated himself into the confidence of a development engineer or had an affair with a secretary from the War Office. As with other countries too, the gathering of information was normally the task of the military attachés in the embassy in London and the officials in the consulates in the major ports and industrial centres. The degree of ignorance about enemy forces, which is documented in the files of the *Wehrmacht*, proves that even these sources produced little useful information. From the prewar period, there are only two mysterious cases known, in which German agents figure. Both occurred in Kent. They are full of contradictions and hardly credible but they do, however, throw a light on the general mood in England.

On 29 August 1935 a Dr Hermann Goetz, a slightly-built man in his forties with two sabre scars on his left cheek. arrived in Harwich from Germany. Together with a nineteen-year-old female companion, he is alleged to have driven by motorcycle from Royal Air Force base to Royal Air Force base over several weeks and, disguised as a landscape painter, to have made drawings and water-colour sketches of the military installations and also taken photographs.

In September the couple drove from Mildenhall in Suffolk to Broadstairs in Kent, where they took rooms for six weeks. Not far from Broadstairs lay the large RAF station of Manston which they obviously wanted to scout out. The six weeks had not yet passed, when Dr Goetz and his companion abruptly left England. Shortly thereafter, the landlady received a telegram from Dr Goetz, in which he bade her to take his 'combination' and camera into safekeeping for him.

By 'combination', Goetz had meant his leather clothing, which he had left behind, not knowing that in English the term can also refer to a motorcycle with sidecar. The conscientious landlady now started to look for a motorcycle and when she could not find one, came to the conclusion that it must have been stolen. She notified the police. In the leather clothing, the officers found Dr

Goetz's camera with a film that later turned out to be highly compromising: it contained pictures of the aircraft installations at Manston.

When Dr Goetz again wanted to enter the country at Harwich on 8 November, he was arrested and brought to trial. He was sentenced to four years in prison for offences against the Official Secrets Act and served his time in Maidstone, even though he protested his innocence. He had only wanted to collect material for a novel.

This Dr Goetz is alleged to be identical to the person who parachuted into Ireland in May 1940 and was supposed to have undertaken preparations for a German landing in the Republic of Ireland with the help of the IRA. He was arrested in November 1941 and detained. On 23 May 1947 he is alleged to have taken his own life by poison.

The second prewar incident was even more obscure and dealt with a Dr Albert Tester who had been living for years with his wife and five children in a large house on the cliffs of North Foreland near Broadstairs. He was suspected of being earmarked to become the head of the Gestapo in Kent after a landing by German troops. There is no documentary evidence supporting this suspicion because, at the time, not even the Gestapo was considering an invasion of England. In the summer of 1939 the family returned to Germany. Only a few days before the war broke out, when the first 'enemy aliens' were being interned, the police appeared at Dr Tester's house, only to discover that the father of the family had also fled the scene, allegedly in a U-boat.

These stories sound even more improbable as there did not appear to be any military necessity to spy on England before the Second World War. In any case, none of the three branches of the *Wehrmacht* had installed a systematic net of agents in the British Isles. How someone's natural military curiosity could be satisfied was demonstrated by Field Marshal Milch and General Udet. In the course of a courtesy visit, both had themselves shown about on British military airbases and even visited the aircraft factories. What else did one need? In 1939, while leafing through British technical journals, Milch came across an advertisement for a book on Britain's industrial capacity. On the letterhead of the *Reichsluftfahrtministerium* [Reich Air Ministry] he had the book ordered from a bookshop in London. It came and was promptly paid for by Department V (the Intelligence Department).

Spying on the 'Germanic brother nation', which he hoped to enlist as an ally in the 'racial struggle' was not in line with Hitler's intentions. The Mosleys, the Mitfords, the Londonderrys and also Winifred Wagner or the visit to the Obersalzberg by the Duke of Windsor, were demonstrating friendly ties, or at least far-reaching possibilities of achieving an understanding, so that spying appeared to be superfluous. That only changed when the Second World War broke out. But even then the efforts by the German secret services were horrifyingly naive. This can best be seen in a report by Walter Schellenberg, a department head in the *Reichssicherheitshauptamt* [RSHA, Reich Central Security Office] of the SS an intimate, as far as there ever was one, of Reinhard Heydrich.

According to his own statements, in July 1940 Schellenberg was supposed to bring the Duke of Windsor, who had had to abdicate as King Edward VIII in 1936, within the sphere of influence of the Nazi regime, because Hitler and Ribbentrop took him to be a friend of Germany and intended to use him for their purposes. The Duke, who was living in Paris with his wife when war broke out, had been acting as a sort of special ambassador to the French Government. In June he had fled to Lisbon via Madrid. From Madrid he attempted to force his and his wife's return to England and laid down financial and other conditions that were unacceptable both for the Royal Family and for the Government. In order to bring him to a place of safety, he was offered the post of Governor of the Bahamas.

In a total misappreciation of the British mentality, Hitler believed he could bring the ex-king over to his side and use him to put pressure on the British. That apparently was at least what Ribbentrop, who also recommended the 30-year-old jurist Schellenberg as the only man who could bring it about, had convinced him of. Schellenberg had been the one who had directed the 'Venlo Affair' in 1939, during which two British secret agents had been abducted in Holland. Among other things, this had been intended to disprove Holland's declaration of neutrality. For this deed, Schellenberg was promoted from SS *Obersturmbannführer* to SS *Standartenführer*, the equivalent of a colonel in the Army.

In June, Ribbentrop summoned the SS leader to his office and disclosed to him that the ex-king's mésalliance had only been an excuse for forcing him to abdicate as Edward VIII. In actual fact, he had had to go because of his social precepts and his friendship for Germany. It was known that the Duke felt very uncomfortable in his present situation. He was being so closely watched by the British secret service that he felt as if he was in prison and had himself already talked about escaping. The *Führer* believed that if the Duke were enabled to live in Spain, he would no longer need to hide his friendly feelings towards Germany. Schellenberg was to find this out and offer the Duke 50 million Swiss francs in the *Führer's* name for moving his place of residence, preferably to Switzerland, or alternatively to some other neutral country, and from there publicly disassociating himself from the machinations of the British Royal Family. 'Should the British secret service try to prevent the Duke from making such an arrangement', Ribbentrop continued, 'the *Führer* orders you to anticipate the British intentions, if necessary by using force and at the risk of your life. The Duke and his wife must be taken to safety in a country of their choice. The *Führer* attaches great importance to this operation.'

And as if all this did not already sound absurd enough and only explainable in terms of Ribbentrop's modest mental endowments, the whole matter becomes totally confused when Ribbentrop speaks of intimidation and force to be applied against the alleged friend of Germany in the eventuality he should prove reluctant to escape.

In any case, on the morning following this meeting, Schellenberg flew to Madrid via Lyon and Marseille. What then followed is a cloak-and-dagger-story which Schellenberg, probably in order to please Ribbentrop and the *Führer*, embroidered so artlessly, that its improbability becomes all the more apparent.

He had, Schellenberg reports, bought an American car and sent it to Lisbon with another fast car. In the Portuguese capital a high-ranking Portuguese official had provided him with quarters with a family of Jewish emigrants from Holland. Before that, he had conferred in Spain with a Spanish friend who was to organise the Duke's unimpeded crossing of the border. The victim was to be kidnapped during a hunting excursion near the Spanish frontier and taken into Spain. Having arrived in Lisbon, Schellenberg then allegedly met a Japanese friend who could obtain detailed information about the ducal couple's residence and habits in Estoril. With the help of a Portuguese police official, Schellenberg claims to have installed a network of informers around and in the house itself, and even placed agents disguised as Portuguese police officers among the guards. A bunch of flowers was delivered to the house with a card saying: 'Beware of the machinations of the British Secret Service – a Portuguese friend who has your welfare at heart!' At night Schellenberg had windows in the house broken in and next day spread the rumour that this had been the work of the British, who wanted to frighten the Duke and his wife into leaving.

After two weeks of this cruel game Schellenberg claims to have received a cable from Ribbentrop: '*Führer* orders, organise abduction immediately.' It was too late. The Windsors did not go on any further hunting excursions but in July boarded a ship of the Royal Navy in order to take up the Duke's new post in the Bahamas. Allegedly Schellenberg observed their departure from a tower in the German Embassy with a pair of binoculars.

Whatever Schellenberg may have been up to in Lisbon, it makes the German Secret Service, whose chief Schellenberg finally became as the successor to General Oster, appear in a bad light. In its political as well as its military operations, it had not progressed beyond the Mata-Hari mentality of the First World War. The boundless rivalry between the intelligence services of the three branches of the *Wehrmacht*, the *Sicherheitsdienst* [Security Service], and the Gestapo, contributed its part in obscuring rather than enlightening the picture of the enemy.

To the present day it is still not clear who had the strange agents sent into England in 1940. What is noteworthy, is the lack of proper preparation and equipment of the 'agents', who either did not speak a word of English or only had a very insufficient knowledge. One is permitted to suspect that they were only sent across the Channel to unsettle the British, in other words that they were deliberately sacrificed. Otherwise, the carelessness of this operation can hardly be explained.

In the early hours of the morning of 3 September, two dinghies containing two men each landed at different places on the southern coast of Kent between Hythe and Dungeness. Sitting in the first boat were the Dutchmen Charles van der Knieboom, 26, and Sjord Pons, 28, in the second boat, the German Rudolf Waldberg and Carl Meier, 24, who claimed to be Dutch. They had probably been disembarked from a larger boat at different places off the coast. Knieboom and Pons landed near the Grand Redoubt in West Hythe. They dragged their dinghy on to the land and picked up their baggage: a case with clothing, a wireless transmitter, and a sack full of food: tinned meat, chocolate and cigarettes. They allegedly had the assignment to spy out the military establishments along the coast and to radio the numbers of troops across the Channel. Both only spoke very little English, and Knieboom had the handicap of looking very Asiatic. His mother was Japanese. It was about 05.00. A soldier of the Somerset Light Infantry could hardly believe his eyes when directly in front of his observation post a civilian wearing highly noticeable white shoes crossed the road. The man had a second pair of shoes slung across his shoulder and in front of his chest hung a pair of field glasses. It was Knieboom, who was intending to scout the area. He made no attempt to run away when he was challenged and arrested. All he did was to keep gabbling the sentence he had learned by heart: 'I am a Dutch refugee and want to speak to the officer in charge'.

Only a few minutes later the sack of food and the case of clothing were found. By 05.25 Pons was also in custody. The two Dutchmen's transmitter was found in the tall grass on a margin of a field, whereupon the refugee story went out of the window.

Waldberg and Meier had landed eighteen kilometres further south near Dungeness in their dinghy. Their equipment was similar to that of the two Dutchmen. They concealed the awkward baggage under a boat jacked up on the beach and looked for a place to sleep further inland. It was already late in the morning when they woke up and felt a powerful thirst. Meier, whose English was passable, set off to find something to drink. He reached Lydd unchallenged, where he went into the first pub he saw, the 'Rising Sun'. It was 09.30. Meier asked for some cider, unaware that in England alcoholic beverages were only permitted to be served after 10.00. The hostess became suspicious and asked him to come back in half an hour. He had hardly left when she informed her husband, who was working a few hundred metres away in a butcher's shop that also belonged to the couple. When Meier actually did return half an hour later, there was an officer of the Royal Air Force waiting for him.

Waldberg waited for his colleague until noon and then went to hide in a shed belonging to an empty house. During the night, he dragged the transmitter along with him and made himself comfortable in some bushes under a tree with low-hanging branches, through which he set up his aerial. Next morning, he set off to reconnoitre the area and ran straight into the arms of a police officer.

On 22 November all four of them were brought to trial. In their defence, the two Dutchmen claimed that they had been forced into spying because of an unpunished crime and had never had any intention of actually carrying out their assignment. The two others apparently did not have any convincing excuse prepared: Knieboom, Waldberg and Meier were sentenced to death and hanged in Pentonville prison in December. Oddly enough, Pons had been acquitted.

Whether they disclosed to the British who had sent them is not known. From the points where they were landed, one can deduce that it was the Intelligence Department of the *Heer* who had sent the unhappy quartet across the Channel. West Hythe formed the eastern, Lydd the southwestern boundary of the Romney Marsh coastline on which, according to the latest valid plan, two German divisions were to land and break through to Ashford. For *Heer* Command it would have been of the greatest importance to learn details of the enemy's defences and troop strength in this sector. Why it was undertaken in such a primitive fashion, which stood no earthly chance of success, still remains a mystery today.

On the British side, fear of espionage produced no less strange effects than did the attempts at spying on the German side. On 1 July an observer near Nettlebed, Oxfordshire, reported an enemy aircraft from which a parachute had been seen to descend. A detachment of Canadian soldiers stationed in the area was sent to the place designated to search for the parachute but failed to discover it. Maybe it had only been a scrap of paper blowing in the air, or a large bird that had flown under the aircraft at an appropriate angle. The Canadians did not have time to make such considerations. Far from any buildings, they stumbled upon a young man who ran away from them. They chased him and took him in. The address in Reading which he gave under police questioning soon proved to be false. Finally he admitted that he had come down with a parachute. He also gave detailed descriptions of other agents who had jumped with him. A map of Wales which he was carrying was taken as a further piece of evidence. The highlight however was, that he was prepared to name his controller to whom he was to have reported after landing: a farmer in the region who had previously enjoyed a blameless reputation and, moreover, was a tenant of the Duke of Marlborough. A detachment of Canadian soldiers immediately took him in as well.

At the headquarters of the Home Force, at the time quartered in the Army Music School at Twickenham, the arrest of the pair caused much excitement. General Ironside, who spoke excellent German, drove to Oxford immediately in order to conduct the interrogations personally. But he arrived too late. The loudly cursing farmer had been sent back home with excellent prospects of being able to demand compensation. The young 'agent' was sitting dejectedly in his cell. In reality he was the son of an English parish priest and had deserted from his anti-aircraft unit stationed in Wales. By admitting to being a spy, he had hoped to hide the fact of his desertion. The farmer, the only person in the area whom he knew by name, had once been his employer for a brief spell before the war. The young man got off quite lightly. He was only sentenced to two years in prison.

Almost all of the German agents who parachuted in or were landed on the coast ended up on the gallows. Most of them gave themselves away, because they did not speak enough English or because they could not sufficiently adjust to their surroundings and were not familiar with the British way of life. The latter sort includes the man who put down food stamps in a restaurant, or the one who, when asked to pay 'ten and six', counted out ten pounds and six shillings.

One trio, consisting of the German Theo Drücke, the Swiss Werner Wälti and the female Russian emigrant Vera Erikson, became famous. They had been landed from a flying boat on Moray Firth near Inverness in Scotland shortly before dawn on 30 September. They had set off in the dark. They had no idea that all of the road signs had been removed throughout the British Isles. They lost their way and asked a station master the name of the station. This cost Drücke and Wälti their heads. Vera Erikson was 'turned around' and henceforward worked for MI6.

It can be said with some confidence, that no German agent remained undiscovered. This partially also explains the fact that the German leadership was completely in the dark concerning the situation in Great Britain.

XIV
Hitler Makes a 'Peace Offer'
An empty gesture

On 19 July, a Friday, three days after issuing Directive No. 16 for the preparation of an invasion of the British Isles, Hitler gave a speech of triumph at a convocation of the *Reichstag* in the Kroll Opera in Berlin on the occasion of the conclusion of the campaign against France. He hoisted the symbols of victory, appointed a *Reichsmarschall* and twelve field marshals and distributed further rewards with a lavish hand. In his speech, however, the overtones of his anger at not being able to pose as a bringer of peace were also discernible. He indulged himself in vicious attacks against the British government and Churchill, who had prevented his becoming one. The war against Great Britain did not fit in with his plans and he would very much have liked to be rid of it. Naturally he knew that in order to save face, Britain would have to lay down conditions, and the first condition would be the withdrawal of German troops from Poland, from where he intended to wage his campaign against Russia.

In his speech therefore, Hitler only saw his way clear to making a half-hearted gesture which, while reflecting his wishful thinking, did not correspond to the political and military realities: 'In this hour I feel it to be my duty before my own conscience, to appeal once more to reason in England as well. I consider myself in a position to do so, since I am not begging for something as the vanquished, but the victor, speaking in the name of reason. I can see no reason why this war need go on.'

For the majority of Germans, this 'peace offer' came straight from their hearts, even though some felt that the *Führer* was letting the English off too lightly. William Shirer who had attended the meeting as an American correspondent wrote later: 'After the meeting I spoke with many high officials and senior officers and none of them had the slightest doubts that the British would accept this, in their honest opinions, generous, even magnanimous, offer by the *Führer*.'

The offer was no less vague and non-committal than the offer of alliance to Great Britain had been in April 1939. Then Hitler had already demanded the politically impossible of the British, this time his offer equated to a demand for political, moral, and military capitulation. The British would have been required to sanction the very thing they had gone to war about.

Already weeks before the start of the campaign in the West, when the German Resistance had stretched out peace feelers, the question had been raised in the Commons: why not simply make peace? David Lloyd George had suggested a closed session in which peace conditions could be discussed. The government should examine any peace offer that was detailed and specific and take all those questions into consideration that had caused unrest in years past.

Minister of Information Duff Cooper had jumped up in great excitement and accused the grand old man of English politics of defeatism. 'The Germans have destroyed a great country', he had cried, 'and wiped it off the map. A country that came into being as a result of the First World War and existed for over twenty years no longer exists. Does that not suggest that they will offer terms which will contain no less than the confirmation of their victory through which they intend to shape the face of Europe? Do they seriously intend to have a truly independent Poland arise anew? And if they did this, what fool could believe in the honesty of their intentions, could trust their word?'

At the time, Duff Cooper had had almost all of the MPs on his side. In the meantime, Hitler had conquered six additional countries and handed the British the defeats of Dunkirk and Norway. In his speech of triumph he had, despite a 'peace offer', also threatened the downfall of the British Empire, for which the British Government would then have to bear the responsibility. The latter impressed the British far more than the appeal to see reason as Hitler saw it and to leave him alone to enjoy his booty.

Brigadier General Raymond Lee, the American Military Attaché in London, was sitting on the terrace of his country house on one of those moonlit summer nights and looking over the hills of Sussex. He noted his impressions in his diary: ' There was not a breath of air, not a sound. Strange to realise that under the same moon only one hundred miles away the Hun hordes were camping, prepared to devastate this country, and that on all these hills and in the valleys armed men were combing the fields for foreigners and the sky for airplanes, gliders and parachutists.' With this description of the atmosphere, he was also reflecting the stance of the British more accurately than many a political commentator could have.

Only one hour after Hitler's speech had gone out over the airwaves, the first unofficial reaction came from London. In a broadcast by the BBC, commentator Sefton Delmer formulated the unequivocal No! of the British: England would never surrender to Hitler. The following day every single British daily newspaper repeated this rejection in an overwhelming display of unanimity. Official London remained mute. The weekend break was in progress. The following Wednesday, Sir Robert Vansittart asked the Prime Minister whether he intended to reply. Churchill answered: 'I have no intention of making any reply to Herr Hitler's speech. We are not on speaking terms.' In the Cabinet, however, Churchill suggested having both Houses bring in a solemn resolution in answer to Hitler's speech. His ministers were able to convince him that this would be doing Hitler too much honour. In his capacity as Foreign Secretary, Lord Halifax had already rejected the gesture in a speech broadcast on 22 July: 'We shall not stop fighting until freedom is secure.' It was decided to leave it at that.

In Berlin the violent reaction caused deep consternation. People were unable and unwilling to accept that the British were presuming to play the champion of morality and preferred a war of life and death to an alliance with the indisputable and undefeatable new major power in Europe. Behind the scenes, a final attempt was made to make the British Government give way. This was to take place via the Vatican, Washington and Stockholm. However, the British ambassadors there had orders not to get involved in any discussions and not to make any replies.

Only the King of Sweden was prepared to act as an intermediary and wrote directly to the British Government. Churchill drafted a reply which Lord Halifax signed: 'These horrible events', it said among other things, 'have darkened the pages of European history with an indelible stain. His Majesty's Government see in them not the slightest cause to recede in any way from their principles and resolves as set forth in October 1939. On the contrary, their intention to prosecute the war against Germany by every means in their power until Hitlerism is finally broken and the world relieved from the curse which a wicked man has brought upon it has been strengthened to such a point, that they would rather all perish in the common ruin than fail or falter in their duty.'

With the rejection of the 'magnanimous peace offer', hate against England was again being incited among the German public. Ruthlessly and by all available means, the war was to be prosecuted in order to force England to her knees and to punish the warmongers in London. Following the occupation of the British Channel Islands by German troops on 30 June, it now appeared to be only logical that the British home country was to be assaulted. Then, or so it was believed, the constant air raid alarms which the population, particularly in northern and western Germany had to put up with, would cease. The song *Denn wir fahren gegen Engeland* ['Yes, we are setting off for England'] became the hit of the season and blared daily from the loudspeakers of the *Volksempfänger* [a radio produced by the Nazis with the idea to make it so cheap, that all Germans could afford one and tune it in to their propaganda], which were always turned on to catch the *Wehrmacht's* 'special announcements'. Nobody wanted to miss the news of the great offensive.

Goebbels' propaganda machine ran at full blast: insecurity and fear were to be instilled in the enemy, the German's willingness to fight was to be strengthened. Besides leaflets, the most important instrument for use abroad were the radio broadcasts directed towards England. From May 1940 onwards, four secret German radio stations were smothering the British with misleading information. Each of these stations claimed to be the voice of a resistance group within the British Isles. Two of the stations attempted to drive a wedge between Scotland and England and fought for the more or less latent desire for Scottish independence. They called themselves the 'New British Broadcasting Station' with the theme song 'The bonnie, bonnie banks of Loch Lomond' and, 'Caledonia', which announced itself by playing 'Auld lang syne'. Both employed gaelic speakers. The third station called 'Workers' Challenge' addressed itself to the British working class with Communist slogans and portrayed the war in terms of a capitalist conspiracy. The fourth station came on the air as the 'Christian Peace Movement'. With its Protestant theology and its pacifist flannel, it left the British completely unmoved.

In their desire to undermine British fighting spirit and to lend weight to their own propaganda, the four stations outdid each other with descriptions of the horrible sacrifices which the air attacks would demand in the British Isles, prophesied terrible secret weapons such as death rays and artificial fog, under cover of which thousands of paratroopers would land, and called upon their listeners to boo Churchill wherever he might appear. As the possible date of invasion approached ever closer, they did not tire in predicting the day and hour and mentioning a different landing area each time. Several times, the secret stations broadcast courses on protection against air raids and gas attacks. Filled with good advice, this cynical campaign only served to describe the terrible effects of a German bomb or gas attack on the civilian population and to produce horror. When English newspapers began to propagate the production of Molotov Cocktails, the stations warned English housewives about the great danger of them exploding: the bottle stored in the house could suddenly go up and kill her children.

From an English report, it had become known in Germany that at Dunkirk 100,000 British Army uniforms had fallen into German hands. Goebbels made use of this to further incite the paratroop hysteria in the islands: on 14 August the secret stations broadcast the news that German paratroopers in British uniforms and civilian dress had landed in northern England and were hiding with members of the fifth column. They were waiting there for their deployment in connection with the landings by German troops. For a time, this information caused considerable excitement among the inhabitants in the north. In actual fact, during the night of 13 August, German aircraft had dropped parachutes with equipment for secret agents in several places in northern England: inflatable boats, tents, maps, emergency rations, and lists with names of prominent people. However, the agents to go with this did not appear and in an official statement, the British government was able to belittle the whole thing as an attempt to deceive.

The English language broadcasts of the *Reichsrundfunk* [Reich Radio Service] attracted more listeners than did the secret stations along the Channel coast. Its studio in northern Germany employed several Mosley Fascists like Baillie-Stewart, Royston and Amery, who were not only to spread German news broadcasts throughout the British Isles but also fear and horror. They did not succeed, any more than did William Joyce, an American of Irish descent, who had managed to swindle a British passport in 1938 and had then gone over to the Nazis. During the 'Phoney War' the British Government over-estimated his effect and appealed to the population not to tune in to him. Many Englishmen listened to the broadcasts in spite of this and were highly amused by his abstruse fantasies and absurd polemics, which he spoke in a contrived Oxford accent, leading to his being nick-named Lord Haw-Haw. He kept his listeners glued to the radio by means of a very simple but highly effective trick: into his broadcasts he sporadically mixed the names of British prisoners of war.

Lord Haw-Haw also repeated the fairy-tale of the fog pills which German paratroopers allegedly carried. With them they could remain up in the air for up to ten hours disguised as clouds. Even though the English had known about gliders for a long time, he tried to talk them into believing that fort Eben Emael near Liège had been eliminated by electro-magnetic rays and then occupied without a fight. Later on, he advised his listeners to have strait-jackets to hand because the bombing attacks would drive many people mad. These clumsy attempts at deception were larded with tirades against the plutocrats, against the 'upper class ruled by Jewish moneybags', just as Goebbels had instructed him to do. This earned him several boxes of cigars which his boss, who was otherwise known to be very parsimonious, had sent to him in August . However, he soon began to bore his English listeners. After the end of the war he himself fell victim to one of his own lies: because of his British citizenship obtained by swindling, in 1945 he fell under British jurisdiction. He was condemned to death by the rope as a traitor and hanged in London in January 1946.

It was only with their news broadcasts that the Germans were able to achieve a modest success. The suspicious British preferred to listen to the German *Wehrmacht* reports, which they then compared with their own propaganda. They added German and British successes and losses, divided by two and thereby obtained an average which was probably closer to the truth.

Goebbels did not think much of leaflets: probably out of a realistic aware-ness that the members of his ministry hardly had the same degree of intuition and power of persuasion as did the German writers and journalists who had emigrated and were working in London for the British Ministry of Information, writing hundreds of pages of very impressive copy which were then dropped by the tonne over the territory of the German *Reich*. Like his master, Goebbels revelled in clumsy threats. He had leaflets dropped containing evacuation plans for the British civilian population in the event that the German invasion were to begin. That he was achieving exactly the opposite effect with this, namely strengthening the population's will to hold out, would never even have entered his mind.

When leaflets containing Hitler's speech of 19 July were dropped over England in August, the British only made fun of them. They became collectors' items and were auctioned off to collect money for welfare or demonstratively used as toilet paper. A whole load of these leaflets is alleged to have landed in the grounds of the Barmey Mental Hospital in Kent, one of the better known institutions for the insane. The attempt by German propaganda to build up the Duke of Windsor as a future British Head of State obedient to the Nazis was just as unsuccessful. It had escaped the German propagandists, like so much else about the mentality of the English, that after having abandoned the throne for the sake of an American woman, the Duke was no longer very popular among his countrymen.

With the exception of the propaganda spread by the 'Christian Peace Movement' station, there was no mention of peace in Goebbels' propaganda. Nor was there in the messages aimed at the population of Germany. Hate against England and the English was fired by means of rumours and deliberately falsified reports. When an epidemic of potato beetles occurred in the Saar and the southern Palatinate, the rumour was immediately launched that they had been dropped by British aircraft. This even sounded plausible, because the RAF was constantly dropping leaflets over southern Germany, so that drops were nothing strange to the inhabitants. It could also be claimed that in the Sieg district, coloured paper balls of two to five centimetres diameter containing arsenic had been dropped, in order to poison the livestock.

The malice of British bomber pilots was asserted, allegedly for dropping their bombs on German cities indiscriminately from great altitude and not even sparing German cultural monuments such as the Goethe house in Weimar or Bismarck's mausoleum, which was a barefaced lie. The propagandists poked fun at the British 'sniper's war' as well as at the Englishman who had been injured during an air raid exercise by a falling steel helmet and then suffered further wounds from a door, slammed shut while he was being loaded into an ambulance. A constantly repeated theme was the 'children of the plutocrats' being evacuated to Canada, while the working population had to stick it out, and that an English anti-aircraft battery had taken seagulls for German aircraft and fired upon them.

However, the German population was nothing like as naive as Goebbels apparently believed. A confidential situation report by the security service of the SS dated 1 August said: 'A number of reports from the *Gauen* [Party administrative districts] indicate that in its polemics against England, the arguments by German propaganda are not always logical. For example, there have been repeated reports about the muzzling of the English press. On the other hand, German propaganda is constantly able to draw upon articles in the English press, in which, despite censorship, the restrictions on the press are being attacked and the English government is openly being criticised.' Furthermore, a certain weariness of the polemics against the English upper class and the portrayals of conditions in England is becoming apparent. The people are 'fed up with the constant carrying on about the plutocrats.'

This however, had less to do with a growing feeling of friendship for the English but was more the result of increasing weariness with the war. A ceiling on wages, a reduction of the bread ration, price increases, and a shortage of textiles caused growing anxiety that the second winter of the war was now being entered. Everywhere, the growing impatience was making itself felt: when will it finally start against England? The people did not want any more propaganda, like the endless repetition of the snide remarks about Duff Cooper's appeal to the English workers: 'sing while you work', they wanted deeds. Special bulletins about spectacular successes of the *Wehrmacht* had not been heard for a long time now. In May, only 77,000 tonnes of enemy shipping had been sunk and the *Luftwaffe* was contenting itself with attacking convoys in the Channel. How was it, people asked themselves, that English ships were still able to navigate there at all, under the very nose of the *Wehrmacht*?

XV

The United States Remains Neutral
With mixed feelings

The time was ripe for the big blow. The British sensed this even more than the Germans, because they felt themselves to have been abandoned and facing an overpowering enemy. What was more reasonable than to look about for an ally, the only one possible, the United States of America? And if the Americans could not prevent an invasion, they could at least supply the urgently needed weapons and offer moral support, even if this were to cost Britain her reserves in gold.

Churchill, whose mother was an American, engaged in a lively correspondence with President Roosevelt, in which he kept inserting appeals for help: 'Give us the tools and we will do the job.' However, the 'Defenders of Freedom and Democracy' were prepared to sacrifice the British to the Nazi moloch and accept an invasion of the British Isles. Still under the effects of the defeat in Norway and the opening of the campaign in the West, in his appeal for aid to President Roosevelt, Churchill had asked for the loan of 40 to 50 old American destroyers, as well as several hundred aircraft, anti-aircraft guns, and ammunition. Roosevelt had replied evasively and procrastinatingly, that he would require an authorisation by Congress, which he felt it was not opportune to ask for at the moment. Furthermore, he had to take the requirements for the defence of his own hemisphere and American commitments in the Pacific into consideration.

Despite all the personal sympathy Roosevelt may have felt for Churchill and the British cause, the Americans had no intention of letting themselves become involved in this war. Even when Reynaud and Churchill had attempted to convince the American President on 15 June that only a declaration of war by America could still save France, the only thing to come from Washington had been declarations of sympathy. In the Senate Foreign Relations Committee Senator Key Pittman stated that an entry into the war by the USA was out of the question; 'because we cannot provide any help for at least one year and the war will be over within six months. By then Hitler will either have won or he will never win.'

At this time, the United States were totally unprepared for a war. The army had a strength of only 75,000 men, the navy and air force combined made about 25,000 men. The weakness of the American armed forces was partly due to a strong isolationist undercurrent which people made no bones about in public. The United States had helped to win the First World War, but the Allies had not repaid their war debts. The Americans had been taken for a ride by one European war. This would not happen to them a second time. Never again were young men to be sent across the Atlantic to fight and die for the British Empire.

Many influential Americans still held their appeasement policies of 1938 against the British. Whereas Secretary of State Cordell Hull had recalled the American Ambassador Hugh R. Wilson to Washington in November 1938 to protest against the pogroms against the Jews during the *Reichskristallnacht*, Chamberlain and Daladier had let themselves be led up the garden path by Hitler and had agreed to a supposed peace arrangement with him. British–American relations reached a low point during the winter of 1939/40: the incidents at sea in the hunt for German sailors, the censoring of American mail on the high seas, the restrictions on agricultural imports from the USA, had angered the Americans; the sending of Sumner Welles of the State Department to the Continent without prior agreement, had angered the British. At this time, the British reputation in the United States was not much higher than that of the Germans or the Soviets.

Conservative observers in America had recognised the dangers emanating from Hitler and his Nazi movement early on. When former Harvard student Putzi Hanfstaengl visited his alma mater during the summer of 1934, the former President of Harvard, Professor Lawrence Lowell asked him to explain National Socialism and the reasons for its success with the Germans. 'One has to consider how the whole thing started', Hanfstaengl began. 'We had lost the war, the Communists ruled the streets. We had to start again at the very beginning. In the end, the Republic had 32 political parties, all of them too weak to get anything done. Finally there was nothing left but to unite them all in a single state party. That was Hitler's accomplishment. If a car gets stuck in the mud, it keeps on sinking deeper, and if the motor stops, one does not quibble about what the man is pouring into the engine, if only the journey continues. It may have been nothing but enthusiasm, but Hitler did it.' Lowell looked him in the eye: 'Fine, if it gets the car moving again, but what if the driver then gets drunk on it?' Such a stance was already so well developed by then that the President of Harvard, James Conant, flatly refused German scholarships for Harvard students, because he suspected that the money was coming from Hitler.

Very soon however, the rapid economic growth and increasing military power of the German *Reich* earned the Americans' grudging respect. The brilliantly staged 1936 Olympic Games and the pompous spectacles of the *Reichsparteitage* [Nazi national party conventions] did not fail to make an effect. President Roosevelt, deeply concerned with improving the living and working conditions of the American workers, kept himself informed in detail about the social programmes of the Nazis by his ambassador in Berlin. Six months before he was recalled, Wilson wrote about a visit to Dr Ley and his *Arbeitsfront* [labour front]: 'I believe there is something in *Kraft durch Freude* [strength through joy], from which the whole world may profit. Without question, one of our greatest problems in the field of employment in almost every country throughout the world, is the fact that increased wages do not enrich life or make it more mean- ingful, but that the additional money is normally wasted on idiotic things. The Germans, who are not able to increase wages because of their monetary situa- tion have, at the same wage level, enriched the lives of their workers by giving them access to music, art, and the beauty of their own and other countries. Even the factories have been made to look better, while the working year is interrupted by pleasure trips. And this has not developed as a philanthropic institution, but the workers have paid for it out of their own pocket. With a turnover of 2.5 billion *Reichsmarks*, *Kraft durch Freude* made a profit of some twenty million last year'. Wilson was also required to contact *Reichsarbeitsführer* [Reich Work Leader] Hierl in order to install a temporary observer in one of the camps of the *Reichsarbeitsdienst* [Reich labour service]. Faced with the army of American unemployed, the idea of a non-profit labour service had fallen on fruitful ground with Roosevelt.

The American press was less naive and as early as June 1938, the State Department was becoming concerned about the possible international reper- cussions of the growing anti-German sentiments which were becoming apparent in the major newspapers. These were initial reactions to the prosecu- tion of the Jews in Vienna and other Austrian cities during the *Anschluß* in March 1938. Only the American press had really understood what the Nuremberg (racial) laws and their practical application would mean for human dignity and human rights and what suffering they would bring to many human beings. This was also the root of the enmity against British and French appeasement poli- cies, and of the strong pressure on American isolationists, which finally forced Roosevelt to agree to the withdrawal of the American Ambassador in Berlin.

Politically however, these forces were not strong enough to entice the Amer- ican Government away from its reservations against the events in Europe. Neither the Polish campaign, nor the occupation of Czechoslovakia, the seizure of Denmark and Norway, the assaults on Holland, Belgium and Luxembourg and the collapse of France brought the 'Defenders of Freedom and Democracy' onto the stage, if one excepts that the Grand Duke of Luxembourg and Prince Felix were taken from Lisbon to New York on the American cruiser *Trenton*. All the calls for help fell on deaf ears. Wilson reduced the American stance to a simple equation: 'Twenty years ago we tried to save the world, and what does it look like today! If we were again to try to save the world, it would look no better after the end of the conflict. By entering into a European conflict, we have nothing to gain and everything to lose.'

In July 1940 in the United States, people had in fact written England off. Nine tenths of all Americans believed that Hitler had already as good as won the war in Europe. Only a very few still gave the British a chance to withstand the assault by the *Wehrmacht*, because alone and almost unarmed, it was facing a superior force, particularly the presumed superior *Luftwaffe*. The decadent island kingdom, as it was perceived to be by many Americans, would soon have to admit defeat and like France, be occupied by the Germans.

The staffs of the American armed forces, whose planning was almost exclusively directed at defending the Pacific region, suddenly saw themselves threatened from the Atlantic by the overwhelming successes of the *Wehrmacht*. With the expected downfall of Great Britain, the security of the American continent was more endangered by the Axis Powers than by Japan. Therefore the American Joint Chiefs of Staff now saw their major task to be the defence of the so-called Western Hemisphere along the Atlantic coast from Newfoundland to the Falklands. In a strategy paper written in May, 'Rainbow 4', a plan was developed to have American forces occupy British and French bases in the western Atlantic, from which an assault by the Axis Powers against South America could be repulsed.

Between 28 May and 18 June the Intelligence Service of the *Kriegsmarine* reported the reinforcement of the US European Squadron by the cruiser *Vincennes* and two destroyers, which were now at anchor in Lisbon next to the cruiser *Omaha*. Cruisers *Quincey* and *Wichita* had been despatched to South America. The former sailed for Montevideo, the latter arrived in Rio on 19 June. The American training squadron, consisting of (battleships) *Texas*, *New York*, and *Arkansas* left Annapolis for a visit to the Panama Canal Zone, Venezuela and the West Indies. It was also announced that the USA intended to put 35 old destroyers back into commission and integrate them into the forces charged with protecting neutrality. Over-hastily German Naval Command concluded from this, that it reduced British chances of obtaining these destroyers.

Together with these fleet movements, the United States increased their political activities in the Americas. Pan-Americanism was the slogan of the times and in the State Department serious consideration was being given to the idea of founding 'The United Nations of America', and even of occupying South American countries in case these did not ask for protection by American troops themselves, whereby Hitler was cited quite openly as an example.

In July, a Pan-American conference took place in Havana under the chairmanship of American Secretary of State for Foreign Affairs Cordell Hull. From

'The United Nations of America' a more realistic concept was developed: the 'Cartel of American Nations'. The idea was to unite the economic and defence forces of the Americas. The assumption was that after Great Britain had been knocked out, there would be a pause, if not peace, on the European continent. An integrated Europe under German leadership represented a gigantic market for the surpluses of the American countries, whose potential was to be exploited. A cartel on the American side as an economic counterweight would not only guarantee price stability, but would also protect the smaller nations against being drawn into the economic wake of a National Socialist Europe.

As much as one might be prepared in America to come to an economic arrangement with a Hitler-led Europe, the military threat to America by the Axis Powers could not be denied. After the defeat of France and Great Britain, the possessions of the former world powers in the western Atlantic would also fall to Germany. It was natural that they would be used as bases against the Americas. Much would depend on what happened to the French and British fleets. Were they to fall into German hands, together with the German and Italian fleet, they would be a deadly threat for the United States. The American Chief of Naval Operations, Admiral William Standley, expected a first show-down in Newfoundland. Germany could already succeed in weakening the British fleet, or at least in tying it down in its home ports. Then Germany could establish a hold on Iceland, set up a base in Greenland and from there, capture Newfoundland, after which Britain's major supply route would be cut off. America would then have to decide whether it could tolerate this attack on North American territory, albeit British.

During these dramatic weeks, the issue for the American planners was not to help the French and British against Hitler, it was to 'prevent a penetration of the Western Hemisphere by the Axis Powers'. General Marshall charged the planners with considering worst cases, namely that the Allied fleets were no longer in the Atlantic. The time was ripe for mobilising the National Guard and discontinuing ammunition shipments to England, in so far as it was needed for American mobilisation. Chief of Staff Strong openly admitted that Marshall's guidelines took an early defeat of the Allies for an accomplished fact and that America did not have the means to decisively alter the situation. He believed that America was next on the Axis Powers' list of victims.

President Roosevelt conferred almost daily with his military advisers. He agreed the about face of American defence plans to the Atlantic, but refused to approve plans that were based on the fact of Great Britain having been defeated. On the contrary, for the next six months, England was to be supported in its struggle as before, insofar as this did not interfere with American defence efforts. A temporary occupation of European possessions in the Western Hemisphere, as well as strategically important positions in South America, was only to take place after consultations with the governments concerned.

Roosevelt was obviously endeavouring to keep America out of a war if at all possible. In November he had to face presidential elections and anything that would speed up entry into a war, like mobilisation, occupation of foreign territories, discontinuation of military aid, would cost him votes. Churchill's exhortations to stand firm and his fervent pleas for delivery of military supplies were therefore politically very welcome to him. In his rare statements on this topic, however, he continued to remain noncommittal and reticent.

On 31 July Churchill asked for destroyers, torpedo boats, and flying boats yet once again: 'The Germans have the whole French coastline from which to launch U-boat and dive-bomber attacks upon our trade and food, and in addition we must be constantly prepared to repel by sea action threatened invasion ... and also to deal with break-out from Norway towards Ireland, Iceland, the Shetlands, and Faroes. Besides this we have to keep control of the exits from the Mediterranean, and if possible the command of that inland sea itself, and thus to prevent the war spreading ... into Africa.'

The answer was not long in coming. In the meantime, the 'hawks' had become active in Washington. The Century Group, an association of prominent interventionists had recommended to the President to let the British have the desired destroyers. The conditions, however, were hardly favourable for the British but were more orientated towards American defence measures. In the event of an invasion of England, the British fleet was to operate out of Canadian and American ports, and concessions should be made immediately for the establishment of American naval and airbases on the British possessions in the Western Hemisphere.

At a meeting of the Cabinet on 2 August the deal was approved in principle and discussed in public on 6 August. On 13 August, Roosevelt wrote Churchill: 'I believe it is possible to provide in the form of immediate aid to the British Government, at least fifty destroyers, the motor torpedo boats already mentioned and five aircraft in each category as test machines.' This could only take place, however, if the American people and its Congress were able to perceive that in exchange, national defence and the security of the United States had been strengthened. Therefore Roosevelt demanded: '1. An assurance by the Prime Minister that, if the waters surrounding Great Britain became untenable for the British fleet, it would not be handed over to the Germans or sunk, but sent to other parts of the British Empire, in order to improve its defence in those areas. 2. The British Government empowers the United States to use Newfoundland, the Bermudas, the Bahamas, Jamaica, St Lucia, Trinidad and British Guiana as naval and airbases in case of an attack on the Western Hemisphere by a non-American nation. In the meantime, the United States have the right to establish such bases and to use them for purposes of exercise and training. The required land may be bought or leased by the United States for 99 years.'

For the British, the demand for bases in exchange for the delivery of destroyers came as an unpleasant surprise. Would that not be perceived as if Churchill were selling off parts of the British Empire for fifty worn out destroyers? Churchill was well aware of the political strictures Roosevelt was under: 'We can', he wrote, 'agree on both points to your demands, which you deem necessary in order to help you in Congress and elsewhere.' At the same time he thanked Roosevelt for his efforts in effusive terms. One week later, however, he asked the American President to consider that offsetting the destroyers against a participation in British possessions could lead to misunderstandings. He preferred to have both transactions regarded as separate gifts. He also drew Roosevelt's attention to the fact that Newfoundland lay within Canada's sphere of influence, which would naturally first have to be consulted.

Shortly before Roosevelt's demand, the British Cabinet had already discussed leasing bases in the western Atlantic. It had just been on the verge of making such an offer because The Pentagon had suggested leasing landing rights to Pan Am on British airports in the Caribbean, which would then automatically be used by the American Air Force to protect the Panama Canal. Now the British Cabinet saw itself confronted by a much more far-reaching demand, which bore no relationship to the benefits the Americans were prepared to provide. Quite apart from the fact that these benefits indirectly also served America's defence, in the minds of the British they had already been materially more than compensated for by Britain having disclosed the closely guarded secret of radar and sent engineers to the United States to build radar stations.

The Americans on the other hand still had Britain's old, unpaid war debt from the First World War on their books. It kept surfacing in the press on any and all occasions. In Washington however, greater weight was given to the presumed weakening of their own fleet. In this, the Americans were particularly touchy, because the forces of their navy were the only really powerful weapons the Americans disposed of at the time. 'Between us and the Nazis', an official in the State Department remarked, 'there is only the British fleet. If it goes, we stand alone!' In this situation, only additional bases could compensate for the giving away of warships. And finally, the British should be thankful that the United States was minding parts of the British Empire for them, instead of Hitler grabbing them as booty.

For Roosevelt the most important thing now was to find out from dependable sources what was really behind Churchill's rhetoric, whether the British really still had a chance in this struggle and if they were capable, in contrast to Kennedy's claims, of seizing it.

In July, secret service agent Colonel William Donovan appeared in London, much to Ambassador Kennedy's annoyance, whom the State Department had not informed about Donovan's mission. Donovan himself claimed that he wanted to study the British draft regulations as a future model for America, furthermore that he was looking for material on the buildup of a counter-espionage organisation. The only thing that is certain is that he was to report directly to Roosevelt on the military situation in the British Isles. Donovan stayed in England until 2 August.

On 15 August a whole troop of advisers to the American President came to England: Brigadier George V. Strong, Army Chief of Operations; Major General Delos C. Emmons, Chief of Operations of the Army Air Corps; and Rear Admiral Robert Ghormley, the Navy's Deputy Chief of Operations. Their mission was secret, as had been Donovan's. But already weeks before, their arrival had been the topic of conversations at London cocktail parties. The reaction by the Intelligence Department of the German Naval Command to the arrival of the American admiral was just as laconic.

The British had been entertaining very high hopes. In this visit they saw the beginning of preparations for America's entry into the war and wanted to sketch supply possibilities and possible joint operations in staff meetings. The generals evaded this. They were only after information. The British found it hard to believe that these senior officers had come to London without precise instructions, but nonetheless managed to adjust to the situation very quickly. The visitors were permitted to look around all the staffs and military units. Churchill himself took the Americans to Dover by train, in order to impress them with the fighting spirit of the British and with the dangers that the island kingdom faced.

To outward appearances nothing changed: America was sitting on the fence and waiting to see how things developed. Before the elections, there were to be no decisions, not even discussions and only a minimum of aid. It remained to the *Luftwaffe* to blow the first breach here.

XVI
The Luftwaffe Begins the Battle
The 'Channel Attack'

The role of the *Luftwaffe* in the preparation of the invasion requires special attention, because with it 'Operation Sea Lion' either stood or fell. According to Directive No. 16 of 16 July, its task was 'to prevent intervention by the enemy's air force', 'knock out ... coastal defences', 'break initial opposition by enemy ground forces', and 'destroy approaching enemy reserves'. In addition, it was to keep the enemy fleet in check and land airborne troops and parachutists.

Despite these clear instructions, which unequivocally tied the start of the operation to the *Luftwaffe* being successful, it was soon to be enmeshed in a battle which only to outward appearances had anything to do with the preparation of an invasion. As the British saw it, retention of air superiority served mainly to be able to beat back an attack prior to actual invasion, whereas the *Luftwaffe* fought with the objective of total destruction of the military and economic infrastructure, while reserving the option to launch terror attacks against the civilian population. If this objective had been achieved, 'Sea Lion' would have become superfluous. As he had already done at Dunkirk, Göring went against all military logic and by acting off his own bat sabotaged the whole operation, even though his ideas did coincide with the plans for 'Sea Lion' to some extent. It is therefore essential to describe the battle between the two air forces in detail, to portray the strengths and weaknesses of both sides, in order to make the fatal outcome for the Germans understandable, despite the self-sacrificing efforts of their pilots.

In June 1940, the *Luftwaffe* was basking in the undisputed reputation of being the strongest air force in the world. Since its successes during the Spanish Civil War it had made decisive contributions to victory in three campaigns: *Stukas* and fighters had blasted the way clear for armour and infantry, bombers had destroyed enemy positions and supply bases, sunk dozens of enemy ships in ports and on the high seas, and with transport planes, paratroops had been taken far behind enemy lines. In the air it had proved itself to be invincible, because in the campaign against France alone, the pilots of the *Luftwaffe* had shot down more than 3,000 enemy aircraft or destroyed them on the ground.

The strategic conditions for the decisive blows had meanwhile been met. The whole coastline of the North Sea and the Channel, from northern Norway to Cherbourg and Brest, was now in German hands and with it, dozens of air bases in the hinterland which could serve the *Luftwaffe* as take-off points. Pioneer detachments were working full out day and night to put the Dutch, Belgian and French bases back into service. Bombed runways were filled in, wrecks of aircraft removed, barracks built, fences put up, anti-aircraft positions dug, and wireless stations installed. Some bases had already been occupied during the fighting; on others, the aircraft transferred there landed just as soon as the grass runways had become serviceable.

The two strongest of the five German *Luftflotten* were stationed on the Channel coast: *Luftflotte* 2 under Field Marshal Kesselring in the area between Rotterdam and Amiens, *Luftflotte* 3 under Field Marshal Sperrle in the Cherbourg area. Together, the two *Luftflotten* disposed of 656 Bf 109 fighters, 769 Do 17, Ju 88, and He 111 bombers, over 248 Ju 87 dive bombers (*Stukas*), and 168 twin-engined Bf 110 fighters. In total, there were 1,841 serviceable aircraft, which according to German estimates, were opposed by 400 to 500 British fighters defending the other side of the Channel.

These numbers, however, do not reflect the true relative strengths. The *Luftwaffe* was not as healthy and full of vigour as it appeared or pretended itself to be. It was the victim of mistaken planning reaching far back into prewar days and mainly attributable to the incompetence of its leaders.

To make matters worse, the Versailles Treaty had forbidden the German *Reich* to have an air force at all. It was only in 1935 that Hitler broke this treaty, and announced the rearmament of Germany and the existence of a *Luftwaffe*, to whose command he appointed the Prussian Minister President Hermann Göring as *Reichluftfahrtminister* [Reich Air Minister].

Nonetheless, the *Luftwaffe* had not grown overnight. Much preparatory work had been carried out in the civil sector. Lufthansa, one of the largest and most successful airlines in the world, was providing a growing German aircraft industry with orders. A large number of different types of civil aircraft had been developed, one of the better known being the Ju 52, the work-horse of the Second World War. In 1935, on the drawing-boards of aircraft designers Messerschmitt, Dornier, Heinkel, and Junkers, one could already see the plans for military machines such as the Bf 109, the Do 17, the He 111, and the Ju 86, all of which had been developed out of civil aircraft. As early as 1937 at the military air show in Zurich, the *Luftwaffe* had aroused admiration with its machines. The Bf 109 held the world speed record for single-engined fighter aircraft. The following year the Ju 88 was to break the speed record for medium range bombers. It was a great advantage for the manning level of the *Luftwaffe*, that by now it could draw upon a large reservoir of highly qualified pilots. Officially, this had continuously been built up from the extremely popular glider clubs. The leaders however, mainly came from the Russian flight training school at Lipzek south of Moscow, where German officers were being trained as military pilots on the basis of a secret treaty with the Soviet Union.

Still, this was not yet an air force. The man who was intended to make it into one was Hermann Göring. As with so many of Hitler's vassals, he was miscast in his role, because he lacked the character traits and the organisational abilities the job required. The highly intelligent egomaniac was as vain as a comic opera figure and enjoyed extraordinary popularity. But he was also obsessed with an unscrupulous lust for power and money, which turned him into one of Hitler's most dangerous blood-hounds. As Minister President of Prussia he had been the actual founder of the Gestapo, and together with Himmler and Heydrich, had installed the concentration camps. He was also responsible for a large number of the victims of the so-called Röhm Putsch. Up until the early years of the war he was the second most powerful man after Hitler, and by far the wealthiest politician in Germany. When he was appointed as plenipotentiary for the four-year-plan in 1936, he made himself the undisputed overlord of German industry. He drew substantial financial benefits from the *Hermann-Göring-Werke*, a concern with 700,000 employees and a share capital of 400 million *Reichsmarks*. His penchant for luxury and the good things in life was boundless, jewellery, castles and hunting were his particular preferences.

All of this had little to do with the term 'Air Force'. Göring's only qualification for the air consisted in his having been a fighter pilot during the First World War, in the end as commander of the Richthofen Squadron, and after the war a civilian pilot for two years in Sweden. Since then, flying and an air force had no longer interested him. His appointment as *Reichluftfahrtminister* and Commander-in-Chief of the *Luftwaffe* meant no more to him than just another jewel in his crown, a symbol of his power, which he displayed to the world by means of fantastic comic opera uniforms covered with medals. His concept of an air force was restricted to two beliefs: fighters were to shoot down as many enemies as possible and, as had been advocated by Italian Air Force General Douhet, the role of bombers was strategic mass bombardment which would inevitably decide a war and relegate the army and the navy to the role of mere bit players. How this was to be achieved and with what, was of no concern at all to Göring. For such matters, he had called Erhard Milch, Chairman and Financial Director of Lufthansa, into his *Luftfahrtministerium* [Air Ministry] as State Secretary.

Milch had the reputation of being an excellent organiser. As a financial expert, he had made a major contribution to the rise of Lufthansa, but a military thinker who would have been essential in this position, he was not. A strategic concept and an aircraft production programme that would have made such a concept possible were never developed. One may well put a large part of the blame for this on Hitler's vague and constantly changing war plans, which never permitted sound planning and preparation, but in any case, arrogant and unpredictable Milch took decisions as *Generalinspekteur der Luftwaffe* [Inspector General of the Air Force], which were determined less by objective considerations than by emotions, and he caused great damage by this.

Aircraft designer Willy Messerschmitt fell into disfavour with Milch because Milch's best friend was killed in an accident with a Messerschmitt plane. Many new *Luftwaffe* orders were therefore withheld from Messerschmitt and his *Bayerische Flugzeugwerke* [Bavarian Aircraft Works] in Augsburg. Instead, in order to humiliate the aircraft manufacturer, Milch had the Messerschmitt factory build Heinkel aircraft under licence, which greatly restricted their production capacity. Milch treated ageing Hugo Junkers, to whom he personally owed much, no better. The staunch National Socialist Milch believed he had to make an example of his former protector because Junkers had refused the Nazis his cooperation. In 1935 Junkers was dispossessed, his factories nationalised and he himself put under house arrest. Six months later Junkers died.

Milch's unfriendly relations with Ernst Udet, whom Hitler had appointed as *Reichluftzeugmeister* [Chief of Aircraft Development], had even graver repercussions. With 62 kills the most successful fighter pilot after Richthofen during the First World War, Udet became a test pilot and stunt flyer when the war was over. He was an upright man and a carefree bon viveur who only lived for flying, but who did not have even the slightest qualification for his office. In connivance with Göring, Milch constantly let him fall into traps until the despairing Udet took his own life in 1941. Milch's lack of military foresight together with Udet's incompetence resulted in chaos in aircraft development and a production output that was lagging behind that of other nations.

The *Luftwaffe* was developed by pilots from the First World War. They were still caught up in their memories of the chivalrous air duels between biplanes, low-level attacks on enemy trenches and artillery positions, and bombs that were dropped by hand. Even though sixteen years of development and use of military aircraft had naturally passed them by, such 'experts' played the key roles in the new *Luftwaffe*. Milch, who during the First World War had been employed as an artillery spotter over Verdun and the Somme, hastened to fall into line: battles are won by fighters and dive bombers.

Udet was obsessed with the Bf 109, whose technical details he knew more thoroughly than many a mechanic. He had far less time for bombers. If there had to be any at all, then they should at least have the attributes of dive bombers. At the head of the class stood the *Stuka*, the Ju 87, which had proved itself so outstandingly during the preceding campaigns. The newly developed twin-engined Ju 88 could also be employed as a dive bomber. The only existing four-engined bomber had to be redesigned several times, because the *Luftwaffe* demanded that this heavy machine should also be capable of diving down on the enemy. In any case the plane was never built in large numbers, because the coupling of two engines to a single propeller did not work properly. The development of the long-range bombers Do 19 and Ju 89, which Udet's predecessor General Wever had initiated, was cancelled in the belief that it would be possible to get by with fast medium-range bombers which required less raw material to build. Recognisable even then, these were serious mistakes. However, they were not able to affect the boundless self-confidence of the young *Luftwaffe*. Up to now no enemy had been able to withstand its great power.

Foolishly, the setback at Dunkirk was ignored. There, the *Luftwaffe* had not succeeded in preventing the exodus by the British, as Göring had boastfully promised. Instead in self-satisfaction, much was made of the many ships sunk and of 105 air victories which German pilots had achieved against the British fighter forces when these had tried to attack German bombers over the rescue ships. Included among the enemy machines shot down were also a fair number of Spitfires, the fastest British fighter, which had made its debut against the *Luftwaffe* there.

The great confidence the German pilots had in their fighter aircraft was not misplaced. With a top speed of 684 km/h, the Bf 109 was not only the fastest fighter in he world, it also had a faster rate of climb, and was armed with two machine-guns and two 2cm cannon. The Spitfire was 20 to 30 km/h slower, had eight machine-guns and no cannon. But already at Dunkirk, several German pilots had learnt to their sorrow that the Spitfire was far more manoeuvrable and only had to fly a series of tight turns in order to wind up in a shooting position behind a German pursuer. This made up in part for the slower speed. The British machine had only one handicap in the beginning: when diving steeply from level flight, the engine stalled because the carburettor design caused momentary fuel starvation. The German machine was equipped with fuel injection which prevented this happening. In the final analysis, who would gain the upper hand in a dogfight depended very much on the skill of the pilot.

Deployment of the two *Luftflotten* on the Channel coast was completed by 24 July, but directive No. 16 was still slumbering on the desks of the staffs. 'Operation Sea Lion' was unpopular with the *Luftwaffe*, because Göring was not alone in believing England could be vanquished solely from the air. Tacitly another directive issued by Hitler on 20 November 1939 was being clung to: 'Once the *Heer* has succeeded in defeating the Anglo-French field army and in occupying and holding a sector of the Continental coast facing England, then the assignment of the *Kriegsmarine* and the *Luftwaffe* to wage war against the English economy takes precedence.' *Kanalkampfführer* [Channel Battle Leader] Colonel

Fink of *Kampfgeschwader** 2 [Bomber Wing], who was to coordinate the battle over the Channel, did not want to wait until all of the units had been assembled in full strength. Already on 3 July, he had undertaken sorties over the Channel off the English south coast with the forces available and thereby begun the air war against England on this front. 'In connection with an armed reconnaissance', as the *Wehrmacht* bulletin on 3 July had cautiously stated, a small bomber force protected by fighters had sunk two freighters totalling 14,000 BRT out of a convoy off the English coast. During the night, other formations dropped bombs on ports along the English Channel coast. As far as the weather permitted these attacks were continued day after day with increasing forces.

The purpose of this operation was to discover the strengths and weaknesses of British air defence. The idea above all, was to draw the British fighters out and to involve them in a battle of attrition with superior forces. Once the British fighter force had been annihilated, the German bombers could fly into England unhindered and deliver the big blow against the British home country.

The leadership of RAF Fighter Command however, did not appear to be falling into the trap and kept its machines back. It only flew sorties against the German long-range reconnaissance aircraft Do 17, which were searching out targets for the bombers. It was only on 7 July that the Spitfires took up the challenge. Towards 20.30 that evening, 45 Do 17s, accompanied by 60 Bf 109s, attacked a convoy off Folkestone. They sank one freighter and damaged three more. Flying high above the bombers the Bf 109s were waiting for the British fighters. Twelve Spitfires of 65 Squadron attacked the bombers who were just in the act of turning back with their job completed. Two Do 17s were damaged, but already the Bf 109s came hurtling down upon their prey and shot down three Spitfires without incurring any loss themselves. Three more Spitfires were shot down over the Manston.

On 10 July, 75 Do 17s from *Kampfgeschwader* 2 and 60 *Stukas* from III Air Division assembled over the French coast where they were joined by a formation of 200 Bf 109s. Colonel Fink was sure that the large convoy air reconnaissance had sighted in the Channel would be defended by British fighters. The attack on the convoy was a failure, only a corvette of 700 tonnes was sunk, because 30 Spitfires came hurtling in among the bombers without letting themselves become involved in a set-to with the German fighters. The result: the Royal Air Force lost six machines, the attackers fifteen.

*Translator's note: In Anglo-American terminology, a 'fighter' is a light, fast aeroplane for attacking enemy aircraft. In German, such an aeroplane is called a Jäger, a hunter. *Kampfflieger*, i.e., 'fighter aircraft', is the term applied to a bomber, following Douhet's theory that the bomber is the weapon with which one 'fights' the enemy by bombing him. Therefore, bomber Wings were called *Kampfgeschwader*, whereas fighter Wings were called *Jagdgeschwader*.

On the German side confidence remained despite this. The *Jäger* even had grounds to celebrate because they were able to book six victories without having lost any machines themselves. The British fighters had shot down the *Stukas* like clay pigeons which immediately resulted in the Ju 87 being nick-named the 'flying coffin'. The *Stuka* was so slow, that its fighter cover had trouble staying with it, particularly if the sky was cloudy. With its load of bombs attached outside it only reached a top speed of 250 km/h. In combat against tactical ground targets in support of the *Heer*, the *Stuka* had performed excep-tionally well, but it was not suitable for the role it was now intended to play. In combat at sea the howling of its siren had nothing like the same demoralising effect as in combat on land, and ship targets require a far greater accuracy in bombing because the attacker cannot depend on the spread effect of his bombs as on land. At sea, there are only direct hits, or misses, and most of the bombs missed.

As much as the British fighters were attempting to concentrate solely on the bombers, the Bf 109s never kept them waiting for long. On 19 July there were no fewer than nine convoys in the waters off the English south and south-western coast. On this day, the *Luftwaffe* only succeeded in sinking one freighter of 5,000 BRT out of one of the convoys. On the other hand, 120 *Stukas* and Bf 109s attacked the ships lying in the port at Dover. On the first sweep, the *Stukas* succeeded in sinking the 12,000 BRT Royal Navy tanker *War Sepoy* by a direct hit. Time and again, the bombers came screaming down on the docks, fountains of water rose up as high as a house, almost completely obscuring vision. Several smaller ships broke apart or foundered under the bombing attacks. It was only when a formation of nine Defiant fighter aircraft threw themselves in between the fighters and bombers with total disregard for death, that the *Stukas* pulled out. The Defiants, however, were the slowest of the British fighters. With a crew of two and a machine-gun turret mounted on the fuselage they were much too unwieldy. Within minutes, six of them had been shot down. Hurricanes that came rushing to their rescue were only able to shoot down one of the attackers.

On 24 July the German bombers and *Stukas* sank five ships totalling 17,000 BRT out of several convoys and damaged three more so heavily that their loss had to be reckoned with. The following day, according to a *Wehrmacht* report, a large convoy was attacked and a total of 63,000 BRT sunk. Nine British aircraft were shot down for a loss of two German planes. The RAF pilots, however, reported shooting down fifteen German machines for own losses of six.

After this, the long-range reconnaissance planes of the *Luftwaffe* had to search far and wide before they sighted a British ship. It was obvious that the British had greatly reduced ship traffic through the Channel. German Intelligence soon discovered that the convoys had been redirected to western ports such as Glasgow, Liverpool and Manchester, because all of these ports were suddenly overcrowded to the extent that one had even gone over to unloading ships by lighter. With this, the *Luftwaffe* had been deprived of easy prey and their bait for the British fighters.

From then on the motto of the *Jäger* became: open hunting season over England. The *Jagdgeschwader* now flew two to three sorties a day attempting to get at the British fighters. The formations assembled at altitudes of 5,000 to 6,000 metres over the French coast and climbed up to 7,000 to 8,000 metres before reaching the English coast, in order to be above their opponents and able to dive down on them. In the ensuing air battles, the British had to accept heavy losses, because they were not only inferior to the Germans in terms of machines, but also in tactics. The German *Jagdstaffeln* [fighter squadrons] flew in *Rotten* [pairs] or in *Schwärmen* [sections] of four. Out of each pair of machines, one acted as leader, the other as look-out, because being surprised by an enemy was normally fatal to a fighter. The greatest German ace, Werner Mölders, had developed this flight formation in Spain.

The British were still following the scheme inherited from the First World War of flying in tight V-formations of three or four planes, in which each pilot had to constantly watch out that he did not collide with the wings of his neighbour. Since they were only able to fly with divided attention, the British pilots were frequently surprised and therefore easy prey. It did not take long before the British changed their formations and adopted those of the Germans.

Major Galland, who at this time was able to have the symbol of his twentieth air victory painted on the rudder of his plane, flew his first sortie over the Channel on 24 July. Over the Thames estuary his group of Bf 109s became involved in a dogfight with Spitfires that were guarding a convoy. The Messerschmitt fighters had the advantage of greater altitude and dived down on the formation of Spitfires from behind. Galland attached himself to a machine flying on the outside and during a wide turn to the right, was able to fire a long burst at it before the other pilot became aware. Galland's adversary fell into the sea like a stone. But two of Galland's comrades were also shot down during this engagement. 'That was bitter', Galland said later. 'The Royal Air Force, there could be no doubt about it, was a very serious opponent.'

The battle, however, could not be won just by dogfights. The German pilots had to recognise this all too soon. The British were evading the great air battle that Göring desired. Nevertheless, they had not abandoned the coastal airbases and withdrawn to the outskirts of London under the assault of the German *Jäger* and *Stukas*. They were well aware of the short range of the Bf 109 and made full use of it. If they wanted to reach their home base, the German fighters could not remain in the air over England for longer than twenty minutes before having to turn back. Their fuel was only sufficient for about 80 minutes' flying time, and they had to calculate 60 minutes for the flight in and back. The British fighters only took off when they were able to assume that their opponents had about used up their fuel. From then on, all they had to do was to prevent the enemy from leaving as long as possible. The trick was quite often successful.

The mood among the German pilots became more and more depressed. Göring called his commanders to a conference at Carinhall. Galland and Mölders were also invited. They received the Pilots Medal in gold with diamonds, and the highest praise for their bravery from the mouth of the *Reichs-marschall*. But bitter words were also spoken, because Göring was highly displeased with his fighter force. That the bombers were suffering such heavy losses was only the fault of the covering fighter forces. They were lacking in the spirit of aggression. And he already knew how to repair the damage. The older *Geschwaderkommodore*, mostly fighter pilots from the First World War who were no longer able to fly, were to be replaced by daredevil younger officers. His motto had become: the officer with the highest score in enemies shot down is also the best *Geschwaderkommodor*. Consequently, Mölders and Galland were therefore promoted to *Geschwaderkommodore*, because Mölders too now had twenty victims to his credit.

This did not alter the situation on the air front in the least. Losses remained disproportionately high. The game of cat and mouse the British were playing continued. Meanwhile, pressure on the fighter pilots grew. There was talk of an impending major sortie by the bombers which would only become possible if the British fighter defence had been beaten to the ground. 'The lack of clarity about how the air war was to continue began to affect every last pilot', Galland remarked. By this time *Führer* Directive No. 16 had also made the rounds within the *Luftwaffe*. Responsibility for an invasion now suddenly lay with the *Jagdflieger*, because it was more necessary than ever before to overcome the British fighter forces.

Göring had given the chiefs of his *Luftflotten* twelve days to let him have their ideas and plans for a concentrated air offensive against England. Field Marshals Kesselring and Sperrle, and Colonel General Stumpf, delegated the planning to the *Fliegerkorps* [air divisions] whose staffs, however, did not prove themselves to be capable of handling this strategic assignment. Only two of these 'plans' still exist in the original, a third has been reconstructed:

Fliegerkorps VIII (v. Richthofen), the only one having three wings of *Stukas*, merely suggested employing these *Stukas* for attacking and destroying Royal Air Force ground installations.

Fliegerkorps II (Loerzer) placed the emphasis on a bombardment of London. The condition on which this was to be based was a prior decisive weakening of Fighter Command's fighting strength. Attacks on London would attract the remaining fighters, which could then be destroyed all the more easily. Thereafter, sorties into the hinterland would become possible. (This suggestion did not stand a chance from the beginning, because at this time, Hitler was not yet prepared to consider bombing attacks against London.)

Fliegerkorps I (Grauert) had given most thought to the matter. It suggested three possibilities:

1. Gaining air superiority by eliminating the Royal Air Force and the aircraft factories.
2. Strikes against the Royal Air Force and the Royal Navy to protect the *Heer* routes across the Channel and support from the air of the troops landed.
3. Blockading and strangling England by destroying her ports.

Independently of these three alternatives, terror raids against major British cities should be ruthlessly carried out.

Hitler was becoming impatient. On 30 July he ordered the *Luftwaffe* to speed up its preparations for its attack against the British Isles in such a manner that within twelve hours of an order from him, the attack could be launched. Two days later he issued Directive No. 17 on the 'conduct of the air and sea war against Great Britain'. It too did not contain any clear operational instructions, but instead named a date for the attack: 5 August was to be *Adlertag* [Eagle Day], on condition that the weather was favourable. The role of the *Luftwaffe* had only been sketched: overpowering the Royal Air Force in the air and on the ground, destruction of the ports in order to cut British supplies. The ports along the southern coast were to be exempted because they would be needed for a possible invasion.

Göring himself put an end to the guesswork in the *Luftwaffe* staffs. At a big conference held at the headquarters of General Christiansen, *Luftwaffe* Commander for Holland, in the Hague, he disclosed his battle plan which had probably been prepared by General Jeschonnek's staff: an attack was to be conducted against southern and southeastern England in a semi-circle around London. During the first five days, the Royal Air Force within a radius of 150 to 100 kilometres was to be assaulted in the air and on the ground, and destroyed by a concentrated attack beginning in the west, then moving to the south and east. In the following three days, the radius of the operation was to be reduced to targets within 100 to 50 kilometres, and during the final five days, to targets within less than 50 kilometres of London. He reckoned with from 400 to 500 British fighters. Execution of this plan would inevitably lead to gaining command of the air and thereby fulfilling the *Führer's* assignment: 'Operation Sea Lion' could then begin.

His field marshals were hardly enchanted by this plan. Neither Sperrle nor Kesselring wanted to commit their bombers before the enemy fighter defence had been overcome. Their pilots had already had to pay far too high a price for the fact that the British defenders concentrated on them and avoided German fighters wherever possible. They reminded Göring that since 1 July, the *Luftwaffe* had lost almost 200 machines. Instead of sending bombers under fighter cover against the London docks by day, the two *Luftflotten* Chiefs preferred to bomb airbases at night and thereby decisively weaken the enemy fighter defence, before going over to concentrated raids by day.

Göring found these objections to be laughable: '*Jagdgeschwader* 51 has already shot down more than 150 enemy machines. That is weakening enough. And given the numbers of our bombers in both *Luftflotten*, this handful of British fighters is contemptible.' He deliberately overlooked the fact that these 150 'air victories' included all of the planes shot down in France as well as the enemy aircraft destroyed on the ground. And Göring did not have his figures straight on the bombers either. Earlier on he had already talked about 4,500 available bombers and was nearly bowled over when he learned that between them, his two *Luftflotten* on the Channel only disposed of barely 1,000 service-able machines.

Finally, the conference reached a compromise. Smaller formations of *Stukas* and bombers were to fly ahead under fighter cover, followed only ten to fifteen minutes later by the main force of bombers under their own cover of Bf 110s. The whole thing was to be repeated twice a day. Targets were still to be the Royal Air Force's bases, aircraft factories and port installations.

The *Reichsmarschall* himself went to the front to take personal command of the coming great battle. Already weeks before near Le Coudray on the railway line Paris–Beauvais and only 55 kilometres from the Champs Elysées, hundreds of workers and German Engineers had closed the northern end of a tunnel, chopped down trees, built anti-aircraft positions and hung barbed wire; sentries were posted everywhere, motorcycle patrols were combing the area, and all because of 'Fatso's' command headquarters, special train 'Asia'. The arrival of the special train was a spectacle in itself, completely suited to the *Reichsmarshall's* pomp. An advanced train came on ahead with guards, equipment and vehicles. Some distance behind came Göring's own train consisting of four cars, preceded by a flatcar with a Flak gun. Göring's saloon car contained a small office, two bedrooms and a bath. It had specially designed soft springs and had been weighted with lead to ensure a smooth ride. The following car contained the command post with map room and telephone exchange, the next housed a kitchen and a dining room, the fourth was designed for adjutants and guests. The crew of the train numbered 171 men, to whom two of Göring's constant companions had to be added: his valet Kropp and Christa Gormanns, a nurse. Göring almost always had guests staying with him, but also often went to nearby Paris.

5 August dawned but nothing happened. Bad weather was preventing take-offs. On the 6th and 7th the weather was also bad along the French coast. On 8 August, 400 German aircraft, *Stukas* and Bf 109s, attacked convoys off Dover and the Isle of Wight. They sank four ships and damaged another six. British fighter defence had been reinforced. The *Luftwaffe* lost 30 planes against 20 of the Royal Air Force On 11 August Sperrle sent 165 bombers of *Luftflotte* 3 under strong fighter escort to attack Portland and Weymouth. 38 German machines were lost, 32 British were shot down.

Nor did the attack order for *Adlertag* come on 12 August. Despite this, over half of the serviceable aircraft flew across the Channel. *Stukas* attacked Portsmouth, the airbases at Manston, Hawkinge and Lympne were heavily damaged. The *Luftwaffe* lost 31 machines, the Royal Air Force 22.

In none of the preceding campaigns had the *Luftwaffe* had to suffer such heavy losses. The fighter pilots were frustrated, the bomber pilots becoming unsure. Medals and promotions were no consolation. And it was soon to get worse, because in all of the tactical skirmishing, the *Luftwaffe* leadership had overlooked the decisive strategic advantage enjoyed by the British. The German pilots were unaware that they were flying across the Channel as if on a platter, because the British radar network was picking up every formation, every single aircraft, even before they had quit the French coast. Each time, Fighter Command was warned just as quickly as the anti-aircraft. In the end, the blind battering of its head against the wall of British radar was to break the back of the *Luftwaffe*.

XVII
The British Warning System
The key to victory

Ever since the German Gotha bombers and Zeppelins had dropped their bombs on defenceless London during the First World War, the fear of bombers had not left the minds of the British. Connected to this, however, was a certain feeling of helplessness: how was one to protect the English coast over all its length? The anti-aircraft guns required to do this would have eaten up the total British defence budget for many years and one would probably have needed half the population to man them. And it would not have been of any use, because without an early warning of approaching bombers, a ring of anti-aircraft guns around the island would hardly have been effective.

During the 1930s, British Air Defence had begun to install listening equipment along the coasts. At Romney Marsh on the southern coast, a curved 8m high and 70m long concrete wall was erected, which being equipped with microphones, was to serve as an artificial ear directed against the French coast. But the heavy diesel engines of large ships in the Channel, the surf, the moaning of the wind, could all smother or distort the noise made by an approaching enemy formation and thereby make the listening installation almost useless.

'The bomber will always get through', Stanley Baldwin, Leader of the Conservatives in the Commons stated in 1934, and suggested that the Rhine should be regarded as Britain's first line of defence. That was the only way to keep the Germans at a distance. Air defence appeared to be becoming more and more hopeless, the more the desires of the German *Reich* to rearm and the existence of a German air force began to make themselves felt. The planners at the Air Ministry were desperately searching for a way out of the dilemma. However, all the mental efforts kept coming back to the absurd idea that a death ray had to be invented. The idea became so overriding, that people seriously began to search and contact all the physics laboratories throughout the kingdom.

Physicist Robert Watson-Watt was at first dumbfounded when Harry Wimperis of the Air Ministry Research Staff asked him out of the blue, whether there was a sort of ray that could be used against enemy bombers. Watson-Watt, 42 years old at the time, was head of the Wireless Research Station at the National Physical Laboratory and had mainly occupied himself with localising atmospheric disturbances in weather prediction. After years of research, he and his team had succeeded in making the disturbances that are normally connected to a storm front visible on the screen of a cathode ray tube (Braun tube) and to measure their distance. X-rays could also be produced with cathode ray tubes, but death rays? Watson-Watt promised to think about it.

Together with his colleagues, he examined the possibilities of influencing the electrical impulses of an aeroplane engine by means of radio waves. They rejected the idea because an aeroplane would never stay within the range of the transmitter long enough. (It was only 50 years later that jet aeroplanes were to be unintentionally caused to crash by radio waves.) The attempt to drastically increase the body temperature of a pilot by means of radio waves was also abandoned by the scientists, because radio waves in part came back in the form of an echo and could therefore damage the sender as much as the receiver.

In principle, with this the basic idea of radar (or Radio Direction Finding, as it was called in those days) had been formulated. Any expert knew, and at the Radio Research Station in Slough in North London they had been annoyed by these disturbances often enough, that aeroplanes reflect radio waves. All that was needed was to apply the knowledge gained in meteorology and instead of atmospheric disturbances, make reflected radio waves appear on the screen of the cathode ray tube, in order to be able to determine the distance and direction of an aeroplane.

On 27 February 1935, Watson-Watt wrote a memorandum to the Research Staff at the Air Ministry in which he denied the existence of death rays while simultaneously offering an alternative. The document bore the title: 'Detection and localisation of aircraft by method of radio'. Cautiously, he only spoke of the possibility that radio waves sent out would be reflected by an aircraft and could be made visible on a screen. He supported his opinion very extensively with all of the known physical details and came to the conclusion that with the data thus gained, a warning system on the ground could be installed by having the data transmitted to airbases and anti-aircraft positions. One could even consider having anti-aircraft guns equipped with their own receivers.

This was just the time when Hitler announced the reintroduction of national service over German radio and when, during a reception on 10 March, *Reichsluftfahrtminister* Hermann Göring informed the foreign air force attachés, that Germany again had a powerful air force. Watson-Watt could not have asked for better support. Sir Hugh Dowding, responsible at the time for research and development in the Royal Air Force, sent for the physicist. Could he prove by a demonstration that this fantastic theory could be put into practice? Watson-Watt suggested having a Royal Air Force aircraft fly along the directional beam of the powerful shortwave transmitter at Daventry. He would make the echo visible on his receiver. Only weeks later the test took place and was successful beyond expectation: the physicists had been able to follow the machine on their screen from a distance of twelve kilometres. The principle worked. What impressed the representatives from the Ministry most was that it could be applied in the pitch dark with the same degree of success. Watson-Watt's Radio Research Station received £10,000 for further research in the field of Radio Direction Finding.

The physicist and his team installed a new station near Aldeburgh in Suffolk on the North Sea coast, because that was where the enemy bombers would come from. Work progressed astonishingly rapidly. On 15 June the masts had been installed, transmitter and receiver calibrated and the next series of tests were under way. This time one reached a range of 23 kilometres. Work continued at a hectic pace, because here no one was in doubt that a war was in the offing. The team next moved into an old mansion in Bawdsey, which stood on a rise of ground. The new site increased the range to more than 80 kilometres in one attempt.

In the ensuing years, Bawdsey became the Mecca of the military. The Admiralty in particular displayed the most intense interest, because such an early detection of enemy ship formations was bound to revolutionise war at sea. Besides Australia and New Zealand, the French also came and people were gladly prepared to help them. Churchill personally fostered the work and cleared aside bureaucratic obstructions. King George VI also visited the station and was impressed by the system.

In the meantime station after station had begun to be built along the south and east coasts. By the time war broke out there were seventeen stations, each with a transmitting tower over 100m high stretching its antennae towards the coast of the Continent. Range was now 165 kilometres. From the stations at Dover and Dunkirk near Canterbury, for example, the whole air space over Amiens, later to be the deployment area of the German *Luftflotten*, could be kept under surveillance.

The tall transmission masts and the sudden demand for cathode ray tubes was bound to attract attention. It was therefore not a coincidence that the government began to take an interest in the work being done by Isaac Shoenberg and to strongly support the complete television system he developed. Several times, the Postmaster General officially announced the impending opening of a television service by the BBC. The press was stimulated to give the new medium wide coverage. This was even more plausible as Germany had opened a regular television/radio service in March 1935. Development could therefore be pushed forward in London with speed, without arousing suspicion. On 2 November 1936 the BBC's first regular television service was opened with broadcasts from Alexandra Palace in London. It served as a welcome disguise for the build-up of the radar stations.

All this had not gone forward totally without friction and problems. Serious difficulties had had to be overcome before a method was found to identify friendly aircraft. Very early on a fatal deficiency had also been recognised: Chain Home, as the system was called, only detected aircraft flying above 300m, which meant that bomber formations flying at low altitude over the Channel were not detected and could penetrate unhindered. The problem was solved by means of a second series of transmitters, Chain Home Low, which covered this area on a different frequency with sensitive equipment and, in addition, was equipped with rotating antennas.

For all the great technical advance radar technology represented, the British did not forget the practical side of the matter. After all, a warning system was but an alarm bell at whose sounding something was required to happen. Here this meant: how can one fight the enemy as quickly and effectively as possible, once he has been detected? To achieve this the information on the screens of the radar stations had to be passed on to the operation leaders of the fighter forces and the anti-aircraft batteries. This was first and foremost a question of communications technology. Because of the danger of listening in, wireless traffic was to be avoided. Therefore, special telephone lines were laid from the stations on the coast to the operations centres. In the Royal Air Force's centres, the incoming information was analysed and entered on large maps by female helpers. Based on this, the operations officers brought their squadrons against the enemy via the ground control stations. Even after the fighters were airborne, they could still be directed by radio. In practical terms this meant that, for example, if an attack was heading for Dover, the whole fighter defence in southern England could be concentrated there within minutes.

Before the system was extended as the war progressed, it had one major disadvantage: the antennae of the radar masts were all directed seawards. Once enemy aircraft had passed the coast they disappeared from the screens. Therefore the Royal Observer Corps was founded whose members, men and women, were recruited from the local population. From fixed observation posts on high points they observed the air space over the hinterland and passed their reports by telephone to the plotting staffs of the fighter groups. The defence system was still in its infancy and there were many mishaps and deficiencies, because in the Royal Air Force too, much had been neglected during the years before the war. But the system did work, because people had proceeded according to the motto: second best is good enough if it can be made available tomorrow.

This was exactly the attitude which gave the British the decisive advantage in their battle with the *Luftwaffe*. In Germany as well, there was radar equipment and the Germans were even ahead of the British in the development of Radio

Direction Finding, but they had been concentrating on the continuous improvement of the equipment instead of thinking about its practical applications in air defence and building up a warning system. As early as 1904, the German high-frequency technician Christian Hülsmeyer had patented a method, which was then forgotten, of detecting metal objects by means of electro-magnetic waves. In 1934, Dr Rudolf Kühnbold, Head of the research department of the *Kriegsmarine*, demonstrated the first detection by radar in Germany. The 'Freya' radar he subsequently developed, which was to serve for the detection of ships and submarines and as a directional aiming device for naval artillery, was therefore totally orientated towards the needs of the navy. The test installation was in Heligoland.

Before the war, there were virtually no contacts between the *Luftwaffe* and the *Kriegsmarine*. Each branch of the service planned and armed itself as it saw fit. Despite this, the *Luftwaffe* came into possession of a 'Freya' set and installed it experimentally in Wangerooge on the North Sea coast. Nobody however, gave a thought to communications systems and the coordination of operations.

On 18 December 1939, 24 Vickers Wellington bombers flew over the North Sea on course for Heligoland. They flew around the island and the radar equipment of the *Kriegsmarine* without anything happening and then set course for Wilhelmshaven. The 'Freya' set belonging to the *Luftwaffe* at Wangerooge detected the formation at a distance of 113 kilometres, about 20 minutes' flying time, off the coast. The lieutenant responsible reported the approach by telephone to the *Jagdgeschwader* at Jever where he was told that what he was seeing was probably a disturbance in his equipment or seagulls. The English were not that stupid to attack under such good weather conditions for flying. The lieutenant was also out of luck with a call to the fighters stationed at Wangerooge: the chief had gone to visit the staff in Jever. The Wellingtons had already overflown Wilhelmshaven and were back out over the sea before the first German fighters finally took off. In the air battle which followed, the British lost 12 out of their 24 machines. All the German fighters returned safely to their base. The people of Wilhelmshaven could thank their lucky stars that the English had not dropped any bombs, nobody would have hindered them.

The criminal neglect of the practical applications of radar may also have been due to the mentality prevailing in the German armed forces at the time: attack, mass attack, was the motto, and for this one did not necessarily need radar, which was regarded more as a technical refinement, a play-thing. Nobody entertained the idea that one would have to defend oneself. Hadn't Göring said he wanted to be called Meier if an enemy bomber were ever to fly over the territory of the *Reich*? For the British, however, it had been clear from the very beginning that their survival depended on a defence directed by radar.

A remark by its *Generalinspekteur* Erhard Milch is characteristic of the attitude of those responsible in the *Luftwaffe*. In 1937 he visited the Royal Air Force in England together with Udet and Stumpf. He was shown quite a lot, aircraft, factories, bases, but no radar stations. Bluntly Milch asked his hosts about this and was greeted by embarrassed silence. 'Come now', he said jovially, 'you needn't be so secretive. We have known for quite some time that you are developing radar. We are too, by the way, and I believe we are ahead of you.'

Major General Martini, Chief of the *Luftwaffe* Intelligence Service, took the matter more seriously. He was obviously the only one in the midst of the shirt-sleeves arrogance of his superiors, who was able to put himself into the opponents' situation. What role did radar play in the British air defence system? On which frequencies did they operate? Were they inter-connected? Were there gaps?

Martini requisitioned airship L 127, *Graf Zeppelin*, for long-range reconnaissance and had it equipped with the most sensitive high-frequency receivers. On 17 May 1939 the ship ponderously flew towards the coast of central England. The radar stations at Canewdon and Bawdsey clearly had its echo on their screens, in the plotting rooms of Fighter Command its course was nonchalantly being followed. The Germans in the gondola were maintaining radio silence; the crew was not transmitting. They were listening into the ether, systematically searching through the frequencies.

The point of the echo showed that the airship was sailing up the mouth of the Humber. Off Hull the German captain broke his silence by sending his position: he was off the coast of Yorkshire. The British on the ground who were happily listening in to him had to hold themselves back not to correct his error: L 127 was already more than 25 kilometres inland. The captain may have realised his mistake, because shortly thereafter the airship turned off east. Half an hour later the bright dot disappeared from the British screens. L 127 brought back no new insights from its voyage. The technicians had not picked up any suspicious radio signals. A second attempt by the airship in August 1939 also failed to produce any results. German interest in the British radar network faded, because there were now other worries. Martini's questions remained unanswered.

XVIII

The Royal Air Force
Parsimony was its strategy

'In comparison with the French, the British have everything with which to build a fantastic air force, especially as far as the engines are concerned', the Director of the Research Department at the *Reichsluftfahrtministerium* declared during a visit to the air show at Hendon in 1937. As far as the engines were concerned, he was certainly right, because the prototypes of the Bf 109, for example, had had to be equipped with Rolls-Royce Kestrel engines because there was no aircraft engine in Germany that was in any way comparable.

The statement contained in the remark, namely that the British did not yet have an air force, hit the nail on the head and a fantastically equipped air force was nowhere in sight for the British. Even more than the *Luftwaffe*, the Royal Air Force had had to suffer from neglect, misappreciation, personal bickering and the overall economic state of the country. After the armistice in 1918, the number of Royal Air Force squadrons had been reduced from 188 to 25, and the annual budget reduced to £11 million, was never to go over £20 million until 1935. A modern air force could not be built up with this.

During the First World War there had only been army and navy airmen until, on 1 April 1918, as a result of the effects of the attacks by German Gotha bombers on southeast England, the Royal Air Force had been formed as an independent branch of the armed services. Its Commander-in-Chief, Sir Hugh Trenchard had to spend the next fifteen years fighting for the very existence of his small force, which by the end of this period disposed of no more than 476 bombers and 156 fighters. During the debates on the budget, the economic feasibility of armament in the air kept being brought up, because when had aircraft ever won a battle! Naturally, there was also jealousy involved: the glory of the flying heroes in the last war was still shining and seemed to grow brighter with every new major aeronautical achievement. On their side, the opponents could always produce the argument of economic need, from which the whole of the western world suffered during the 1920s and early 1930s. As late as 1936 a hunger march by needy workers took place, during which hundreds of thousands from all over the British Isles marched to attend protest meetings in London. Against such a background, flying appeared as a luxury, an expensive sport, which only the sons of the upper and upper middle class could afford. This impression was fostered by the élitist behaviour of the smart flying clubs. To be a bomber pilot counted more than holding officer's rank in a traditional regiment of the Guards.

Within the armed forces, the bomber fleet therefore came under additional fire. Why does one need a fleet of bombers when their job can just as readily be handled by army and navy airmen? Time and again the press seized upon this topic and took sides for the Army and the Royal Navy. The campaign only ebbed away after Sir Hugh Trenchard himself went to the public with a brilliant idea: he recommended that in future 'police actions' throughout the Empire should be carried out by bombers instead of by punitive expeditions by the Army. Convincingly he proved with how little effort and how quickly a squadron of bombers could make a tribe of natives see reason, compared to wearisome marches by infantry and artillery formations, who also had the unfamiliar terrain against them as well. The suggestion was widely acclaimed. In 1934, 25 squadrons of the Royal Air Force were even stationed overseas and mainly employed in Iraq and on the Afghan-Indian border. With this, the continued existence of the Royal Air Force had at least been secured.

The Royal Air Force's budget, however, was not increased. It stayed at under 17 per cent of defence spending. Preference for the bombers remained as well, which Trenchard defended against all opposition, even within the Royal Air Force: 'Final victory will only be achieved after the enemy's industrial base has been destroyed and the morale of his population thoroughly shattered.' In a much quoted speech in 1932, Stanley Baldwin was even more outspoken:'... that one is forced to kill more women and children faster than the enemy can in order to survive.'

In 1933 Sir Hugh Trenchard was replaced as Chief of the Air Staff by Sir Edward Ellington. In the development plan of the Royal Air Force for 1933, a cautious change of direction becomes apparent: the strength of the bomber formations was to be increased from 316 to 476 machines, that of the fighters however, from 156 to 336. The idea was percolating that the enemy could also send over bomber fleets, which it would be the job of the fighters to defend against.

For Hitler's birthday on 20 April 1935, a huge air parade was held in Berlin. For the first time, Göring showed off 'his *Luftwaffe*'. Fighter and bomber formations roared over the rooftops of the capital while Hitler gazed admiringly upwards. Göring, who was standing next to him, was all smiles. The British Military Attaché pulled a long face. His report, and the loud echo it found in the press, produced a wholesome shock in London. Now it was

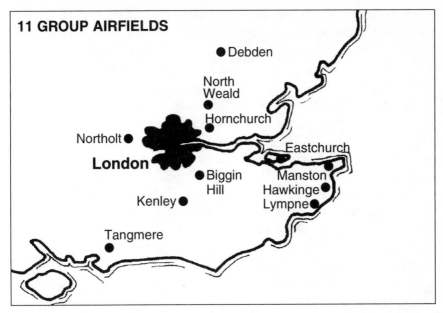

11 GROUP AIRFIELDS

- Debden
- North Weald
- Hornchurch
- Northolt
- **London**
- Eastchurch
- Biggin Hill
- Manston
- Hawkinge
- Lympne
- Kenley
- Tangmere

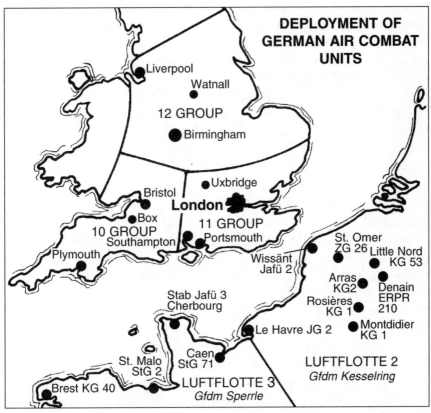

DEPLOYMENT OF GERMAN AIR COMBAT UNITS

- Liverpool
- Watnall
- 12 GROUP
- Birmingham
- Uxbridge
- Bristol
- **London**
- Box
- 10 GROUP
- Southampton
- 11 GROUP
- Portsmouth
- Plymouth
- St. Omer ZG 26
- Little Nord KG 53
- Wissänt Jafü 2
- Arras KG2
- Denain ERPR 210
- Rosières KG 1
- Stab Jafü 3 Cherbourg
- Le Havre JG 2
- Montdidier KG 1
- St. Malo StG 2
- Caen StG 71
- LUFTFLOTTE 2
  Gfdm Kesselring
- Brest KG 40
- LUFTFLOTTE 3
  Gfdm Sperrle

no longer a question for debate whether bombers were needed in remote areas, or fighters for the protection on one's own country. Air defence became the key word in Home Defence. The Air Ministry finally, if still slowly, began to set the switches for a development that was to lead directly to the Battle of Britain and the defeat of the *Luftwaffe*.

Months went by before the planners were able to agree. The Royal Air Force was decentralised, because the future tasks facing the air force were too far-reaching to be overseen by a single man. The bomber fleet, coastal defence, and air defence were made into independent parts of the armed forces. In June 1936, Sir Hugh Dowding was appointed Commander-in-Chief Air Defence. He was responsible to the Chief of the Air Staff for fighter defence, anti-aircraft formations, searchlight units, and barrage balloons.

As a fighter pilot during the First World War, 52-year-old Dowding had advanced from squadron leader to brigadier general. His nickname was 'Stuffy', the unapproachable one. A very reticent, very difficult man with a brilliant technical and organisational intelligence, Dowding was an incorruptible, tenacious defender of his convictions. His loyalty to the job at hand took precedence over all else, even if this brought him into conflict with his superiors. Dowding was not really popular anywhere, even though he never paraded his rank as air marshal and preferred to work in a team. His subordinates respected, revered him, but his superiors kept putting obstacles in his path whenever they could. Churchill was an exception, but he too could not really warm to him. He did not even help him when Dowding's superior sent the victor of the Battle of Britain into early retirement. But until then, four more years were to pass, four years that were decisive for the existence of Great Britain.

Dowding established his headquarters at Bentley Priory in Stanmore, Middlesex not far from London. Bentley Priory had actually once been the home of a prior and after changing hands many times, had been converted into a girls' boarding school at the beginning of the century. During the economic crisis, the school went bankrupt, was subsequently bought by the Royal Air Force and designated as headquarters of Fighter Command. The stylish mansion with its great hall and many rooms became the office building. Underneath a new building that was taken down, a command post was built ten metres underground, from which the fighter defence was to be directed during a future war.

The new Commander-in-Chief of Fighter Command was a hard worker. The task he was faced with was hardly manageable and required all his strength. With 356 outdated fighter aircraft – even the newest model, the Gloster Gladiator, was a biplane – and about 2,000 anti-aircraft guns, he was to protect an area of 242,000 square kilometres from a massive attack by bombers. Dowding's demands for money, *matériel*, and personnel led to constant fights with the comptrollers of the Air Ministry, in which the air marshal lost most of the rounds.

The Royal Air Force having been reorganised and the emphasis placed on air defence was thought enough. It was a piece of bad luck for Dowding that Stanley Baldwin, the bomber enthusiast, became Prime Minister in 1934. Not that Baldwin actively fostered building more bombers, but his opinion alone was enough to prevent any preferential treatment for fighter defence.

Even after the shock which the openly proclaimed German rearmament caused in Britain, and Hitler's bragging to Anthony Eden that the *Luftwaffe* was already equal in power to the RAF, in England people were still not totally convinced of the need to increase rearmament. Many Britons believed that an arms race would only provoke a conflict and that the danger of war could be avoided by remaining quiet. This already became apparent with the deployment of the anti-aircraft batteries: nobody wanted to suffer the guns in his neighbourhood, as if the village, the golf course, the school, the factory nearby were particularly endangered by their presence. People moved heaven and earth, played upon their connections, appealed to their MPs to have the guns installed somewhere else. General Sir Frederick Pile, commander of anti-aircraft defences, sorrowfully noted that they mostly got their way.

Dowding even had to battle for months to have the most important airbases equipped with concrete runways. Higher up, people refused to realise that the existing grass runways became soggy during periods of heavy rain, thereby degrading his fighter force to a mere fair-weather weapon.

It was lucky that in Sir Wilfred Freeman, his successor as Chief of Research and Development on the Air Council, Dowding found an important ally. Freeman thought along the same lines as Dowding and it was his job to bring the modern fighter aircraft, the Hurricanes and Spitfires, from the drawing board to production in as large a number as possible. Both were single-seater monoplanes, fast, elegant machines, which were far superior to any fighter aircraft known at the time. The Hurricane was cheaper and easier to build than the Spitfire, but it was somewhat slower as tests with the proto-types showed.

Freeman succeeded in having both machines rapidly brought into production and also in enabling the aircraft manufacturers Hawker and Supermarine to extend their production facilities, but the number of Spitfires produced lagged far behind that of the Hurricanes. The first Hurricanes were delivered to the forces in December 1937; the first Spitfires followed in

September 1938. Up to October 1938, 26 Hurricanes were delivered each month and from then until war began, 44 machines a month. During the same period the production of Spitfires went from 13 to 32 per month.

When war began, many things became easier, the bureaucratic obstructions less. Orders for 3,500 Hurricanes had already been placed, 497 machines delivered. The monthly production of fighter aircraft now lay at over 200. Some Hurricanes were even exported to Belgium and Yugoslavia. The situation in which the Royal Air Force found itself, however, was not satisfactory, because Great Britain had also stationed an Advanced Air Striking Force with 474 aircraft with the BEF in France. These machines were missed at home. Dowding only disposed of 36 fighter squadrons for defence.

When the catastrophe in France began to develop in May, the situation for Fighter Command became precarious. Losses at the front were horrendous. During low-level attacks against the bridges over the Meuse on 13 May alone, the Royal Air Force lost six of the seven machines to flak. The total losses on that day came to 67 aircraft. The British bombers also had to suffer incredible losses. Within only one hour on 14 May, 40 out of 71 bombers were shot down. During the first five days of the campaign in France, the Royal Air Force lost 268 of the machines deployed in France and Belgium.

In his desperate attempts to stem the German tide, Prime Minister Reynaud demanded ten additional fighter squadrons from Churchill. The British War Cabinet discussed the request during a meeting on 15 May. Air Marshal Dowding had been asked to attend. He presented Churchill with a diagram showing accumulated losses of Hurricanes to date and declared that if things continued as before, he would not have a single Hurricane left within a matter of days. Churchill, however, did not respond and Dowding believed he had convinced him. This was a misunderstanding on both sides. Churchill had not taken Dowding all that seriously, because he believed he recalled that Dowding himself had told him earlier that he needed only 25 squadrons for the defence of the British Isles. Therefore, given a strength of 39 squadrons, the situation could not be critical. The problem was that Churchill had got this important number turned around, and he clung on to it. What Dowding had actually calculated to be the absolute minimum required was 52 squadrons.

The following morning the War Cabinet met again, this time without Dowding, and decided to send at least four squadrons across the Channel, with which Dowding's deficit in the number he would need for home defence increased to seventeen fighter squadrons. Churchill himself flew to Paris the same day to stiffen the spine of the French and to inform himself first hand about the situation. During the discussions, Reynaud insisted on ten British fighter squadrons. Churchill, who was impressed by the desperate situation of the French, cabled to London that same evening and asked whether this would be possible. The answer was to be given by telephone and because of the danger of listening in, in Hindustani (Lord Ismay, who spoke fluent Hindustani was with Churchill). In an immediately convened night meeting, the War Cabinet gave in to the demand. Only Air Chief Marshal Sir Cyril Newall voted against. This time, he was on Dowding's side, particularly since Air Marshal Arthur Barratt, the commander of the Royal Air Force in France, had informed him that there was only room for three squadrons on the few remaining French airbases and, moreover, that it had now become senseless to sacrifice further British pilots and aircraft for a lost cause. Newall was unable to prevail against the Cabinet decision, but did, however find a way to prevent the worst: the additional six squadrons were to operate from England, three in the morning and three in the afternoon, and to return to their home bases. With this, there was a chance to keep them out of the French débâcle. Fighter Command in England, however, had been trimmed down to 29 squadrons. This bleeding of the Royal Air Force, which Churchill had so carelessly set in motion, was not to be the last before the big battle. Dunkirk cost Dowding over 100 machines. And so in early June, the Royal Air Force had only 331 Hurricanes and Spitfires left, which were opposed on the other side by 850 Bf 109s and Bf 110s and the whole might of the German bomber fleets.

But Churchill had already compensated for his mistake in a different way. When forming his Cabinet on 10 May, he had appointed Lord Beaverbrook, the press baron, as his Minister for Aircraft Production. The diminutive 60-year-old Canadian intervened so ruthlessly in the slowly grinding mill of the air force bureaucracy and created such a whirlwind, that he soon had the whole establishment up in arms against him. This did not affect him in the least. He did not even let himself be influenced by the 'bloody air marshals'. He had only one goal: build more aircraft. He called managers and engineers from industry into his ministry and speeded up production. In his newspapers, he launched a propaganda campaign which culminated in a vast action to collect cooking pots and other aluminium utensils for the production of Spitfires. It is a fact that within only a few weeks he was able to double the production figures for fighter aircraft, also in comparison to German production. Now, over 400 fighters came from the factories each month. Already on 1 July, Fighter Command again disposed of 591 serviceable fighter aircraft.

Dowding and Beaverbrook got on very well together, even became the best of friends in their joint efforts to provide the greatest possible number of fast fighter aircraft. The dynamic Beaverbrook not only brought aircraft production into top gear for the Spitfire alone 1,500 sub-contractors had to be organised – he also thought of repair facilities. Experience in France had shown that many machines that had come back from sorties shot up, or had been damaged by other causes, had had to be given up because there were either no repair facilities available or these were overloaded. Beaverbrook created a civilian organisation, which only occupied itself with the maintenance and repair of aircraft. In the end, 25 per cent of the serviceable machines were ones that had been patched up in one way or another, instead of having been scrapped and melted down.

But already a new problem was becoming apparent: who was to fly the machines? The pilot training schools were not prepared for the huge output of new aircraft, nor had anybody been able to foresee the heavy losses on the Continent and over Norway. And it took a whole year before a pilot was trained and qualified to fly a fighter. Even counting Polish and French pilots who had come to England, Fighter Command was short of 300 to 400 fighter pilots. The transfer of 51 pilots from the Royal Navy was only a drop in the bucket.

On paper, it did not look good for the British fighter defence. Attacks by German bombers on central England during the moonlit nights in June appeared to confirm this. Only very few of the attackers were shot down. In the whole Royal Air Force there was only one formation of night fighters, twin-engined Blenheims that had been experimentally equipped with radar. On 20 June the newspapers came out with sensational headlines like 'Beginning of Mass Bombing', or 'The Hun was Here', but such attacks remained few and far between.

When towards the end of June German bombers attacked the Bristol area night after night for two weeks, damage was surprisingly light. Many bombs fell on the open countryside or did not explode. An air raid warden summarised: 'In our sector they only hit a lemonade factory. But woe betide us if the bombs had come down a bit further on, then they would have got the brewery.'

In Kent, where not only Fighter Command had expected heavy air attacks in preparation of the invasion, there were only four bombing attacks until mid-July. A chapel and several houses were destroyed. Five civilians were killed when shortly before midnight on 18 July bombs fell on the little town of Gillingham and caused a row of houses in Nelson Road to collapse. Rescue teams worked until early morning to dig out the people who had been buried in the ruins. An eighteen-year-old wormed his way through the wreckage to a couple trapped by the debris and protected them from falling rubble with his body for four hours while the rescue workers were digging through. He became the hero of the hour.

A farm on the boundary of the airbase had received four bombs. One had exploded next to the barn, the others on the open field close by. The neighbours reported with relish that the Germans had not even damaged the window panes, only a pig had been pierced by a splinter of wood and a rooster struck dead.

For Fighter Command, the quiet month of June was a more than welcome pause which was utilised to the full extent: formations were filled up, emergency take-offs practised and patrols increased. Dowding was able to confirm with satisfaction that his fighter control system worked. The radar stations had detected all of the machines flying in and the information had promptly been passed on to the fighter squadrons via the operations centres, despite the fact that they were unable to take off at night. That the voluntary observers could only depend on their ears during darkness and therefore much mistaken information about the further course of the enemy bombers crept in, had to be accepted as inevitable.

There was a further test that the Royal Air Force was able to conduct during this relatively calm period. Towards the end of 1939, two Messerschmitt Bf 109Es had fallen into British hands undamaged and been taken to Orléans Bricy for examination. One of the two machines crashed during a test flight, the other, which stemmed from Jagdgeschwader 54, Grünes Herz [Green Heart], was flown to England in early 1940. In May the Royal Air Force began to test the machine seriously for its strengths and weaknesses. Its manoeuvrability on the ground was also tested in order to determine its speed in an emergency take-off. It proved to be relatively cumbersome in comparison to the Spitfire.

A team of the best fighter pilots was brought to Farnborough to compare the machine with the Spitfire and the Hurricane in flight. For days, dogfights were simulated and it soon proved that both British fighters were able to out-turn the Messerschmitt simply because they could fly tighter turns without stalling. In flight straight ahead, however, the Bf 109 could not be caught and above 6,000m it was indisputably superior to the two British fighters.

It was also possible finally to test under flying conditions the Bf 109's already known capability for allowing the pilot to enter a steep dive without the carburettor cutting out due to centrifugal force. The British pilots compensated for this deficiency by first turning their machines on their backs and then following the Messerschmitt in a loop. But this cost them precious seconds. The Rolls-Royce Merlin engine could not be converted to fuel injection overnight. This led, once again, to bringing the British ability to improvise to the fore: within only a few days, the engineers at Rolls-Royce designed a carburettor without a float which solved the problem.

Dowding mobilised the final reserves of pilots by rigorously reducing training time at the schools. Every additional man in the squadrons now counted double. By the end of June nobody doubted any more that 'he', as they referred to Hitler in a contemptuous tone, could pounce on them any day, any hour.

Tension was highest at 11 Fighter Group in Kent and Middlesex, which now lay closest to the enemy. When Fighter Command was created in July 1936, Dowding had split the British Isles into three zones of defence and assigned a Fighter Group to each zone. The north, together with Scotland, became the area of 13 Fighter Group; 11 Fighter Group was to defend southern England, including London. Now Dowding was preparing a division of the southern zone: the south and southwest, on a line running west of the Isle of Wight through Cornwall to South Wales, was to be taken over by a newly created 10 Fighter Group from 16 July on, whereas the area of 11 Fighter Group now extended from the Isle of Wight to Norfolk, including London. The coastal sector on the Continent facing 11 Fighter Group stretched from Amsterdam to Cherbourg. It therefore had almost the whole deployment area of the German *Luftflotten* on its front.

11 Fighter Group was the strongest of the four fighter groups: 196 fighter aircraft spread over 24 main and satellite bases in Sussex, Kent, and Middlesex, a semicircle around London. Without radar and the fighter control system they would not have stood the slightest chance against German superiority in numbers. After all, this little band was faced by two *Luftflotten* with 656 Bf 109s, 168 Bf 110s and almost one thousand bombers. What cannot be expressed by numbers was the motivation of the British pilots and their helpers on the ground. For them, every enemy machine was a deadly threat: at issue was the continued existence of their country, their homes. This gave them that measure of dedication and willingness to sacrifice themselves with which they would be able to make up for the superior numbers of the attackers.

On the German side, the air battles were seen more as sporting events even though it was a matter of life and death, like in a bullfight. And in the German *Luftflotten* everyone was so thoroughly convinced that in the Bf 109 they had the best fighter, that they assumed the British would have to feel themselves inferior and therefore have the lower morale. Not all of the Germans realised as quickly as Galland that they were facing an enemy who had to be taken very seriously.

Shortly after take-off from Tangmere, the leader of a group of six Hurricanes flying at 3,000 metres detected twelve Bf 109s above him flying in the opposite direction. At his command, the Hurricane pilots pulled back on their sticks and curved in among the Germans. During the ensuing dogfight, one Bf

109 almost literally offered itself on a silver platter to the leader of the Hurricanes, John Simpson: 'He appeared to be dreaming', he reported later. 'I gave him a short burst in order to damage him and flew closer to give him another, and then I saw him drop down into the sea like a stone'. Seconds later, three more Bf 109s crossed his course. He could clearly recognise the black crosses on the fuselages and opened fire at the tail machine. 'I continued shooting, while we were flying tighter and tighter turns. Pieces of his wings blew off, black smoke was coming from his cockpit.' At this moment, Simpson's ammunition ran out, while at the same time he became aware that the other two Messerschmitts were attacking him. They were flying at 6,000 metres. Simpson flew turns, zig-zagged, but the two pursuers were not to be shaken off and opened fire. 'I heard the dull thumping of their bullets hitting the armour plating behind me. I saw pieces of my wings being blown away, the engine began to stutter. The steering was blocked and black smoke began to fill the cockpit.' Simpson bailed out. Hanging by his parachute, he was drifting towards a long row of villas on the coast at Worthing. One of the Bf 109s began circling around him. 'He was so close that I could see the face of the pilot. I thought he was going to shoot me down. But he behaved splendidly. His machine was making a hell of a noise and kept circling. Suddenly he waved to me.'

Such behaviour could not always be taken for granted. On the contrary, British pilots were sometimes shot while on their parachutes. In the Royal Air Force the opinion was that the Germans were well within their rights to do this. Dowding had made it clear that a German pilot who had bailed out would most likely become a prisoner of war and should therefore be immune, but British pilots over England or the sea remained potential combatants even when hanging from a parachute. One could therefore not fault the enemy if he shot at them. The German side, however, vigorously denies that such conduct occurred.

British attacks against German He 59 air-sea-rescue aircraft over the Channel were based on the same principle. 'We could not tolerate this means of rescuing pilots that had been shot down, because they would have returned to bomb our civilian population', Churchill wrote, even though at the time there could be no talk of a systematic bombing of civilian targets. But in the situation in which Great Britain found itself, the re-employment of pilots was a key issue, because one hundred rescued pilots meant one hundred additional enemy machines over the British Isles.

The Geneva Convention had expressly declared rescue services to be immune, and Dowding's attack order took this into consideration: in principle, the white rescue planes were to be immune. However, the twin-engined biplanes with an observer's position far forward in their nose, flew over British ships and approached military installations on the coast. They could therefore also fly reconnaissance, something that had to be prevented at any cost. Many Royal Air Force pilots obeyed the order with mixed feelings, because the ungainly flying boats with their clearly visible red crosses on the fuselage and wings also fished British airmen out of the Channel. So they only attacked the rescue aircraft when they believed that there were no Britons on board.

J. E. Hubbard of 601 Squadron stationed at Tangmere was accompanying a convoy about ten miles southwest of Selsey Bill when he saw one of the white planes below him. Hubbard called his operations controller and asked him whether he should shoot the machine down. He received the cryptic answer: 'if hostile'. Hubbard circled above the rescue aircraft for about five minutes and tried to force it towards the coast. For a time, it looked as if he would succeed, but then the German suddenly turned off and flew doggedly south towards the French coast. Hubbard fired a burst across his nose to force him down into the water. As he was pulling up again, he noticed two other Hurricanes approaching. One of them shot the rescue aircraft down, which immediately burst into flames. Four Germans jumped into the sea – no parachutes were seen to open.

The *Luftwaffe* continued to send its rescue aircraft to the English coast, but they armed the He 59 and covered it with camouflage paint. The British watched the German rescue efforts with some degree of envy because their own rescue organisation remained very much improvised. The Royal Air Force itself had only eighteen motorboats along the whole of the southern coast with which to search for pilots who had been shot down. Frequently the (civilian) sea rescue organisations did the job with their rescue boats. Mine-sweepers and fishing boats at sea had also to be relied upon to pull the men who had been shot down out of the water.

Seventeen-year-old Peggy Prince, who lived in a bungalow on the Channel coast with her mother and siblings, was woken one morning shortly before 06.00 by a loud hammering on the front door. Two soldiers wanted to borrow the rowing boat that was laid up next to the garage: an aircraft had crashed out at sea, the crew had to be rescued and there was no other boat to be found. They were probably Germans, one of the soldiers remarked. Peggy Prince still insisted on going along. They dragged the heavy three-metre-long carvel-built boat over a concrete wall and through barbed wire barriers to the beach. The aircraft had sunk meanwhile, but after searching for some time they succeeded in fishing a man from the sea. He was a sergeant of the Royal Air Force His two comrades were pulled out of the water by a fishing boat. They belonged to the crew of a returning bomber, which having been damaged by German flak, had no longer been able to make the coast. They had been lucky that it had already been light enough and the sentries on shore had seen the plane.

Despite the fact that hardly a plane went down unobserved, many pilots still drowned because they had been wounded or had not been able to free themselves from their machines. From the first day of the battle, on those stretches of the coast that were inhabited, hordes of curious onlookers were apt to gather on the cliffs, beaches, and promenades at the first wail of the sirens, in order to watch the German attacks on shipping in the Channel and the ensuing dogfights in the air. Dover became the Mecca of the international journalists who came down from London by the dozens to experience the war first hand.

The BBC, too, had sent a reporter, young Charles Gardner. To protect himself from shrapnel from the anti-aircraft guns, he had tied a mattress on the roof of his car and obtained a steel helmet for himself. And so, on 14 July, there occurred the first broadcast of the Second World War of a live report directly from the front. The hand holding the microphone may have trembled when, as excited as a reporter at a major race meeting, he shouted: 'Now the Germans are attacking the convoy out at sea. One, two, three, four, five, six, seven German bombers, Junkers eighty-sevens, there's one coming down on his target, bomb, no, there! he missed the ships... he did not get a single ship... there's one coming down trailing smoke. You can't follow these fighters for long, you hardly identify them before they disappear again... there is a dogfight up there... there are two, three, four machines, they're circling. Watch out! Machine-gun fire! Watch out! One, two, three, four, five, six... and now they're gone. Yes! They're being chased, and how they are chasing them home: three Spitfires are after three Messerschmitts. Oh boy! Just look at that! How the Messerschmitts... Oh this is really fantastic... and one Spitfire after the two in front... He's got them!' Gardner's voice cracked with excitement.

When the report was broadcast at 6.00pm that evening, it caused a storm of outrage: 'Must we', a clergyman wrote to *The Times*, 'when human lives are at stake, stand for such a commentary, which is on the same level as a steeplechase or a cup match?' The BBC was swamped with letters of protest: too dramatic, too much lacking in self control, war is not a game, was the theme. In secret, however, the British enjoyed this report, which was so much more exciting than anything they had heard about the war so far. 'We have never heard anything as good as this', wrote the *Sheffield Telegraph*. Gardner's broadcast became one of the great mementoes of the Second World War. Later, with growing experience, the war reports by the BBC became cooler and more factual.

The German bombers and fighters now came almost every day, the 'Channel Battle' was in full swing. It was being fought almost exclusively by 11 Fighter Group. The defence zone was divided into six sectors, each of which contained a large airbase as operations control. Therefore, only those sectors in which something was really going to happen needed to be put on alert, and even then there was seldom more than one squadron in the air. Keith Park was in complete agreement with Dowding that they should not let themselves be provoked into a mass engagement by the Germans and should husband their own forces. The bombers remained the main target. Sometimes a few Spitfires were sent up to distract the German fighter cover, which was always lurking at great altitude, so that the Hurricanes could attack the bombers.

On 19 July there were nine convoys sailing off the coast. Fighter defence on the forward bases had been reinforced for all emergencies. Many of the curious had again gathered at the lookout points and refused to obey the friendly requests by the police. The police were powerless, because there was no law forcing people to seek protection in an air raid shelter. Some claimed to have observed that the seagulls in the harbour had been particularly numerous and excited that morning, even before the sirens had started howling.

This may have been an omen. It is more probable, however, that the Luftwaffe leadership did not know the number of convoys at sea that day, because the Royal Air Force had shot down several Do 17 long-range reconnaissance planes during the preceding days. In any case, the Stukas ignored the convoys and instead launched a surprise attack on the harbour in Dover. Dover radar had detected and reported the 120 machines long before, but their intentions had been misinterpreted because people were concentrating far too much on the convoys. The Stukas came in two waves, high above them the Bf 109 fighter cover. The dive bombers with their screaming sirens hurtled themselves down on the ships lying in the harbour. Bomb after bomb rained down and raised huge dirty brown fountains of water between the ships.

This was the day on which 141 Squadron of Defiant fighters was the only defence to take off and to lose six machines. A squadron of Hurricanes was sent off after them and, flying through the flak without regard for life or death, threw itself against the Stukas. But it was already too late to save anything. Their deed done, the Stukas turned off. A secret weapon which the British employed here for the first time did not quite fulfil the expectations placed in it. Instead of normal shells, some of the anti-aircraft guns had shot cable parachutes into the path of the Stukas. These were small parachutes from which hung a long steel cable into which the enemy was intended to fly. However, far too few were shot into the air to have any effect. In one case, the parachute had not opened. The cable had fallen back to the ground and had entangled itself over the entrance of the railway tunnel on the London line. Navy experts had to be called in, because there was an explosive charge dangling from its end.

The onlookers in Dover had only observed one Defiant being shot down, but everybody believed that at least ten German machines had gone down. That the tanker *War Sepoy*, which had supplied the evacuation ships at Dunkirk with fuel, had become a victim of the bombs was also not visible from the cliffs and the city. 'The water in the harbour was white with dead fish', one eye witness reported, 'and swarms of seagulls took their share from the richly decked table.' From then on the sailors in the port believed that the seagulls circled above the harbour with more excitement and clamour than usual when German bombers were approaching, long before the sirens sounded.

The Germans appeared off the coast of Kent almost every day now. In London heads were shaking and people were wondering what they hoped to achieve by this. The convoys were not so important as to merit such vicious and risky attacks. In the War Cabinet the assumption was voiced that possibly the Germans actually did hope to starve Great Britain out by this means, but they were not aware that the few convoys were not of great importance for the supply of industry or the population. By adopting such methods, Göring could not seriously hope to gather enough strength for a decisive mass attack, let alone an invasion.

Winston Churchill was all in favour of continuing to use coastal shipping, which was mainly hauling coal, as bait, even though he was forced to admit that 'the remaining bait' was slowly becoming fed up with this cruel game. Admiral Sir Dudley Pound was able to reassure the Prime Minister: the merchant marine had more coastal ships than it needed and the Royal Air Force could prove its tactical superiority in this way. Churchill remarked that perhaps the *Luftwaffe* was less 'all powerful' than had been assumed, but it was indisputably superior in numbers and it would be a great mistake to let twenty Spitfires or Hurricanes fight against 50 or 100 Messerschmitts. The motto therefore remained: exercise restraint, avoid the German fighters, and concentrate only on the bombers. Moreover, a coal freighter was easier to replace than a fighter aircraft.

The little band that Keith Park was sending against the enemy had soon discovered that the *Luftwaffe* was not impregnable. Between 10 and 31 July, the Royal Air Force shot down 138 German machines, mostly *Stukas*, against

57 of their own losses. By 'Eagle Day' on 12 August the ratio was to shift even more against the *Luftwaffe*: during the six weeks preceding this date, the *Luftwaffe* lost 274 aircraft. The Royal Air Force lost 124 fighters, but had the advantage that many British pilots were rescued or only crash landed and could be reemployed the following day.

The tally of aircraft shot down, which was such an influence in Germany, did not mesmerise the British. While air heroes such as Al Deere, Peter Townsend, Max Aitken and Douglas Bader did begin to distinguish them-selves, they did not stand out from the mass of the other pilots to the same degree as their German counterparts Galland, Wick, or Mölders. Nor did the Royal Air Force make the mistake of taking derring-do as the qualification for leadership. There were no spectacular promotions or glittering prizes awarded. The pilots were, after all, only doing their duty, and this is how they themselves saw it. The more successful among them only received the Distinguished Flying Cross and the clasps that went with it. Only the flight commanders were not permitted to be older than 26 years of age.

Bravado was not in demand, this would already have gone against the cool, factual demeanour of the British. Max Aitken wrote action reports of such brevity that they were hardly comprehensible and one gains the impres-sion today that he just did not want to hear any more about the matter. He shot down a Do 17 over the sea after he had approached to within 100m and fired four three-second bursts into it. He described the rest of the battle against the enemy formation in the following words: 'Flew attack No. 1. Cartons with wire were thrown out at me when I attacked and enemy turned away steeply. After attack, I turned off. Our other machines continued attack and shot e/a (enemy aircraft) into the sea. (signed) Max Aitken'. The Hon Max Aitken, 30, son and heir of Napoleon-sized publisher Lord Beaverbrook, now Minister for Aircraft Production, was awarded the Distinguished Flying Cross for 'great daring and bravery' and for having shot down eight enemy aircraft.

The British had no inkling that they were in for 'Eagle Day'. They only knew that the Germans would attack with all their power and that the blow had to be parried until the enemy lost any interest in setting foot on British soil. More than their German opponents, who had no clear ideas about the objectives of the war, the thought of an invasion was awake in the minds of the British fighter pilots. Every enemy machine was a German over their country, whom the others would soon follow, with ships, tanks, artillery, and infantry, who would devastate their gardens and penetrate into their houses.

Long before Göring lifted *Adlertag* out of the baptismal font, the British knew the German words *der Tag* (the day). It stood for invasion and it could be read in the newspapers almost every day. On 14 July, John Colville noted in his diary: 'There is an uncanny stillness. For the first time this month there was no air raid alarm last night. With two exceptions, all German U-boats have returned to their home ports, and it appears that *der Tag* is imminent. The Prime Minister considers this to be highly likely and keeps repeating: Hitler must attempt invasion or he will fail. If he fails, he will be forced to turn to the East and will go down for good.'

XIX
Dover Suffers
The initial blows

Dover became a front line city. The 'Gateway to the Continent' was now like a hole in a fence that had to be defended. It had been tacitly assumed that the Germans would attack the port town. It had been sufficient that on 6 June, four German torpedoes had been washed ashore on the beach north of the harbour basin. The six-metre-long black projectiles were taken to be a new weapon with which the Germans had intended to blow up the port. In actual fact, they stemmed from misses by German torpedo boats, intended for the last evacuation ships from Dunkirk. Navy explosives experts defuzed them and burned the charges on the beach, in the same way as they did with mines that had been washed ashore. But the feeling of being exposed remained awake in the minds of the inhabitants: after having received the defeated army which had streamed over the piers in the harbour, all eyes were now turning ever more frequently to the German-occupied cliffs of the French coast on the other side. Between them and the enemy now only lay a narrow strip of water.

In London as well people began to worry about the port town, which has always been the most heavily protected spot on the southeastern coast, near which the Romans had landed long ago. During Napoleon's day, the battlements from the castle overlooking Dover had been removed to make room for guns. In the twentieth century however, these cannons, which were distributed along the promenades, served only for display and were show pieces on which children played. During the First World War the Royal Engineers had dug new emplacements for heavy and light artillery, because a German invasion was feared. During the 'twenties, however, these too had been abandoned and were now smothered in weeds.

At the outbreak of the Second World War nobody had seriously considered the need to have to defend Kent and its coastline, true to Baldwin's motto that the first line of defence of the British Isles was the Rhine. Only the shock of Dunkirk changed this self-satisfied stance. Winston Churchill proved that he was sensitive to the symbolic value of Dover, which disguised its function as an advanced base behind the comfortable Victorian façades of its hotels along the seafront. The Prime Minister gave his personal attention to the defences on the heights above the port and along the valley of the river Dour, which flows into the sea there. This valley splits the steep cliffs and opens the town's only road inland. Several times during July and August, Churchill visited the Admiral in command at Dover, his old friend Ramsay, whose Dynamo Room in the caverns beneath the castle had become the centre of the naval coast defence.

The harbour had long been secured by anti-submarine nets and mines, the beaches bristled with steel beams and concrete humps. The artillery on the cliffs above the port was finally beginning to be reinforced. There had not been much to be found after the bloodletting at Dunkirk. Nevertheless three, albeit outdated, 9.2-inch guns were being installed on Castle Hill, seven 6-pounders and one 12-pounder had been mounted elsewhere. None of these weapons could reach Calais where the Germans, clearly visible through a good pair of field glasses, were making themselves at home. The Admiralty soon had photographs taken from the air to hand, proving that on the other side of the Channel between Calais and Boulogne, giant long-range guns were being cemented in. These were in fact four 38cm guns south of Cap Gris Nez, three 30.5cm guns north of Boulogne, and six 28cm as well as two 24cm guns between Blanc Nez and Calais. Distributed along this whole sector of the coast, there were an additional 35 batteries of heavy field artillery.

Churchill was alarmed. He immediately ordered the emplacement of two 14-inch former ships' guns which had been rusting away in a naval depot since the battleship they had belonged to had been dismantled. Only one of them was quickly made serviceable after a brief overhaul and transported to Dover with much effort. In order to be able to do this, a special railway line had to be built to St Margaret-at-Cliff, a position three kilometres north of the harbour. There next followed voluminous excavations and the laying of foundations. Earthworks and concrete walls were put up in great haste, before *Winnie*, as the gun was baptised after Churchill's nickname, could be lifted into place with heavy cranes. But when it came to calibrating the gun with its barrel of over two metres in diameter on its target, there was much bafflement. There were no English maps which showed the exact relative position of the English to the French coast. It was only with the help of French maps that an Engineer officer was able to determine the topographical points. By the end of August the other gun *Pooh* had been made ready, so that it could be brought to its prepared position on the other side of St Margaret-at-Cliff.

Originally, Churchill had intended using the two guns to hinder the build-up of the German batteries. All the haste, however, had been in vain. The German long-range guns opened fire first. On 12 August the heavy shells landed in the western sector of Dover and caused considerable damage. *Winnie* returned fire on 22 August with salvos against ship targets off the

191

French coast and not against the German positions. An evaluation of the detonations observed came to the conclusion that 'further practice' was required. Furthermore, the guns could only be fired at long intervals, because the powerful force of the shells was putting far too much strain on the barrel of the gun. It was not reckoned that more than a total of one hundred shots would be fired with the gun. And so the major effect achieved remained psychological: fire was being returned. However, this did not comfort the inhabitants who saw the gun as a provocation, following which the enemy would fire into the city even more.

While there were several batteries of heavy and light anti-aircraft guns in the harbour and on the heights, their fire-power was not sufficient to put up an effective barrage. This too was an outcome of the widely held opinion before the war that money spent for defence was money spent for a war. In May 1938, the severe neglect of air defence had led to a scandal. Thirty-year-old Conservative MP Duncan Sandys had questioned Minister of Defence Hore-Belisha on the condition of AA defence and only received an unsatisfactory answer. Duncan Sandys, himself a lieutenant with an anti-aircraft unit, thereupon wrote the Minister a letter in which he confronted him with secret statistics clearly proving the miserable state this service was in: far too small a number of anti-aircraft guns, poor equipment and training of the troops, and low morale resulting from this.

Hore-Belisha immediately had an investigation started: how had Duncan Sandys got hold of the secret statistics? The MP named an officer who was immediately transferred to the Far East and was to spend the rest of the war there. Duncan Sandys had to fight for his immunity as an MP because Chamberlain had set up an investigating committee. The events did not escape the notice of the press. Sandys made the headlines, because he was not just an ordinary lieutenant or an ordinary MP, but Churchill's son-in-law. Two years previously he had married Diana, the First Lord's eldest daughter. Churchill brought his influence to bear and helped him out of the mess. Later on Duncan Sandys became among other things Air Minister and Minister of Defence. With his quarrel in 1938 he had shaken public opinion awake, even if late in the day, and rendered a valuable service for future developments. While there was no Beaverbrook in the offing as with fighter aircraft, sufficient guns and searchlights for AA defence were still to be lacking for quite some time. At least production was increased substantially thereafter.

As far as the important barrage balloons were concerned, the situation was not much better either. These silver-grey balloons, firmly anchored to the ground, had the shape of a small airship and were about 20m long and 10m high. Their oversized tail unit with its three bulbous fins made up about one third of the total length. The hull, filled with hydrogen gas, consisted of heavy cotton material coated with rubber. When sent up, the balloons rolled about playfully in the wind somewhat resembling drunken elephants and the English lovingly gave them names like *Matilda*, *Romeo* and *Bessy*. One that had frequently been a target for German fighters was named *Hermann* by its crew. Another one which hung over Lambeth Palace was disrespectfully called *Archblimp*. Colloquially the inflated sleeves were known as 'Blimps', after an equally inflated legendary Colonel in the British Army. 'The balloon goes up' became a standard phrase for 'it's going to start'.

Barrage balloons had already proved themselves to be an effective defensive weapon during the First World War and had been used successfully as an air barrier over London. In March 1918 German pilots had reported that the number over the city had increased enormously and was still growing daily. They made an attack against the British capital almost impossible, because they forced the German bombers and airships to fly at such altitudes that an aimed bomb drop was no longer possible.

After the First World War the balloons were almost forgotten. There was only one experimental station still in existence when the Air Defence Staff decided to install a balloon barrage over London. For lack of funds the work required was only begun in 1938. One year later, planning was begun for installing such barrages in those provinces, in which industrial sites and ports had to be protected.

Despite the importance of its port for the protection of the Channel, despite its radar masts, despite the degree of exposure of its long-range guns, Dover did not have a single barrage balloon before June 1940. The Admiralty had insisted on first equipping the escort vessels for the Channel convoys with them. The result was that the *Luftwaffe* again turned its attention to the port insufficiently protected by AA guns.

On 24 July German bombers attacked a minesweeper flotilla lying off the port without anybody being able to prevent them. On 25 July they went after the ships in the harbour, but were only able to sink the coal freighter *Gronland* which was moored to the pier, and coastal motor vessel *Newminster*. From a convoy passing Dover and steering south, four ships were sunk and damaged; the 600-ton motorboat *Summity* had to be run aground under Shakespeare Cliff. The two destroyers escorting the convoy, *Boreas* and *Brilliant*, were so heavily damaged that they had to be manoeuvred into the harbour later by tugboats. For the first time, the inhabitants of Dover sat for over five hours in the air raid shelters that had been dug into the soft chalk of the cliffs.

On 27 July the German bombers returned yet again. 120 aircraft attacked the southern pier near the station. *Stukas* dived down through the sparse anti-aircraft fire on the destroyers lying in the harbour, sank *Codrington* and heavily damaged two more. Burning oil spread over the harbour basin and heavy clouds of black smoke rose into the brilliant blue July sky: oil tanks on the cliffs had burst under the fire of the aircrafts' guns and were pouring their contents into the docks. It took hours before the firemen had the blaze under control. The destroyers were withdrawn from Dover.

On 28 July Dover was left in peace, but already next day the sirens sounded again. This time British fighters came out in support of the AA and shot down twelve of the attackers, losing only three machines themselves. What was even more important was that the *Stukas* had been prevented from aiming their bombs so that the damage stayed within bounds. On the other hand, a number of the explosive charges fastened beneath bridges and cranes as a measure against invasion, had gone up and turned parts of the port facilities into ruins.

On 31 July the first barrage balloon finally rose over Dover to the applause of the inhabitants. Fighter Command had not been idle in the meantime. Hugh Dowding had made sure that after Bristol, Birmingham, Coventry, Liverpool, and other industrial centres, Dover was now also given balloon protection. For Dover and its harbour, Balloon Command which reported to him, had provided 23 balloons together with a supply of spares and their anchorages were being prepared during these hectic days.

Balloon technology had made great advances since the First World War. Instead of only several hundred metres up, they now flew at altitudes of 1,200 metres and more from a strong steel cable that ran through a motor winch. The balloons were anchored to a wire ring cemented to the ground by two thin wires, one of which was attached to the tail because the balloons had to be kept constantly turned into the wind. If they were caught sideways by a strong gust of air they invariably tore themselves loose. During a storm over London in November 1939 half the balloons had been lost in this way. Thunderstorms posed a further danger because the steel cable acted as an excellent lightning conductor. When hit by lightning the hydrogen gas-filled hull caught fire and fell like a burning torch. In February 1940 there were only two bolts of lightning registered in all of Great Britain: both hit barrage balloons.

It was soon seen that balloon barrages were an excellent weapon of defence and feared by the enemy. First of all they provided outstanding protection against low-level attacks. If an aircraft flew against a cable, its wing was cut through like butter and severed. Simultaneously, the contact set off an explosive cartridge attached to the wire, which finished the bomber or fighter concerned. And this occurred more often than might be expected because this treacherous target held an irresistible attraction, particularly for the fighters. Attempting to shoot down balloons, or even just to fly between the cables of a barrage, cost many German pilots their lives.

But balloon barrages also forced approaching bombers to remain at greater altitudes, which made aiming more difficult, especially at night. The concentrically positioned balloon barrages, with an inner and an outer ring of balloons standing very close together, could also become a deadly trap for bomber pilots. One who managed to escape by sheer luck was Lieutenant Hollinde, who was flying against the Filton aircraft plant near Bristol in his Ju 88. In order to be able to hit his target, he had to dive down inside the inner ring from 3,000 metres up. This alone required all of his skill as a pilot and a fair amount of courage. Getting out of the ring was another matter entirely. Flying in tight circles very low over the ground – he could see the faces of the anti-aircraft gunners – he desperately attempted to gain altitude while his gunner was strafing the AA positions and trying to shoot down at least one of the balloons in order to open a gap for his pilot. When this did not succeed, Hollinde turned his machine on its side and slipped through between two balloon cables, only to find himself in the same situation inside the outer ring. Twilight had fallen and the steel cables were hardly visible any more. Against all reason which told him that he could not again bring the machine into the dangerous sideways position without stalling, he repeated the manoeuvre and was again lucky.

The balloons which rose over Dover on 31 July were partly attached to motor winches in the harbour, partly on the cliffs, and anchored at irregular intervals. A plane that got in between the cliffs and the balloons in the harbour could hardly have found a way out. However, the Bf 110 which appeared over Dover in the early morning hours of 11 August, paid no attention to the silver-grey giants. It dropped its bombs on the harbour at a steep angle and then went over to strafing attacks in the suburbs and along the railway line outside of the balloon barrage. The balloons were peacefully tugging at their lines against the blue sky. The first shelling next day by the German long-range guns near Calais could not affect them either, because at such altitudes they were far safer than on the ground.

For the inhabitants of Dover the shelling marked the beginning of a siege that was to last for almost four years. Besides the constant bombing attacks they were to suffer almost three thousand hits on their town by the heavy calibre shells of the German long-range guns, and with constantly reduced food rations, to live with the ever present thought that the German troops might still cross the Channel.

From the very first day Dover was the showcase of the war for foreign correspondents, mainly Canadians, Australians, South Africans, and Americans. The American Military Attaché in London, Brigadier Lee, personally took the correspondents from Hearst Press, United Press, and the *Chicago Daily News* to Dover. They were even permitted to visit the secret defence installations so that they could gain an impression of how calmly and firmly the people in Dover were facing the German threat, and that they were anything but defeatists, as Ambassador Kennedy was constantly trying to convince the American President. They included such famous reporters as Knickerbocker, Beatty and Stoneman, and had all just returned from the war in Abyssinia. Their reports contributed much to the gradual volte-face of American public opinion and the coming into being of American aid.

Much later, this was to console Bevington-Jones, publisher of the *Dover Express*. The British press was under strict censorship: neither place names nor any details of actual engagements were permitted to appear in the dailies or weeklies. Enraged, Bevington-Jones observed the activities of the foreign journalists. Even in provincial newspapers in Australia there was more to be read about the events of the war than in his paper. In protest, he sent the censor his identity card and press card as a means of drawing attention to this injustice. He pointed out that the lack of information for the people could cause great harm. It was to no avail. The people in Dover and along the coast only learned what they could see with their own eyes: ships sunk, aircraft shot down, the increasing number of victims, and the growing destruction of their town. The readers in London, Manchester, Edinburgh, learned nothing. For the foreign correspondents, however, the employees in the central post office in Dover had to send up to one hundred cables per hour.

As was the case for the town administration, the hospitals, the police, and the firemen, for the employees of the post office the relatively calm life during the 'Phoney War' had turned into pandemonium during the past few weeks. With the arrival of the troops and refugees from Dunkirk, the atmosphere of the front had spread into the post office as well: day and night hundreds of soldiers wanted to call their families, send telegrams or letters. Belgian and French refugees insisted on contacting the Continent and obstinately refused to believe that it was not just the poor linguistic abilities of the staff that prevented the calls going through. Bags of soaked mail that originated from damaged ships or had been fished up elsewhere piled up in the sorting room, where the hardly legible consignments were dried, repacked and readdressed. When the catastrophe in Dunkirk had become known inland, the telephone lines were blocked for days on end because anxious mothers and wives were searching for their sons and husbands. Hardly had this excitement died down, when by its report on the air battles the BBC set off a veritable storm of enquiries and the men and women in the telephone exchange patiently passed on information, as far as they were able or permitted to do so. Then the artillery shells contributed their bit, machine-gun fire whipped along the façades of the houses, bombs fell, and one wing of the post office was destroyed.

In August, the post office had nearly burned down. One morning shortly before 09.00 fifty German aircraft flew over the port at an altitude of about 6,000 metres. Suddenly six Bf 109s peeled off from the formation and hurled themselves at the barrage balloons. Despite the vicious fire of the light AA batteries they succeeded in shooting down all 23 balloons within six minutes. One of the burning balloons fell on the central post office, remained hanging in front of the window of the telephone exchange and was threatening to set the whole building on fire. One of the operators found this to be 'quite unsettling' and pushed the shreds of the burning hull off the windowsill into the street before hurrying after her colleagues down to the emergency exchange in the cellar. The assault cost the German attackers dear: three Messerschmitts were shot down and fell into the sea. One of them had fallen victim to rifle fire by the crews of the balloons.

The barrage balloons were replaced more quickly than the *Luftwaffe* liked. The men of Balloon Command (later on women auxiliaries were to take over the balloon positions) eagerly filled new hulls with gas and brought them to their anchorages. Under conditions existing then a balloon could be inflated in 40 minutes, later this was to take only 20 minutes. And so two hours later, there were again eleven, by afternoon eighteen, balloons standing in the sky. At 1930 the same day the German fighters came back again and shot down fifteen of them. Next morning, sixteen new balloons were swaying above the town as if nothing had happened. Two of these fell victim to the next German attack, and again three of the attacking machines were shot down. This time the rifle fire by the crews had caught one attacker when he was shooting at a rising balloon only 200 metres up. The balance sheet of this senseless balloon battle: 40 easily replaceable barrage balloons for the price of ten precious fighter aircraft and their pilots. After this, the barrage balloons were seldom attacked, because the *Luftwaffe* leadership had expressly forbidden this form of sport, much to the relief and astonishment of the inhabitants of Dover, who were now spared low-level attacks by aircraft. Many years later thirteen holes from machine-gun hits which had occurred before the balloons had been put up still adorned one of the pillars of the main entrance to the post office.

During these days the authorities in Dover were still busy trying to convince those civilians who up to now had not joined the evacuation, to move away. The results were meagre. These were mostly elderly people who refused to leave their town. When the schools and many factories were shut down, parents and some of the younger people let themselves be persuaded to move to towns lying further inland. However, nobody could be forced to leave the danger zone. In the end, about 15,000 stayed in the town and were then enjoined to obey a new rule: if the Germans come, stay where you are! The people in Dover took all of this in their stride, just as did the people in Ramsgate, Deal, and Folkestone. They had always been the advanced outpost against the Continent and were determined to fight to the last come what might. In Deal, the suggestion was even made in the town council to put up a plaque with the names of all those who had turned tail in this critical hour and left the town.

XX

'Eagle Day'

A near victory for the *Luftwaffe*

From 5 August onwards the *Luftwaffe* was becoming nervous because the weather was turning worse and the *Großeinsatz* [major effort] kept having to be postponed, literally from one hour to the next. In his Directive No. 17 Hitler had clearly and unequivocally ordered: 'The German air forces are to overpower the English air forces as quickly as possible with all the power at their command:' That is what they all wanted to do and more than 1,000 bombers were ready to destroy the enemy's airbases, industrial plants and supply centres. Hitler had said: the air war could be intensified from 5 August onwards. Göring was convinced that his *Luftwaffe* would be able to do the job within only a few days. Two weeks would be enough to force the British to their knees. On a desert of ruins they would literally beg for peace. All he needed was a three-day period of fair weather in order to start the all-out attack rolling.

But the sky stayed overcast. Low clouds, whose hazy billows hung down to the ground over the coast, were keeping his forces tied to the ground. Göring had to console Hitler, who was becoming impatient. Tension also mounted among the waiting pilots. When on 8 August the cloud cover broke, everybody believed that things would now start. But after a few sorties by the occasional squadron, visibility was again as poor as before. The *Luftwaffe* meteorologists were unable to give the green light: a low-pressure area in the north was pushing one bad weather front after another across the Channel. And the more time that went by, the closer came autumn with its fogs and storms.

The discussion about the landing in England continued. It also signalled a certain degree of uncertainty stemming from the fact that a complete success by the *Luftwaffe* would make an invasion superfluous. This is why Kesselring was not able to convince Göring of his ideas. Kesselring did not only want to fly to England and drop bombs, he wanted to land there. Airborne troops were to take airbases and ports by a coup-de-main and with the support of the *Heer* and the *Kriegsmarine*, build up a front in southern England. In Göring's view, this would have been an admission of the *Lufwaffe*'s lack of capability. He was a convinced adherent of Douhet's bomber theory and his bombers would, so he had promised Hitler, bring England to the edge of ruin. With Sperrle, he refused even to discuss the matter at all, because the commander of *Luftflotte* 3 was well aware of the limitations of the *Luftwaffe* and considered it to be highly unlikely that it alone would be able to strike the decisive blow.

The difference of opinion continued straight down through the ranks and in the officers' messes often led to heated discussions during which the tensions of the waiting men were released. It was only in the daily routine of the pilots and the ground crews that the debate ebbed away. Work and the condition of constant alert did not permit time for heavy thinking. Here the assignment to utterly defeat the British was enough, and there was no lack of commitment. The targets for the individual squadrons had long been minutely listed in Chief of Intelligence Major Joseph Schmid's 'Study Blue'. The bomber pilots whiled away the time by studying their targets.

The attack against the radar stations in southern England on 12 August raised the curtain on *Adlertag* [Eagle Day]. The operation was more an expression of the growing impatience in the two *Luftflotten* than a serious tactical measure, because much to the relief of the British it was not repeated. Without radar, the British fighter forces would not have been able to counter the assault by the German formations as effectively as they did in the ensuing weeks. When scrambled, a Spitfire needed all of twelve minutes to reach its attack altitude, a Bf 109 took six minutes to fly across the Channel. Without advanced warning the German fighters would in every case have been above their opponents and in the better shooting position, because they were already at great altitudes when flying in. The opinion is widely held that the air battle had already been decided when the *Luftwaffe* abstained from attacking the radar stations until they were completely destroyed.

The attacks during these days against the airbases close to the coast, Manston, Hawkinge, and Lympne also had little effect. In Manston there were only a few Blenheim night fighters, whereas the Hurricanes based at Hawkinge were already airborne and the small former sports field at Lympne now served as an emergency base. Bombs and guns only caused minor damage.

The ban, however, had been broken. The *Luftwaffe* meteorologists were able to predict the longed-for good weather period from 13 August onwards. Already in the afternoon of 12 August therefore, Göring set the date for the beginning of *Adlertag* at 07.30 the following morning. However, during the night the weather again worsened and the attack was postponed to the afternoon. *Kampfgeschwader* [Bomber Wing] 2 at Arras did not receive this order in time. 50 Do 17 bombers with *Geschwaderkommodore* [Wing Commander] Colonel Johannes Fink at their head had taken off punctually at 07.30.The formation's target was the airbase at Eastchurch on the island of Sheppey in the Thames estuary.

Over the coast several Bf 110s appear in front of them, circle around the formation, go over on their noses and dive headlong under the bombers. Fink shakes his head about these 'stupid antics' and flies doggedly on. The twin-engined fighters finally drop back. Off the English coast the bombers go down below the cloud cover and fly towards their target at an altitude of only 500 metres. There are no fighters to be seen, neither German nor British.

At Eastchurch on the eastern side of Sheppey there are reconnaissance aircraft and other aeroplanes belonging to Coastal Command, but no fighters. But an airbase is an airbase and the German attack plan has been prepared very meticulously. In the approach path within sight of the island lies the little port town of Whitstable. The rearmost machines unload their bombs there, right over the town centre. The leading bombers concentrate on the airbase. They chop up the runway, destroy five Blenheim bombers on the ground and hit several hangars and storage dumps. Over the radio-telephone Fink gives his pilots the order to return to base. At this moment a squadron of British fighters appears. They shoot down four German bombers before the formation can disappear in the low-hanging clouds and escape. Only after landing in Arras do they learn that the Bf 110s had been attempting to make the formation turn back.

After this inauspicious beginning, *Adlertag* began in earnest that afternoon, even though the weather had not markedly improved. Fighter-bombers, *Stukas* and Ju 88 bombers attacked south and southeast England. The port facilities in Southampton, the airbases at Andover, Middle Wallop and Detling were bombed and strafed. The biggest success was achieved by about 40 Ju 87s, which attacked the base at Detling near Maidstone in Kent not far from the mouth of the Thames in the afternoon. Detling was not part of Fighter Command but served a reconnaissance unit with twin-engined Ansons. There were far more important bases near by, so that at Detling they believed themselves to be fairly safe from attack. After duty hours at 17.00 the canteens began to fill up for the evening meal and the crews were looking forward to their evening time off. Only operations control and the anti-aircraft guns were still manned. A member of the WAAF happened to look out of the window of a barrack and suddenly noticed soldiers running across the field. She had not attached any great importance to the sound of aircraft, because this was always to be heard, but seeing soldiers running so fast was unusual. Then she realised that the noise stemmed from enemy aircraft and that she was the target for an attack. She rushed outside and just reached the air raid shelter when there began the earsplitting screaming of the *Stukas* who were hurling themselves down on the airbase almost vertically. For many minutes all hell broke loose, the earth shook under the bombs and the sound of the detonations and falling ruins intermingling with the cutting noise of the *Stukas'* sirens became almost unbearable.

After the *Stukas* had flown away and the dust had settled, the survivors were presented with a picture of total devastation. The hangars and workshops had been levelled, the operations centre destroyed, and one of the air raid shelters had received a direct hit. Rescue work continued long into the night: 67 soldiers and civilians had been killed, 22 Ansons had been destroyed on the ground and the runway looked like a lunar landscape. Despite radar, the observer network, and the excellent communications system, Detling had not been warned and Keith Park had not sent any fighters. On that afternoon the sky over southern and southeastern England had been full of German aircraft and Fighter Command's fighters could not be everywhere.

Several hundred kilometres away, at the time Detling was being attacked, a squadron of Spitfires was in the air above Weymouth waiting for the enemy, whose approach over the Channel from the south had been reported: a large formation of *Stukas*, Bf 110s, and Bf 109s. Already over the coast, the Bf 110s fell victim to a squadron of Hurricanes. The Spitfires fell upon the oncoming *Stukas* and broke up the formation but were forced to retire in the face of attacking Bf 109s. Then what the British had been speculating about happened: the Bf 109s had to turn back for lack of fuel while the *Stukas* flew on alone. Nine machines attacked the sector main airbase at Middle Wallop. Six of them were shot down by the Spitfires.

On 13 August, the *Luftwaffe* flew a total of 1,485 sorties, but it was not the big blow for which they had been hoping. The defenders were able to book the day as their victory and reported 78 German machine shot down against the loss of three British pilots. In actual fact, the British lost thirteen fighters in the air battles in addition to the 40 machines destroyed on the ground, while 34 German aircraft did not return.

14 August brought a worsening of the weather which permitted only a few sorties. As the forecast for the following days was also not good, Göring ordered the chiefs of his *Luftflotten* and Field Marshal Milch to a meeting. The *Reichsmarschall* was enraged because the results of *Adlertag* were in no way comparable to the effort made. The bombers were being thrown away uselessly over difficult targets because the fighter cover was failing. It was the old familiar story of the difficulties the fighter formations were having to stay with the bombers, who had the tendency to disappear somewhere in the haze because of the poor weather conditions. The ensuing search was costing even more fuel than was already being spent on the constant circling above the slow bombers, Kesselring remarked. With attacks on targets further inland, the German fighters had already reached the limits of their range. Göring also had nothing better to suggest than to install a radio-telephone link between fighters and bombers. This however, could not be done at such short notice. The only result of the

meeting was the decision to withdraw the lame duck Bf 110 from the battle and only employ it when a fighter cover for it was available.

While the gentlemen of the *Luftwaffe* were arguing about the deficiencies of their weapon at Carinhall, the weather situation on the Channel had surprisingly taken a turn for the better. The Chiefs of Staff of the *Luftflotten* acted without notifying their superiors. Göring had said he did not wish to be disturbed. Anyway, the operational plans for each day had been worked out to the last detail so that the staff Chiefs only needed to give the order to attack.

Bomber formation upon bomber formation rolled down the runways. The fighters followed in precisely calculated intervals. With 1,786 sorties they set a record on this day. For the first time, *Luftflotte* 5 (Norway) also entered the battle. From Stavanger two groups of He 111s of *Kampfgeschwader* 26 and one group of Bf 110s from *Zerstörergeschwader* 76 [Fighter-bomber Wing], totalling 110 machines, set off. Towards noon they were approaching the coast of Northumbria where they were to attack Fighter Command's airbase at Usworth and two bomber airbases further south. The British radar stations, however, had detected them long before. Already over the sea, the formations of the Royal Air Force attacked them and made full use of their superiority over the slow bombers and fighter-bombers. They broke up the formations and shot down fifteen machines with no loss to themselves. The bombers did not reach their targets.

Half an hour behind, 50 Ju 88s had taken off from Aalborg and had penetrated across the North Sea into Yorkshire near Scarborough. They seriously damaged the bomber base at Driffield and destroyed ten Whitley bombers on the ground. Eight Ju 88s were shot down. With this, *Luftflotte* 5 had lost 23 out of 160 machines employed on one day. From then on it was no longer deployed in the Battle of Britain, because without fighter cover it was hopelessly inferior to the British fighters.

In the meantime the rolling mass attacks by *Luftflotte* 2 had started in the south: 40 *Stukas* accompanied by fighters headed for Essex and Suffolk, 100 bombers escorted by fighters flew into Kent. The airbases at Martlesham, Eastchurch and Hawkinge, as well as two others near Rochester were hit. In late afternoon *Luftflotte* 3 appeared with 200 machines including 47 *Stukas*, and bombed Portland and the airbase at Middle Wallop, causing only light bomb damage however. Shortly after 18.00 *Luftflotte* 2 hit again: 60 aircraft penetrated to the outskirts of London. The airbase at West Malling and the civilian airport at Croydon were heavily damaged, as were the aircraft works there. On this day the *Luftwaffe* lost 75 machines against 34 for the Royal Air Force

On 16 August the battle continued remorselessly. Even without *Luftflotte* 5, 1,700 sorties, of which 400 were by bombers, were flown. The attacks were

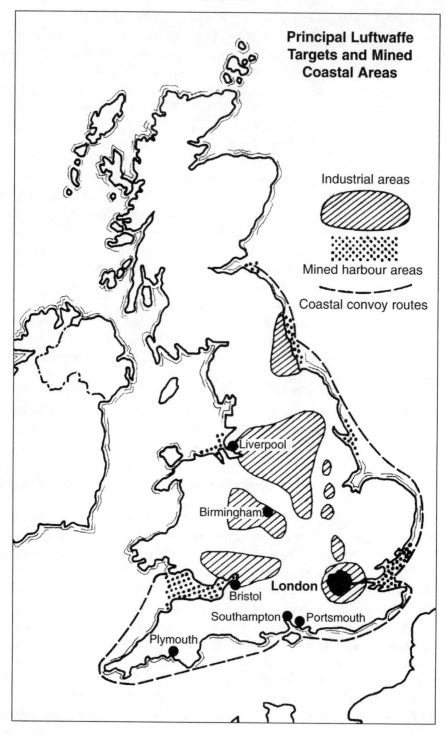

Principal Luftwaffe Targets and Mined Coastal Areas

Industrial areas

Mined harbour areas

Coastal convoy routes

Liverpool

Birmingham

Bristol

London

Southampton   Portsmouth

Plymouth

mainly directed against airbases and caused great damage. Heavy cloud hindered dogfights. Despite this, 45 German aircraft were shot down. The Royal Air Force lost 21.

Stukas had reduced the airbase at Tangmere, which had been built by German prisoners of war during the First World War, to ruins. All the hangars, workshops, storage buildings, the infirmary, the officers' mess, the Salvation Army hut, and the pumping station had been hit. Furthermore, three Blenheim bombers and seven Hurricanes were destroyed or heavily damaged on the ground.

On 17 August the *Luftwaffe* only flew 77 sorties. The British were astonished because the weather over the island was good. The German bases on the other side of the Channel, however, were hung with heavy rain clouds. On 18 August the *Luftwaffe* flew another 750 sorties. These were successfully directed against several airbases and in Kenley, for example, destroyed half a dozen Hurricanes on the ground and caused the radar station at Poling to shut down for several hours. Losses on the German side were almost as heavy as on 15 August: 71 machines against 27 of the Royal Air Force. Lieutenant Colonel Hans Seidemann, Chief of Staff of VIII Air Division called this Thursday the 'black day of the Battle of Britain'. His division had lost 30 *Stukas* on just this one day.

The débâcle of the *Stukas* continued and the day could clearly be seen coming when there would be no more *Stukas* left. On 19 August Göring threatened his fighter pilots with court-martial if they continued to neglect the bombers. But the *Luftflotten* had already withdrawn the *Stukas* from the battle the day before.

Out of a squadron of nine Do 17s from *Kampfgeschwader* 76, only two machines returned to base. They had taken off from Cormeilles-en-Vexin in the early afternoon for an attack against the fighter airbase at Biggin Hill in Kent. At their head flew Lieutenant Lamberty. The bombers with their long, pencil-shaped fuselages flew over the water at only 30 metres, below the horizon of the radar aerials on the English coast. Therefore they did not appear on the radar screens. The German pilots did not know this, however. They were flying low in order to escape the British fighters which they assumed to be at great altitude. Even after having flown over the coast of Kent they maintained their low altitude. They disappeared between the hills of the undulating landscape and appeared over the airbase before the enemy could be warned. The fire of their guns and their bombs hailed down on the completely surprised British. Between the detonations the crews of the Bofors anti-aircraft guns ran to their positions and began shooting at the German bombers who were already turning off.

Lamberty had the tip of his left wing shot off and the aircraft caught fire. While he was searching for a place to crash-land, he saw another Do 17 from his squadron plummet to the earth. Carefully, Lamberty pushed his aircraft down towards an open field. He hit the ground with a crash. The burning machine bounced three times and then tore into a hedge. The flames had now reached the cockpit. Behind him his crew crawled out of the fuselage.

Lamberty saw a group of uniformed men who were pointing their rifles at him. The cockpit was glowing hot and metal began to melt. With bare hands, he pulled himself over the edge of his seat. In his desperate struggles he did not feel any pain, but only smelled burning flesh. He managed to free himself from the cockpit and to let himself fall outside. He staggered towards the men who were still holding their rifles aimed at him.

Subconsciously the German lieutenant wiped his hands on his flying suit and then raised them above his head. The Englishmen saw burnt shards of flesh dropping from his hands and lowered their guns. When they led him away he asked for cigarettes from the top pocket of his blouse which they willingly gave him. These were English cigarettes which he had bought in Guernsey.

While Lamberty was crash-landing, in the air above him another drama was being enacted. One of his Dorniers kept flying low circles over the bombed airbase without paying any attention to the firing of the anti-aircraft guns. The dead pilot was hanging in his seat and his body had jammed the controls. The flight mechanic was working like mad to pull his dead comrade backwards off the seat. The body only moved centimetre by centimetre. He could still have bailed out, but he had no desire to become an English prisoner and maybe be shot. The airstream was cutting through the shattered cockpit, but his exertions in the confined space drove the sweat out of every pore. After he had finally succeeded and laid the dead man out in the back, he quickly jammed himself into the seat. It was not a second too soon, because the aircraft was rapidly losing speed and the nose was rising slowly but surely. The mechanic had never flown himself, but he knew all the instruments and their functions. He pushed the nose down slightly and steered left with the rudder until he was flying south. He was in luck that the sun was shining and he could navigate by it. He had to work hard because his hands on the controls were much too heavy and he constantly had to correct for direction and altitude. However, he was able to bring the heavy machine across the Channel, even found the base at Cormeilles-en-Vexin, and managed a passable landing. His commander pinned the Iron Cross on him the very same day. One week later he was shot down over London and became a prisoner of war after all.

Even though Biggin Hill was again attacked by a squadron of Ju 88s the same day, the airbase remained relatively undamaged. The runway had been ploughed over by bombs, but operations control and the telephone lines remained serviceable. The attack had cost two dead and three wounded. The craters were soon filled in again and smoothed over.

In the days following until 24 August, the weather was hazy and there were only sporadic attacks by German bombers with little effect. At Fighter Command Headquarters, Dowding made use of the time to fill up his badly thinned ranks. During the ten days between 8 and 18 August, 183 fighter aircraft had been lost in air battles and another 40 destroyed on the ground. That was more than even Beaverbrook could pull out of a hat in such haste. Even though the machines coming from the factories were missing everything that was not essential for flying and fighting, production could not be increased any further, barely more than 100 fighters per week. Added on to this were the Spitfires and Hurricanes that had crash landed and been patched up again. But at this rate of loss there remained a gap and it was possible to foresee when the reserves, and finally the capital, would be used up.

Even worse was the lack of pilots. During the ten past days, 94 British fighter pilots had been killed or listed as missing, and 60 were wounded, including many that had suffered severe burns. In 11 Group alone, eleven squadron leaders had been killed. Faced with such a situation, Air Chief Marshal Dowding could not afford the flippant optimism of a Lord Beaverbrook. Beaverbrook had said: 'The Almighty is certainly not against us. On the contrary, He is our Minister for Aircraft Production and I am only his deputy.'

Dowding was a pragmatist, self-opinionated maybe, but he possessed an instinct for the needs of the moment and was able to get things done. It would have been understandable had he now ordered his most experienced pilots to the rearward bases to speed up training of new pilots. However, he seemed to sense that there was no more time for this and began to drum up pilots from the Navy and the Army indiscriminately. For better or for worse, they were put into the Spitfires and Hurricanes and had to fly these fast machines without any experience in action. This emergency measure did not have much effect, because those responsible in the Air Ministry believed that the Germans would soon begin the invasion anyway, regardless of the outcome of the air battle. Therefore Dowding was only sent 53 pilots. By way of a consolation, however, he received an unexpected tribute which Winston Churchill paid him and the members of Fighter Command on 20 August: 'Never in the field of human conflict was so much owed by so many to so few.'

The fighting spirit of the pilots in Fighter Command was unbroken. They fought against the intruders above their homes to the very limits of self-sacrifice. For them it was simply a matter of survival. Flight Lieutenant J. S. Nicholson of 249 Squadron was flying a patrol in his Hurricane at 5,000 metres in the cloudless sky over Southampton. He was probably thinking of his wife who was expecting their first child within a few days, or maybe only that, after landing, he would again have to fight for something to eat because the new regulation said that no meals would be served outside meal times.

Nicholson had not yet had to fight an air battle. He was burning with desire to 'spray' a German. And there they came: a formation of about 20 Ju 88s crossed his course far ahead. Nicholson and two other pilots were given permission to go after the Germans but they were too late. A squadron of Spitfires was already diving down on the bombers and breaking up their formation. Nicholson turned off in a wide curve in order to fly back to his squadron.

Nicholson looked behind him to search for his comrades and found himself looking straight into the muzzle flashes of the cannon and machine-guns of a Bf 110 that had attached itself to his tail. A terrible blow like an explosion made Nicholson's Hurricane shudder, fire erupted from a petrol tank and quickly spread to the cockpit. Instinctively Nicholson turned off. He clutched the stick with clenched teeth. 'Bail out!' flashed through his mind. He felt blood running over his face and blinding his right eye. There was something wrong with his right leg, when he stepped on the rudder pedal to bring the machine back on a straight course a burning pain shot through him. He had flown a complete circle and the Messerschmitt was now flying in front of him. 'I'm going to get you!' Nicholson shouted. The heat in his cockpit was almost unbearable. Through the smoke and flames he saw the enemy machine only as a shadow. The acrid stench of burning rubber and textiles stuck in his nose. The shadow ahead of him was growing bigger. Nicholson pulled his burning aircraft slightly up and fired a full volley from his eight machine-guns into its belly. The German fell off over one wing and spiralled into the ground. With his last remaining strength, Nicholson turned his machine on its back and let himself fall out of his cockpit.

His flying suit was in flames which, however, the updraught of his fall extinguished. His face grimacing in pain, Nicholson pulled the rip-cord of his parachute. Both hands were covered in burns. An enemy fighter flew past very close. Nicholson let himself hang forward in his lines. One never knew...

Then he was approaching the ground. Below him lay a little village. He fought against becoming unconscious and tried to mentally prepare himself for the landing. Suddenly rifle fire blasted up at him from below – brave men of the Home Guard, who were giving vent to their hatred of the Germans. And with success. Nicholson was hit, but still did not lose consciousness. Somehow he must have mastered the landing, because he woke up in a hospital, badly but not mortally injured.

The battle went on. On 24 August the *Luftwaffe* attacked again. This time the bombers flew with reinforced fighter escort: there were as many as three Bf 109s to one bomber. And again they concentrated of the airbases of 11 Group. Manston, North Weald, and Hornchurch were heavily damaged. The British fighters appeared to be fighting a hopeless battle: 24 of them were shot down, 16 the following day, and another 24 the day after. One of the pilots, the New Zealander Al Deere, had had to save himself from his Spitfire by parachute for the third time already.

The Luftwaffe bombers flew attack after attack from early morning until late at night. Biggin Hill was a target for the sixth time: the operations room was destroyed, all telephone connections cut, and there was not a single building on the whole base that was not damaged. Warmwell and Manston were also without any communication. The radio-telephone frequencies for communications with the pilots had to be taken over by rearward bases. A lucky hit on a major switching station cut off electricity in a large sector of southeastern England and shut down seven of the main radar stations.

And the bombers kept coming, in formations of 50, 100, 200 machines. The British fighters found no rest. Completely exhausted they scrambled, fell asleep as soon as they landed again, only to be driven back into their planes a short while later. Five sorties a day was the rule for most of them. And the ratio of machines shot down slowly began to turn: on 31 August the Royal Air Force lost 34 fighters against 28 German aircraft shot down, on 3 September it was 34 to 29.

Between 24 August and 6 September the Luftwaffe flew dozens of heavy attacks against the installations of the Royal Air Force, which registered 4,523 sorties by its own forces in this time period. It was not only Fighter Command's airbases that suffered under this assault by the enemy, the aircraft factories were also included among the favourite targets of the German bomber formations. Besides the Spitfire works at Castle Bromwich, the Vickers plants at Brooklands and Weybridge, where Wellington bombers were produced, were also attacked. At Brooklands there were 88 dead and over 600 wounded. Production came to a halt for a time. The Short Brothers factory in Rochester was also bombed several times. Besides the big Sunderland flying boats, this was where the new Stirling bomber was being built. Because of the heavy bomb damage, delivery of the bomber was delayed by many months. If this were to go on, British aircraft production would soon collapse.

The Heer was beginning to show signs of optimism, despite the heavy losses of aeroplanes. During a conversation with von Brauchitsch, Field Marshal von Bock stated that this time the Luftwaffe was really 'performing'. With this he was closer to the truth than many of those responsible in the Supreme Command of the Luftwaffe were; because of the toughness of the battle, people were unwilling or unable to recognise the achievements.

Among the German population, the results of the great air battle so far were seen with satisfaction, even with enthusiasm. In its 'reports from the *Reich*', the secret studies on the situation prepared by the security service of the SS, it said on 29 August 1940: 'The conviction is becoming firmer and firmer that it cannot now be much longer before command of the air over England will be achieved and the English attacks on Germany will stop. A particular impression was made by the report by the OKW that during one night over England, 1,500 bombs amounting to 150,000kg of explosives had been dropped. People were surprised that the German attacks had already reached such proportions.'

On 5 September 1940 the security service reported: 'It is absolutely certain that England will not be able to stand the daily blood-letting in aeroplanes as well as the destruction of her airbases, port facilities, and industrial plants for longer than another four weeks. The firm hope continues to grow that the war will be over this year.'

For Fighter Command the situation was serious, but not so desperate as it was seen to be from the German side. Dowding was not so much worried about the numbers of aircraft lost – from 24 August to 6 September the Royal Air Force had lost 292 aircraft in the air or on the ground as against 331 for the *Luftwaffe* – it was more the lack of pilots and the damage to the airbases that were hindering the deployment of the fighter groups. Despite the constant German attacks the high rate of production and repair of fighter aircraft was continuing. All Dowding needed was a little time, a breather, in order to replenish and repair the sector operations rooms from which the sorties were controlled.

The reports of successes by the German bombers were exaggerated and the damage caused nothing like as heavy as even English sources claimed. A high percentage of the bombs missed their targets or came down as duds. Many a bomber fleeing from formations that had been broken up dropped its load somewhere over the countryside or on any town that happened to be handy. The inhabitants of Kent and Sussex suffered particularly from this, even though the majority of such bombs fell on open fields.

The number of civilians killed by such bomb drops was relatively high, however, because very many insisted on watching the air battles instead of seeking cover. They wanted to see the intruders being shot down and applauded any trail of smoke rising from a German machine, whereas the crash of one of their own aircraft only served to deepen the bitterness and hatred of the Germans. The many Junkers, Dornier, Heinkel and Messerschmitts which soon disfigured the landscape became the objects of outings. A cartoon in *Punch* from those days has a man asking for directions being told: 'When you reach the Junkers, turn right, then straight on until you get to the Messer-schmitt...'

There was hardly an area in Kent where bombs did not fall. During an attack on the airbase at Manston, many bombs landed in the centre of Ramsgate only five kilometres away. The inhabitants had been warned, however, and had sought shelter in the extensive tunnel system under the town, so that there were no casualties to be mourned. In Gravesend several bombs fell on the town centre and killed two civilians. One bomb fell next to the church during a service, and shattered the valuable stained glass windows. In Ashford a number of bombs exploded near the railway station, but only one house was ruined. In Maidstone, Folkestone and many other places, private homes were destroyed and their inhabitants killed. And the shock was always accompanied by the fear that this could be the curtain-raiser for the invasion.

Despite this, everyone was concerned with proving to himself and to others that life would go on. The thought of surrender was as far from their minds as the Continent. In early September in Kent, the hop harvest begins. Because many of the inhabitants of the county had been evacuated, the hop farmers had to recruit pickers from all over England and more than had been expected turned up. The harvest did not go forward without disruptions, because time and again low-level aircraft shot at or even bombed the people in the fields or the farm buildings. Therefore air raid shelters had to be dug for the pickers alongside the fields. The men and women doing the work took this in their stride and did not complain. They considered their work also to be a contribu-tion to the defence of the country. Major S. C. Berry, a hop grower in Brenley near Faversham, donated the harvest of two hectares of hops to the 'Spitfire Fund' with which Faversham wanted to finance a new fighter for the Royal Air Force. Voluntary helpers from the city worked for five weeks in the fields and with the hops harvested, achieved a profit of over £1,000.

The population was well aware of the difficult situation Fighter Command was in. The attacks on the airbases were visible far and wide and the inhabitants of Kent saw the dogfights over the roofs of their houses every day. They well knew that the machines shot down from the sky trailing smoke were not only German. People mistrusted the slanted daily figures of planes shot down put out by the BBC, because according to these, during the two weeks from 24 August to 5 September, the *Luftwaffe* would have had to have lost 562 aircraft, almost double the actual numbers.

XXI
The Attack on London
Göring throws away the final chance

A minor mistake in navigation by a German bomber formation was to bring on the defeat of the *Luftwaffe* and thereby prevent an invasion of the British Isles. During the night of 24/25 August, a Saturday, one of the formations of German bombers operating over England was on its way to the aircraft factory at Rochester and the oil storage tanks at Thameshaven. The crews had flown this sortie before and dropped their deadly freight on the targets. This time they blithely flew past their target and only when thirty kilometres further west, dropped their bombs. Instead of the oil tanks on the Thames estuary and the Short Brothers aircraft plant, they hit the city centre of London. Oxford Street with its many department stores was badly hit, a church was destroyed and fires broke out in the city over a large area.

Initially Hitler did not learn that London had been attacked against his express will. Göring was at pains to anticipate an outburst of rage by his master and sent a cable to the *Luftflotte* the following morning, which it immediately passed on to the formations that had been deployed: 'It is to be reported immediately which bomber crews dropped bombs on the restricted London area. The O. *d*. L. [*Oberbefehlshaber der Luftwaffe*, i.e., Göring] reserves the right to punish the commanders in question personally and to transfer them to the infantry.'

But this was not enough to avoid disaster. The Chief of Air Staff in London called Churchill at his weekend residence at Chequers and obtained his permission for a retaliatory strike. During the Sunday night, 81 Wellington and Hampden bombers flew to Berlin and unloaded their bombs over the capital of the *Reich*, in part at least. More than twenty of the machines brought their bombs back home, not having been able to identify a target, whereas most of the others dropped their bombs on open country. 150 incendiary bombs landed on a group of allotment gardens. The Berlin auxiliary security service counted only 80 hits and estimated property damages to be 3,000 *Reichsmarks*. Some of the bombers dropped leaflets instead of bombs. Among other things people could read: 'Berliners! Have you taken leave of your senses? Have you forgotten that there is a British Empire in which 492 millions are united against Hitler? Have you forgotten that out of Hitler's 200 million slaves, at least 80 million are conquered peoples who hate their oppressor and are only awaiting their chance? And 44 million are only Italians?! Have you forgotten our air force, which flies about over Germany just as it pleases and in July alone dropped 37,000 bombs on military targets on the Ruhr and in the Rhineland? The bombs that are being dropped together with this leaflet tell you: the war that Hitler started will go on. This long war, which started in 1933, because war is the only objective of the National Socialist Dictatorship, will not come to an end when Hitler wants it to. When and how this war will end, will be determined by us and with us, by the rest of the world.'

There was nothing said in the leaflet about this attack being in retaliation for the nightly bombing of London, because the leaflet was already several weeks old and had originally been intended as an answer to Hitler's 'peace offer' of 19 July. The staff of Bomber Command had not paid any attention to the content of the leaflets, particularly as the idea of retaliation had not found much favour there. Sir Charles Portal, Chief of Bomber Command had not been able to deny the necessity of such an action but, unlike Churchill, he was not the sort to let himself be carried away by a given situation and to work himself up emotionally into almost biblical dimensions. After the single night attack on 25 August therefore, the British bomber fleet went back to its agenda which had Leipzig as the next target.

When Churchill returned from the weekend on 26 August and learned of the intention to bomb Leipzig instead of Berlin, he immediately called Air Marshal Portal: 'Now that they have started molesting our capital', he said, 'I want you to hit back hard, and Berlin is the place where you can hit them hard.' Sir Charles Portal obeyed, and on 28 August the Royal Air Force bombers flew to Berlin. On 30 and 31 August they repeated their attacks. On the German side nobody had an inkling that this was intended in retaliation. The *Wehrmacht* report had kept silent about the mistaken attack on London and now merely reported: 'Attacks on the *Reich* capital with light damage'.

Hitler, who was spending these days on the Berghof near Berchtesgaden, allegedly only learned about the air attacks on the capital on 30 August. Instead of flying to a conference in Vienna, he flew to Berlin beside himself with rage. In the *Reichskanzlei* [Chancellery] he indulged himself in violent insults against the British. At the OKW, General Jodl 'translated' the tirades for General Warlimont: 'The *Führer* now intends to have retaliatory attacks carried out with concentrated forces when the weather is favourable.' In a speech on 4 September Hitler became more outspoken: 'If they attack our cities, then we will wipe out their cities.'

Ever since 25 August, when the first bombs had fallen on the city, the inhabitants of London had been waiting for the Germans to come back. Now they had the confirmation that they were to be the next target and that German bombers could appear over their heads at any day, any hour. They knew what this meant, because 25 years previously between 1914 and 1918, many of them had already experienced days and nights of bombing.

Then too, the German *Reich* had wanted to bring Great Britain to her knees with its *Luftwaffe*, and as in 1940, the initiative for this had come from the *Kriegsmarine*. In September 1914, the former Chief of Staff of the German Navy had demanded in a memorandum: '... we should not leave anything untried that could bring England down... in view of the nervousness already existing among the population there, air attacks on London would be a valuable means of reaching this objective.' On 19 January 1915 *Kaiser* Wilhelm II gave his permission to carry out such attacks which should 'expressly remain restricted to shipyards and arsenals, harbour basins and general military installations.' 'London itself shall not be attacked', the Supreme Warlord decreed in a temporary fit of magnanimity. This decree, like that of his successor two and a half decades later, was to remain a pious wish. On 9 September 1915, a sunny day, the German airship L13 under *Kapitän-Leutnant* Heinrich Mathy appeared towards noon over the rooftops of the crowded inner city of London. Purring leisurely, it flew in circles like a creature from another world. Its appearance caused great excitement among the Londoners. Then the apparently peaceful spectacle turned into brutal reality: from the belly of the gondola, ten 50kg bombs fell one after the other into the swirling life of the metropolis and caused what in those times was considered to be horrible devastation. There were dozens of killed and injured.

In those days to drop bombs on civilians was against all concepts of the chivalrous conduct of a war and the Germans incurred severe odium in the eyes of the world. This however, did not deter the men in the airships from continuing their attacks. In January 1916, nine Zeppelins attacked the Midlands; in April navy Zeppelins flew all the way to Scotland. Both attacks cost 150 men, women and children their lives. In September 1916, eleven airships attacked the British Isles and L32 was shot down by British air defence. The burning hull of the Zeppelin buried the gondola beneath it when it crashed on the south coast near Dungeness.

In June 1917 the air offensive was intensified by deployment of the new Gotha bombers, huge four-engined biplanes: 21 of these monsters attacked the capital unhindered and killed 162 people, injuring a further 426. In July they again dropped ten tonnes of bombs on the city, whereby 250 civilians were killed. From then on the airships and bombers continued their attacks on London by day and night until 18 May 1918, when for the last time during that war, 43 Gotha bombers dropped their loads on the city. Six of the attackers were shot down by British fighters and the newly developed anti-aircraft guns.

After some initial bafflement, from 1917 onwards the British had desperately worked at some form of air defence. And with success, because by summer of 1918 London was the first major city in the world with a modern air defence system, consisting of 284 guns, 371 searchlights, eleven fighter squadrons and several dozen barrage balloons. During the 'twenties and 'thirties, however, not much changed in this respect. In 1939 air defence under the command of General Sir Frederick Pile was made up of seven AA divisions which were spread throughout the whole of the British Isles. While Duncan Sandys' initiative had set some things in motion, it had come far too late. Despite this the Londoners faced the coming German air attacks on their city with astonishing, in hindsight even alarming, composure.

7 September was, as 'Zeppelin day' in the First World War had been before, a very sunny and warm autumn day. Because it was a Saturday, the shops had all long been closed when at 16.43, the sirens began to echo through the streets of the inner city. Only hesitatingly did people seek shelters. In the parks, people reading newspapers sat unmoved on the benches and the lawns, women with baby carriages continued knitting, and flirting young couples stood leaning against trees. They would all have been less carefree if they could have cast an eye across the Channel.

On the steep coast of Cap Gris Nez stood Göring and his generals. They watched his *Walhallas** disappear westwards high above the cliffs of Dover; 625 bombers together with 648 fighters and fighter-bombers had been deployed against the British capital on this day and the following night. In wave after wave for fourteen consecutive hours, they were to retaliate for the attacks against Berlin and bring the decision in the great air battle a big step closer. 'I have personally taken over command of the *Luftwaffe* in the battle against England', Göring had announced. He was unshakeably convinced that his *Luftwaffe* could handle the English all by itself and make an invasion unnecessary.

The leading bombers reached London unopposed shortly after 17.00. In vain did the anti-aircraft batteries open continuous fire, while in between the white burst of AA shells the first condensation trails of British fighters appeared, their machine-gun fire intermingling with the detonations of the bombs. Formation after formation unloaded its deadly freight over the docks at Woolwich, Deptford, Poplar and Wapping; the docks, that were the gigantic basin of the port of London, the largest in the world. From Woolwich to Tower Bridge in the heart of the City, they lined both sides of the Thames for over ten

---

* Translator's note: This is a confusing term, as frequently happened under the Nazi mania for all things 'Germanic'. What Göring actually meant was 'Einherier', namely the hero warriors gathered by Odin in 'Walhalla' for the final battle of Gods and men against the Frost Giants, i.e., the 'Ragnarök' or 'Götterdämmerung', after which the world as man knows it will come to an end.

kilometres, surrounded by the slums and workers' living areas of East London, and they lay directly in the approach path of the bombers coming from France. The bombardiers only needed to wait until London and the first bend of the Thames came into sight before they pressed their triggers: their load then almost automatically fell into the docks and any bomb that missed, fell equally automatically into the slums and poor peoples' living areas which crowded against the docks.

The operations department of 11 Fighter Group had detected the direction of the concentrated attack too late. The old tactic of holding back with the intention of only attacking the enemy formations where this was worthwhile had worked against the British and kept an approach path open for the *Luftwaffe*. When German intentions had finally been recognised, Keith Park hastily deployed 21 squadrons. He ordered two further squadrons of Canadians and Poles stationed west of London up to protect 11 Group's airbases. However, he came too late, his fighters were unable to intercept the massed attack. All they could do was to go after the retiring enemy and pursue him past the coast. While they still succeeded in shooting down 38 German bombers and fighters, they lost 28 machines themselves.

The attack by the first wave of German bombers lasted less than half an hour and, far too prematurely at 18.15, the all clear was sounded in central London. High in the sky over Woolwich there was a condensation trail in the form of a gigantic eight. However, those that had seen the sign were only to understand its significance afterwards. Rescue work was in full swing when the sirens sounded the alarm again. It was 20.00 and shortly thereafter the engines of German bombers again roared over the city. The light of the fires caused by thousands of incendiary bombs dropped in the afternoon stood like a shining beacon over London against a sky which was now pitch dark. The barrage balloons shone pink against the black wall and when darkness had fallen completely, the city centre remained so bright that one could still have read a newspaper in Shaftesbury Avenue.

The AA guns were only able to fire at the sound of the engines because the concentrated beams of the searchlights lost themselves in the clouds of smoke. The Spitfires and Hurricanes were condemned to stay on the ground. There were only two squadrons of Blenheim night fighters, one of which – 600 Squadron at Hornchurch – was unable to take off due to heavy smoke billowing over their base. And so during the night the bombers from *Luftflotte* 2 were able to fly 250 sorties over London almost without interference. Again it was the docks, the Royal Arsenal at Woolwich, and the surrounding residential areas that were hit by the weight of the attack. But Victoria and Charing Cross stations, Battersea power station, a tunnel under the Thames, and one of the bridges over the Thames were also hit, in addition to many other buildings in the city centre.

Frightened people, many of whom had been surprised during dinner in the restaurants, crowded into the air raid shelters in the city. At 22.00 there was still no all clear. Some of the diehards were still cracking jokes: the pubs would soon be closing and one would not even be able to have a comforting drink after all the excitement. Towards midnight, however, morale began to reach rock-bottom and some faces began to show people's fear. Nobody had reckoned on having to spend more than an hour in the shelters, there were no blankets and only a few people were wearing overcoats because it had been such a warm evening. They sat pressed together on benches, stood about shivering or cowered down on the floor on outspread newspapers; they were hungry and tired, and the air was becoming more and more stale. Was the rumbling of the bombs to go on like this forever until nothing was left? Was this the beginning of the end? Would the paratroops and the panzers appear tomorrow morning?

How close to home this thought was had already become apparent that evening at 20.07 and it was lucky that the people in the shelters and cellars were not aware of it. At this time the code word 'Cromwell' had gone out over the communications links of Home Defence. 'Cromwell' was the signal that the conditions for an invasion had now come into being and that all units who received the word were to repair to their defence positions. From 3 September onwards the ships and barges along the Belgian and French coasts had been detected on air reconnaissance photographs and it had been discovered that they were 'rapidly increasing in numbers'. And then somebody had drawn the wrong conclusion from the attack against London. The tension which had been mounting for so long unloaded itself in a false alarm which included all of England and parts of Wales. 'Cromwell' had not only been sent to selected units of the Home Defence, but had gone out over all the wires and lines of communication.

That night, the church bells were rung in many villages and towns. Following orders from higher up they had remained still since 13 June. Only when the day came were they to sound the alarm against the invaders. A typical example was a little village in Dorset where the telephone of the parish priest rang at 23.45. The caller, an admiral personally known to the priest, requested the priest to ring the church bell and hung up without further explanation. 'That means invasion', the priest said tonelessly and ran over to the church where he began pulling the bell rope with all his might. His sister had hurried after him and was holding a storm lantern. As if in answer, the bells of the neighbouring communities began ringing shortly thereafter. The priest then got in his car and drove around to the surrounding farms in order to mobilise the Home Guard. At home his wife asked her sister-in-law: 'I'm supposed to set up a first aid station. How should I do this?' 'Well, treatment for shock. First of all, put on the kettle!' 'What? Tea? For the Germans?', the nonplussed wife answered.

It was a night of bewilderment. The signal had not been intended for the Home Guard, but everywhere men with armbands appeared and manned the pillboxes and road barriers. Several bridges that had been mined went up into the air because over-zealous pioneers had misunderstood the signal. On the east coast a road was blown up and several officers of the Home Guard killed. A messenger raced through the night on his motorcycle and set the church bells ringing in five villages. On the beaches sentries armed with rifles appeared and listened into the darkness in order not to miss the crunch of boats coming ashore. As late as 04.00, army officers were being called from their beds: 'Cromwell is here!' It was only when two Engineer officers wanted to blow up the LNER railway track in the station at Lincoln that the mess began to be cleared up. The stationmaster insisted on first calling his defence centre for confirmation and learned that it had been a false alarm.

When at 06.15 on 8 September Londoners were emerging from their cellars pale, over-tired, and hungry, 'Cromwell' was also being cancelled throughout the countryside. 'Cromwell' was destined never to emerge again, but for Londoners the nights of bombing had just begun. Firemen, air raid wardens, Home Guard, the police, and hundreds of voluntary helpers had worked all night under the hail of bombs to put out the fires, dig people out of the ruins, and take the wounded to the hospitals. The attack had cost 448 dead and more than one thousand injured. Besides the East End, the docks had also been hit, many of them seriously. At Victoria Station there hung a large sign: 'Closed due to disturbances.' This rather cool statement characterises the stance of the inhabitants after the initial shock had worn off: the Germans had not succeeded in destroying the Royal Air Force's bases, nor in affecting industrial production. If they now believed they could demoralise the population, they were going to be mistaken.

The following night the bombers came back again. This time the streets emptied within minutes. Anybody not needed above ground sought protection in the nearest cellar or air raid shelter. In the overcrowded poor areas and slums in the East End the houses had no cellars, nor were there any air raid shelters in this area. Following the experience of the preceding night, thousands set off for the protecting tunnels of the Underground. In the ticket hall at Liverpool Street station they pressed against the closed gates of the barriers. The Tube officials called in soldiers to quell the mob, but the press was too great and the soldiers had to withdraw as the first wave of bombers thundered overhead. When the bombs began falling the officials gave in and had the gates opened. With shouts of triumph, the frightened people streamed down the moving staircases into the protecting depths and occupied the platforms of the station. 'Victory for the working class!' some of them yelled. It was the first sign of an approaching revolt, which stemmed from the deeply rooted class-consciousness of the British. They were making 'those up there' responsible for the fact that the poor sections in the East End were having to bear the full brunt of the German attack. 'Why us and not the rich buggers in the West End?' the workers and unemployed from the slums were asking. It was only after Buckingham Palace had been hit and thick smoke began billowing around St Paul's Cathedral that emotions began to die down again. King George had returned to London from Windsor with the Queen on 13 September, just when the German bombers were coming in for an attack. Because several windows in the King's private apartments had been shattered by previous bomb detonations near the Palace, the Royal Family moved into rooms on the second floor from where they had a view over the spacious lawns of the Palace. Suddenly they heard the screaming of an aeroplane coming down in a power dive. The bombs detonated on the lawn only about seventy metres away and made gigantic craters from one of which a heavy stream of water sprayed against the façade of the opposite wing of the building, whose windows had all been broken. It had been a piece of good luck that the windows in the room of the royal couple had been open, so that they escaped injury from flying splinters of glass. Hastily the King and Queen sought shelter in the corridor because Buckingham Palace had no air raid shelter.

In all six bombs had fallen on the palace grounds: two on the lawn, two in the courtyard, one in the garden, and one which devastated the Royal Chapel. King George made no secret to Churchill of the fact that he was pleased to be sharing the dangers which his subjects faced. The news that the palace had been bombed and the stance the royal couple had taken spread throughout the city like wildfire and social peace was completely restored when King George and Queen Elizabeth began to visit the most heavily hit areas of the city each day and in midst of the ruins and debris, to speak words of comfort and encouragement to the Londoners in complete disregard of the danger they themselves were in.

The tunnels of the Underground became the home of the people bombed out and the air raid shelters those of the people who crept out each morning to see if their houses were still standing. The air in the shafts was heavy with the smell of disinfectant which wafted through the air conditioning system of the tunnels. Armed with blankets and pillows, sleeping bags and newspapers, the families that had found a place to stay set up camp closely pressed together, drank tea from thermos flasks, and lived on sandwiches. Soldiers forced the people constantly pushing in from behind into the trains, which were still regularly rumbling over the tracks and disappearing into the black tubes to unload their passengers at the next, or the following, or the third, the fourth station, wherever there was still room.

During the ensuing months and years a spirit of togetherness developed here. However, this was only true for a very small percentage of the total population of London. Most of the Londoners living in the single family or rows of town council houses without cellars, had to make do with so-called Anderson shelters which rose up like mole-hills above the lawns in all the gardens. Already long before the outbreak of war the air raid defence authorities had encouraged the building of these shelters and even supplied the material. During many weeks of neighbourly support, men had helped each other excavate the 2 x 2 metre wide and about 80 centimetres deep dugouts in which huts made of corrugated iron were set up and covered with earth. People with horticultural ambitions planted cucumbers and marrows on these mounds, others just let grass and weeds grow over the ugly spots in their gardens.

Whenever the sirens sounded families moved into these burrows with sleeping bags, blankets, and tea kettles and spent the night there. They were to suffer this torture for four and a half years, because after the bombs came the VI and V2 rockets. In particular those people who lived in the approach path, so-called Bomb Alley, dared not spend the nights in their houses, and the Anderson shelter became a part of their daily lives.

The Home Office, which was concerned with the health and the fighting morale of the population, issued a directive in the winter of 1940 for the improvement of the garden shelters which required, however, that the corrugated iron walls had been replaced with brick, something that only applied in rare cases. 'Paper the walls and paint the ceiling white. A self-made auxiliary heating system can consist of two large flower pots with their openings facing each other with a burning candle inside.' As protection against the cold one should wear a head protector and make sleeping bags out of old army blankets that had been filled with newspaper. However, there was nothing that could make a stay in an Anderson shelter even the slightest bit comfortable.

Far more important to most Britons than their own comfort has always been that of their pets, the four-legged members of the family, but also the budgerigars and canaries. Dogs did not need to be accustomed to the shelters. 'Our dog Stumpy became nervous long before the sirens sounded', remembers one London lady, 'he scratched at the door to the garden and wanted to go into the shelter. Even if the family decided to ignore the alarm and stay in the house, he disappeared inside it. He was able to tell our own planes from those of the enemy, and if the word "Hitler" fell in the course of a conversation he would start to bark.' Cats normally went their own way. The shelters were too damp and cold for them, because in summer as in winter condensation dripped from the corrugated iron walls. Instead of a door the only protection for the entrance against shrapnel was an open embankment.

Professor Julian Huxley, Chairman of the London Zoological Society, observed the reactions of the animals in the zoo and found to his surprise that most of them quickly became accustomed to sirens, bombs, and anti-aircraft fire. Camels did not even get up any more when bombs came down only metres away from their pens. Chimpanzees were also not disturbed by the blasts of the detonations, but did start screaming horribly when the sirens began their infernal wailing. Birds, however, went completely out of their minds from the noise caused by bombs and gunfire, and in particular crows, jays and magpies needed a long time before they calmed down again. The parrots in the zoo began to imitate the sirens, and, because they often did this long before the actual alarm was sounded, the assumption was that they could hear the aeroplanes long before their keepers. This, by the way, also applied to dogs, geese, ducks and seagulls.

Observations of this kind were typical for the British. Even in moments of the greatest danger they did what came naturally. The animals were an important part of their everyday lives, members of the family and not just the objects of a maudlin sentimentality. Their dog or their cat was closer to them than the intruder in the sky and contributed much to the fact that no panic developed under the blows of the *Luftwaffe*. This is also expressed in the wills made by the pilots of Fighter Command which they deposited in the office or left with a comrade: almost invariably these mentioned a dog or a cat which shared their quarters and for whose care they wished to provide. As a psychological connecting link this was as important as the fact that they were fighting above their own home ground.

XXII
Heer and Kriegsmarine are Set
No jump across the Channel

The south coast of England lies basking in bright sunshine. Playfully seagulls circle from the white cliffs over a deserted beach. Near a sentry box stand two British soldiers with steel helmets and rifles, deep in conversation.

When the camera then sweeps out across the open sea to the East, the seemingly peaceful picture changes: out of the haze on the horizon long rows of stormboat carriers appear (speedboats with a stormboat hanging outboard to port and to starboard), behind them flotillas of Siebel ferries carrying panzers and 88mm guns on their broad decks, and a whole armada of landing craft, stuffed full of troops. The air is filled with the thrumming of approaching bomber squadrons, in the lead the feared *Stukas*. Zero hour of the German invasion of England has broken assures the voice of the commentator, which almost breaks from the excitement of describing the details.

Shortly before reaching the beaches the stormboats drop from their lines and run towards shore under a fine spume. Enemy defensive fire sets in. Machine-gun bursts whip across the water, artillery shells raise huge fountains between the boats. However, the German *Gebirgsjäger* [mountain troops] are not to be daunted: with mines exploding all around they take the beach and storm forward towards the steep coast behind, while the bombers cover the enemy coastal defences with their loads.

Under enemy fire the first wounded are laid out in the sand and treated. Captured British soldiers are being led away in long rows, a 'defeated army'. Slowly now the treads of the panzers are grinding across the beach and eating their way into the soil of the hated island, over which the German flag will soon fly everywhere.

Then the screen went dark and the audience, mostly junior officials of the *Reich* Propaganda Ministry, squirmed in their seats and some nodded to each other with enthusiasm: that is the way it would happen, exactly like that.

The film was a fabrication. The first picture report of the landing on the English coast could hardly have been filmed on site under enemy action and the probably very poor lighting conditions. Goebbels had therefore sent a camera team to the French coast, where since August the preparations for the invasion were running in high gear and individual units were constantly practising landings. He had the landing scenes filmed and exciting action sequences staged.

The bombers were added later. There was enough footage of air war material available from the Spanish Civil War, Poland, and the campaign in the West. The British prisoners had fallen into German hands a few weeks previously at Dunkirk. The film had been intended for the *Wochenschau* [News of the Week] some time after 15 September, but it was only 30 years later that reporters of the BBC unearthed this masterpiece of Goebbels' propaganda in the *Deutsche Filmarchiv* [German Film Archives].

What the film did not, could not, show, was the extent of the preparations and the gigantic effort that stood behind the operation. Within only two months, the German side had made virtually everything that could float or fly available in order to enable the *Heer* to land on the British Isles.

The German General Staff was quite well informed about British defensive measures. German Army Intelligence was constantly monitoring British Army radio traffic, so that the positions and deployment areas of the British divisions was known: a weak Coastal Defence Force had the assignment to delay a landing from small defensive positions, while a Mobile Defence Force had built up the actual line of defence on a line running Leicester–London–Midhurst–Salisbury. From the intercepted radio traffic as well as from articles in the press it was known that the British were not considering the possibility of preventing a landing, but only intended to oppose it with all available forces further inland. They had also to reckon with mass landings by paratroops and airborne troops. The *Heer* leadership could therefore assume that bridgeheads could be won with relatively light losses. The first phase of the invasion was therefore more of a transportation problem: to bring the largest possible number of troops to the English coast as quickly as possible in order to extend the bridgeheads before the enemy could crush them.

For the crossings five routes had been marked over which 145 steamers, 1,939 barges, 422 tugboats, 994 motorboats, and a number of Siebel ferries were to take the reinforced regiments of the *Heer* to the other side of the Channel. Area A was the coast from Deal to Ramsgate, crossing from Ostende. Area B stretched from Folkestone to Dungeness, crossing from Dunkirk and Calais. Area C from Dungeness to Cliff End, crossing from Calais. Area D reached from Pevensey to Beachy Head, which was to be approached from Boulogne, and area E lay from Brighton to Selsey Bill with Le Havre as the port of departure. The steamers which had been distributed among the jump-off ports were not only to be loaded with troops and equipment, but were also to take two loaded barges in tow, accompanied by tugs each towing two barges, and motorboats that were to act as assault boats and ferries during the landing. Six such convoys formed a group under a group leader in a fast motorboat (customs speedboats). The Siebel ferries loaded with heavy equipment and panzers had their place behind the troop trans-ports.

On S-Day, the day of the landing, this gigantic armada with about 100,000 men was to set sail and fall upon the English coast like the Romans and Normans of yesteryear. S-Day had last been scheduled for 21 September. The order for the invasion was to be given no later than S minus 10 days. That would have meant on 11 September, in other words four days before the date the *Kriegsmarine* intended to have its preparations completed.

Already in mid-August, the *Heeresleitung* [Army Command] became impatient and had its naval liaison officers enquire of the *Kriegsmarine* when ships would finally be made available for practice. In order to be able to hold to the schedule it was important to know what could be loaded in which time span. Loading procedures had to be practised with men, equipment, and horses. But Naval Command had continually to put the *Heer* off because many of the ships were a long way from being marshalled at their intended stations. Coordinated exercises only began in September. In the short time remaining until 15 September, to say nothing of 11 September, it was left up to the initiative of individual unit commanders to reach agreements with local port commanders and *Kriegsmarine* officials and to practise loading and unloading of ships with their units on their own.

Results were not encouraging and showed how necessary such exercises were. The loading of large ships turned out to be relatively easy. By using four hatches it was possible to load 854 men, 62 horses, 88 motorcycles, 21 cars, 34 lorries, five anti-tank guns, eight field kitchens, six waggons, 28 carts, and 30 bicycles into a steamer within seven hours. Loading of a barge with 150 men and their equipment required only one to one and a half hours. Difficulties were caused by the horses which had already been provided in great numbers. About 60,000 of the four-legged creatures were to be taken along in order to pull ammunition and supply carts, guns and field kitchens, over the hedged-in country lanes and through the orchards of southern England. During the loading exercises many balked when they were supposed to step onto the loading ramps, others shied when they heard their hoofs ringing on the steel plating of the ship's bottoms. Chief-of-Staff Halder therefore gave the order to put the cavalry squadron on bicycles and to leave their horses behind.

Naturally *Heer* Command placed great emphasis on throwing as many panzers as possible onto the British coast and in the familiar B*litz* manner, having them run over the defenders. There was no lack of panzers and battle-proven crews, but never before had panzers been transported across the sea and landed on an open coast. Loading them with dock-side facilities was no problem, but hardly any of the ships had their own loading gear with which to unload them again, something that would not have been possible anyway on an open coast. The problem was solved by putting them on barges from which the panzers could be unloaded via a ramp over the cut down bows. However, when driving ashore on the open coast they had to go into water at depths of between four and six metres – therefore amphibious panzers were required for the operation.

There were already underwater armoured vehicles in the Soviet Union where this type of tank had been successfully experimented with for years for use in river crossings. In Germany such experiments had just begun. A number of Panzer III had been equipped with rubber seals and long flexible schnorkels which were held above water by a buoy. It was particularly difficult to make the turrets and the eye slits watertight and it was only very gradually that panzers were being turned into submersible vehicles.

Experiments in the Jade estuary at Schillig proved that while the panzers could penetrate into the sea to depths of about six metres and drive out again, when they tried to make a turn on mud-flats at low water the inner tread sank into the mud and the panzer became stuck. And time and again there were problems with the seals, so that the panzers became flooded and their crews had to bail out with the help of rescue divers. In one such case, two first lieutenants, a corporal and a mechanic claimed the loss of two wrist-watches, a pocket watch, a shirt and a pair of trousers, for which they were generously compensated.

At the final approval tests in the Baltic at Neuruppin in June, the commander of the test group drove into the sea with panzers that had only been fitted with new covers for the eye slits the night before. After a short drive parallel to the coast the panzers came charging onto the beach again with throttles wide open. The eye slits did not open. Blind, the panzers roared through several gardens of seaside villas and into a group of trees, causing much damage before they came to a halt. However, there were no serious delays. During July and August the conversion of Panzer IIIs and IVs was pushed forward. The first Panzer IIIs were loaded for the Channel coast already on 15 July and by 1 August another 90 Panzer IIIs and 29 Panzer IVs had been made ready, with a further 90 Panzer IIIs following a fortnight later. By 15 September, Army Group A disposed of 250 amphibious panzers for employment against the British coast.

Thanks to the good maps provided by the *Kriegsmarine* it was also possible to avoid difficulties in the terrain during the landing, for example the steep pebble beaches which can be found all along the English coast. Off Deal, one of the originally preferred landing places whose unsuitability even the OKH finally had to recognise, there were loose pebbles piled up on the beach metres high forming a barrier unsurmountable by tanks. Even such unusual hindrances as the petrified forest with soft mud between St Leonard's and Dungeness were known, so that it was possible to concentrate on the more motorable sand beaches.

The organisers of this campaign had not forgotten anything at all. Even carrier pigeons in their boxes had been planned for in the loading lists. They were to bring news of victory back across the Channel. One day 72 guard dogs arrived at Dunkirk and were distributed among the divisions. They were to hunt for snipers. Food for these animals was provided, just as was the fodder for the 60,000 horses. And the food for the troops? The quartermasters worked over-time to portion out the rations according to the *Einsatzwehrmachtsverpfle-gungsvorschrift* [Wehrmacht-Directive-For-Food-Supply-During-Deployment-For-Battle] and wrap it in waterproof packs. Rations were generous because in addition to regular rations, each man received 250 grams of meat per day, a second portion for supper, an additional portion of beverages and tobacco, and 100 grams of chocolate.

Rations for two weeks were provided because the armies had been instructed to live off the land as far as possible in order to minimise supply across the Channel during the initial phase of the battle. 'The needs of the troops take precedent over those of the civilian population', stated the order by the Commander-in-Chief of the *Heer*. For all 'things taken or confiscated (food, vehicles, etc)', only correct receipts in German should be handed out. At the same time the warning was issued: 'Taking of goods for personal use without payment will be punished as plundering.' That was normal practice in war. However, particularly because of the blockade, all deliveries of food to Great Britain would come to a halt after occupation. The occupied Channel Islands provide an interesting case study of such a situation. Therefore, to get rid of superfluous mouths to feed the OKH ordered that 'all prisoners of war are to be deported to the Continent in empty transports as quickly as possible.'

The only thing nobody seems to have thought of was medicine against sea-sickness, even though a large percentage of the soldiers becoming incapaci-tated in this way had to be reckoned with. In any case, the thirteen hospital ships that had been provided were not destined for those suffering from sea-sickness. They were to sail behind the landing fleet in order to pick up wounded and ship-wrecked in case the landing fleet were to be attacked. They disposed of a total of over 1,000 beds and were especially equipped for the transport of badly wounded. For operations on land, field hospitals had been provided.

Equipping the force, loading it, and transporting it were basically matters of routine for the *Heer* staffs. Forty years previously a whole army had been sent to China in ships and everything had gone well, and only months ago ships had brought German troops to Norway and even defied the British Navy while doing so. Compared to this the thirty kilometres of Channel really did look like a river crossing. But even after the development of the amphibious tanks, unloading on the open enemy coast remained a big problem, because that was something nobody had practised before.

After about thirteen hours of crossing, unloading had to be done at dawn. First the speedboats, released from their motorboats and with the advanced elements on board, were to charge high up onto the beaches. Everybody knew that the mud-flats and the beaches had been mined and that the time could not be taken to defuze all the mines beforehand. One of the tasks of the advanced elements was merely to open mine-free passages. The OKH was calculating with losses of between 30 and 50 per cent among the troops to land first.

In the meantime the steamers were to anchor in line abeam off the coast and transfer their loads to the barges they had brought across. These would then be landed under their own power or pulled by motorboats, alongside the barges which had been towed over by the tugboats. As soon as the barges had grounded, the ramps attached to the bows were to be lowered and the troops with their equipment – machine-guns, artillery, rocket launchers, and vehicles – were to disembark and immediately engage in the battle being undertaken by the leading troops.

One of the few exercises in full formation took place off Boulogne. About 50 ships – steamers, tugs, lighters, motorboats, stormboats – were involved. They marshalled far out in the roadstead and then cruised south at a speed of five knots. Only a few kilometres south of its starting position the formation turned towards the coast and began the landing. For many of the spectators, including General von Manstein and Colonel General Strauß, it was an imposing spectacle when the armada silently and threateningly approached the beach, the barges opened, and hundreds of soldiers began climbing the surrounding hillocks like ants.

However, the appraisal of the exercise showed that many more would be required before the intentions of the *Heer* and the capabilities of the *Kriegsmarine* were to be in tune. The ships' masters – civilians, like almost all of the ships crews – had for example, let the intervals between ships become wider and wider even on this short distance, because they feared collisions. In the real event this would have made escorting the landing fleet during the crossing virtually impossible. Furthermore, one of the major conditions for the success of the landing would have been called into question, namely landing as many troops as possible on the beaches simultaneously.

The soldiers on the towed barges also made many mistakes. They crowded together in the bows of the barges and thereby obstructed the crews in the handling of the tow lines. They preferred exposing themselves to the dangers of being injured by a parting tow line to waiting in the darkness inside for the barge to go down. During the subsequent exercises strict attention was paid to ensuring that the troops stayed below deck with their equipment and only came on deck in small groups to have some fresh air. Escape hatches and ventilation shafts were intended to give the landlubbers the feeling that they were not locked into a floating coffin. When the weather rose all army personnel had to go below decks and the hatches were closed. The only relief that could be provided for them was that they were permitted to lay down their equipment during the crossing.

A much greater risk was run by the troops assigned to the stormboats, into which they had to transfer when they had been lowered into the water shortly before reaching the coast, and run towards the beaches in them. Many boat masters were afraid of damaging engines and screws while running up onto the beach and therefore shipped the powerful outboard motors while still in the surf. The boats broached, turned over, and dumped the troops into the water. The landing manoeuvre had to be practised time and again until everybody had found the courage to run through the surf at a right angle at high speed and let themselves be carried high up onto the beach so that the men they carried could then land with dry feet.

The landings by the barges caused fewer problems. Those with their own power had no choice but to steer for the beach at a right angle in order to be able to lower their ramp. Barges without engines depended on the skill of the tugboats, who all too frequently cast off their lines too soon so that the barges were thrown on to the beach broadside and foundered, or else grounded at an angle, so that the ramp could not be lowered and in the event, guns, tanks, and other vehicles would be sitting uselessly stuck in the mud with their ship.

From barges without bow ramps the troops had to disembark on to floats via ladders; this system also applied to troops who were to be taken off steamers and barges by motor boats.

Everything had been thought of. This included life jackets of which thousands had been provided. These, however, were only sufficient for the first wave and they were to brought back again by the boats for the second wave. How this was to be done was not quite clear to anybody, because the life jackets were worn beneath the combat packs and for those landing and immediately engaging in the battle, there would hardly be time to shed this piece of clothing on the unprotected beaches. On the other hand, the life jackets could not be taken away from the troops in the stormboats, on rafts, or from men who had to land in deep water while they were still on their ships or barges. There was also the question of who was to collect them on land and bring them back to the ships. Once the bridgeheads had been established the problem would probably have solved itself, because the landings by the following troops would have been far less hectic and not carried out under enemy fire.

There was a serious conflict between the Heer and the Kriegsmarine about the employment of smoke, or artificial fog. For tactical reasons the Heer wanted to have as much as possible, because on the open beaches it would offer the only form of protection. For seamen, however, smoke or fog – be it artificially produced or natural – has always meant a particularly grave danger. The cumbersome landing fleet could be paralysed for all practical purposes if an artificial fog bank were to drift out to sea instead of towards land. During a planning exercise at Ninth Army, a heated argument arose between Colonel General Strauß and the responsible officers of the Kriegsmarine. Strauß insisted that the order to make smoke should be solely the prerogative of the unit commanders to be given out of tactical considerations, whereas it was the opinion of the Naval Staff, that in order not to endanger the fleet, only the flotilla commanders were able to take such a decision depending on weather conditions. The only point on which agreement could be reached was that smoke generators should actually be employed.

At 10 Downing Street fog was also being thought about during these days. Lord Ismay, Sir Hugh Dowding, and Lord Gort were having dinner with Churchill and the conversation soon turned to the invasion. Churchill said that the most threatened sector of the coast was from North Foreland near Ramsgate to Dungeness, and the most dangerous weather conditions for the British would be heavy fog. While Ismay believed that the Germans would hardly be able to maintain contact among themselves under such conditions, Lord Gort was prepared to swear that he himself could carry out a landing even in the densest fog. All the Germans needed to do was to advance inland immediately. What was important was to let them through and not stubbornly insist on holding a defensive line as the French had done, thereby suffering their terrible defeat. Lord Gort even had the idea – which agreed with the German planning – that the forward elements would only be lightly armed and would be landed in fast boats, the follow-up panzers from landing craft with bow ramps, and as a third wave, artillery and the mass of the infantry set ashore. The first two waves would reach their initial objectives before daybreak and before the fog had lifted. Churchill showed himself to be greatly disturbed by such a prospect. He continually kept calling the Admiralty and enquiring about the weather situation in the Channel. The following day analysis of air reconnaissance photos showed that the Germans were making themselves independent of the weather and using artificial fog in their landing exercises.

The impression that there were very intensive preparations for invasion going on on the French Channel coast was also confirmed by other aerial photographs which clearly showed the massive Siebel and Herbert ferries under construction. The analysts believed that with these large platforms, the Germans could succeed in bringing hundreds of panzers across the Channel with great speed and land them directly on the beaches. A conversation with the experts from the *Kriegsmarine* would easily have dispelled these fears, because the latter had very little time for these ferries. They had been conceived and built by H*eer* Engineers, reason enough to be a thorn in the flesh of the *Kriegsmarine* which had the sole responsibility for the transport fleet. Although the ferries were later put under the command of the *Kriegsmarine*, this was not enough to dispel its fundamental objections against the ferries.

The shipbuilding department at O. *d*. M. [*Oberbefehlshaber der Marine*, i.e. Navy Command] had studied the Herbert ferry and concluded that with this 'rectangular vessel' one had to reckon with 'hard movements in all directions and wet decks even in a light sea'. 'The connecting beams between the pontoons will... not hold up to the dynamic pressures at sea', the report went on to state. The wooden platform also made the naval experts uneasy, because it lay only one metre above the surface of the water so that even the lightest waves beat upon it from below and could lead to damage that could cause the ferry to sink. The water pressure that would build up between the pontoons when in motion would increase this danger. The very much larger and more powerfully motorised Siebel ferry was better able to withstand the criticism by the naval experts, even though because of its square bow it was very difficult to manoeuvre and could only be employed in a widely spaced formation, provided the sea was calm. During transhipment from Rotterdam to Le Havre the pontoons of one ferry filled with water in light seas and the vessel sank. Another ferry was shattered against the steep coast near Boulogne in a heavy sea.

For the ordinary soldier who was to storm the enemy beach with his rifle in his fist, such problems were as remote as the English coast. He was neither aware of the operational plans nor the logistic problems of the 'river crossing'. In early September the German troops along the Channel coast from Biskins in Holland, through Ostend, Dunkirk, Calais, and Boulogne, to Le Havre and Cherbourg were all set and ready to go. Infantrymen and Engineers were everywhere in evidence along the beaches and in the ports. Everywhere huge amounts of war material were being unloaded, from waggons onto ships, from ships onto lorries and vice versa. The soldiers were driven from combat exercise to combat exercise and through the surf in practice landings. They stormed dummies of coastal defence installations, tore up and down off the beaches in speedboats, practised on the ships and barges in the ports, shot at moving targets from rocking boats, and looked with envy upon their comrades in Paris and elsewhere in the hinterland, who were enjoying the life of occupation forces to the hilt.

The fact that they had to brave the water in order to get at the enemy also contributed to the envy. Most of the officers and men had never even seen the ocean before and had no concept of the power of the sea. Ebb and flood tides were so new to them that the drivers of a Bavarian transport unit, for example, parked their lorries far out on the mud flats at low tide, because they felt they would be safe from saboteurs, and then set off in search of quarters. The sentry they had left behind conscientiously kept watch towards the land, until suddenly water lapped around his feet. When he went around the vehicle against which he had been leaning, the water was already up to his knees. Calling for help the non-swimmer ran for his life and barely managed to save himself on the beach. The lorries were lost. The staff car decorated with its pennant belonging to General von Manstein took an involuntary bath for the same reason.

The OKH had recognised the problem as far back as July and issued a directive signed by Field Marshal von Brauchitsch entitled 'Familiarisation with the Sea' which said: 'The means to do this are, among other things, riding in storm and motorboats at sea and in the surf, bathing, swimming, instructions in the use of rescue equipment (life vests, life belts, small floats).' Conscientious company commanders therefore first undertook to have their men taught how to swim in the sea, something the troops took to with enthusiasm during the bright summer days. Unfortunately tides and work schedules did not always coincide: if it happened to be low tide at 07.00 one jogged across the mud flats to reach the water until one could swim. Experience gained with the incoming tide soon put an end to this game, because non-swimmers were always in danger of their lives.

In general the feeling was not good, namely everything was happening much too fast. Any day the order S minus 10 days could burst into all these preparations and exercises and set the huge machine, even if with much groaning, in motion towards the enemy coast with irresistible force. By day and night the *Luftwaffe* bombers thundered westwards over the Channel, and the *Heer* had no doubts that the *Luftwaffe* would soon gain the upper hand over its adversary and keep the air over the landing beaches clear of enemy aeroplanes. In any case, the attack armies were ready: six divisions from Sixteenth Army, with three divisions from Sixth Army on the left flank.

General Loch's 17th Infantry Division of Sixteenth Army had marched to Ostend and Dunkirk from Dijon in August. During the initial days on the Channel nobody had known exactly how things were to continue. Orders and counter-orders followed each other, strange units appeared whose commanders claimed

231

to have been assigned to 17th Division with immediate effect: engineers, artillery, paymasters, crews of schnorkel panzers without tanks. It was only after a temporary Corps order had been issued that the confusion was cleared up to some extent and everybody was assigned his place. Now it had also become clear: 17th Division would fight next to 35th Division between Hythe and Dymchurch on the open right flank. The battle sector would be supported by paratroops.

The ships and barges that were to take them across were already lying side by side like cigars in a box in the ports at Ostend and Dunkirk. In Dunkirk alone, there were already 180 ships ready to sail. Each barge was to carry 70 to 150 men with their weapons and vehicles. The vehicles were mostly horse-drawn carts, because neither 17th nor 35th Division were fully motorised. General Loch had set up his headquarters in Bellem near Ostend. Almost daily he conferred with Captain Lehmann, chief of the naval command station in Ostende, because he too was a newcomer to transport by sea and landing operations. At his level of command cooperation with the Kriegsmarine was far less problematical than at OKH or Army Group. During the practical daily routine of loading and 'familiarisation with the sea', questions of prestige and prejudices did not surface. Loch learned from Lehmann that the captain had recommended sinking medium-sized steamers off the English coast to act as breakwaters, but that his superiors had been against it. Therefore the idea of an artificial port in the landing area was nipped in the bud. It was only during the Allied invasion in 1944 that this idea was to play a major role and contribute decisively to the success of the overall operation.

17th Division's staff had received information on the enemy situation from Corps which they could not make much use of. The defensive line staked out by the British armies stretched at least 60 kilometres inland from the coast and it was obvious that at the moment of the landing they would be set in motion and their forces advance against the bridgeheads in pincer movements. In what strength and from which direction they would come could not be predicted by the attackers.

In order to tie down defending forces in other places, the OKH had planned elaborate diversionary manoeuvres. Case 'Green' had to do with a diversionary landing in southern Ireland. A large convoy of the Kriegsmarine was to take elements of Fourth and Seventh Army from the coastal sector Lorient–Loire estuary to the southeast coast of the island. On the open coast between Wexford and Dungarvan it was hoped to be able to establish a bridgehead with relatively weak forces, because it was not reckoned that the neutral and rather pro-German Irish would offer resistance. The bridgehead was to be rapidly expanded northwards and the ports on the east coast taken. They were intended as additional jump-off ports against England.

Further diversions in the North Sea had been planned under the code name 'Herbstreise' [Autumn outing]. From the Oslo–Bergen area XXI Group was to land between Newcastle-upon-Tyne and Edinburgh in force and carry out a simulated advance in order to tie down strong enemy forces. A similar assignment had been given to XXXVII Group, which was to land on the English coast between the Wash and Harwich from Dutch ports up to the Western Schelde, and then advance westwards in the rear of the British lines of defence.

There were enough troops and *matériel* available for all three operations, but sea transport could not be as readily provided. The *Kriegsmarine* had already marshalled all the reserves of suitable shipping for 'Operation Sea Lion'. After many negotiations with the *Heer* about reductions of troops, the *Kriegsmarine* now scraped together the last remaining tramps – ten steamers for the Norway sector and four for the Bay of Heligoland – whose seaworthiness could only be confirmed if one was a cockeyed optimist, and brought them to the departure ports. Securing the convoys at sea was just as much of a headache, because all three diversionary operations had to cross waters mined and controlled by the Royal Navy. And since the defeat of *Luftflotte* 5 on 15 August, it had also become questionable if the diversionary forces in the North Sea could be protected from the air.

General Loch was not informed about these planned diversions, to which only the higher staffs of the *Heer* units involved had been initiated. He had to prepare himself for meeting with concentrated resistance. The terrain he would encounter was most unsuited for a rapid advance as in Poland or France: a marshy area with many ditches, few settlements and consequently few roads, the best of which ran along the coast. Behind the beaches they would find only a few recreation spots with more beach stands than houses, hardly suitable as bases. In front of the little village of Dymchurch the approximately ten-metre-high Dymchurch Wall made of granite blocks stretched for miles, a fortified dyke which had only very few ramps for boats and could be covered by cannon and machine-gun fire from the Martello Towers. The towers were to be taken first, if the *Luftwaffe* had not already made short work of them. One of his officers had drawn Loch's attention to the Military Canal that ran right through Romney Marsh from Hythe to Rye. For Napoleon this might have been an obstruction, the Engineers would easily be able to deal with it.

Loch's divisional staff had worked out the operation down to the last detail. 21st and 55th Infantry Regiment were to attack first, while 95th was to be kept in reserve. Behind 55th Regiment near the Grand Redoubt, the mightiest of the Martello towers, the German schnorkel panzers would creep out of the sea and decide the expected battle for the way north. Long before this the *Stukas* were to have eliminated the artillery positioned at Sandgate and Folkestone.

1,250 infantrymen from each of the attacking regiments had been planned for the first wave, together with Engineers armed with flame-throwers and rocket launchers, light field guns, and a communications team. The motto was: clear the beaches and gain the heights behind the canal. Before nightfall a bridgehead at least five kilometres deep had to be won. Thereafter the division, together with reinforcements landed in the meantime, would advance northeast towards Dover and north towards Ashford. To Loch's and his staff's disappointment, the occupation of London was therefore reserved for Ninth Army. However, one could never know, and in any case the campaign in England would be over just as quickly as the ones against Poland and France, because the *Luftwaffe* would soften up the British. Only occasionally did thoughts trouble him about the 'artificial oil fires' which had to be reckoned with during the landing. Lehmann had told him that every port command had been provided with 50 motor fire pumps after Intelligence had discovered that the British intended to pump oil into the sea off the beaches and set it afire. Lehmann voiced the opinion that this would be very difficult to do and probably only succeed at a few isolated spots, but to be sure the troops should be prepared for this before embarkation and be given the appropriate instructions on what to do in case.

XXIII

The Royal Air Force Gains the Upper Hand

London remains uncowed

The German pilots flying against London in these decisive days were missing being tied to a home base, the support of familiar surroundings. They were setting out from a foreign country that was only able to offer the superficial diversions in the life of an occupation force and they were flying across the sea, in other words with a wet death constantly below them, and from the moment they flew over the enemy coast they had to reckon with being shot down at any minute. If Churchill was able to claim of the British that during these days they stood alone, this was even more true for the German pilots. After they had taken off they did not even have the moral support of a radio-telephone link to their base: they were completely cut off and forced to depend solely on their fighting spirit and courage in the face of death. While this may be true of any conquering force, here the growing realisation was added that their own means were not sufficient to fulfil their assignment. As clear as their battle assignment may have been, experience and the high rate of losses was proving that they were neither sufficiently armed nor prepared to carry it through.

As fighter cover for the bombers, the Bf 109 was too fast and not sufficiently agile in air battles, so that after his initial sorties over England Galland confronted his Commander-in-Chief with the demand: 'Give me a *Geschwader* of Spitfires!' The short range of only 80 minutes' flying time of the Bf 109 proved to be another handicap. When a bomber formation over England was forced by anti-aircraft to make a long detour on the way home, for thirteen of the covering fighters the flight ended with empty tanks and stopped propellers in the waters of the Channel, while several more were only able to crash-land their planes on the beaches of the French coast.

On 7 September 21 squadrons of Spitfires and Hurricanes had hurled themselves against the Germans and shot down 35 bombers and fighters. The empty places in the pilots' messes were demoralising and it was no help knowing that 31 enemy machines had been shot down, nor that in an air battle with 60 Bf 109s, 249 Hurricane Squadron had lost six aeroplanes without having achieved a single air victory. Frustration in the *Luftwaffe* increased day after day. In a letter written after 7 September, Theo Osterkamp said: 'It was depressing when the *Geschwaderkommodore* came to me for meetings and explained time and again: "We can shoot down as many as we like, they do not get any fewer!"'

Among the leadership of the *Luftwaffe*, however, wishful thinking prevailed. General Jeschonnek was convinced that it would be one final bomb that would break the camel's back and force the British to the negotiating table. The German bomber formations were sent against London in wave after wave, and some of the formation leaders believed they could already detect a let up in the British fighter defence. This however was not because Fighter Command had been beaten to the ground, but was due to the fact that fighter defence and anti-aircraft defence had not yet achieved complete coordination of their efforts.

The British had not expected such massed attacks on London. General Pile was forced to recognise that his defence was not strong enough and on 8 September ordered every anti-aircraft gun in the British Isles that could possibly be spared brought to London. With this he succeeded within 48 hours in doubling the number of anti-aircraft batteries in London. On the evening of 9 September, after the new guns had been emplaced, Pile called all of his commanders and fire control officers to a meeting and swore them to a new tactic: from now on, the air over London would be kept clear of their own fighters so that with the next attack the flak could put up a barrage.

On 10 September for the first time, the German bombers flew against a 'curtain of steel and iron'. When the leading machines reached the outskirts of London all hell broke loose below them. All of the batteries fired what their barrels could stand. The Londoners, who up to now had heard more bombs than flak and had felt themselves to be very poorly protected, drew a deep breath. At last they were shooting back, at last they would show the Germans. 'This was the first night when I slept peacefully' a reader wrote to *The Times* next day.

The military effect was small and those responsible had to be satisfied with the psychological effect on the inhabitants. Because of bad weather, only smaller formations had flown in, even though the following day the *Wehrmacht* reported: 'Installations vital for war in the city and the port of London were again the most important targets for German reprisal raids yesterday. Many new fires were added to those burning already. In addition, other vital targets, particularly port installations, air bases, and industrial plants in the southeast of the British Isles were bombed.' The latter was only true in so far as a number of the attacking bombers had got rid of their loads in the approach paths because of the heavy anti-aircraft fire.

Fighter Command's airfields had now not been attacked for over one week and people were working feverishly to repair runways, workshops, and other buildings. The protective earth walls for the parked machines and the operations centres were strengthened and the communications networks renewed.

For Keith Park it was a more than welcome breather during which he also succeeded in replenishing the number of his pilots, withdrawing exhausted squadrons or reinforcing them with rested squadrons from the North. Among the new pilots there were a fair number of Poles and Frenchmen. The Poles in particular distinguished themselves during the forthcoming sorties by their flying skill and daredevil courage. Thanks to Lord Beaverbrook, the high losses in machines were more than made good.

There were still some mishaps because the increased AA intervention had confused the fighters' tactics. When during attacks on 11 September the fighter squadrons had been deployed too late and at too low an altitude, the German fighters were able to shoot down 31 Spitfires and Hurricanes with only 22 losses themselves. After this Dowding and Pile developed a new tactic which exactly defined areas and altitudes of deployment for both types of weapon. From now on fighters would only operate far ahead of the anti-aircraft barrage and, if necessary, fly over it at very high altitudes. The test of the new tactics took place four days later.

After the preceding rainy and stormy days the morning of 15 September, a Sunday, broke with a light haze over the English Channel coast, which soon dissipated, giving way to a beautiful late summer day.

That morning Winston Churchill had 'driven to the front' with his wife, to Uxbridge, one of London's western suburbs. Here, more than ten metres under the ground, was the control centre of 11 Fighter Group, headquarters of Air Vice Marshal Keith Park, who had taken over command of the Group's 25 squadrons six months previously.

There were dozens of telephone cables along the walls of the passage down which Park led his guests to an approximately 100 square metres large room that was lighted as bright as day. On two huge tables lay maps of the operations area. Seated on either side of each table were ten women auxiliaries, (Women's Auxiliary Air Force).) They wore earphones and had microphones around their necks. From the filter room, in which the reports coming from the radar stations and from observers were collected, they received the positions of the enemy formations. With long pointers they pushed coloured wooden counters displaying a large Swastika across the squares on the maps.

On a gallery running around the room about 5 metres higher up sat other helpers, who passed the movements on the table on to various offices. Higher up again behind and separated from these by a balustrade, sat the officers of operations control who directed the squadrons from the various airbases against the enemy. Churchill and Keith Park took seats beside them. On the wall opposite hung a large board with long rows of coloured lights. They lit up as soon as a squadron was airborne, but also showed the state of readiness of the machines at any given moment, so that the controllers always knew which squadron's turn came next. This unique and extremely effective fighter control system had already been developed with great foresight before the war by Air Marshal Dowding. Without this method of controlled deployment, the Royal Air Force would not have been able to withstand the onslaught by the *Luftwaffe*.

'I do not know if anything will happen today', Keith Park told his visitors after he had explained the system to them. 'For the moment everything is quiet.' That was shortly before 11.00. Only minutes later the plotters at the tables suddenly came to life. The pointers darted across the tables. More than 40 enemy aircraft had been reported approaching from the Dieppe area. At other places as well, counters were being pushed across the coastline: 'More than 20 here', 'more than 60 there', two Swastika counters symbolising 'more than 80' appeared. The lamps on the board lit up: the battle could now begin.

Twelve squadrons of Spitfires and Hurricanes attacked the Germans already over Canterbury, six additional squadrons were circling high over London. There were now 200 Royal Air Force machines in the air. Air Vice Marshal Park was still not satisfied, because soon the first of his fighters would have to land to replenish fuel and ammunition. In order to reduce weight, the British did not fly with full petrol tanks. Park asked 12 Group for reinforcements and within minutes Wing Commander Douglas Bader, the legless but most famous fighter pilot, was over the city with another 60 Spitfires and Hurricanes. Under the assaults of the British the German bomber formations broke up. An aimed bomb drop was no longer possible. Many dropped their loads over the open countryside when they saw their comrades' machines exploding in the air or crashing in flames. One after the other turned away and, still being chased by the fighters, tried to save himself by diving low towards the coast.

Towards 14.30, 300 German bombers came back again. They crossed the coast between Dover and Dungeness in two waves, attentively watched by British radar. This time, almost all of the fighters were deployed outside London. By the time the first wave approached Chatham and the area of the Thames estuary, 50 machines had already been forced away. In a tight formation, the remaining Do 17s flew directly towards the positions of the heavy anti-aircraft batteries at Malling, which began firing a dense barrage at exactly the right moment. The bomber formation immediately split up to avoid the dangerous white puffs of smoke.

Forty machines were flying towards Chatham, altitude 6,000 metres, speed 340 kilometres. From the battlements of an old fortress that had once been built to turn back an invasion by the Dutch, AA control officers were watching the spectacle. In the bright afternoon sun the city and the port lay beneath them as if deserted. The only thing to be heard was the constant thrumming of the bombers.

When the anti-aircraft guns opened fire the bombers were greeted by an inferno. The leading aircraft fell steeply over its wing, trailing a thin line of white smoke from its cockpit. The second machine also met its fate. The bombers changed course and pulled up steeply, whereby the formation fanned out and made an imposing sight. The AA shot a third Dornier out of the formation, which was now approaching the batteries at Dartford. The sound of battle was earsplitting and seemed to be growing by the second.

The Dorniers' formation now dissolved completely. Individually some tried to get rid of their bombs. And this was the moment the Spitfires and Hurricanes fell upon their prey. The anti-aircraft guns fell silent, the fighters came down out of the sun and pounced upon individual machines. More and more parachutes of the German crews that had bailed out hung in the sky.

A wave of He 111s following behind fared no better, if not actually worse. This time the gunners at Chatham shot down three bombers within thirty seconds. The leading Heinkel received a direct hit in its bomb load. The machine exploded in a ball of orange fire which stood out brightly against the sunny sky. Like the Dorniers before it, the Heinkel had underestimated the range of the English AA and had been hit at an altitude of 6,500 metres.

The tumult continued throughout the whole afternoon. British fighting morale was now as high as never before. The dreaded *Luftwaffe* had lost its sting. The enemy machines fled back out to sea at low altitudes. Towards 17.30 the final Do 17 appeared over Faversham in the Thames estuary. It was flying so low that it almost brushed the rooftops. With its guns it strafed the main street of the little port before turning out to sea in a curve to the right. At the town exit there was a Bofors battery which immediately opened fire and hit both engines. After a few hundred metres the bomber crashed in neighbouring Whitstable Bay. 'It was like an exclamation mark at the end of this day', one of the gunners recalled even 45 years later.

On this day the *Luftwaffe* lost 56 aircraft. With this the spell had been broken. Ten such days would have annihilated half a *Luftflotte*, and the *Luftwaffe* could not afford this.

On Monday, 16 September, the *Wehrmacht* reported: 'On the 15th and during the night to the 16th, reprisal raids against London continued under difficult weather conditions. Bombers attacked the docks and port facilities, hit the Bromley gas works with a bomb of heavy calibre, set fire to an oil storage depot, and achieved hits on railway stations as well as important industrial installations in Woolwich and other city districts. During the attacks heavy air battles took place. The total loss by the enemy yesterday came to 79 aircraft. 43 of our own aircraft are listed as missing.'

From now on not a day would pass on which the *Wehrmacht* was not able to report 'retaliatory attacks' on London. During the second half of September, Londoners were still convinced that these attacks were the prelude to the dreaded invasion which contributed to the fact that they suffered them with equanimity, believing that worse was to follow. John Colville, who returned to Downing Street at noon on 15 September from a short holiday in the country, remarked: 'I came back to London just in time for the air attack and the noise of guns and bombs throughout the night was deafening. The house shook and the blasts of the anti-aircraft guns were so loud you thought they were standing in the garden next door.'

The American Raymond Lee made similar statements: 'And if I were to stand on my head, I would still not understand what the Germans are after. Here they have this huge air force and they waste it in fruitless and pointless attacks all over England. They must have an exaggerated idea of the damage they are causing and of the effect on the morale of the population. After a whole month of this "Blitzkrieg" the British are stronger and in a better position than before.' The only thing he found remarkable in the continuous bombardment that was shaking London during these days was the Irish maid, who after having turned down the beds took a stroll to Victoria Station to see the German bomber that had crashed there.

He was certainly not intending to belittle the human suffering that the bombs were bringing to London. Lee was avid to convince his superiors in Washington of the strong fighting morale of the British in order to set US aid in motion. The Londoners made his job easy for him. Lord Gort had already been bombed out twice, and had moved into a hotel without batting an eye. Churchill had only succeeded after great effort in convincing the mortally ill Chamberlain to leave the city centre. But also the workers and their families in the East End, who in the beginning had picked up all their belongings when an alarm sounded and gone to the West End because they believed they would be safer there, now stayed in their damaged houses or crowded into the shelters for the bombed out, which had rapidly been installed in large sheds and warehouses in order to take care of those who no longer had a roof above their heads. The German bombs had achieved exactly the opposite of what had actually been expected: to make England desire peace. The impotent rage of the initial days had turned into pure hatred when the *Luftwaffe* had started to drop aerial mines. These floated aimlessly down from the sky on parachutes and all too often landed in housing or shopping areas where they caused terrible damage. Nobody believed any longer that the Germans were after militarily important targets.

'Timers' were regarded as being particularly dastardly. An MP was on his way home from the Commons, which continued to stay in session despite the bombs. The all clear had long sounded when very close by a gigantic explosion shattered the air. A policeman believed he had seen a bomb fall on Buckingham Palace and now claimed it had been a time bomb intended to kill the Royal Family. It turned out however, that a team of explosives experts had blown up a dud that had landed in the palace gardens. It should be noted that the number of duds among the German bombs was horrendously high.

Soon there was no district, no famous building in London that had not been damaged. Hardly any of the great streets was still unaffected. St Paul's Cathedral, Buckingham Palace, the Houses of Parliament, had all received heavy hits, Leicester Square resembled a pile of ruins, Pall Mall was damaged, and the Carlton had fallen down. Bomb craters and shattered façades adorned the Government buildings in Whitehall. Despite this, Churchill and his staff stayed on in Downing Street as if they were holding a fort. Cabinet meetings were held in the concrete protected Central War Room and when it became really bad, the Prime Minister sent his employees to the air raid shelter across the street while he and his immediate staff doggedly continued to work.

On 17 October Churchill was having a late dinner with friends in the garden room at 10 Downing Street. The steel shutters over the windows had been closed but hardly deadened the blasts of the bombs exploding near by. When one, as it seemed, exploded less than 100 metres away on Horse Guards Parade, Churchill abruptly got up and went into the kitchen where the staff were still at work as if the noise had nothing to do with them. The kitchen was extraordinarily high and had a gigantic approximately six metre high window. Churchill instructed the butler to put the dishes on the warming plate in the dining room and to go immediately into the shelter with the rest of the staff. He then sat back down at the table with his friends.

A few minutes later a loud detonation very close by shook the room, the furniture swayed dangerously, glasses fell over, and from next door glass could be heard shattering, and a dull crash. Churchill and his friends went over and looked at the damage: the pantry, the kitchen and the offices on this side lay in ruins. A heavy calibre bomb had hit the Treasury building opposite and its air pressure had blasted the gigantic kitchen window into the room in a thousand splinters. Black-brown debris had covered ovens, tables, and the pots and pans were torn from their shelves. Churchill's premonition had saved the kitchen staff from serious injuries.

Without further loss of time, host and guests put on their steel helmets and climbed up onto the roof of the annex in order to have a look at the extent of the attack which was still going on. The night was clear and before them lay the panorama of the burning city. Half of Pall Mall seemed to be in flames, St James's Street and Piccadilly were also brightly lit up by fires, and across the river the glow of many fires could be seen over the docks. Later they would learn that this night had cost 500 people their lives and that about 2,000 had been injured.

The 'Blitz' was in full swing, and it was not only directed against London, but also aimed at industrial centres and aircraft factories in Southampton, Bristol, and Liverpool. Production at the Supermarine works in Woolston was interrupted for a short time after a formation of Ju 88s succeeded in making a surprise attack which caused heavy damage and cost 98 people their lives. These attacks, mainly carried out by *Luftflotte* 3, did not have any appreciable effect on British industrial potential.

After British fighter defence had achieved coordination with the AA it again took command of the air over Britain during the day, attacked the German bomber formations in greater concentrations of numbers during their approach over Kent, and hindered them in reaching the metropolis. The inhabitants of this county, who had already had to suffer the battles for the airbases of Fighter Command, now had to witness dozens of machines falling from the sky each day. Morale was also reflected in the exaggerated official numbers of enemies shot down which were broadcast over the BBC: in September alone, the *Luftwaffe* had allegedly lost 1,005 aircraft. In actual fact, between 7 September and 31 October, 647 German machines were shot down, while the Royal Air Force lost 373.

Because of the far smaller number produced, the *Luftwaffe* was unable to stand such a high rate of loss and it would slowly but surely have been completely wiped out, a fate that it had actually had in mind for its opponent. Daylight attacks by bombers became less and less frequent. Instead, Göring sought recourse in a measure of desperation which would then put his beloved fighters in front of the British guns. With Hitler's permission he had the Bf 109 converted to a bomb carrier and deployed it in daylight attacks against London. The results were catastrophic: because of the added load, the Messerschmitt became cumbersome and slow and could barely reach altitudes of 5,000 metres. Only one out of three or four machines managed to get past the British fighter defence, which had discovered far too quickly that the loaded Messerschmitt was helpless in a dogfight. As a result, one after the other was shot down during approach.

Theo Osterkamp, Chief of Fighters with *Luftflotte* 2 complained to Chief-of-Staff Jeschonnek, who rejoined: 'I can't do anything about it, the *Führer* himself has ordered it'. This was the standard alibi in the *Wehrmacht* for any mistaken decision. Osterkamp let his bitterness show without restraint, which later on was to cause him to fall into disfavour and cost him his position and rank: 'Until proven otherwise, I take our *Führer* to be a man who would not order such an idiocy if he knew what effect it is having. I suggest the following: by God's grace I still have about 384 fighters left at the moment, that makes 96 sections. Out of these I will send a section off twice a day at different times, with bombs under their bellies. They will reach their targets because such small formations can slip their way through anywhere. Above their targets, they will dive down to 400 metres, bail out with their parachutes and let the aircraft with its bomb crash into the docks. The pilots will go into captivity. Result No. 1: the bombs will land in the docks, which you all consider to be "decisive for the war". Result No. 2: You will at least all know exactly when the fighter weapon will have been completely destroyed, namely in 48 days. On the 49th day I will go the same way with my adjutant. Then you will all finally have peace. But one thing will at least have been accomplished: my boys will not have sacrificed their lives for a daydream.'

Soon thereafter the 'fighter-bomber' attacks on London were discontinued and the Battle of Britain slowly began to dwindle without fanfare. For all practical purposes the *Luftwaffe* was now only fighting for its own survival and nobody talked about gaining command of the air any more.

Still during the war, in the spring of 1944, Captain O. W. Bechtle prepared an analysis of the 'Battle of Britain' as a staff exercise for the Air War Academy in Gatow. His conclusions, with all the due circumspection required in those days, clearly identify the weaknesses to which the *Luftwaffe* owed its devastating defeat. He draws upon the opinions of the British: 'The enemy has attributed decisive importance for the course of the war to the "Battle of Britain" and lists the following reasons for the failure of the *Luftwaffe*: 1. Insufficient defensive power of the German bombers, 2. their insufficient bomb loads, and 3. fragmentation of effort, respectively insufficient follow-up against a specific target.' For the deeper underlying reason for the failure, Bechtle also cites an enemy source: 'The aircraft designer Seversley who is appreciated in America... claims... (that) Germany neglected to develop the required weapon in time.' In these opinions Bechtle was able to discover 'a grain of truth.' He goes on to say that from the point of view of those days, it is not possible to criticise the building programme nor the *Luftwaffe* leadership. Instead, Bechtle points to the short time span of only two months that was available to gain command of the air, and that one had 'possibly underestimated' British fighter defence against which German daylight attacks, and thereby the objective, failed.

At the time, the results of the lost battle were not to be recognised, because the fight continued, if with different objectives and at a different level. Bechtle continues: 'After the struggle for air supremacy was broken off, the economic war was begun by almost uninterrupted attacks against London. The power of the air war can be seen from the fact that in the time span from 7 September to 17 November attacks against London were carried out during each night (excepting seven) with an average strength of 166 per night.' But even at the time, Bechtle was forced to concede: 'The enemy's power of resistance was stronger than the means of attack. Maybe the effects of an air war with regard to the morale of the civilian population are being overestimated.' Nothing further need be added to that.

The analysis contains all of the factors that, even seen from the present, explain why at the time the *Luftwaffe* failed to achieve its objective, albeit not by much: the production programme was not up to modern requirements and was not commensurate with the war aim, because the Bf 109 had too short a range and could not operate over London, the Ju 87 and Bf 110 were too slow, the bombers too vulnerable. The unstinting efforts by the pilots went a long way to make up for this, but the inept leadership negated this. They were waging the wrong war at the wrong time with the wrong means.

Those to blame for this débâcle were never called to account. Nobody lost his job, except accuser Osterkamp. On the British side, however, the victors in the battle, who have been rightly called the saviours of England, fell victims to an intrigue. In November 1940, Sir Hugh Dowding was retired against his will, while Keith Park was transferred to the Royal Air Force Training Command and later sent to Malta. And what became of the invasion? The *conditio sine qua non* had not been met, the *Adler* had been plucked, and only dared to leave his nest at night, before he was then to make another blood sacrifice on the battlefields in Russia and there find an unworthy end.

XXIV

Occupation of the Channel Islands
A taste of what might come

Independently of 'Operation Sea Lion', German troops had occupied British territory in the Channel on 1 July: the Channel Islands of Jersey, Guernsey, Sark and Alderney. The islands, lying off the coast of the French Cotentin peninsula in the Gulf of St Malo, were tiny, dreamy paradises. Protected by steep coasts, their softly rolling fruitful garden landscapes produced vegetables, mainly tomatoes, and the famous breeds of cattle, fishing being only a secondary source of revenue. Because people paid only minimal taxes on the islands and the cost of living was cheap, many well-to-do Englishmen and Scotsmen preferred to spend the final years of their lives in country houses with well-tended gardens, in an idyll high above the sea, a mild climate, and a pleasant mixture of British and French life styles, which attracted thousands of tourists to the islands in the summer.

This tranquillity lasted until 18 June 1940. On that day the British Government announced the demilitarisation of the islands and withdrew the small naval command stationed there. Faced with the threatening situation as the French coast is only about 50 kilometres from Guernsey and 25 kilometres from Jersey as the crow flies, during the next two weeks several thousand children, young people and mothers with babies were evacuated to England and Scotland. There was much unrest among the approximately 90,000 inhabitants of the islands, and understandable fear of the Germans ever since the sounds of battle could be heard coming from Cotentin, so that many of the adults also took advantage of the offer to leave the islands. The Royal Navy had provided 22 ships and ten barges for this purpose. In total, about 20,000 people set out for England in panic, including many who had made their living in France, now lost, and were therefore in fear for their means of support.

On Friday 28 June, hundreds of the inhabitants of Guernsey had gathered in Smith Street in St Peter Port, the small port on the east coast, in order to hear an address by the Bailiff on the subject of evacuation. Suddenly the sounds of aircraft were heard and shortly thereafter a bomb whistled down and fell into the harbour. Machine-gun fire barked over the heads of the gathering, which broke up in panicky fear and sought shelter in the houses. Two to three hundred men, women, and children who had been waiting to board the mailboat down on the quay, were taken to safety by port officials between the concrete pillars of the harbour dyke which was dry because of the ebb tide.

Six German aeroplanes swooped down on the defenceless town. By sheer luck, most of their bombs fell into the harbour and the sea. Flying low, they attacked with their guns, boats anchoring in the harbour and a column of lorries standing in front of the port warehouse. Windows and doors of the hotels and shops on the promenade splintered under the hail of bullets. While the aircraft were still circling above them, firemen and ambulances of the Knights of St John rushed down to the harbour to rescue the wounded, and themselves came under machine-gun fire from the planes. The attack lasted fifteen minutes, during which 31 people were killed and 47 wounded. At the same time almost the identical scene was being enacted in the port city of St Helier in Jersey, where eleven people were killed and many injured in an air attack. On this the *Wehrmacht* reported: 'Particularly effective were bombing attacks on troop concentrations and embarkations on the British Channel islands of Jersey and Guernsey, where large fires and heavy explosions were observed in the harbour installations.'

Intermingled with the mourning and shock of the inhabitants was the worry that this sort of thing would now continue until the towns on the islands had become ruins and the last inhabitant killed. On 1 July, German transport aircraft landed on the small airstrips of the islands and disembarked troops. On Guernsey there were problems because a farmer had driven a herd of cows onto the runway and the pilot of the leading machine had to make several passes to first shoo the leisurely browsing animals away. The soldiers who then landed first had to act as herdsmen to keep the runway clear for the following transports, before they could set up their machine-gun positions and occupy the airfield. In the report by the *Wehrmacht* next day, the whole thing sounded far more dramatic: 'On 30 June and 1 July respectively the British Channel islands of Jersey and Guernsey were taken in a coup-de-main by the *Luftwaffe* and subsequently occupied by assault units of the *Kriegsmarine* and *Heer*. In the course of this, a German reconnaissance aircraft shot down two British Bristol Blenheims in an air battle.'

The group of *Luftwaffe* officers that set out for the town in a captured car can hardly be described as an assault unit: with the greatest politeness imaginable they asked the notabilities of the island gathered in the town hall to surrender, which was then accomplished within a matter of minutes. Then the occupation statute was read out loud and its publication in the next edition of the island's newspaper required. The sequence of events took place in the same way on both islands and was synchronised.

The intimidated civilians had no recourse but to bow down and agree to everything. There was no violence, nobody was raped, beaten, or shot. The

German officers were hard and factual and demonstrated emphatically that they were now masters of the islands. A curfew from 23.00 to 06.00 was imposed, alcohol was prohibited, weapons had to be handed in, petrol was rationed, all private cars and boats shut down. After protests by the island authorities, the fishing boats were allowed to sail under German supervision. The schools were converted into quarters for the troops and private homes, many of which now stood empty, confiscated for the officers.

In the beginning, the inhabitants of the islands could hardly complain about their occupiers: officers and men were polite, low-key and gave the impression of strict discipline. They did not believe they would be on the islands for long, because they would soon occupy the British home country. One *Luftwaffe* officer exchanged *Reichsmarks* for £100 at the post office, because he intended to buy presents for his fiancée in Bond Street in London in a few days' time.

However, the Germans stayed on and began to let the inhabitants, a mixture of Britons and Norman-French, feel what it meant to be occupied. The first measure, which affected everybody in the same way, was censorship of the islands' newspapers. The *gleichgeschalteten* [literally: same-switched, Goebbels' euphemism for only letting newspapers print what he told them to] papers were now filled with German directives and carried the reports by the *Wehrmacht* together with propagandist commentaries. The local editors of the English and French editions had to bring their articles to the offices of the German press officers for approval, which often led to grotesque situations. An instruction on how to repair a hammer intended for hobby craftsmen was cut out, because it was to appear next to an advert entitled 'Be prepared' and therefore could have been taken for incitement to commit sabotage. Despite such things, people still bought the newspapers, because they did still contain enough news about the islands and one had, after all, to learn what the Germans had now put under threat of punishment.

For the occupation of the home country after 'Operation Sea Lion', the *Reichssicherheitshauptamt* [RSHA, Reich Central Security Office] of the SS had already planned to take over the Ministry of Information in London, to close down the major news agencies, and to take control of the editorial offices of all of the newspapers, insofar as these were not also to be shut down because of former 'anti-German incitement' (for example, the Beaverbrook press). However, since there were 900 newspapers in Great Britain at the time, the planners ran into a problem, because among the 'intellectuals' of the RSHA there were hardly any who were experts on England. All that remained was the vague hope of finding collaborators. It was known, for example, that *The Times* had kept quiet about the persecution of Jews in Germany and Poland, from which it was deduced that the paper had editors with pro-Nazi sympathies.

Goebbels would probably have broken up the BBC and manned it with personnel from the English language service of the *Deutsche Rundfunk* [German Radio Network], in order to bring the doctrine of *Germanentum* [German racial ideology] home to the British and to make the advantages of the New Order in Europe palatable to them. In the Channel Islands, reception of the BBC was still permitted for quite some time, until Lieutenant General Graf von Schmettow, Commander of the Channel Islands, stopped it by a very simple measure: in order to eliminate this focus of enemy propaganda, he had all wireless receivers confiscated, because in the face of increasing German defeats, the broadcasts by the BBC were becoming more and more embarrassing. The first order to hand in wireless receivers was issued on 27 September 1942, shortly after U-156 had sunk the *Lakonia* in the Atlantic with 1,800 Italian prisoners of war and 1,200 additional passengers and crew members on board, which again set off a world wide wave of protest against the German war leadership. The timing for the confiscation had been well chosen, because shortly thereafter, the Allies landed in North Africa and beat back Rommel's *Afrikakorps*, and two months later, the German Sixth Army with 250,000 soldiers was encircled at Stalingrad, the sort of news best kept from a hostile population.

This loss of their last link with the home country was a severe blow to the inhabitants of the islands. Out of fear of punishment, which had been set at 30,000 *Reichsmarks* or six months in jail, many wrapped their receivers in blankets or cartons and handed them in for 'safekeeping', as the term had been. The German military authorities noticed that the number of receivers handed in, bore no relationship to the number of households, and conducted rigorous searches which, while leading to discovery of several receivers incensed the inhabitants even more against the occupation forces. The BBC was still listened to in hideaways in attics or sheds, often with self-made primitive crystal receivers, and the news passed on by word of mouth. This led to denunciations which poisoned the atmosphere even more. Suspicion was mainly directed against those men and women who worked for the Germans because of the higher pay and better rations. Included here were the many prostitutes that had been brought over from France and housed in the brothels newly installed for the troops. People no longer dared to talk about political or military events even when queueing up at the shops to buy milk and bread. A waitress was denounced to the Germans by a foreign colleague for having made some very unfriendly remarks about Hitler, and was sentenced to several months in jail. The prisons were soon overcrowded, despite the fact that prisoners were constantly being deported to the Continent and to Germany.

Normally the denunciations were based on personal jealousies or the hope of currying favour with the German troops, and there were only very few true collaborators acting out of conviction, none of which were in positions of responsibility. The military authorities on the islands did not depend on such, because the numbers of the inhabitants could easily be overseen and military pressure was sufficient. The civil administration had simply been put under the authority of the commanders, as had already been practised successfully in other occupied territories.

In the British home country, however, a properly working government and administration as in France, where Marshal Pétain and Laval were willing collaborators, was not going to be found. It had to be assumed that the King and the Government would have left the country. Who was one then to deal with? During these days consideration were being given to this at the OKW, in the RSHA and the Foreign Ministry and even lists prepared of people who it was believed were sufficiently pro-German to be entrusted with forming a government, as had been done in Norway with Quisling. Naturally, the list was headed by Oswald Mosley, the 43-year-old leader of the British Blackshirts, who was still being held in jail in the autumn of 1940 because of his political unreliability. Mosley would have turned out to be a bitter disappointment for the occupiers, because he was a Briton first and only then a Fascist. 'I would have escaped from jail', he admitted later, 'put on my old army uniform and fought against the Germans to the last.' Among the British Fascists imprisoned with Mosley by Churchill, there was not one who could have headed up a government, and most of them thought like Mosley. Sir Alexander Cadogan, State Secretary in the Foreign Office claimed later that former Foreign Secretary, Sir Samuel Hoare, might possibly have become a Quisling, because, for example, he had intended, in agreement with Laval in 1935, to cede parts of Abyssinia to Italy, for which he had had to resign. But it is more than doubtful whether Cadogan's suspicion was valid, because Hoare was Jewish. In misapprehension of Harold Nicolson's true convictions, the RSHA also placed high hopes on the former diplomat, further proof of how little was known about the leading British politicians and their mentality. The list could have been extended as long as anyone liked without any better results. In the end, Ribbentrop, after Hitler and Göring the exponent of the Nazi regime most despised in London, would probably have become *Reich* Protector for Great Britain.

Even when fear of invasion was at its peak, in Great Britain people still had no conception of the effects an occupation would have. People with experience and foresight like Harold Nicolson were the exception, because under the impressions left by the military power of the Germans, the majority of the population was expecting a battle of life and death, which would be fought for every street, every house, and Churchill was doing his best to fortify this ultimate will to resist. The word 'occupation' did not occur in the vocabulary of the times, which is why the 'poor Channel Islands' were simply written off as a temporarily unreachable prey of the Germans.

Resistance was all the more easy to organise, as there was nothing being offered by the aggressor that could be defined as a temptation or a liberation. *Germanentum*, which in British eyes was rather weird to begin with, offered nothing except brutal force, destruction of the traditional ways of life, and the loss of private property. German diligence and love of order, which was respected throughout the world, was being misused by Hitler for the destruction of Europe, so that he could establish his dictatorship under the guise of a 'New Order'. That was 'the curse of this man', from which Churchill intended to free the world.

As little as the British were willing to consider life under the Germans, in Berlin they were considering all the more how life on the British Isles could be *gleichgeschaltet*. Since they had no concept at all of the humane way of life of the British, they were concentrating on administrative measures. While these never got beyond amateurish fragments, they would still have had devastating consequences for the British. The RSHA of the SS was planning 'purification' of public life from all 'harmful elements', leading personalities in politics and business who were known for their anti-German stance, or were members of institutions the Nazis despised, such as the Salvation Army, the Freemasons, or the Quakers. Various departments in the RSHA had prepared lists of people to be arrested, which give the impression that they had simply copied the telephone directories. The list was headed by Winston S. Churchill, followed by Beaverbrook and Vansittart. The latter was believed to be the Chief of the Secret Service, probably due to the fact that Chamberlain had removed him from the Foreign Office because of his opposition to appeasement policies and put him into a dubious function as a consultant.

Home Secretary Anderson in particular was to be apprehended at all costs, because he was assumed to be Head of the Security Service, which did not even exist. Harold Nicolson also appeared on one of these lists, next to other members of the Foreign Office who had made themselves unloved by the Nazis. For worst cases Nicolson had already provided himself with 'a pinch of poison' in correct premonition that the Nazis would smell out their enemies and lay them by the heels. The Munich office of the RSHA advised: 'What is important is to secure the servants of the captured Englishmen. Every prominent Englishman has a butler, often a former soldier, who is extraordinarily well informed about the private and official affairs of his master.' The author had obviously come to this conclusion from having read detective stories, and it again proves how little was known about the true state of affairs. What is also striking, is the large number of names from the British upper class that appear, and that cannot be fitted into any political or military context and had probably simply been copied from *Who's Who* to make the lists more impressive. It goes without saying that the SS cast a particularly strict eye on the Jews. The Rothschilds were all listed, as was Sigmund Freud, who had already died back in 1939.

Much to its chagrin, the SS did not have a list of the emigrants who had been interned by the British. It would have provided them with a rich harvest of Jews and opponents of the regime. They wanted to get hold of 'Putzi' Hanfstaengl and Brüning, *Reich* Chancellor from 1930 to 1932. Since 1935, however, Brüning was a professor at Harvard in the United States. Heydrich instructed Dr Franz Six, the head of Department II in the RSHA, to form a task force and immediately secure the files on the emigrants in the Home Office in Whitehall, after London had been occupied, and to bring the refugees back to Germany.

Dr Franz Six, a professor of constitutional law, had been earmarked to become the Security Service Chief for Great Britain. Six was one of Göring's favourites with whom he shared his love of the art treasures from conquered countries. During the autumn, Six was busy not only with planning the installation of Security Service offices in London, his headquarters, Birmingham, Bristol, Liverpool, Manchester, and Edinburgh, he had also been entrusted with 'securing aero-technological research results and important equipment'. Under his direction, 'Germanic works of art' were to be secured, among whose creators Holbein, Rubens and Rembrandt were also numbered. In plain language this meant the art treasures of the British were to change ownership. The SS intended to sift through the British Museum, the National Gallery, the Ashmolean Museum, and was even toying with the idea of transporting Nelson's Column from Trafalgar Square to Berlin and setting it up as a symbol of victory, as Napoleon had once done with the Egyptian obelisk on the Place d'Étoile in Paris.

At the OKW the plans for occupation were being treated in a less dilettante manner. Even though installing a military government in an occupied country had by now become almost routine, the directives for the application of military law and the procedures for field commanders were set out in minute detail. As opposed to the conduct by the military authorities in France, where much was left to the Vichy Government, there was no intention to handle the civilian population in Great Britain with kid gloves. The OKW took the 'snipers' more seriously than the Propaganda Ministry and reckoned with the armed resistance of the civilian population, which it was hoped would be broken by taking all men between age 17 and 45 prisoner and immediately deporting them to the *Reich*. This measure would have affected eleven million Britons, almost 25 per cent of the population and have paralysed British industry, apart from the many younger doctors, chemists, lawyers, priests and members of other vital professions.

In the Channel Islands, where there was no need to fear snipers because there was no Home Guard, in the course of time even more draconian measures were imposed, which proved how seriously these considerations by the OKW were to be taken, and that deportations were a fundamental part of the German way of waging war. For the Channel Islands, Field Commander Colonel Knachfuss issued the order on 15 September 1942 that all Britons between age 16 and 70 who had not been born there, had to leave the islands with their families. The order was published on the front pages of the islands' newspapers the following day. Groups of two *Feldgendarme* [military policemen] and a local policeman served the order on all the families concerned. The first transport with 1,200 people from Jersey and 450 from Guernsey was to leave the islands on 21 September, a further 1,000 people were to follow two days later. German officers promised they would all be brought to England within two weeks via Spain and Portugal in exchange for German internees, but nobody believed them.

The shattered victims learned that they were only to be allowed to take clothing and articles of personal use with them. Cameras and jewellery, in so far as it was not being worn, had to be left behind, and nobody was to take more than ten *Reichsmarks* with him. The *Feldkommandanturen* [military field command offices] were besieged by excited weeping people who were trying to have an exception made in their case. Most were turned down and only a very few were able to achieve a postponement. Doctors Rose and Sutcliffe from Guernsey volunteered to accompany the transport, but the Field Commander insisted on deporting two other doctors. One of these was Dr McGlashe who had fallen into disfavour with the Germans, because as head of the health service he had refused to let the Germans have the mental hospital as an aid station and had only given in under vociferous protest.

The people remaining behind had to witness in impotent rage how their friends and neighbours were driven from their homeland. For the poorer deportees who often had many children, they organised a collection of shoes and warm clothing and also collected £1,500 for their support. Those deportees who were better off tried to sell their possessions in great haste so that they would not fall into German hands during their absence.

When the first of them began to board, there were heart-rending scenes in St Peter Port and aboard the first of the two ships stood a small group and sang 'There will always be an England'. In St Helier the German authorities had taken precautions: soldiers had blocked off the access roads and only let the deportees through. If there had formerly been people in the islands who had had a good word to say about the Germans, from now on there was only hatred to be felt among the local inhabitants, because it was also remembered that only a few short months before, the Jews living in the islands who were mostly small shop owners and artisans, had first been registered, then forbidden to work, and finally deported in small groups. While the Jews had to set off on their march of pain through the concentration camps, the Britons were interned in camps at Biberach, Laufen and Compiègne.

The inhabitants of the Channel Islands were tied hand and foot. They could only defend themselves by passive resistance and individual actions of little effect. Later in the war, for example, the V for Victory sign appeared on all German installations, something which even the most massive threats by the *Feldkommandanturen* were powerless to prevent. It was only after the *Wehrmacht* began to decorate all of its buildings and vehicles with its own V sign in a laurel wreath, that the islanders stopped. In the spring of 1945 the slowly developing Resistance succeeded in blowing up the Palace Hotel in St Helier with 24 German officers inside. By comparison, the Resistance in Great Britain had already been organised when the OKW was still occupied with planning the crossing of the Channel.

XXV
'Operation Sea Lion' Is Put to Bed
Until D-Day

Even if 15 September brought a turnabout in the air battle and it became clearer day by day that the *Luftwaffe* was not going to be able to gain command of the air over the British Isles, in England fear of invasion continued to live on, just as on the German side 'Operation Sea Lion' continued to exist. 'If he does not come by 15 September, it will start to go downhill with Hitler', an American observer in London had stated. But that had been more wishful thinking hinging on a magical date, which by the way, would be declared to be 'Battle of Britain Day' and a public holiday in Great Britain, because the extent of the British fighter defence's victory was not yet recognised at the time.

In a secret session of Parliament on 17 September, Churchill described the coming weeks as being serious and threatening. The Germans had prepared themselves for a major assault on the islands with astonishing thoroughness and on a huge scale. There were 1,700 powered barges and 200 large ships available in the occupied ports. During bombing attacks by the RAF, several of these ships had blown up in huge explosions, which proved that they had been loaded with ammunition for the invasion troops, ammunition for half a million men who were just waiting to defeat the British and make them their subjects.

Churchill had made no bones about the fact that the Germans would be able to establish bridgeheads, even if many ships were sunk during the crossing and many soldiers drowned. But everything had been prepared for their reception and also, that their supply would be cut off. 'As sure as the sun will rise tomorrow, we shall win', he said at the end of his speech, and was possibly thinking of the huge amounts of mustard gas that had been stored in Kent and East Anglia and which the Royal Air Force had already practised dropping along the coast weeks before, using a pink powder. MP Harold Nicolson laconically remarked on the Prime Minister's eloquence: 'At least he is not attempting to keep our courage up with false promises.'

It was only after the daylight attacks stopped and the autumn storms set in that the fear of invasion began to ebb away and was only reawakened by occasional false alarms. Late at night on 22 September, the office manager woke up one of Churchill's private secretaries with a telegram from Roosevelt, who claimed to have learned from a 'reliable source' that the invasion was to take place that morning at 3 a.m. Churchill was not woken up, because it was raining cats and dogs and a westerly storm was raging over the Channel. The unanimous opinion of Churchill's office was that if the Germans really wanted to commit suicide, the Prime Minister would have plenty of time to go and watch this after breakfast. Later on it turned out that the 'reliable source' had been the American Chargé d'Affaires in Berlin Kirk, who had predicted the invasions of Holland and Belgium to within 24 hours, but this time had entangled himself in the underbrush of the various 'S-Days'.

The Americans were 'sitting on the fence' as before, a stance to which Joseph Kennedy's pessimistic reports contributed a great deal. When the British announced that they intended to reopen the Burma Road during the coming month, the Secretary of State had the statement issued that it would depend very much on progress in the Battle of Britain during the coming weeks, whether the United States would support Great Britain in this matter if it came to a conflict with the Japanese. 'The Americans have still not realised that their own fate as well as that of the civilised world depends on the outcome of this battle', John Colville noted in his diary. 'It is of no avail just to exude "goodwill" and to say, as did one of their journalists recently, that the attacks on London are making the Americans "sick with rage".'

At the same time Churchill was giving his warning speech in the Commons, the German Security Service was noting in its 'reports from the *Reich*': 'Almost daily the *Volksgenossen* [literally 'national-racial comrades', i.e. the Germans] are waiting in front of the loudspeakers for the decisive and "relieving" special bulletin on the beginning of the invasion.' The growing impatience among the German population did not stem from the lust for conquest or a particular hatred of the British. Invasion meant an end to the war, because the average *Volksgenosse* was reckoning on a victorious campaign in England lasting maybe three or four weeks, which would bring the war to a good ending. One did not want to live through a second winter of war. This hope, however, evaporated very quickly and already on 24 September, the Security Service was reporting a 'certain disappointed impatience': 'In the absence of major battle actions, rumours and speculations have increased substantially during the past few days. The focuses are the landing preparations on the Channel coast and the Russian question. Particularly the constant movement of troops to the East, which is being watched with interest by the population, is an ongoing source of new assumptions about an imminent change in German–Russian relations.'

The rumours also made the rounds on the Channel coast, because already in August the first divisions from France had been moved 'to the East', including two (the 56th and 299th) on 10 September from Army Group A, for which they were to have acted as reserves for the landing operation. This obviously did not effect the invasion, however, because on 25 September a planning exercise for

'Operation Sea Lion' took place in St Germain, headquarters of Army Group A, in which von Rundstedt, Halder, von Sodenstern, the Commanders of Sixteenth and Ninth Army, the Chiefs of *Luftflotten* 2 and 3, as well as the Admiral Commanding France, and the Chief of Naval Group West took part. The great task of a landing on the British coast was solved according to the book and General von Sodenstern, leader of the planning exercise, concluded: '... even if the political leadership does not consider this operation to be necessary, it can still be ordered by the *Führer* at any time after a further softening up of the enemy, particularly the civilian population.'

The bitterness which speaks in von Sodenstern's closing comment was understandable. For more than two months the *Wehrmacht* had worked on the preparations under high pressure, had staged a huge operation, organised it down to the last detail, and nothing had happened to let the *Heer* throw this decisive blow of the war. From 10 to 13 September, von Brauchitsch and Halder had held the final preparatory meetings with Army Group and the Commanders of the two Armies, so that Army Group was able to issue its initial orders for the 'execution of Sea Lion' on 14 September. On 15 September, the deadline, everything was prepared for the jump-off, only the *Luftwaffe* had still not wiped the British from the sky.

Quite the opposite, the British were now coming over every day and night and attacking the ships marshalled in the Channel ports. Admiral Schniewind had seen this coming as early as 4 August because a British pilot shot down on 20 July had allegedly said in a conversation that his bomber unit had orders to attack the barges being collected in the region of Rotterdam, the first of the assembling invasion fleet. Schniewind had warned of the dangers such attacks posed for 'Operation Sea Lion': 'Given the deadline now set, there is no time reserve available... a *matériel* reserve to any degree worth mentioning cannot be provided, so that any damage to or any loss of transport space will have a weakening effect already on the first wave of the landing.'

The Admiral made use of this statement to again point out the urgency of 'achieving command of the air quickly' over England, urging the *Luftwaffe* on even before the expected A*dlertag*, so to speak. None of this had any effect. After British air reconnaissance had discovered the growing number of ships in the Channel ports towards the end of August, Bomber Command had received the order to systematically bomb these assemblies. The attacks began around 13 September and produced surprising results because without radar, German fighter defence could not be forewarned and regularly came too late. Only with the flak could one hit back during the day. On 15 September alone, the Royal Air Force sank four steamers in the harbour at Antwerp. Army Group A's war diary notes 'substantial' or 'heavy' damage for each day. Many ammunition dumps, including much captured ammunition, were blown up, the fires in the port facilities lit up the night far and wide. The British bomber crews called these night sorties the 'Blackpool run', because the coast was so brightly and colourfully lit up as had formerly been the pier of the Lancashire holiday resort of Blackpool. Within a few weeks the invasion fleet lost almost ten per cent of its transport space: 21 steamers, 194 barges, many tugboats, coastal motorboats, and motorboats fell victim to the enemy air attacks. In order not to lose the whole fleet, the naval commands were directed to move the vessels into the hinterland via the canals connected to the ports and also to ensure that they were loaded there.

For the time being, Hitler learned nothing about all this. During a *Führer* conference on 14 September, he insisted that preparations were to continue on the same scale as before. Raeder reported that on 13 September Hitler had toyed with the idea of calling the whole operation off, but had then reconsidered. The day before, Göring had been to see Hitler privately and had boasted to him of the power and successes of his *Luftwaffe*. He had therefore not needed to attend the meeting next day and had been content to send Jeschonnek instead. When Hitler then announced in front of Raeder, Jeschonnek and von Brauchitsch, that the *Luftwaffe* had already achieved substantial results and that with good weather, there would have been even greater successes, he was only repeating Göring's blandishments. Nevertheless, Hitler had actually reconsidered the matter. For reasons of prestige however, 'Sea Lion' was only to be dismantled at the moment of the greatest success in the air, because then 'Sea Lion' would no longer be necessary. Both Raeder and Jeschonnek knew that one would still have to wait a long time for any such successes and pleaded for permission finally also to bomb residential areas, because the attacks to date had not been able to produce 'mass psychosis and emigration' among the British. Hitler, however, rejected systematic terror attacks against residential areas, he wished to reserve this means of pressure as a reprisal for English attacks against German cities. Finally, he intended to decide on 17 September about postponing S-Day to 27 September.

It never came to that, because in the meantime von Brauchitsch had complained to the OKW that the British air attacks on the Channel ports had not only raged against the ships but had also led to 'unusually high losses in soldiers and *Wehrmacht* equipment'. OKW reacted immediately and answered, after Keitel had spoken with Hitler: 'The *Führer* and Supreme Commander of the *Wehrmacht* has ordered that all measures are to be taken in order to immediately prevent such grave results of enemy air attacks. For this, concentrations of troops and *Wehrmacht* goods marshalled in this area for reasons other than waging war are to be removed. The measures taken in connection with the waging of war against England are to be relaxed to a substantial degree. In so far as this leads to an inability to adhere to the formerly valid starting date for 'Operation Sea Lion' of S–10 days, this is to be accepted.'

Shortly thereafter, the advanced warning date for the operation was extended to S–15 days. With this, 'Sea Lion' had temporarily been put on ice, because the planning exercise on 25 September had demonstrated that one month of transportation time would be required before all thirteen divisions could be brought across the Channel. With a starting date of 15 October the landing fleet would have sailed into the autumn storms and been lost. Despite this, the loading and landing exercises were continued with great diligence. On 1 October at least six soldiers from 6th *Gebirgsdivision* [mountain troops] lost their lives in this context, one of many accidents which were accepted as inevitable and were not important in comparison to the losses inflicted by the enemy.

On 12 October a convoy of twelve Siebel ferries with tugs was transferred from Antwerp to the departure ports of Boulogne and Le Havre. They had been loaded with the anti-aircraft batteries which they were to take to England later on. Ahead of them sailed minesweepers, while guard boats and speedboats circled the little flotilla, which was only advancing at a speed of 5 knots and only reached Vlissingen in the evening. On the second day they managed to reach Dunkirk, where they ran into an air attack but did not suffer any damage. From there on because of minefields, they had to sail right to the middle of the Channel where they were again attacked by British bombers before they reached Boulogne. A number of them were then towed on to Le Havre.

This voyage, which was partly carried out in poor weather, was a masterpiece of seamanship and organisation, which proved how well *Heer* and *Kriegsmarine* were able to work together. The ferries, which were difficult to manoeuvre, had been safely brought to their destinations in formation without loss, against wind and currents, through mines and enemy bombs, and in view of British coastal artillery. They could just as easily have set course across the Channel for the coast of Kent, and have reached it.

The *Kriegsmarine* remained unimpressed by this great success. Not all of the ships had been demagnetised as a protection against mines as these ferries had, and mines were more dangerous than fog. The British dropped them from the air both inside and off the Channel ports at night. German minesweepers were constantly underway to clear them but could not prevent several ships which ran into these dangerous explosive devices from being sunk. The 'time requirement for minesweeping preparation of the transportation routes in the absence of enemy interference on the water, in the air, and from the enemy coast' had been calculated at three weeks, and then only in calm weather. When several minesweepers made a direct run from Cap Gris Nez to Dover during daylight, they were driven off by British torpedo boats and aeroplanes before they had even reached the enemy minefields. The problem was never solved. Had Hitler given the order to attack during late summer, a part of the landing fleet would most probably have fallen victim to mines, both British and German, which had been dropped off the English coast in great numbers by naval aircraft.

On 12 October the admission could no longer be avoided that the lack of command of the air and the onset of bad weather had made the operation impossible for the time being. Keitel had the three branches of the *Wehrmacht* informed: during the winter 'Operation Sea Lion' will remain in effect only as a means of exerting political and military pressure on England, its execution will remain as a possibility for the spring or early summer. The winter was to be used to improve the preparations.

'Operation Sea Lion' had not been buried but only gone into hibernation. The exercises continued, although no longer as intensively as in the preceding weeks. In any case, the Commander-in-Chief West applied to the *Kriegsmarine* on 24 October for the provision of a practice formation of 22 steamers, 202 barges, 81 tugboats, coastal motorboats and motorboats, which was to be divided among the ports between Rotterdam and Caën. To make such a demand had become necessary, because the *Kriegsmarine* had begun to send shipping, above all tugboats, back to the *Reich* where it was urgently required for the economy. The landing barges, however, whose bottoms had mostly been reinforced with concrete, were of no further use for inland traffic and therefore remained in their assembly areas in the various canals in Belgium and northern France.

Personnel problems also began to make themselves felt. The *Kriegsmarine* had deployed 329 qualified seagoing officers for the organisation of 'Sea Lion'. Most of them were urgently needed for manning battleships, destroyers, and U-boats, or for training, and were therefore withdrawn bit by bit. The *Heer*, which now had 'other important duties', could no longer do without the officers it had detached for the operation. 'Sea Lion' was slowly being reduced to a skeleton.

In the staffs and the officers' messes despondency was obviously making the rounds, because the Admiral Commanding France found reason to advise his subordinates on several occasions that 'Sea Lion' had not been dismantled. On the contrary, one had to reckon that 'at any time at a moment that appears to be favourable to the *Führer*, the order to execute the operation may be issued'. He explained the dispersal of the formations in terms of a deception tactic which was designed to leave the enemy in the dark about the intended focal point. On 21 November, the OKW came to the Admiral's aid by ordering exercises in loading operations for 'Case Green' (the diversion against Ireland), which this time Sixth Army was to conduct on the western Channel coast and the Bay of Biscay.

From mid-November on, the *Kriegsmarine* began to concentrate on the spring and reported development of a self-propelled barge with a speed of 13 to 15 knots for the transport of three panzers. It pointed out that the Engineers were working on a similar barge for one panzer that could only do 5 knots, and that Colonel von Schell was even building a hydrofoil boat in competition to the *Kriegsmarine*. Again Raeder demanded from Hitler that all new construction was to be put under the control of the *Kriegsmarine*. The directive was issued, but nobody paid any attention to it.

Raeder's respect for the Royal Navy was almost boundless. His recurring nightmare was probably that the overpowering British fleet would penetrate into his landing fleet one fine night and make short work of it. He therefore let the Commander-in-Chief of the *Luftwaffe* know: 'Air attacks against England have not yet achieved the conditions for the execution of "Sea Lion". Ports such as Portsmouth and Plymouth still have warships stationed in them. Before "Sea Lion" can begin again, this will have to be altered. Furthermore, the new construction of battleships on the slipways on the Clyde etc. must now be attacked, in order to make the situation at sea more favourable for next year.' Naval Command did not receive any answer to this, because already weeks before during a conference at the OKW, Göring had announced that 'Operation Sea Lion' did not interest him because he did not consider it to be possible.

It would have been the job of the OKW to reconcile such differences of opinion and to coordinate the operations of the individual branches of the *Wehrmacht*, but Keitel and Jodl only acted as Hitler's mouthpieces, and he always preferred only to talk to one commander-in-chief at a time and then play them off against each other, or to present their opinions as his own.

Churchill had his commanders-in-chief with him almost constantly, together with their chiefs of staff and other important people, either for informal meetings, for drinks, or for dinner, and when it got late, one or the other of them slept in one of the guest rooms at 10 Downing Street. This would have been unthinkable for Hitler, apart from the fact that Keitel, Göring, Raeder, and von Brauchitsch could not stand each other.

In July, Hitler had assigned the Commander-in-Chief of the *Heer* to prepare plans for a possible attack against Russia, which he would have preferred to have begun already by the autumn of 1940. However, preparation time was too short and winter fast approaching. By December, the deployment plans were ready and had already been tested in planning exercises. On 18 December, *Führer* Directive No. 21 was issued for the campaign against Russia, 'Case Barbarossa'.

'Operation Sea Lion', however, was still alive. On 28 December 1940 the Admiral Commanding France decided that 'the originally envisaged time-span of 30 days for the renewed start-up of "Sea Lion" is not sufficient'. While 100 transport steamers, fishing steamers and ocean-going tugs, as well as 200 barges, could be brought forward from their preparation areas within this time, other types of ships would require 45 days. The Admiral recommended bringing the approximately 500 motor fishing boats to Emden at intervals of ten days beginning in early March and starting with those in the most remote Baltic ports, and then taking them to their ports of embarkation in groups. The dead-lines for 'Sea Lion' were growing longer and longer, because shortly thereafter, the Commander-in-Chief of the *Kriegsmarine* reported a start-up time of two months, and was taking into consideration the development programme for new barges of six months, which had been conceived in the meantime.

None of this concerned the Commander-in-Chief of the *Heer*. On 4 February 1941 he pointed out that it was particularly important to have the deployment in the East to appear as long as possible to be a great diver-sionary manoeuvre intended to distract attention from 'Sea Lion'. Shortly thereafter he even ordered that the experts on the British economy which the Office for War Economy had earmarked as consultants for 'Operation Sea Lion' be informed of their impending call-up. None of this fooled anybody, and yet 'Sea Lion' was still alive.

On the Channel coast yawning boredom broke out. Nobody believed any longer that the operation against the British Isles would take place, and people quietly began to adjust themselves to a permanent 'state of readiness'. There were hardly any distractions to be found in the devastated port cities. In Dunkirk, for example, the crews of the ships and the troops were shown movies three times a week with newsreels that were at least ten weeks old. From time to time a variety show made an appearance, or sound trucks drove up and filled the foreign surroundings with music from home.

There was little reading material in the quarters. The leaflets the British aero-planes had dropped by the bale during the preceding summer had long lost their attraction. To read them was strictly forbidden anyhow, because the British had played macabre jokes on the German *Landser* [common soldier]. These had been tips for travellers to England containing English phrases: 'Where is the next tank?' 'Was that a bomb – a torpedo – a shell – a mine?' 'How much do you charge for swimming lessons?' 'We are seasick. Where is the basin?' 'See how briskly our captain burns!'

The handbooks on England returned to the lockers and cases, because what use was the town map of Dover or Hastings any more, or the topographical maps that showed Salisbury Plain to be ideal for panzer attacks, but the hedgerows in Devon to be avoided. Interest in the British Isles ebbed away, and men turned – mostly with the help of bicycles – to the pleasures offered by the hinterland, the towns in Flanders and the Pas de Calais, whose inhabitants were friendly and did not like the English.

'Sea Lion' continued to slumber, because nobody gave the order that there was no longer any need to be ready. On 5 February 1944 Naval Command pulled itself together for a final 'Sea Lion' order: 'Constructions (but only these) in preparation for "Sea Lion" are to be discontinued for the time being'. The preparatory time span of between eight and ten months was extended to twelve months, against which the Admiral immediately protested. Twelve months was too short, and he demanded: 'It must be decided whether the planning for "Sea Lion" is to continue or not'. The only answer to this was: 'The provisions made in personnel and material may be dissolved for other urgent purposes.' But 'Sea Lion' was not even cannibalised until six months later when it was overrun by its counterpart, the invasion by the Allies.

XXVI
Conclusions from a Fatal Omission

This – in terms of the dimensions of its preparations – greatest operation in German military history, made the world hold its breath during one summer: an invasion of the British Isles by the *Wehrmacht* after the rapid overthrow of France was but a logical next step, because Great Britain was the only opponent still left. In London the invasion was considered to be absolutely inevitable. On 30 June during Sunday lunch at Chequers in idyllic Buckinghamshire, Churchill and General Thorne, Commander of XII Corps stationed in Kent, discussed the invasion and the possibilities of defence. Thorne believed that the Germans would land about 80,000 men between Thanet, Kent's easternmost projection, and Pevensey near Eastbourne in Sussex, the two opposite endpoints of his line of defence. Churchill interjected that the Royal Navy would also have a word to say about that, but had to admit however, that the whole length of the coastline could not be held. The enemy would find the soft spots and break through. Thorne, who had once been Military Attaché in Berlin, believed he understood the German mentality well enough to predict that the Germans would concentrate their main force against a single point and only carry out diversionary attacks elsewhere. Guderian's break-through at Sedan probably served as his example. Thorne knew that under these circumstances he would only be able to hold his left flank at Ashdown Forest, but could not prevent the Germans on his right from driving through Canterbury directly towards London. There was apparently no salvation.

The American Ambassador Joseph Kennedy described an even darker scenario in his reports to Washington. He not only questioned the effectiveness of the military defence, but considered the island kingdom to be in such a state of decadence and decay that any moral resistance would collapse under a German assault. His cries of woe found willing listeners in Secretary of State Cordell Hull and among the American Joint Chiefs of Staff. During the second half of July, the Joint Chiefs believed that they had to prepare themselves for worst cases: the defence of their own hemisphere without the British and their fleet. General Marshall, Commander-in-Chief of the American Army found the time had come to mobilise the reserves and to stop military aid to Britain, because he would need the ammunition and weapons for the mobilised formations. A situation report by the military planners came to the conclusion in late

June: even an active participation by the United States in the war in Europe cannot prevent Great Britain's defeat.

Against this background it is remarkable how difficult it was for the German military leadership to come to a decision. Greatest haste appeared to be called for if the unique opportunity was to be seized and the war ended with a short campaign in England, the British Army having already been defeated at Dunkirk. As late as August, however, the debate between Heer and Kriegsmarine about the extent of the invasion front still raged and forced the Kriegsmarine leadership to fragment the transport fleet between a large number of embarkation ports and to disperse their protective forces over so wide an area that they threatened to become useless.

It was demonstrated here how novel amphibious operations were for the Heer, and that the planning and coordination of the branches of the Wehrmacht left more than much to be desired. Basically, what had been neglected was the development of a strategy that was valid for both branches of the service: either the modern concept of a spearhead with mobile fast troops, or the establishment of a broad front with many bridgeheads. The Heer had success-fully practised the modern concept in France with the Manstein Plan; for the invasion, however, the OKH again insisted on the traditional strategy. Halder demanded from the Kriegsmarine: 'sufficient means of transport for quickly throwing across numerous points of attack on a wide front', whereas Raeder kept pleading for a narrow crossing area. Hitler first agreed with the Kriegsma-rine, then with the Heer, and finally with the Kriegsmarine again. Someone should have asked Churchill who had greater experience in such matters: 'The diffi-culty', he said, 'of defending an island against invasion from the sea, has always lain in the fact that the attacker may always appear with superior forces at some point or other. If he spreads his forces too widely, upon reaching the coast his main force will be facing an equal or even superior defence on that coast.' A compromise for 'Operation Sea Lion' was only set down in the volu-minous OKH directive of 30 August.

Despite all of these obstacles, the fleet and the troops were ready to be launched on 15 September. As had been the case at Dunkirk, the troops clearly saw their objective and raised their arm for the blow; they were just waiting for the Luftwaffe. And they waited patiently. Nobody complained that command of the air had not yet been won. On the contrary, one gains the impression that the condition of preparation was preferred to the condition of execution, possibly because 'Sea Lion' was seen as a guarantee that one would not have to go to Russia. Neither Heer nor Kriegsmarine appeared to take note of the Luftwaffe defeat. All that was ever said was: 'since the Luftwaffe has not yet gained command of the air', and Jeschonnek was not the only one who believed already 'the next bomb could be the one to make the barrel run over.' With this, the favoured launch date in the third ten days of September passed. The next date at the end of October was no longer possible because of the expected bad weather. In actual fact, 'Operation Sea Lion' was therefore postponed to the spring or early summer of 1941 on account of weather conditions and not because of the failure by the *Luftwaffe*, since such an admission – failing rearmament of the *Luftwaffe* – would have made any later attempt illusory anyway.

In retrospect it appears that 'Operation Sea Lion' only became the victim of a *Luftwaffe* that was poorly led and not properly equipped for its task. If one considers how close the *Luftwaffe* came to winning command of the air over England, and was only prevented from doing so by the senseless attacks on London, then the question arises whether a timely planning and coordination within the OKW would not have brought the battle to a different conclusion. As early as June none of the three branches of the *Werhmacht* had the slightest interest in an invasion; on 13 June Raeder was convinced that he had buried 'Sea Lion' for good. And then the unbelievable occurred: within a matter of days, the *Heer* had drawn the military deduction from the preceding triumph over France and elicited agreement for an invasion plan from Hitler. Two months later, 150,000 men and many seagoing vessels stood ready to cross over to the English coast. Had the three commanders-in-chief been able to agree on a plan in early July, and instead of letting it sink ships in the largely senseless 'Channel Battle', had the *Luftwaffe* be concentrated against radar stations, fighter bases, and aircraft plants from 10 July on, 'Operation Sea Lion' would have already have become a campaign in England by August.

Left to themselves, the three commanders-in-chief would certainly never have reached an agreement, only a *Führer* order could have forced them to do so, but in June Hitler was thinking even less about an invasion of the British Isles than Raeder, von Brauchitsch and Göring. And once it had been set afoot, 'Operation Sea Lion' remained the only one of all the major operations during the war for which he showed no interest and which he did not attempt to improve on personally. While he had imposed each of the preceding campaigns on his generals against their will and interfered on even the minutest details, this time the Supreme Commander of the *Wehrmacht* was content to accept the plans in their totality and only to provide the political background music, that is to shower the British with threats. Hitler never had the intention to invade Great Britain!

Göring, who from many years of intimate association knew Hitler far better than did Raeder or von Brauchitsch recognised this and kept himself well clear of the operation. The other two, however, had taken the great orator at his word and set a fearsome war machine in motion, prepared to send thousands of soldiers to their deaths in order to make a basically empty threat come true. They had become the victims of an excusable political ignorance: they had not read *Mein Kampf* thoroughly enough, nor listened attentively enough when Hitler expounded the topics of his second book.

Ever since he had decided to become a politician, Hitler had dreamt of ruling the world together with the 'Germanic brother nation' across the Channel. Next to Italy, he considered England to be 'the only possible ally in Europe'. The content of the possible alliance, however, never went beyond a mutual tacit tolerance: Great Britain was to rule its Empire at sea, he intended to erect his *Großreich* on the Continent. 'I admit openly, that even in the prewar era [Hitler meant pre-First World War] I believed it would have been better if Germany had renounced its senseless colonial policies as well as its merchant and fighting navy and positioned itself against Russia in an alliance with England, and thereby moved from a weak worldwide policy to a strong European policy of acquiring territory on the Continent.'

Hitler never renounced this point of view. It was a basic part of his ideology and therefore stamped his practical policies. For him, who suffered from a Germanic mania, the British were a Germanic *Herrenvolk* [master race] which was equal in value to the Germans. He attributed all of the clichés to the British, which culminated in the 'gentleman in uniform', who had demonstrated for centuries that he knew how to conquer and rule. He admired British parliamentarianism as 'a sublime self-government by a nation', the stability of British foreign policy, the public schools, and time and again, the courage and great self-confidence of the British, which he claimed he had first experienced in the trenches in Flanders, where a British gas attack almost cost him his sight.

The self-taught Hitler flattered himself that he had recognised the mistakes made by the 'God-punish-England-politicians', as he derisively called the members of the governments during the time of the *Kaiser*: Germany's participation in world economics, its struggle for colonies, markets, and sources of raw material had been utopias. Any such attempts by Germany had to draw England's mortal enmity down on its head. He would not make the same mistake. 'How hard it is to beat England, we Germans have learned to our satisfaction.'

In his second book Hitler wrote that his objective for the future was to provide his people with sufficient *Lebensraum* [literally 'life room', i.e. territory for growth] for the next hundred years, and this room could only lie in the east. This required great military strength but would not bring Germany into conflict with all of the other major European powers. That he was in error here was demonstrated during the war in Abyssinia and during the Spanish Civil War, both of

266

which severely strained Anglo-German relations, particularly when the German aerial attack against Guernica was condemned in the British press.

At the time, King Edward VIII's abdication also led to angry reactions in Berlin, because people assumed there were anti-German machinations by Baldwin behind it. When the ex-king visited Hitler on the Obersalzberg as Duke of Windsor, Hitler assured him repeatedly that under Edward VIII an understanding on spheres of interest between Germany and Great Britain would before long have been reached. Hitler was unable to obtain Baldwin's sanction of his expansion plans and complained bitterly about this to Lord Lothian who had come to Berlin in May 1937 for exploratory talks. Hitler showed himself to be bitter about the 'pig-headedness' and 'unreasonable-ness' of the British Government. But he still clung doggedly to his ideal and attempted to seduce Lord Lothian, who remained completely unmoved: 'The united strength of 120 million Germanic people would form an irresistible power'. British sea power and the unsurpassable German army could jointly provide a strong guarantee for peace. That he himself was anathema for the Briton never even entered his mind.

Hitler's assaults against the British Government increased. They were the blind rage of a disappointed lover who does not, however, forswear his love because of this. He never gave up his preference for the British: 'They are of an impertinence without equal, but still I admire them. We have a lot to learn there', he once remarked during a dinner conversation at the Wolfsschanze [Wolf's lair, Hitler's main military headquarters during the war], when his troops were already deep into Russia.

He never understood English mentality, nor why Great Britain could not agree to his clean division of Europe into a sea empire and a land empire, and had declared war on him on his very first attempt to put his ideas into practice. He would not even have dreamt of occupying the British Isles, because until further notice, he would then have had to give up his great objective of Leben-sraum in the east. 'We appear to draw back automatically from taking the awesome task upon us of desiring power both in Europe and in the British Empire. Let us conquer England – but what then, and why?' He assured Heydrich's confidant Walter Schellenberg: 'I do not wish to destroy the British under any circumstances. I want to cut them down to size and they have to learn to see things from our Continental-European point of view as we see them.' Like Bismarck formerly with Austria, Hitler wanted to compel Great Britain into an alliance by force of arms.

Hitler's arch-enemy was France. After France, it was not England which stood next in line as the military successes in May and June 1940 appeared to dictate, but Russia, as he had already outlined in Mein Kampf : 'As clearly as we all recognised the necessity of a conflict with France today, so ineffective would it be for its overall line, if our foreign policy objectives were to be satisfied with this. It can and will only have made sense if it clears the way for the enlargement of the *Lebensraum* of our nation in the East. We stop the constant *Germanenzug* [literally: voyage of the Germans, i.e. referring to the medieval emperors' constant squandering of their military and financial strength in the attempts to establish themselves in Italy] to the South and West in Europe and turn our eyes to the East.'

How strongly this concept ruled him can be seen from a remark he made while the French campaign was still in full swing. On 2 June he had driven to Army Group A headquarters in Charleville to inform himself about the beginning second phase of the campaign in France, the massive attack south and southwest. While the commanders and staff officers were gathering in the conference room, he walked up and down outside the building with von Rundstedt and his Chief of Staff von Sodenstern. Right in the middle of the conversation about deployment plans and questions of supply, Hitler said by the way: 'Now that England is probably ready to make peace, we can begin thinking of settling accounts with the Bolsheviks.' The sentence made von Rundstedt uneasy, even though one must assume that he had heard about Hitler's geopolitics before. On the evening of that exciting day, which had been fully occupied with problems closer to home, he confided in von Sodenstern: in his opinion, a campaign against Russia would overtax Germany's military strength.

Hitler had far fewer scruples. On 31 July, two weeks after the directive to prepare an invasion had been issued, Halder noted in his diary: 'England's hope is Russia and America. If hope of Russia eliminated, America will also be eliminated, because Russia's elimination will lead to gigantic upward evaluation of Japan in the Far East. Russia need do no more than to tell England that it does not want Germany great, then England will hope like a drowning person that in six to eight months the matter will be completely changed. Has Russia been destroyed, however, then England's last hope will have been crossed out. Master of Europe and the Balkans will then be Germany. Decision: In the course of this conflict, Russia must be eliminated. Spring 1941.'

With this conclusion, Hitler carried his generals with him, by giving them a new theatre of war as an alternative to 'Sea Lion', and holding out the bait of mastership of all continental Europe including the Soviet Union. He no longer needed to fear contradiction, because no later than the triumph in France, it had become clear even to many of the doubters that he must have 'providence' on his side. Nobody could question that a threat against Germany by the Soviet Union aided the British. However, this threat only existed in the imaginations of Hitler and his followers. In London people saw matters quite differently: ever since the failure of British–Soviet negotiations in 1939, Churchill feared nothing more than an alliance between Germany, the Soviet Union and Japan. Stalin was obviously making great efforts to keep on a good footing with Hitler, sent congratulatory addresses after every German victory, had not a good word to say about the British, and supplied the German *Reich* with food and raw materials.

During a visit by Molotov to Berlin in November 1940, Ribbentrop offered the Soviet Foreign Minister the partitioning of the British Empire, since Britain was as good as beaten and only needed the coup de grâce. Molotov did not respond to this and only commented that one could not speak of victory as long as British bombs were still falling on Berlin – the meetings took place in part in the air raid shelter of the *Reich* Foreign Ministry. In all seriousness, a quadripartite Germany–Italy–Japan–Soviet Union pact was envisaged, whose conditions were hardly satisfactory for the Soviets, so that Molotov returned to Moscow empty-handed. The coalition so dangerous for Great Britain, however, was still possible. Hitler could not do Churchill a bigger favour than to open a front against Russia.

Hitler did not see the big danger threatening Germany from the British Isles. After the collapse of France and long before 'Sea Lion' had been decided upon on the German side, the British General Staff was planning an offensive army of 55 divisions for operations on the Continent. The Royal Air Force was to be brought up to the same strength as the *Luftwaffe* in order to win command of the air on the Continent.

The means to do this were available, because Great Britain still disposed of substantial resources world wide: Canada, Australia, South Africa and India represented a hardly exhaustible reservoir of men and *matériel*. From the Dominions and the colonies a constant stream of steel, rubber, cotton, food, and other valuable goods was flowing, which the German U-boats could painfully disturb, but which could be made good without much trouble. London was negotiating with Washington about construction of 3 million BRT of cheap new transports, which together with 1.25 million BRT of British new construction were to compensate for the calculated loss of 4.5 million BRT of shipping sunk by U-boats.

Already in October 1940 the Admiralty was working on landing craft for tanks, of which more than one thousand were built in the USA alone. Later on a whole industry grew up in Great Britain, which employed 70,000 people in the building of landing craft of all types for the landing in Normandy. The process of creating the huge fleets of bombers with which the Allies were soon to attack Germany had also begun: since June 1940 production of long-range bombers in Great Britain had been increased to 1,600 machines per month.

As opposed to Hitler, who had told the English in August: 'Don't worry: He is coming!', Churchill did not boast, but his associates knew how tenaciously he was pursuing the idea of attack: 'Even if the man stood on the Caspian Sea, and there is nothing to prevent him from going there, we will bring him back and he will find his back yard in flames. We will turn Germany into a desert, yes a desert!' And even if Hitler were to reach the Great Wall in China, it would avail him nothing as long as Great Britain were not defeated.

What Hitler was unwilling or unable to see was that the moment he turned against Russia, he would be leaving a deadly enemy in his rear. He had woken the sleeping British lion, but he believed he could hold him down with his *Luftwaffe*, which was still flying its nightly bombing attacks, and with the *Kriegsmarine*, whose U-boats had increased their blockade in the Atlantic. He wanted to let the British 'stew in their own juice' while he turned to his actual great task and made the east into what 'India was for England'.

In the reasons he gave for the start of the campaign against Russia, Hitler deliberately ignored all of the dangers. He not only made the mistake of which he himself had always warned, namely beginning a war on two fronts, whereby he left the Western Front completely open before he began building an Atlantic Wall after this had already become useless. He underestimated the determination of the British to bring him to bay, just as he did the military power of the Soviets, despite the fact that they had been the ones who had trained his tank and air crews. And he underestimated the danger threatening Germany from the United States of America.

Hitler succumbed to the delusion that Japan, having become more powerful through an 'elimination' of Russia, would keep the USA tied down and fully occupied in the Pacific. The idea certainly has some justification and found expression in the strategic planning of the US Navy and Army. What proved to be decisive, however, were the close economic, political and blood ties between the British and the Americans. Many of the wives of the British upper class were Americans, as for example was Churchill's mother, and there were close personal relations to the American leadership class. Added to this were the historical ties, the respect held in America for Old England. British and American business enterprises had always been closely knit, so that there was a brisk traffic in money and goods across the Atlantic, and then there was the common language.

In Germany people have always underestimated these ties, possibly also because the German element in the USA only maintains such links to the country of its origin to a very minor degree. On the other hand, disagreements in Anglo–American relations were always played up, thereby masking the actual relationships. When Churchill exchanged British possessions in the western

Atlantic for 50 old destroyers, this was noted in German leadership circles with much gloating and shaking of heads. They would probably have rubbed their hands in glee if they had known that the cruiser *Emerald*, whose sailing from Greenock with course set for Canada German Naval Intelligence had reported on 24 June, had the British national reserves in the form of gold bars and negotiable securities on board. These reserves stayed in the New World and were used to pay for American aid shipments. At this time, an American warship also sailed to Capetown and took on board British gold reserves stored there. During the winter of 1940 the British were in dire financial straits because the Americans insisted on cash payment for every screw, every bullet. In the end the British were so deeply in debt that they had 'probably mortgaged their future forever', as one British author wrote.

On the other hand, the neutral Americans did everything possible to circumvent their own laws and help their cousins. The Pentagon ordered the production of far more ammunition than it would ever need and sold the 'surplus' to the British. Simultaneously, it bought up British arms factories in the USA and let them continue to work under British control for British accounts. Many American ships crossed the Atlantic for the British and some were sunk by German U-boats without there being a hue and cry raised in the United States. Nor was the enormous, still unpaid debt which the United Kingdom owed from the First World War seriously a matter for discussion. It was all in the family. The rich relations are always taken advantage of, that was nothing new, but they were also prepared to help one another unselfishly in times of need, like now, and when such a brilliant orator as Churchill had convinced them of the need. And soon tens of thousands of bombers and the best equipped army in the world were to cross the Atlantic and, together with the rest, crush Germany.

Hitler preferred to ignore the United States. He was still living in the confines of 1914 to 1918 and the confusion of the postwar era. He was still fighting the First World War to a conclusion: after France, it was now Russia's turn. And after the Soviets had been eliminated, there would be only one enemy left, as Hitler proclaimed at a dinner conversation in 1941: 'I will not live to see it, but I am happy for the German nation that one day it will see how England, united with Germany, will confront America. By then Germany and England will know what they can expect from each other. And we will have found the right ally.' This was not a prophetic inspiration or an attempt at distraction, it was the economic-political wisdom of the 'twenties. In *Mein Kampf* Hitler had written at the time: 'All the of blood ties are not able in England... to prevent a certain envious worry about the growth of the American Union in all sectors of international economic and power politics. Out of the former colony, the child of a great mother, a new master of the world appears to be developing. One can under-

271

stand why England is examining its old alliances today and British statesmanship is staring in trepidation towards a point in time when it will no longer be said: "England rules the waves", but "The oceans of the Union".'

The American press appeared to agree with Hitler. In July, *Time* magazine in New York had still made mysterious prophecies that a Great Britain occupied by Germany would, in bitterness, join Germany against America. How was militarily underdeveloped America ever to pose a threat to Germany? In Hitler's view, the delivery of the 50 old destroyers did not alter this. He, who was still caught up in the mentality of the First World War, could well recall the schematic, hardly effective presence of the Americans on the battlefields of Flanders. But he should have known that times had changed and that America now had a gigantic economic potential that would soon be at the complete disposal of the British.

The about face in public opinion in the United States can be traced back to the fact that 'Operation Sea Lion' did not take place and to the defeat of the *Luftwaffe* in September that this entailed. On 16 September the British flying boat *Clare*, a mail and passenger aeroplane, landed in the port of New York coming from Poole in Dorset. The captains were surprised at the overwhelmingly hearty welcome they received. They were showered with congratulations, because that morning it had become known in New York that the day before the Royal Air Force had shot down 185 German machines and decisively beaten the *Luftwaffe*. The German Embassy had tried in vain to correct this exaggerated number. A wave of sympathy for their struggle broke over the British. In a full-page advertisement in the *New York Times*, a group of pro-British Americans demanded a political union with the 'six British Democracies', because they were no longer dealing with George III but with Adolf.

At the same time, the American Army's Chief of Plans, Strong, returned to the States from London and confirmed the positive developments: 'The Royal Air Force is strong enough and the bomb damage to those military installations vital for British survival minute compared to the claims by German propaganda.' His, and Admiral Ghormley's, report on British military strength and fighting spirit formed the basis for an analysis by the Chiefs of Staff of the American Navy, which was handed to Roosevelt on the eve of the elections: 'America's security depends to a large extent on the fate of Great Britain', said the first key sentence of the analysis. 'If Great Britain wins decisively against Germany, we can win everywhere, but if it loses, we will be faced with very serious problems. We will then not lose everywhere, but hardly be able to win anywhere.' For the British, this statement meant more than the declaration of a political union. For the first time, an active participation by the United States in this war was being discussed: the British would not be able to win the war on their own, therefore

American potential in troops and *matériel* had to be deployed. 'I believe', said Admiral Stark, 'that in addition to the support at sea, the United States must send large land and air forces to Europe or Africa, or both, in order to participate in the land offensive (which will become necessary).' The focal point of American military presence was shifted from the Pacific to the Atlantic. The planned war objective corresponded exactly in diametric opposition to Germany's 'Operation Sea Lion': to bring about the military defeat of Germany by air attacks and an invasion of the Continent.

Hitler could only have counteracted this development by an invasion of the British Isles. 'He will have to come, or go under', Churchill had said during the critical weeks and thereby only expressed what many were thinking on both sides of the Atlantic. One cannot pick up a sword only to lay it down the moment one's opponent raises his. Göring's arrogance had made the operation a thousandfold more difficult, nevertheless a landing should have been attempted. From the reactions of the British one can conclude today that it would have been successful. To forego it, however, was suicide, a military declaration of bankruptcy on the eve of the beginning of the campaign against Russia.

All of this was already predictable from the point of view of the times. The former German Ambassador in Rome, Ulrich von Hassell, an active member of the resistance movement centring on Goerdeler, Beck, and Oster, noted in his diary on 29 September 1940: 'In every conversation... we ask ourselves in vain, whether the Generals have not finally now realised the game being played and how terrible a responsibility they carry, both for internal developments as well as the outcome of the war. It is clear to all of us that everything must now be done to convince them that they cannot just let things go on if we do not suddenly want to find ourselves faced with, or already fallen into, a catastrophe.'

The landing in Great Britain would have ended the war for the time being and possibly saved the lives of millions of people, but made millions of others into slaves and cemented the rule of a megalomaniac over Europe, an alternative that is beyond any evaluation. 'Operation Sea Lion' too, was a product of the inhumanity that ruled Germany for twelve years.

Appendix
Documents

The *Führer* and Supreme Commander   F.H.Q., 16.7.1940
of the *Wehrmacht*
OKW/WFA/L No. 33 160/40 sec. Comm. Chiefs only

Secret Command Document!   7 copies
Chiefs only - only via officer!   2 copies

Directive No. 16
On the Preparation of a Landing Operation
against England

Since England, despite its militarily hopeless situation, still has not shown any signs of being prepared to negotiate, I have decided to prepare a landing operation against England and, if necessary, carry it out.

The objective of this operation is to eliminate the English home country as a base for the continuation of the war against Germany, and if this should become unavoidable, to occupy it to the full extent.

For this purpose I order the following:

1) The landing must take the form of a surprise crossing on a broad front, approximately from Ramsgate to the region west of the Isle of Wight, whereby elements of the *Luftwaffe* will play the role of artillery and elements of the *Kriegsmarine* the role of Engineers. Whether it is appropriate to conduct partial operations in advance of the main one, such as occupation of the Isle of Wight or the county of Cornwall, is to be studied from the point of view of each branch of the Wehrmacht and the results reported to me. I reserve the right to decide.

Preparations for the total operation must be completed by mid-August.

2) Included in these preparations is the bringing about of those preconditions which make a landing in England possible:

   a) The English air force must have been beaten down to such an extent morally and in actual fact that it can no longer muster any power of attack worth mentioning against the German crossing.

   b) Mine-free routes must have been created.

   c) The Straits of Dover on both flanks, as well as the western entrance to the Channel approximately on a line Alderney–Portland, must have been blocked by a dense mine barrier.

   d) The coastal foreland must be dominated and secured artillery-wise by a strong coastal artillery.

   e) Tying down of English naval forces shortly before the crossing both on the North Sea and in the Mediterranean (by the Italians) is desirable, in the course of which every effort must now be made to reduce English naval forces stationed in the home country through air and torpedo attacks.

3. Organisation of leadership and preparations. Under my command and in accordance with my general directions, the Commanders-in-Chief will command the forces to be deployed from their branches of the *Wehrmacht*.

As of 1.8., the operations staffs of O. *d*. H., O. *d*. M., and O. *d*. L. [C-in-C *Heer*, *Marine* and *Luftwaffe* respectively] must be within a radius of no more than 50km from my headquarters (Ziegenberg).

I consider it appropriate to house the immediate staffs of O. *d*. H. and O. *d*. M. together in Gießen.

Therefore the O. *d*. H. will have to employ an Army Group for the command of the landing armies.

The operation will carry the code name 'Sea Lion'.

During the preparation and the conduct of the operation the branches of the Wehrmacht will carry out the following tasks:

a) *Heer*:

prepares operations plan and plan for crossing, initially for forces to be shipped in 1st wave. The anti-aircraft artillery to be shipped with the 1st. wave will be under the command of the *Heer* (individual groups crossing) until a division of assignments into support and protection of ground forces, protection of disembarkation ports, and protection of the airbases to be occupied becomes possible.

Furthermore, the *Heer* allocates the means of crossing among the groups to cross and decides the embarkation and landing points in cooperation with the *Kriegsmarine*.

b) *Kriegsmarine*:

secures the means of crossing and, within the limitations of seamanship, brings them up to the embarkation areas in accordance with the wishes of the *Heer*. As far as possible, ships from the overthrown countries are to be drawn upon.

It provides each point of crossing with the naval staff, including escort vessels and security forces, required for advising on matters of seamanship. It protects, in addition to the air forces deployed for surveillance, the whole Channel crossing on both flanks. An order on the regulation covering command structure during the crossing will follow. Furthermore, it is the task of the *Kriegsmarine* to install the coastal artillery, i.e. to emplace as a unified whole and to organise overall fire direction of all of the batteries from both the *Kriegsmarine* and the *Heer* that can be employed for combat against targets at sea. The greatest possible number of the most heavy artillery is to be deployed as quickly as possible to secure the crossing and the protection of the flanks against enemy interference at sea. For this the railway artillery (augmented by captured guns), except those batteries earmarked for engaging targets on the English mainland (K5 and K12) are also to be employed and emplaced with the help of railway turntables. Independently of this, the heaviest batteries available are to be emplaced under concrete opposite the Straits of Dover in such a manner, that they will be able to withstand the most heavy air attacks and thereby, within their range of effectivness, command the Straits of Dover for the duration under all circumstances. The technical work will be carried out by Organisation Todt.

c) It is the assignment of the *Luftwaffe*:

to prevent interference by the enemy air force.

To knock out coastal defences that can affect the landing areas, to break initial resistance by enemy ground forces, and to destroy approaching reserves. For this task, closest cooperation between individual formations of the *Luftwaffe* and landing groups of the *Heer* are required.

Furthermore:

to destroy important roads over which enemy reserves can be brought up, and to attack approaching enemy naval forces well ahead of the crossing points. I request recommendations on the employment of paratroops and airborne troops. In this context it is to be studied in conjunction with the *Heer*, whether it is appropriate to keep paratroops and airborne troops back as a reserve that can quickly be deployed in case of emergency.

4) The necessary preparation of communications links between France and the English mainland will be carried out by the *Wehrmacht* Chief of Communications.

Installation of the remaining 80km of cable from East Prussia is to be planned for in conjunction with the *Kriegsmarine*.

5) I request the Commanders-in-Chief to provide me as quickly as possible with:

a) the plans of the *Kriegsmarine* and *Luftwaffe* showing how they intend to create the conditions for crossing the Channel (see No. 2),

b) details on the installation of the coastal batteries (*Kriegsmarine*),

c) an overview of the shipping space to be deployed and the method of provision and preparation. Involvement of civil authorities? (*Kriegsmarine*),

d) organisation of air protection in the marshalling areas of the troops and the means for crossing (*Luftwaffe*),

e) the crossing and operations plans of the *Heer*, composition and equipment of the 1st wave,

f) organisation and measures of the *Kriegsmarine* and *Luftwaffe* for the execution of the crossing itself, its protection, and the support of the landing,

g) recommendations for the deployment of paratroops and airborne troops, as well as for the chain of command and leadership of anti-aircraft artillery once sufficient gains have been achieved on English soil (*Luftwaffe*),

h) recommendations for the location of the operations staffs of the O. *d*. H. and O. *d*. M.,

i) an opinion by *Heer*, *Kriegsmarine* and *Luftwaffe*, if and which separate operations they consider appropriate in advance of the main landing,

k) recommendations from *Heer* and *Kriegsmarine* on the chain of command during the crossing.

(signed) Adolf Hitler

Distribution:

O. *d*. H.	1st copy
O. *d*. M.	2nd copy
O. *d*. L.	3rd copy
O. K. W.	
WFA	4th copy
L	5th-7th copy

The Führer and Supreme Commander   F. H. Q., 1.8.1940
of the *Wehrmacht*
OKW/WFA/L No. 33 210/40 secr. Comm. Chiefs.

Secret Command Document
Chiefs only   10 copies
Via officer only   4th copy

Directive No. 17
On the Conduct of the Air and Sea War
Against England.

In order to create the conditions for the final overthrow of England, I intend to wage the air and sea war against the English homeland in a more intensified form than before.
For this I order the following:

1) The German air force is to beat down the English air force with all available forces as quickly as possible. Attacks in the first instance are to be directed against airborne formations, their ground bases, and lines of communication, furthermore against the air armaments industry, including the industry for the production of anti-aircraft equipment.

2) After a temporary or local air superiority has been achieved, the air war is to be continued against ports, and here particularly against installations for food supply and furthermore, against installations for food supply in the interior of the country. With regard of our own intended operation, attacks against ports on the south coast are to be kept at the barest possible minimum.

3) Compared with this, the battle against enemy warships and merchant ships from the air can be postponed, unless it is a matter of particularly favourable targets of opportunity, or unless an additional effect can be achieved within the framework of attacks to No. 2), or unless it is necessary for training of crews for future deployment in battle.

4) The increased air war is to be conducted in such a manner that the *Luftwaffe* can be called in with sufficient forces at any time against favourable targets of opportunity in support of naval operations. Furthermore, it must be available in battle strength for operation 'Sea Lion'.

5) I reserve the right to order terror attacks as a form of reprisal.

6) The increase in the air war may begin from 5. 8. on. The *Luftwaffe* may set the exact date itself, depending on when preparations are completed and weather conditions permit.

Simultaneously, the *Kriegsmarine* will initiate the intended increase in the war at sea.

(signed) Adolf Hitler

[P] K[eitel]

	Distribution:	
O. *d.* L.	1st copy
O. *d.* M.	2nd copy
O. *d.* H.	3rd copy
OKW *Chief* WFA	4th copy

Chief WIRüAmt*	5th copy
Chief L	6th copy
IL	7th copy
IK	8th copy
IH	9th copy
K*tb*	10th copy

|P| W|arlimont|

* Chief of Armaments Industry Office

APPEAL
To the Population of England

§ 1
English territory occupied by the German Armed Forces will be placed under German Military Administration.

§ 2
The military Commanders will take all necessary steps to ensure the security of the Armed Forces and for the maintenance of public order and security.

§ 3
Provided that the population behaves in an orderly manner, the Armed Forces will respect person and property.

§ 4
Provided that they maintain an honourable attitude, the local authorities will be allowed to continue to function.

§ 5
Any ill-considered act, any form of sabotage, any resistance, active or passive, against the German Armed Forces will be met with the sharpest possible reprisals.

§ 6
I hereby warn all civillians against the commitment of any hostile acts against the German Armed Forces. Such acts will be remorselessly punished by sentence of death.

§ 7
The orders of the German Military Authorities are to be obeyed. Disobedience will be severely punished.

The Commander-in-Chief of the Army

Bibliography

Afte Kameraden, Jg 11 Nr. 2,4, 1963
Ansel, Walter, *Hitler Confronts England*
Ardizzone, Edward, *Diary of a War Artist*, Bodley Head, London, 1974
Army Quarterly, Jan 1952, July 1957
Assmann, Kurt, *Unterriehmen Seelöwe*, Wiesbaden, 1951
Bevan, Aneurin, *In Place of Fear*, Heinemann, London, 1952
Bishop, Edward, *The Battle of Britain*, George Allen and Unwin, London, 1960
Blake, John W., *The Threat of Invasion*, Belfast, 1956
Blaxland, Gregory S. E., *Britain Eternal Battleground*, Maresborough Books, London, 1981
Blond, Georges, *England im Krieg*, Berlin, 1942
Boberach, Heinz (Hrsg), *Meldungen aus dem Reich Bd 1–17*
Boorman, H. R. P., *Hell's Corner*, Kent Messenger, Maidstone
Brassey's Naval Annual, 1948
Bullock, Alan, *Hitler: A Study in Tyranny*, Odhams Press, London, 1952
Carr, Edward H., *Conditions of Peace*, Macmillan, London, 1942
Churchill, Winston, *The World Crisis*, Four Square Books, London, 1960
Churchill, Winston, *Great Contemporaries*, Fontana Books, London, 1959
Churchill, Winston, *The Second World War*, Vol. II, Cassel, London, 1951
Churchill, Winston, *Blood, Sweat and Tears*, Putnam, N. Y., 1941
Ciano, *Diaries 1939–1943*
Codestey, Peter G., *1940: The Story of No. 11 Group Fighter Command*, Robert Hale, London, 1983
Collier, Basil, *The Defence of the United Kingdom*, London, 1957
Collier P./Horowitz D., *The Kennedys*, Secker & Warburg, London, 1984
Colville, John, *The Fringes of Power*, Hodder & Stoughton, London, 1985
Cooper, Duff, *Old Men Forget*, London, 1954
Cortvriend, V. V., *Isolated Island*, Guernsey, 1947
Cottrell, Leonard, *The Great Invasion*, Readers Union, 1960
Damals, Jg 10 H8, 1978
Deighton, Len, *Luftschlacht über England*, Heyne, 1982
Der Nürnberger Prozeß, Delphin, 1947
Deutsche Rundschau, Jg 69 H3; 1946 Jg 70 M516, 1947
Die Wehrmachtberichte 1939-45, Bd 1–111, DTV Stuttgart, 1985
Donnison, F. S. V., *Civil Affairs and Military Govt.*, London, 1966
Dover Express
Eade, Charles (Ed.), *Reden 1940–41 Winston S. Churchill*, Zilrich, 1947
Eade, Charles (Ed.), *Secret Session Speeches*, London, 1946
Erfurth, *Die Geschichte des dt. Generalstabes*, 1918–45, Göttingen, 1957
Fest, Joachim, *Hitler*, Ullstein 1978
Fleming, Peter, *Invasion 1940*, Rupert Hart-Davis, London, 1957
Foot, Michael, *Aneurin Bevan*, Vol. I Readers Union, 1963

BIBLIOGRAPHY

Foster, Jane, *An Unamerican Lady*, Sidgwick & Jackson, 1980

Galland, Adolf, *Die Ersten und die Letzten*, Schneekluth, 1955

Gallo, Max, *La cinquième colonne*, Editions Complexe, 1980

Gegenwart Jg 2, 1947

Gillman, P. and L. *Collar the Lot*, Quartet London, 1980

Goebbels, Josef, *Tagebücher*, Hoffmann & Campe, Hamburg, 1977

Graves, Charles, *The Home Guard of Britain*, London, 1943

Greiner, Helmut, *Oberste Wehrmachtführung 1939–45*, Wiesbaden, 1951

Grinnel/Milne, *The Silent Victory*, Bodley Head, London, 1958

Guderian, Heinz, *Panzer Leader*, Fortuna, 1974

Guedalla, Philip, *Mr Churchill – A Portrait*, Pan Books, 1951

Hall, H. D., *North American Supply*, London, 1955

Hanfstaengl, Ernst, *Zwischen Weißem u. Braunem Haus*

Hanfstaengl, Ernst, *Hitler in der Karikatur der Welt*, Berlin, 1933

Hassell, Ulrich v., *Vom Andern Deutschland*, Atlas Freiburg, 1946

Hay, Ian, *The Post Office Went to War*, H.M. Stationery Office, 1946

Henke, Josef, *England in Hitlers politischem Kalkül*, Boldt, 1973

Hitler, Adolf, *Mein Kampf*, Volksauflage, 1936

Hitler, Adolf, *Monologe im Führer-Hauptquartier*, Knaus, Hamburg, 1980

Hitler u. die Industrie, Hrsg. Bundesvorstand des dt. Gewerkschaftsbundes, 1963

Hubatsch, Walther, *Hitlers Weisungen für die Kriegsführung 1939–45*, Bernard u. Graefe, 1983

Hyde, H. M., *Zimmer 3603*, Blick u. Bild, 1965

Irving, David, *Die Tragiödie der Deutschen Luftwaffe*, Ultstein, 1970

Isherwood, Christopher, *Goodbye to Berlin*, Penguin, 1945

Jones, R. V., *Most Secret War*, Hamish Hamilton, London, 1978

Julian, Marcel, *The Battle of Britain*, London, 1956

Kesselring, Albert, *Soldat his zum letzten Tag*, Bonn, 1953

Kent, Roberts, Greenfield, *Command Decisions*, USA, 1960

Klee, Karl, *Das Unternehmen Seelöwe*, 1958

Klee, Karl, *Studien u. Dokumente zur Geschichte des 2.Weltkrieges*, Bd 4a

Knopp/Wiegmann, *Warum habt ihr Hitler nicht verhindert?* Fischer, 1983

Kozaczuk, Wadyslaw, *Enigma*, London, 1984

Kuehncr, Otto-Heinrich, *Wahn und Untergang*, Stuttgart, 1956

Ladd, J. D., *Assault from the Sea*, 1939–45, Vancouver, 1976

Langer/Gleason, *The Undeclared War*, Royal Institute of Int. Affairs, 1953

Leasor, James, *The Clock with Four Hands*, N.Y., 1959

Lee, Raymond E., *The London Observer*, Hutchinson, London, 1972

Legerkocrier Jg 2

Le Mois Suisse A3 No. 27 Juin 1941

Leverkuehn, Paul, *Der geheime Nachrichtendienst der dt. Wehrmacht im Kriege*, Frankfurt a. M., 1957

Lewin, Ronald, *Hitler's Mistakes*, Cooper, London, 19 8 4

London Illustrated News, Vol. 197, 1940

Londonderry, *England blickt auf Deutschland*, Essen, 1938

Longmate, Norman, *If Britain Had Fallen*, Arrow, London, 1975

Longmate, Norman, *Home Front 1938–45*, Chatto & Windus, London, 1981

Lord, Walter, *Das Geheimnis von Dünkirchen*, Scherz, München, 1982

MacKensey, A. J., *Propaganda Boom*, Right Book Club, London, 1938
Macksey, K., *Invasion: The German Invasion of England, July* 1940, London 1980
Marine Rundschau Jg S7 Nr. 1, 1960
Maugham, R, C. F., *Jersey under the Jackboot*, Allen, London, 1946
McAllister, Ralph, *Report on England*, USA, 1941
Military Affairs, Vol. 38, 1974
Montgomery, Field Marshal Bernard, *Memoirs*, Fontana, London, 1960
Mosley, Leonard, *Göring*, Desch, Munich, 1975
Munson, Kenneth, *Die Weltkrieg II Flugzeuge*, Motorbuch, Stuttgart, 1984
Newcastle Herald & Miners' Advocate, NSW, 1940
Nichaus, Werner, *Die Radarschlacht*, Motorbuch, Stuttgart, 1977
Nicholas, H. G., *The United States and Britain*, University of Chicago Press
Nicolson, Harold, *Tagebücher und Briefe*, 1930–41, Fischer, 1967
Nicolson, Harold, *Diaries & Letters*, Vol. II, N.Y. 1967
Nürnberger Dokumente, Hamburg, 1947
Official Story of Britain's Anti-Aircraft Defences 1939–40, H. M. Stationery Office, 1943
Osterkamp, Theo, *Durch Höhen u. Tiefen jagt ein Herz*, Heidelberg, 1952
Piekalkiewiez, Janusz, *Spione, Agenten, Soldaten*, Munich, 1969
Pioniere H. 1, 1967
Pont, *The British Carry On*, Collins, London, 1940
Raeder, Erich, *Mein Leben*, Tübingen, 1957
Reynolds, Quentin, *A London Diary*, Random House N.Y., 1941
Roeseler, Joachim, *Die dt. Pläne für eine Landung in England*, 1964
Roosevelt–Churchill Secret'Wartime Correspondence, London, 1975
Roores, Andrew, *Front Line County*, London, 1980
Rowland, John, *The Radar Man*, London, 1963
Schellenberg, Walter, *Memoirs*, London, 1956
Schramm, Percy (Hrsg.), *Kriegstagebuch des* OKW, Band I
Shulman, Milton, *Defeat in the West*, Secker & Warberg, 1947
Spiegel Nr. 21, 22, May 1957
Süddeutsche Monatshefte Jg 25 H7, Munich, 1928
Teissier du Cros, Janet, *Divided Loyalties*, London, 1962
Thomas, Leslie, *Ormerod's Landing*, London, 1979
Townsend, Peter, *Duel of Eagles*, Weidenfeld, 1970
Toynbee, Arnold, *War and Civilisation*, Oxford University Press, 1951
Unimare Jg 1 H2/3, March 1951
War Monthly, Vol. 7 No. 67, 1979
Wehrwissenschaftliche Rundschau Jg 17 H7, 1967
Wheatley, Denis, *Stranger Than Fiction*, London, 1959
Wheatley, Ronald, *Operation Sea Lion*, Clarendon Press, Oxford, 1958
Widemann, *Unser Kampf in Frankreich*, Munich, 1941
Williamson, James, *The English Channel*, London, 1959
Wilmot, Chester, *The Struggle for Europe*, London, 1952
Wilson, Hugh R., *A Career Diplomat*, USA, 1948

Bundesarcbiv – Militärarchiv, Freiburg
Public Record Office, London
Imperial War Museum, London

Index of Personalities

Aitken, Max, 188
Alexander, Albert Victor, 1st Earl of Hills-
    borough, 66, 102
Amery (broadcaster), 144
Anderson, Sir John, 41, 43, 250
Anzanis, Secretary General, 47
Atlee, Lord Clement, 56

Bader, Douglas, 188, 278
Baillie-Stewart (broadcaster), 144
Bake (chief engineer), 115
Baldwin, Stanley, 167, 174, 177, 190,
    267
Barker, R. G. K., 74
Barrat, Arthur, 99, 179
Bartley (Lieutenant), 61
Baudouin, Paul, 97, 100
Beatty (reporter), 196
Beauvoir, Simone de, 11, 12
Beaverbrook, Lord William, 179, 180, 188,
    192, 207, 237, 250
Bechtle, O. W., 243, 244
Beck, Ludwig, 273
Beraud (journalist), 97
Bernstorff, Count Albrecht von, 38
Berry, S. C., 211
Bethel (Major), 48
Bevington-Jones (publisher), 196
Billotte, Gaston Henri Gustave, 24
Bismarck, Otto von, 9, 145, 267
Blanchard, Jean G. M., 24, 27, 58
Bland, Sir Neville, 40
Blond, Georges, 105
Blum, Léon, 103
Boadicea, Queen of the Iceni, 78
Bock, Fedor von, 209
Brauchitsch, Walter von, 9, 83, 84, 95,
    120, 127, 132, 209, 231, 256, 257,260,
    265
Braun, Max, 42
Broh, Richard, 41

Brüning, Heinrich, 251
Burfeind (Captain), 47, 48

Cadogan, Sir Alexander, 249
Carol II, King of Rumania, 45
Cavendish-Bentinck, Sir William, 40
Chamberlain, Neville, 11, 15–17, 148,
    240, 250
Chateaubriant, Alphonse de, 97, 98
Churchill, Winston Spencer, 13, 15, 16,
    18, 20, 23, 24, 26, 31, 33, 43, 44, 54,
    58, 62, 63, 68, 70, 77, 97, 99–103, 105,
    107, 109, 111–113, 140–143, 147,
    152–154, 169, 176, 178, 179, 183, 187,
    190–192, 207, 212, 213, 229, 235, 237,
    240, 241, 249, 250, 254, 255, 260, 263,
    264, 269–271, 273
Ciano, Count Galeazzo, 90
Coats, J. S., 55
Colville, John, 12, 103, 189, 240
Conant, James, 148
Cooper, Duff, 141, 146
Cunningham, Sir Andrew, 108

Daladier, Edouard, 97, 103, 148
Darlan, François, 99, 102, 103, 108,
    110–112
Deere, Alan, 61, 188, 209
Degenhardt (Captain), 88
Delmer, Sefton, 141
Dietl (General), 25
Dill, Sir John, 24, 99
Donovan, William, 154
Dornier, Claude, 156
Douhet, Giulio, 157, 166, 199
Dowding, Sir Hugh, 168, 176, 178, 179,
    181, 186, 194, 207, 210, 229, 237, 238,
    244
Drücke, Theo, 139
Dufay (Lieutenant), 110
Duponselle, Simone, 59, 62

283